The Convention on Modern Liberty

The British Debate on Fundamental Rights and Freedoms

Edited by Rosemary Bechler

This collection copyright © Open Democracy, 2010
Individual contributions copyright © their authors, 2010
The moral rights of the contributors have been asserted.
No part of this publication may be reproduced in any form
without permission, except for the quotation of brief passages
in criticism and discussion.

Published in the UK by
Imprint Academic, PO Box 200, Exeter EX5 5YX, UK

Published in the USA by
Imprint Academic, Philosophy Documentation Center
PO Box 7147, Charlottesville, VA 22906-7147, USA

ISBN-13: 978184540 200 6

A CIP catalogue record for this book is available from the
British Library and US Library of Congress

TABLE OF CONTENTS

Acknowledgements   vii
Editor's Introduction   viii
    Rosemary Bechler
Foreword   ix
    Guy Aitchison with thanks to Clare Coatman

Run-Up to the Convention   3
    Sunny Hundal blogs the Convention on Modern Liberty
    on Pickled Politics   4
    An invitation to participate   6
        Anthony Barnett
    This is Britain, for Heaven's Sake   8
        Henry Porter
    The Database State   10
        Phil Booth
    The Abolition of Freedom Act of 2009   11
        UCL Student Human Rights Programme
    Are such things done on Albion's shore?   24
        Philip Pullman

Morning Sessions   29
Opening Plenary
Citizens and the state: the crisis of liberty
    The state is here at our behest   32
        Helena Kennedy QC
    The delivery of public services   36
        Sir David Varney
    The Mega Snooper State   39
        Ken Macdonald QC
    This rather unpleasant place   42
        Dominic Grieve QC MP

Session 1: Judges and Politicians
    Relight the candle   47
        Lord Bingham
    Can there be liberty without legal aid?   51
        Sir Geoffrey Bindman

Session 2: Human Rights and Global Responses
    Calmly pulling down our eternal rights   55
        Timothy Garton Ash

Standing up for repugnant views   59
Jo Glanville
Incidents in Fallujah   62
Paul Rogers
A single human community, arms and oil   66
Mary Kaldor

Session 3: Business gets Personal – Can Privacy have a Future?

A tempting honey pot   72
Caspar Bowden
Realising the value of your personal information   74
Iain Henderson
Acknowledge the commercial imperatives!   76
Peter Bazalgette

Session 4: Faiths and Freedoms

It has begun to get serious   81
Vaughan Jones

Session 5: The Conservatives and Civil Liberties

The liberal conservative case for human rights   87
Dominic Raab
Liberty doesn't come from liberalism   89
Phillip Blond

Session 6: Press Freedom

The Prevention of Electronic Crimes Act   94
Fatima Bhutto
The press needs to start getting angry   96
Andrew Gilligan
When matters become undiscussable   99
Alan Rusbridger

Session 7: The Police

Where it all went wrong   105
Steven Powell
"All for two good holidays a year..."   108
Harriet Sergeant

Session 8: Liberty and the National Question

Some thoughts on sovereignty, voice and power   115
Gerry Hassan

Session 9: Xenophobia
    The backlash against Macpherson   121
        Tufyal Choudhury
    Racialising rubbish collection   123
        Stuart Wilks-Heeg

Session 10: Democracy and Liberty
    Democracy is an untried adventure in the modern history of the west   128
        Ivo Mosley
    Organise!   132
        Neil Jameson

Session 11: Freedom and working people
    Imagine CCTV in the boardroom   138
        Jerry Hicks

The Event in Photographs   146

Afternoon Sessions   169
    Digging for victory   170
        Sunny Hundal

Session 1: The Database State
    Tell us everything   175
        Sam Talbot Rice
    The Stockholm Programme   178
        Tony Bunyan

Session 2: Parliament's Role
    Human rights and liberty   184
        Stuart Weir
    "Parliamentary difficulties"   185
        Andrew Blick
    Towards a culture of justification   190
        Murray Hunt
    Parliament's role in the Abolition of Freedom   194
        Jonathan Butterworth

Session 3: Protecting rights
    They are our servants   198
        AC Grayling
    The quango state   202
        Douglas Carswell MP

Scoring Points   207
Francesca Klug
A balance has got to be struck   211
Michael Wills MP

Session 4: The Left and Liberty
Embracing the collective   219
Michael Rustin

Session 5: Liberty, Sovereignty and Republicanism: Can the Leveller Tradition be Revived in the 21st Century?
The elephant in the room   226
Excerpt from Geoffrey Robertson's speech
Secure freedom is the only freedom there is   229
Quentin Skinner
Levellers and the good life   233
Melissa Lane

Session 6: Torture and the Decline in Fundamental Human Rights Standards
Jacqui Smith vs. Mitting   240
Victoria Brittain
A desire to seek justice   243
Moazzam Begg
Torture is absolutely wrong   247
Edward Fitzgerald QC

Session 7: Are Human Rights Universal or a Privilege of Citizenship?
Bringing socio-economic rights back home   254
Geraldine Van Bueren
Liberties with teeth: lions parallel to the throne   257
Roger Smith
Freedom from want   260
Andrew Dismore MP
Human rights fundamentalism   264
David Goodhart

Session 8: Love and Liberty
Standing up for sissies   268
Marina Warner
The prison in which we have placed ourselves   271
Michael Edwards

Session 9: Who Rules? Is there a Media-Political Class?
    Healthy bacteria   277
        Liz Forgan
    A conspiracy against society   281
        Peter Oborne
    Are they all devious, venal liars?   284
        Simon Jenkins

Session 10: Child's Play? Equality and Young People
    Children in the media spotlight   290
        Sam Dimmock
    Keeping tabs on every child   294
        Terri Dowty
    A sick society: that's enough   297
        Jenni Russell
    Giving respect back   299
        Alex Gask

Session 11: Can Liberty Survive the Slump?
    The neglected constitution of capitalism   307
        Will Hutton
    Paranoia?   310
        Vince Cable

Keynote Addresses and Closing Plenary
    The Freedom Bill   317
        Chris Huhne MP
    On the imagination   320
        Brian Eno
    We are a better people   324
        Philip Pullman
    Is that a police state, Jack?   328
        David Davis

Elsewhere in the UK...   335
Cambridge Union Society Debate
    David Howarth proposes   338
    Bill Rammell opposes   342
    Bill Rammell sums up   347
    David Howarth wraps up   350

In the Days that Followed... 355

Joni Mitchell was right, you don't know
what you've got till it's gone 357
Suzanne Moore

England: nothing to be scared of 360
Paul Kingsnorth

No broken society here 362
Henry Porter

The database state and the true cost of Labour's free lunches 364
James Graham

Publisher's foreword to *The pro-Israel lobby in Britain* 367
by Peter Oborne and James Jones
Tony Curzon Price

Britain's new Internet law - as bad as everyone's been saying, and
worse - much, much worse 369
Cory Doctorow

An Afterword from Anthony Barnett 371

Contributor Biographies 384

Index 404

Acknowledgements

Warm thanks go to all who have contributed to making this book happen, in particular to,

Rosemary Bechler—editor
Helen Coskeran—assistant editor
Michael Rebehn—transcription
Alexandra Dunn—layout and design
Leon Harris—cover design
John Barker—index
Keith Sutherland—publisher

Photography
Mike Goldwater
Georgia Haseldine
Miki Yamanouchi

Peter Steadman—for a kind contribution to its funding

We would also like to thank all the sponsors, our funders, staff and volunteers of the Convention on Modern Liberty itself. Their names can be found at modernliberty.net

and in particular

The Joseph Rowntree Reform Trust for its initial approach and its sister trusts the Joseph Rowntree Charitable Trust and the Joseph Rowntree Foundation

The *Guardian* and Comment is Free for great sponsorship

openDemocracy and OurKingdom for looking after us

NO2ID and its network for support on the ground

Editor's Introduction

It was a daunting prospect, putting together the book of this event. I worried about the sheer amount of good material - written, video, audio - to be left out! How to choose and, even more challenging, how to preserve some of the brio and warm reciprocity of the moment in the written word? In the event I omitted all the gems from the chairs of sessions - John Jackson, Tom Porteous and Joanne Cash immediately spring to mind - and most of the video, the parallel events around the UK and the coverage. My primary concern has been to invoke the huge range of different issues and voices that came together on February 28, 2009, in central London, just up the road, as Anthony Barnett pointed out in his morning greeting, from the place where the hunger marchers arrived and were attacked by the police in 1934, an event which led in response to the creation of the National Council of Civil Liberties, 'to protect our freedoms'.

But as I began to sift through the discussions, an unfamiliar feeling took over: one that I personally don't remember experiencing for years. I can only describe it as the novel sense of being proud to be British - proud and glad that there are so many vigilant people thinking long and hard about the quality of our liberties today, for ourselves and for those we live with, and how best to guard our human rights. The quality of the speech-making was impressive: where has it come from, like water in the desert? And even more unusual is the feeling that Henry Porter captured in his column three days later, dubbing it the 'good nature' of the event. The sober relief and real pleasure of this convention is evident on the faces in the terrific photographs you can browse through on Flickr. If this volume succeeds in sending you back for more to **www.modernliberty.net** and beyond into the debate spaces of the blogs and campaigning organisations you will find there, it will have done its job.

ROSEMARY BECHLER

DECEMBER 23, 2009

Foreword

One year on from the Convention on Modern Liberty and the political situation is at once familiar and profoundly altered. The attack on rights and liberties continues apace alongside the construction of a hyper-intrusive database state. In the last 12 months alone we've seen: measures to allow secret inquests in cases which may embarrass the state; the creation of a new body to vet every adult who has regular contact with children outside the home; plans to hand Government arbitrary powers to punish copyright infringement; the criminalisation of protesters as 'domestic extremists'; the appearance of new 'super-injunctions' to protect the wealthy from free speech; the Government's refusal to abide by the rule of law when it comes to innocent people on the DNA database; and the attempt to cover up the United Kingdom's complicity in torture. And that's just the start of a very long list.

But the last 12 months have also seen a shift in the waters. An issue macho Home Secretaries could once confidently dismiss as the preserve of the 'airy fairy' chattering classes is now the object of general concern and attention. From tabloid campaigns against hectoring 'Big Brother Britain', to prime-time documentaries on police use of surveillance, anxiety at the condition of liberty in this country has entered the mainstream. Culturally, this can be seen in the popularity of near-future dystopian thrillers, like *V for Vendetta*, or the huge queues outside Bristol Museum to see Banksy's artistic subversion of the all-seeing authoritarian state. Together they point to a growing malaise at the direction in which our society is heading.

What role did the Convention play in this awakening? It's a hazard for any deputy director writing a personal reflection such as this, one year on, that one assigns a certain neatness and inevitability to events which they never actually possessed. As Co-Director Anthony Barnett notes (in his account of making the Convention on Modern Liberty) - from the very start it was marked by a high degree of uncertainty and the lingering worry that the financial crisis would overshadow what might be seen as a 'luxury' issue.

That's certainly how it felt from my perspective, relatively new to this kind of organising. I was in the final stages of an MA at University College, London in the summer of 2008 when I first spoke with Anthony Barnett, Henry Porter and Stuart Weir about working on a 'teach-in' they were planning, with the backing of the Rowntree Trust, to sound an alarm at the threats to civil liberties and discuss what could be done to counter them. David Davis's spectacular resignation and by-election campaign had brought 42 days and the threat of growing state authoritarianism to public attention in a way which the media had signally failed to do. Opinion on the liberal-left, however, was divided over how to respond to Davis's cross-party call. Some questioned his sincerity and pointed to his own party's dubious record on civil liberties; the Greens stood a candidate in the by-election on a more pro-liberty platform than Davis, and the Lib Dem decision not to stand a candidate was controversial within the party.

I shared the view of Barnett and Weir, writing on *OurKingdom*, that the constitutional and ethical importance of the issues required that they be treated in a non-partisan fashion: the left would need to make common cause with the libertarian right if the last twenty years of illiberal legislation was to be successfully challenged and reversed. This analysis would inform the Convention's approach and the distinctive way in which it brought the civil liberties and human rights communities together.

The alliance of people and organisations that would ultimately head up the Convention first came together at a meeting at the *Guardian* in September. The headline sponsors, it was agreed, would be openDemocracy, Liberty and the Rowntree Trusts with the *Guardian* as media partner – NO2ID would later join them. A team was put in place. Clare Coatman, whom Anthony had met campaigning for David Davis, was brought on board to oversee the ticketing system, the email database and to provide general administrative assistance. Claire Preston, working from Cambridge, was Production Manager dealing with accounts. From the start, Porter's energy, enthusiasm, and unrivalled knowledge of the issues, made his input invaluable. When he agreed to become Co-Director of the Convention alongside Barnett, the core-team was complete: organisation could begin.

My work involved conceiving the different sessions, and inviting speakers. Each session was to be supported by a different organisation. These included organisations actively involved in the civil liberties sector, such as the British Institute of Human Rights or Open Rights Group, but also organisations not traditionally associated with the cause, such as the Citizens Organising Foundation and the Football Supporters' Federation. The idea was to get an interesting and surprising mix which reflected the spectrum of political opinion and the breadth of opposition to the loss of privacy and freedom. Some choices proved controversial. The Countryside Alliance's inclusion, for example, provoked many emails and blog comments claiming that their support for hunting precluded them from a campaign for civil liberties. After concerned emails from two of our speakers, who had been pressured by one especially vocal animal rights activist not to attend, we issued a formal statement on the website defending their inclusion and justifying the need for broad-based civil society support.

Nearly everyone we asked to speak accepted the invitation enthusiastically, saying that this was an event whose time had come. Between the Convention team and the supporters of the sessions we decided who would speak on the panel and who would chair them, the only rule being that there had to be at least one woman. As well as organisation, my role involved providing strategic and political input. Even though this was my first time working on such a project, and I was surrounded by people with far greater knowledge and experience, I always felt that my views were listened to respectfully and taken seriously. If ever there was a case of serious disagreement within the team, this would usually be resolved at one of the strategic meetings which took place roughly once every fortnight. Alongside the core team, regular attendees of these meetings included Stuart Weir, Phil Booth, John Jackson, Sabina Frediani, Tony Curzon Price and Stephen Taylor who assumed charge of logistical planning for the day itself. Also in attendance were some of the Convention's partners and volunteers, people like Christina Zaba or Georgina Henry from the *Guardian*, who had an interest in various aspects of our agenda. Meetings grew over time, with the increasing difficulty of fitting everyone into our small conference room more than compensated for by the feeling of being part of a growing movement.

At all times there was an extraordinary level of creativity and excitement at these meetings, assisted by some able chairing by Barnett. In addition to practicalities, the meetings would look at the tone of the Convention and how to make its message effective. What does 'modern liberty' mean? What exactly is 'a Convention'? It was during a session of group editing, for example, that we agreed that the Convention should be a 'call to all concerned with attacks on our fundamental rights and freedoms under pressure from counter-terrorism, financial breakdown and the database state'. The idea was to have a strong message with a clear narrative whilst being open to debate and not dogmatic.

On 15 January, the Convention launched publicly with a party hosted by *Vanity Fair* at the Foreign Press Association. It was a great success with an impressive turnout, graced by such luminaries as Bob Geldoff, actor Sam West and Channel

4's Jon Snow. Our media presence was boosted by the *Guardian's* 'modern liberty' series which launched at the beginning of 2009 alongside their fantastic *liberty central* site and Porter's blog. On 11 February, we were able to purchase the full backpage of the *Guardian* at a reduced rate and fill it with a wonderful image of the full Convention programme designed for us by Leon Harris – an image which became his design theme for the Convention.

From the outset, the project had become steadily more ambitious. Now, we were determined that the Convention should not be London-only, but take place across the nations and regions of the UK. Booth turned his formidable organising prowess to making this a reality, energising his NO2ID network into organising parallel Conventions in Bristol, Cambridge, Glasgow and Manchester. In Belfast, Amnesty Northern Ireland's Patrick Corrigan did a fantastic job organising a strong programme which included its own civil liberties discussions specific to the situation there. In Wales, Caroline Oag of the United Nations Association (UNA) of Wales: Vale of Glamorgan responded to our call for an area organiser, stepping in at the last minute to put together a great event in Cardiff. These parallel meetings took the webcast of the London plenaries and held their own sessions. In so many ways, they were vital to the body language of the event, bringing people from across the country together in one virtual Convention as a visible demonstration that, contrary to the self-serving myths of the political class, rights and liberties are not solely a metropolitan concern but common to all of us.

The most inspiring thing about being part of the organising process was witnessing the talent and energy of the many volunteers who offered their time and commitment to a cause they believed in. As well as the parallel convention organisers, there was Dan Collier who designed the website, Ellen Velacott who organised the camera crews, and Portia Barnett-Herrin and her crew who shot the wonderful talking heads videos which you can still watch on the website. Plenty of the people who pitched in were members of the public, many of them new to political activism, who had felt inspired by the Convention and wanted to help.

One such offer came from Jonny Butterworth of the UCL Student Human Rights Programme (UCLSHRP). Under Porter's guidance, Butterworth's team of bright young lawyers produced 'What we've lost: The Abolition of Freedom Act 2009' which catalogued all the rights-violating legislation introduced in recent years. The document won great media coverage for the Convention, raising our profile, and a copy was placed in every speaker's pack. It remains a useful reference document for anyone who needs to see the legislation set out in detail.

In the final few months, our team expanded to include Matthew Brian and Miranda Porter who researched for the series of press briefings, followed by Alice Dyke and Phoebe Dickerson who provided vital support as the workload mounted and nerves started to kick in. Rosemary Bechler, editor of this collection, was also brought on board to take care of partner outreach, which, with over fifty partners, had become a full-time job.

The day itself was a stunning success. Apart from a few very minor hiccups, the technology went smoothly; all but two of the 150 speakers turned up and every single session was packed with a lively and engaged audience. Perhaps the true significance of the Convention lay in crystallising a feeling that was already there, bringing it to the surface and giving it voice and form. Over 1,500 people participated in London, hundreds in the parallel conventions at venues across the UK, and many more via the web, leading the *Observer* to dub it 'by far the largest civil liberties convention ever held in Britain'. They came together from all different walks of life and political backgrounds in a spirit of mutual concern and understanding. Talking to people who were there on the day and reading the many blogs and responses, perhaps the most important reaction this mobilisation stirred in people was the feeling that they were weren't alone; that concern at the state of liberty doesn't mark them out as strange or paranoid, that others feel the same way. As one gentleman put it on the *Voices of the Crowd* video on the Convention website, 'Over the past ten years or so, I found rights being drip-drip, slowly taken away from us, which is why I came here today, to find a sense of not being alone in that'.

The Convention did not start a movement but it was an important 'line in the sand' moment, which helped raise awareness and shift opinion. Sources in Downing Street privately credited the Convention for the reversal of Clause 152 in the Coroner's and Justice Bill which would have quietly reversed data protection legislation allowing people's data to be shared across government departments without their consent. The Tories took on board some of the arguments they heard at the Convention from the likes of Lord Bingham, Philip Pullman, Baroness Helena Kennedy and Brian Eno. Dominic Grieve MP has promised to scrap ID cards and the National Identity Register, cut back the 'database state', adopt the Scottish system of limited DNA retention, and review the vetting system for adults who have contact with children. These commitments don't quite amount

xiii

to a Freedom Bill, equivalent to Chris Huhne's, which Grieve hinted may be on the cards during the Convention, and the rumour that David Cameron agreed to replace the dovish Grieve as Home Secretary with Chris 'less rights, more wrongs' Grayling in return for support from the *Sun* and the Murdoch clan does not bode well. But these commitments nevertheless reflect the British public's growing concern at the creation of a highly controlled society; a concern which means that civil liberty is now an electoral issue. Measures which invoke terrorism, crime and the protection of children as their justification are no longer unanswered or unanswerable.

Looking back at 2009, future historians will also no doubt wish to emphasise the role of events - none of which we could have foreseen or predicted at the start of the year - in shifting the terrain of debate. Two in particular stand out: the policing of the G20 protests in April and the tragic death of Iain Tomlinson as a result of police violence; and the parliamentary expenses scandal, and its exposure of the political system as venal and dishonest.

The first of these showed in the most dramatic way possible the dangers of raw unchecked state power. The release of amateur footage, obtained by the *Guardian*, showing Iain Tomlinson being pushed and beaten by a Territorial Support Group (TSG) officer as he walked away, hands in pockets, provoked an outpouring of public anger and disgust prompting the media to switch editorial lines faster than you could shout 'police cover up'. Newspapers, like the *Evening Standard*, that had initially parroted the Met's spin that police medics had been attacked by a mob of braying anarchists whilst aiding Tomlinson, now condemned the police action and called for a review of training and tactics. Ultimately, the backlash led to a critical review by the police watchdog, Her Majesty's Inspectorate of Constabulary. Although it did not call for an end to 'kettling' (the tactic of penning protesters in with lines of police) it deemed the Met's approach unlawful and made a number of recommendations for reform.

The arbitrary violence directed at Tomlinson by the young TSG officer and the cold indifference of his colleagues seemed to signal that no one, not even an 'innocent' member of the public, was safe. Along with football supporters, minorities, and others, protesters have, of course, always known that police will act like thugs given half the chance. But it took the tragic death of a passer-by to alert the wider public to the dangers of a semi-militarised and unaccountable police force possessed of an ever-growing armoury of sweeping anti-terror powers.

Hot on the heels of the G20 came the *Daily Telegraph*'s revelations of MPs' abuse of expenses. The scandal sent shock waves through the system, exposing the central institutions of the state as corrupt and dysfunctional and highlighting the need for thoroughgoing reform and new checks and balances. The party leaders scrambled to respond. Gordon Brown informed us that he was a long-time fan of constitutional campaign group Charter 88 and made noises about 'a written constitution'; David Cameron called for giving 'power to the powerless' and Nick Clegg pointed out that he had long distinguished himself with calls for reform of a 'rotten' Westminster system.

Finally, it felt like a breakthrough. Opponents of draconian government laws from across the political spectrum had consistently drawn attention to the failure of Parliament, a 'Bazaar' in Diane Abbott's memorable phrase. Following the expenses scandal this was now the orthodoxy, with polls reporting a record 75% of voters in support of serious changes to the system.

In their own different ways, the G20 and the expenses scandal drew attention to the true nature of key institutions in British public life, contributing to a mood, heightened by the banking crisis, of inchoate anger and distrust. In response to this crisis of legitimacy, the Rowntree Trusts came together, once again, to launch POWER2010, a unique campaign to renew democracy and defend civil liberties that gives everyone a chance to have a say in how this country should be run. Clare Coatman and I from the Convention team are involved in the organisation and implementation of the campaign.

As many pointed out at the Convention, on the panels and from the floor, there is now an overwhelming case for having a democratic written constitution which entrenches, beyond the reach of the state, the rights we have as citizens. The old order, which has permitted government to ride roughshod over liberty through its control of a supine and semi-corrupt Parliament, is bust beyond repair.

Key to any successful movement for better democracy and liberty will be public education and open discussion. This book brings together many of the inspiring speeches and talks from the Convention on Modern Liberty with photos from the day. Alongside the videos and podcasts on the CML website, it is hoped the collection will provide an ongoing educational resource and an encouragement.

The battle against arbitrary state power is one that needs to be continually re-fought. It is clear that whatever shifts in attitude have been achieved are elusive, sometimes evanescent and vulnerable to easy reversal. As I write this, at the end of the decade, the 24 hour news media is abuzz with news of a foiled 'Al Qaida' attack on a US airplane. Photos of a Nigerian student who studied at UCL are played endlessly on 24 hour news networks. As fragments of his past are pieced together, various pundits are wheeled out to say how an intervention here or there in the young man's life could have prevented this from happening. Unfailingly, when politicians respond, it is not to defiantly re-assert our values or refuse to be cowed by this botched attack, but to call for ever-more intrusive measures of dubious value in enhancing security.

Without doubt, the decade ahead will see more battles fought to protect rights and liberties against the creation of a hi-tech authoritarian state, battles which we cannot yet conceive of. It is hoped that this collection will play a modest part by re-asserting the values of liberty and privacy and setting out the issues at stake.

GUY AITCHISON WITH THANKS TO CLARE COATMAN

CHRISTMAS 2009

RUN-UP TO THE CONVENTION

Photo courtesy of Miki Yamanouch

Sunny Hundal blogs the Convention on Modern Liberty on Pickled Politics
30TH JANUARY, 2009

Friends, readers, citizens and small furried animals. I'm going to this (and will be chairing an event). I hope you will come too, because it's a bloody important event, especially with all the growth in terrorism-related legislation.

The Convention on Modern Liberty (28 February 2009) will bring together well over a thousand people representing nearly fifty organisations, and is a call to all those concerned with the increasing threats to our fundamental rights and freedoms – from our own State, from terrorism and the responses to terrorism, and from the escalating financial crisis.

From being imprisoned without charge, to bailiffs entering our homes without a warrant, to unlicensed surveillance and officials extracting your information from wherever they want and passing it to whomever they like – our liberties are being violated. The convention organisers will publish audits of these violations, show how they are connected, ask why they are taking place and suggest how they might be reversed.

The convention's co-directors, Anthony Barnett and Henry Porter, said 'We want three things. First, we want the public to ask why these violations are happening and see that they are not isolated events. Second, we want the violations to be stopped in a way that ensures they do not happen again.'

'Third, by asserting the right to manage our identities and to share between its agencies deep dossiers of information about us, the government trespasses on the first claim of democracy: that the State is the servant of the people. We want to ensure that the tradition of public freedom in our country is renewed, not suffocated, that our fundamental rights are secured, and that the agents of the state understand their powers exist to serve, not control, the citizens of Britain.'

Amen to that. The list of convention speakers is shown below:

run up to the convention

Yasmin Alibhai-Brown
Lisa Appignanesi
Mohammed Aziz
Anthony Barnett
Simon Barrow
Peter Bazalgette
Moazzam Begg
Sir Geoffrey Bindman
Lord Bingham
Andrew Blick
Philip Blond
Caspar Bowden
Billy Bragg
Victoria Brittain
Tony Bunyan
Jean Candler
Malcolm Carroll
Douglas Carswell MP
Joanne Cash
Shami Chakrabarti
Tufyal Choudhury
Nick Clegg MP
Nick Cohen
Linda Colley
Philip Collins
Tony Curzon Price
Iain Dale
David Davis MP
Andrew Dismore MP
Cory Doctorow
Oliver Dowlen
Terri Dowty
Michael Edwards
David Elstein
Brian Eno
Keith Ewing
Peter Facey
Edward Fitzgerald QC
Liz Forgan
Sabina Frediani
Edie Friedman
John Gardiner
Juliet Gardiner
Edward Garnier QC MP
Timothy Garton Ash
Alex Gask
Pam Giddy
Paul Gilroy
Jo Glanville
Lord Goldsmith
Zac Goldsmith
David Goodhart
A C Grayling
Colin Greer
Dominic Grieve QC MP
Gerry Hassan
Iain Henderson
Georgina Henry
Savitri Hensman
Guy Herbert
Becky Hogge
Chris Huhne MP
Sunny Hundal
Murray Hunt
Saghir Hussain
Will Hutton
John Jackson
Simon Jenkins
Vaughan Jones
Mary Kaldor
Yasmin Khan
Sunder Katwala
Helena Kennedy QC
Paul Kingsnorth
Francesca Klug
Satish Kumar
David Lammy MP
Tim Montgomerie
Suzanne Moore
Ivo Mosley
Peter Oborne
Tom Porteous
Henry Porter
Philip Pullman
Dominic Raab
Geoffrey Robertson QC
Alan Rusbridger
Paul Rogers
Meg Russell
Mike Rustin
Laura Sandys
Quentin Skinner
David Smith
Roger Smith
Trevor Smith
Sam Talbot Rice
Chuka Umunna
Geraldine Van Bueren
David Varney
Sarah Veale
Hilary Wainwright
Marina Warner
Stuart Weir
Stuart Wilks-Heeg
Michael Wills MP
Gareth Young
Christina Zaba
Simon Zadek

An invitation to participate
ANTHONY BARNETT

It was one of the great missed opportunities of recent times. Twelve years ago we had our own 'Obama moment'. A young, untried leader was swept to power on a wave of popular desire for the renewal of our political system, all the more possible in benign economic circumstances. Now, for all the good things it has done, Labour's legacy includes:

- The misuse and abuse of 'the War on Terror' to extend arbitrary police power
- The development of a surveillance society that undermines privacy
- The creation of a database state that tracks and controls the lives of its subjects
- The collapse of parliament as a check on the executive power of government

Why? What is the problem to which the billions being allocated to the database state and the surveillance society is the solution? I know of no coherent and persuasive answer.

Is it because, as a senior figure in Westminster suggested while himself supporting identity (ID) cards, a 'deep state' is at work, especially in the Home Office? Is it because surveillance and information sharing provide juicy contracts ensuring years of cash flow for mainly United States (US) corporations skilled at lobbying at the highest levels of the bazaar (as Diane Abbott described the House of Commons in an unchallenged speech)? Is it because our media has been too flattened to expose and sustain coverage that is not fed by official press releases? Is it because the European Union (EU) seeks to create a 'single market' for commercial and official information sharing? Is it because the Westminster establishment, led by Blair, bought into George Bush's 'War on Terror'? Is it because, since it backed the Iraq war, the Whitehall elite knows that it is no longer wiser than the people, and seeks to sustain - by electronic means - the legitimacy it has lost, even in its own eyes? Is it because ID cards will be British and thus provide a hi-tech means of countering the threat to the

run up to the convention

> "Remember that we are powerful together—and if you don't feel this to be so, perhaps it is because this is how they want you to feel."

United Kingdom (UK) as governments gain popularity in Scotland, Wales and Northern Ireland? Or is it because a governing class hankering for the global reach of empire is simply desperate to control the natives by any means possible?

It makes it harder to stop something if you do not understand why it is happening. So investigating the reasons for the assault on our liberties is important ongoing work.

It needs to be public, concerted, open-minded and enjoyable. Henry Porter and I want the convention to be a convivial event. If it is, it will be thanks to the energy and confidence of a generation under 35 and, in some cases, under 20. Their talents and voluntary dedication have created the website, the videos, the research and briefing papers, the design, the local meetings, and its spirit of constructive resistance.

The original idea was for an 'alarm call'. When asked 'what next?', I feel like saying: don't look to the smoke alarm to put out the fire. Look to yourself and what you can do in concert with others. Remember that we are powerful together - and if you don't feel this to be so, perhaps it is because this is how they want you to feel. Many organisations are already combating the four-fold undermining of liberty as we can see. Please join and support them.

Any such movement will include strange bedfellows and contain differences. Some fear the right to privacy strikes at the right to know. Some see human rights as an infringement of democracy, not its support. Party antagonism runs deep across those brought together by the convention. But as the financial crisis moves in, and as the police seem to be preparing to act 'pre-emptively' to control everyone they deem unruly, from football fans to music lovers, this is all the more reason to act together in whatever way we can.

A profound transformation of our government and political culture is needed to defend the causes of liberty, fundamental rights and freedom in our country. People say this can only happen from below. It's true. Usually it is said in Britain in a tone of voice that suggests such a movement is therefore impossible and can never happen. I hope the Convention shows that it can.

SOURCE: CML PROGRAMME,
FEBRUARY 2009

This is Britain, for Heaven's Sake
HENRY PORTER

Looking through the thirty odd Acts of Parliament responsible for so much of the erosion of British liberty, you have a feeling of unreality: how could this happen in *our* Parliament, under the gaze of the press and the British public with its innate respect for justice and freedom and addiction to privacy?

It seems incredible to find that MI5 developed the torture policy in Pakistan, that Britain is one of the two liberal democracies in the world to be named by an international panel of jurists as having actively undermined International Law, that the Constitutional Committee of the House of Lords has condemned the culture of surveillance and data collection in the United Kingdom as 'undermining the long-standing traditions of privacy and individual freedom which are vital to democracy.'

This is Britain, for heaven's sake. These things don't happen here.

But they do, and perhaps the most remarkable part of the story is that the Human Rights Act (HRA) - a bill of rights by any other name - came into law in 1998 at the exact moment the government began to reveal its hostility to constitutional rights and the Rule of Law. The HRA may have brought justice to many individuals but even its most ardent supporters cannot now argue that it has protected the public - as a true bill of rights would - from a government that received just a third of the popular vote at the last general election, yet behaves as though our rights and freedoms are privileges that may be withdrawn at the government's leisure.

The presence of the HRA on the statute book has prevented us from seeing the wart on the end of our nose: namely, that we are a substantially less free society than we were a decade ago, and that the individual is on the point of being encircled by the state's apparatus of surveillance.

If the HRA really worked as a Bill of Rights we would not be here today.

Perhaps the most difficult aspect for many to face is that we are as responsible as the government for what has happened. Over the last decade a change came about in Britain that allowed people to think that only *their* liberty and comfort mattered and to forget that a system of rights must be universally applied and respected in order for it to work. The very expression "human rights" became an object of scorn in the popular press and led those in power to believe that we did not care about rights and liberty and we would not guard our privacy. It's difficult to know whether fear of terrorism, apathy or exuberant consumerism caused this mood but it is clear that this selfish mood was disastrous for society - and for politics. For government can only function properly and serve the public if people pay attention to what's happening and demand proper coverage of politics from the media.

When people ask me 'what next?', I reply that reading the newspapers would be a start. Find out who your MP is and pester them; set up a local group to discuss

> **Unless we involve ourselves in the political process, ours will be the first generation in centuries of British history to pass on a less free society than the one we inherited."**

the attack on liberty and what you can do about it, which is exactly how my co-director, Anthony Barnett, and I began three years ago. Activated opinion can be a great force for good and not just on this issue. We need to re-engage with politicians and they with us, not in the bogus consultations that always produce the result the government wants, but with meaningful exchange in which we hold our politicians to account.

It's no exaggeration to say that, unless we involve ourselves in the political process, ours will be the first generation in centuries of British history to pass on a less free society than the one we inherited. That is a shocking thought, but we still have time to act. What we need is a movement, especially among young people, to make the public at large understand that we have only a few years before the changes wrought by this government become a permanent part of life in the United Kingdom. A movement cannot be born in a day of speeches and discussion, however notable the speakers, but it can provide that spark of inspiration and that is what we will do today.

SOURCE: THE CML PROGRAMME
FEBRUARY 2009

The Database State
PHIL BOOTH

Hi there! I am Phil Booth and I am the National Coordinator of NO2ID. When NO2ID started – as a public campaign in 2004 - Guy Herbert, our General Secretary, coined the phrase 'the database state' to clearly articulate a particular problem. This problem was the tendency to try to control society by collating and observing people's data - whether it be through the use of identity (ID) cards or ContactPoint, the National DNA Database, the centralisation of medical and passenger records, use of internet and phone records – your data, your family's data, your car, your kids, the list goes on.

If it were another individual obsessively tracking you, monitoring your movements, taking notes on you, snooping and following you wherever you go, we would call them a stalker! There are laws against it.

Unfortunately, however, we have a government that is passing law after law to create a stalker state. The Convention on Modern Liberty offers us an opportunity not only to identify *what* needs to be stopped but to suggest *how* this could be done. Because we can stop this and we will stop this.

They can only take our liberties if we let them. They cannot achieve this if we refuse to comply. If you submit to the government's demands, then it is not just you who is losing out. Join the hundreds and thousands of other people who have already acted by exercising their right to opt out of certain procedures like having their personal medical records placed under central government control. Inform yourself: inform others.

When NO2ID started, we were just a handful of concerned citizens – a few people working in privacy and human rights organisations. Now we are 60,000 strong and growing every day. Join us! Join a group. There are groups across the UK. There's probably one in a town near you. And if there isn't, why not start one? We are just people like you, standing up for freedom. It's time to demand control. It's time to withdraw consent. It's time we made a choice.

SOURCE: CML VIDEO

run up to the convention

The Abolition of Freedom Act 2009

BROUGHT TO YOU BY THE UNIVERSITY COLLEGE LONDON STUDENT HUMAN RIGHTS PROGRAMME IN COOPERATION WITH THE CML

One of the problems with the erosion of liberty in Britain over the last decade was that the public failed to pay attention to what was happening in Parliament. Laws that fundamentally challenged our traditions of rights and liberty and flew in the face of the Human Rights Act (HRA) were passed with relatively little debate. Few grasped the impact they would have on our society and Ministers were able to brush aside protests with assurances that their desire to protect us was equal to their respect for civil liberties.

The difficulty campaigners faced was to press home the argument about the scale of the loss. An account was needed to show that the legislative programme, which swept away centuries-old rights and transferred so much power from the individual to the state, actually existed. Now we have that evidence and the Convention on Modern Liberty can demonstrate with confidence what Britain has lost and discuss how this crisis of liberty took root in one of the world's oldest democracies and what to do about it.

This report by the UCL Student Human Rights Programme (UCLSHRP) is a concise and approachable inventory of the loss. It is a profoundly disturbing document, even for those who thought they knew about the subject, for it not only describes the wholesale removal of rights that were apparently protected by the HRA and set down nearly 800 years ago in Magna Carta, it also shows how the unarticulated liberties that we assumed were somehow guaranteed by British culture have been compromised. The same is true of constitutional safeguards that were once considered beyond the reach of a democratically elected legislature.

▶

The attack is as broad as it is deep. Over 25 Acts of Parliament and some 50 individual measures are involved. This document is organised around the articles of the HRA and also draws on the guarantees of Magna Carta, but it is important to remember that many of the freedoms that are disappearing have never been codified, which makes it all the more difficult to keep track of the ongoing attack on liberty. Part of the future assignment for those associated with the Convention must be to continue to monitor and report on these dangerous trends. Opposition can only begin when we are in full possession of the facts. These facts are what the UCLSHRP provides in this first exhaustive account of what we have lost.

SECTION 1: EUROPEAN CONVENTION ON HUMAN RIGHTS

The Human Rights Act 1998 incorporates the European Convention on Human Rights (ECHR) into United Kingdom (UK) law. As a result, these rights can be enforced by individuals in UK courts. Individuals need no longer take their claims to Strasbourg, the home of the European Court of Human Rights. Despite boldly claiming to be 'bringing rights home' through the HRA, the UK has since then introduced a contradictory legislative scheme that in fact erodes our rights.

Life, Article 2, ECHR

'Everyone's right to life shall be protected by law. No one shall be deprived of his life intentionally.'

The obligation to investigate violations of the right to life

Coroners' Inquests
1. The right to life can only be secured if the executive investigates suspicious deaths to determine whether a violation of that right has taken place. New proposals will end the independence of coroners who, until now, have been able to investigate the cause of suspicious or uncertain deaths and criticise government departments and agencies, (for example in the death of Iraqi civilians under the control of the British Army). Jack Straw's Coroners and Justice Bill trespasses on this independence by granting the Executive power to suspend the inquest even when it may involve a homicide. The inquest may be forced into secret session by a minister for reasons of national interest, to protect relations with a foreign country or if the hearing threatens to harm the public interest.
2. There is a further erosion of accountability in the measure that will allow the Executive, acting through the Lord Chancellor, to suspend an inquest when the death is being investigated under the Inquiries Act 2005. (Coroners and Justice Bill 2009)

No Torture, Article 3, ECHR
'No one shall be subjected to torture or to inhuman or degrading treatment or punishment.'

Prohibition of degrading treatment and enforced destitution
3. Asylum seekers were denied state support in 2002 unless they make their claims as soon as reasonably practical after their arrival in the United Kingdom. The Home Secretary may withhold support from these applicants, who are not given the opportunity to explain how they came into the country and how they have been living since their arrival, as well as from anyone who does not cooperate with the authorities. Lord Bingham found this application of the Nationality Immigration and Asylum Act 2002 to be a 'deliberate action of the state' which 'denied shelter, food [and] the most basic necessities of life'.
(Nationality Immigration and asylum Act 2002)

Liberty, Article 5, ECHR
Article 5(1), Right to Liberty and Security of the Person
'Everyone has the right to liberty and security of person. No one shall be deprived of his liberty save in the following cases and in accordance with a procedure prescribed by law: the lawful detention of a person after conviction by a competent court;…the lawful arrest or detention of a person effected for the purpose of bringing him before the competent legal authority on reasonable suspicion of having committed an offence.'

Individual liberty is an ancient right recognised by English law as early as 1215 AD in the Magna Carta, Article 39, 'No free man shall be captured, and or imprisoned, or robbed of his freehold, and or of his liberties…but by the lawful judgment of his peers, and or by the law of the land.'
4. Control orders were introduced to confine terrors suspects who have not been found guilty of any crime by a conventional court of law. The orders include measures such as house arrest and electronic tagging. They also restrict movement, association and the use of phones and the Internet. The act allows control order proceedings to be held in closed sessions with security cleared 'special advocates' representing the accused, who do not even have the right to see or rebut the evidence against them. The evidence may consist of secret intelligence, or even information obtained from torture outside the United Kingdom.
(Prevention of Terrorism Act 2005)
5. Immigration officers were given police-like powers, which include increased detention, entry, search and seizure.
(UK Borders Act 2007)

ECHR Article 5(1)(c)
'No arrest or detention unless it is for the purpose of bringing them to court because there is reasonable suspicion they have committed a criminal offence'

▶

6. Immigration officers were given the power of arrest without a warrant.
(Asylum and Immigration (Treatment of Claimants) Act 2004)
7. Police were given powers in two different acts to stop and search people and cars without suspicion at airports and within designated areas. Currently, 180,000 people are being stopped and searched every year.
(Terrorism Act 2000 and Anti-Terrorism, Crime and Security Act 2001)

No detention without charge, Article 5(2)

8. Police have the power to hold a terrorist suspect for 28 days without charge. This power was to last one year but the Secretary of State was given the authority to continue 28 days detention by statutory instrument. (Terrorism Act 2006)

Right of detained individuals to legally challenge their detention within a reasonable period of time, Article 5(4)

9. Automatic bail hearings for those detained under immigration legislation was abolished. The same piece of legislation also made it possible for an asylum seeker to be detained in accommodation centres at any time during their application, for up to six months. (Nationality, Immigration and Asylum Act 2002)

Fair Trial, Article 6, ECHR
'In the determination of his civil rights and obligations or of any criminal charge against him, everyone is entitled to a fair and public hearing within a reasonable time by an independent and impartial tribunal established by law.'

Criminal standard of proof, Article 6(1)

10. To restrict an individual's liberty, it must be proven in a court of law that the individual is guilty beyond reasonable doubt. This is the criminal standard of proof. The lower standard of proof for a civil trial is that of the 'balance of probabilities'. The important distinction between criminal and civil law was eroded with the introduction of Anti-Social Behaviour Orders (ASBOs). These orders are granted based on a civil burden of proof, which requires only the 'balance of probabilities'. However, a person breaching an ASBO is likely to incur criminal penalties and, even though the actions or behaviour for which the ASBO is granted may not be against the law, breaching an ASBO can lead to a sentence of up to five years in prison. (Crime and Disorder Act 1998)
11. Parenting Orders were introduced. These can result in prosecution if a parent does not meet the conditions of the order. (Crime and Disorder Act 1998)
12. Civil orders that allow courts to impose post-sentence restrictions on those convicted of violent offences were introduced. (Criminal Justice and Immigration Act 2008)

13. The Serious Crime Prevention Order (SCPO) can be used to restrict where an individual can live as well as to limit their work and travel arrangements. SCPOs can last for up to five years and breaching them can result in up to five years' imprisonment. The House of Lords Constitutional Committee expressed doubts about using SCPOS to target organised crime. 'Whether or not the trend towards greater use of preventative civil orders is constitutionally legitimate (a matter on which we express doubt), we take the view that SCPOs represent an incursion into the liberty of the subject and constitute a form of punishment that cannot be justified in the absence of a criminal conviction.' (Serious Crime Act 2007)

The presumption of innocence until guilt is proven, ECHR, Article 6(2)

14. The presumption of innocence was weakened with a new law that allows a jury to make inferences about the guilt of a defendant if he or she fails to give evidence when charged with the new offence of causing or allowing the death of a child, either by murder or manslaughter. (Domestic Violence, Crime and Victims Act 2004)
15. The right to silence was further eroded by terror legislation that allows post-charge questioning of terror suspects and the courts to draw an adverse inference from a defendant's silence. (Counter-Terrorism Act 2008)

Right to a lawyer of one's own choosing, ECHR, Article 6(3)(c)

16. Under the Terrorism Act, an individual and his/her lawyers may be barred from court proceedings. The Act also states that material contrary to the public interest may not be disclosed, that state-appointed special advocates, with limited ability to communicate with the individual, are to represent his/her interests in the closed proceedings, and that the written determination of the court may be withheld from the defendant, if in the public interest. (Counter-Terrorism Act 2008)
17. Free speech and freedom of association were both reduced by terror laws. Any support for a proscribed organisation became illegal. (Terrorism Act 2000)

Privacy, Article 8, ECHR
'Everyone has the right to respect for his private and family life, his home and his correspondence.'
'The Database State'- intercepting, collecting, storing, sharing private information
The right to privacy has been eroded, perhaps permanently, by broad powers to intercept, collect, store and share our private information.

Surveillance and Interception
18. In 2004, the Secretary of State was given the power to authorise the electronic monitoring of individuals.
(Asylum and Immigration (Treatment of Claimants) Act 2004)

19. Regulations of Investigatory Powers ACT (RIPA) laws came into force in 2000 and specified the circumstances in which various authorities and agencies could mount surveillance operations. RIPA defines five broad categories of covert surveillance: directed surveillance (including photographing people); intrusive surveillance (including bugging); the use of covert human intelligence sources (informants and undercover officers, including watching and following people); accessing communications data (records of emails sent, telephone calls made) and intercepting communications (i.e. reading the content of emails, listening to telephone calls). The Act also allows the Home Secretary to issue an interception warrant to examine the contents of letters or communications on grounds of national security, or for the purpose of preventing or detecting crime, preventing disorder, ensuring public safety, protecting public health, or in the interests of the economic well-being of the United Kingdom. (Regulation of Investigatory Powers Act 2000)

20. An end to rules banning government departments from sharing personal information has been proposed in the Coroners and Justice Bill. An amendment to the Data Protection Act of 1998 contained in the new bill will allow personal data to be shared by ministers by executive order, to achieve what are vaguely termed the government's 'policy purposes'.
(Coroners and Justice Bill 2009)

Collection and Acquisition

21. Over 50 pieces of personal information will be transferred from the private control of the individual to the authority's National Identity Register (NIR) under the Identity Cards Act. Information placed on the NIR will include date and place of birth, principal place of residence, every other place of UK or overseas residence, a head and shoulder photograph, signature, fingerprints, and other biometric information (which may include iris scans, and a facial measurement template). Individuals may be forced to register their details in order to receive certain public services and may be fined for not keeping their NIR information up-to-date. A record of all the important transactions in a person's life will be created by the electronic verification of their card. (Identity Cards Act 2006)

22. The freedom to communicate in private has been effectively extinguished by RIPA laws. The state may demand that telephone and internet providers hand over detailed communications records for individual users, including: names and addresses; phone calls made and received; source and destination of emails; internet browsing information and mobile phone positioning data which records the user's location. This power may be exercised by many public bodies, ranging from Revenue and Customs to the Royal Mail Group.
(Regulation of Investigatory Powers Act 2000 and Regulation of Investigatory Powers (Communications Data) (Additional Functions and Amendment) Order 2006/1878)

23. The loss of the right to communicate privately by post also ended with RIPA. Postal service providers may now be forced to intercept and retain postal items; maintaining a system of opening, copying and resealing of any postal item carried for less than £1. Secrecy is written into the law. Postal services are under strict obligations to intercept with as little

impact as possible to ensure the individual remains unaware of the intrusion. (Regulation of Investigatory Powers (Maintenance of Interception Capability) Order 2002/1931)

24. A further serious loss of privacy will occur when a person crosses UK borders. Anyone entering or leaving, or even expecting to leave, the UK must - under the e-Borders Scheme - supply the government with their name, gender, nationality, type of travel document held, and vehicle registration number if travelling in a vehicle. In all, 53 pieces of information may be taken from British citizens before they are permitted to leave the country, even though the new Draft (Partial) Immigration and Citizenship Bill asserts the freedom of a person to leave the UK unimpeded. Those coming into the UK will be expected to provide information and biometrics. Yachtsmen leaving British waters for the day and returning to shore will be expected to provide information about all those on board. (Immigration, Asylum and Nationality Act (2006) and the Immigration and Police (Passenger, Crew and Service Information) Order 2008 /5)

25. The right to check into a hotel in the United Kingdom anonymously and without the state being informed, may end with the introduction of compulsory registration measures proposed in clause 30 of the draft of the new Draft (Partial) Immigration and Citizenship Bill. This will allow the Home Secretary to keep records of people, 'whether or not they are a British Citizen', and require them - on pain of a £5,000 fine or a year in prison - to provide the information to an unspecified list of people whom the Secretary of State considers 'expedient'. (Draft (Partial) Immigration and Citizenship Bill 2008)

26. The privacy of non-UK nationals has also been compromised. Asylum seekers must supply a personal record containing physical characteristics, photos and fingerprints and an inventory of a detainee's possessions must be made. Photographs and fingerprints may be retained until they become British citizens, even if they have a right to residency in the UK. (Nationality, Immigration and Asylum Act 2002, Immigration and Asylum Act 1999, Immigration (Provision of Physical Data) Regulations 2006/1743, Detention Centre Rules 2001/ 238)

27. The line between guilt and innocence has been blurred with preventative orders, under anti-terrorism and social disorder legislation (see below). One result is that personal information concerning those who are merely suspected of involvement in terrorist-related activities which are held by public bodies, may be demanded by police and security services carrying out criminal and terrorist investigations. Individuals placed under control orders may now be forced to provide police with fingerprints and DNA samples. (Anti-Terrorism, Crime and Security Act 2001 and Counter-Terrorism Act 2008)

Storage and retention of personal information

28. Children are being groomed for a life in the database state. Alongside the gradual introduction of biometrics and CCTV in schools, is the children's database 'ContactPoint', which went live in January 2008. It contains 20 pieces of information on all children resident in England. Over 400,000 people will have access to the database but parents will have no

right to check the data held on their children. (Children Act 2004)

29. The concept of innocence unless proven guilty by a normal court of law was eroded when it became possible for police in England, Wales and Northern Ireland to retain indefinitely DNA samples and fingerprints from anyone arrested for a recordable offence, even if they were released without charge, or found not guilty. This also included the DNA of people who were witnesses to a crime. The ECHR ruled in December 2008 that the retention of DNA from two innocent men in Yorkshire, breached their human rights, which has implications for the samples of one million innocent people on the Police National DNA Database. (Criminal, Justice and Police Act 2001)

30. The imposition of compulsory biometric identity documents for non-EU immigrants was introduced in 2007 in a law which grants the Secretary of State wide-ranging powers to retain and share biometric information. This law requires those subject to immigration control to apply for a biometric immigration document which can contain over 15 pieces of information, including details held on a radio frequency electronic microchip (RFID) embedded in the document. The information can be retained by the Secretary of State as long as is deemed necessary.
(UK Borders Act 2007 & Immigration (Biometric Registration) Regulations 2008/3048)

Data sharing

31. The sharing of information on the National Identity Register (NIR) is the first step in a government-wide project to make all information on private citizens available to the government and its agencies. The Security Service, Secret Intelligence Service, GCHQ, Serious Organised Crime Agency and HM Revenue and Customs will all have access to the NIR. Information on the NIR may be passed on to any public authority where it is deemed necessary for security, law enforcement, prevention of crime or government efficiency. No member of the public will be allowed access to his or her file. (Identity Cards Act 2006)

32. Information about parents and children is required to be shared between public authorities before an application for a parenting order is made. (Anti-Social Behaviour Act 2003 & Education (Parenting Contracts and Parenting Orders) (England) Regulations 2007/1869)

33. The enhanced Criminal Records Bureau (CRB) check system infringes the right to privacy and the presumption of innocence. Charges for which one has been acquitted and even conduct unrelated to crime may be disclosed. The Chief of Police is empowered to disclose to potential employers anything that in his or her opinion 'might be relevant' to an individual's job application. This is in spite of the disproportionate effect that disclosure might have on the individual's employability. This promotes a 'no smoke without fire' approach.
(Police Act 1997)

The privatisation of the database

34. The government's drive to use private companies to hold information on private citizens began in 2001 with anti-terrrorism legislation. It requires airlines to provide information about passengers and enables communication service providers to retain data, so that it

can be accessed by law agencies investigating terrorism or criminal activities. The law also obliges financial institutions such as banks to contact law agencies when they believe there are 'reasonable grounds' to suspect terrorist financing. The Act allows for the retention of communications data by service providers, who must retain information on who called whom for extended periods of time. (Anti-Terrorism, Crime and Security Act 2001)
35. In 2000, the government took measures to force internet service providers (ISPs) to fit equipment to facilitate surveillance, and to allow the government to demand that the ISP give secret access to a customer's communication.
(Regulation of Investigatory Powers Act 2000)

Freedom of Expression, Article 10, ECHR
'Everyone has the right to freedom of expression. This right shall include freedom to hold opinions and to receive and impart information and ideas without interference by public authority and regardless of frontiers.'

36. New laws affecting the freedom of expression will be introduced by Jack Straw's Coroners and Justice Bill: the discussion, criticism or discouragement of sexual conduct or practices will become an offence of stirring up hatred on grounds of sexual orientation.
(Coroners and Justice Bill 2009)
37. Terror laws make it a criminal offence to encourage terrorism by directly or indirectly inciting or encouraging others to commit acts of terrorism. This includes an offence of 'glorification' of terror - people who 'praise or celebrate' terrorism in a way that may encourage others to commit a terrorist act. (Terrorism Act 2006)
38. The freedom to take photographs of police who are engaged in anti-terrorist operations was removed by laws that make it a criminal offence to elicit or attempt to elicit information about a member of the armed forces, the intelligence services or a constable, which is likely to be useful to a person committing or preparing an act of terrorism. (Counter-Terrorism Act 2008)
39. To glorify terrorism in a way that may encourage others to commit a terrorist act was made a criminal offence in the Terrorism Act 2006.

Freedom of Assembly, Article 11, ECHR
'Everyone has the right to freedom of peaceful assembly and to freedom of association with others, including the right to form and to join trade unions for the protection of his interests.'

Right to peaceful protest
40. The right to freedom of assembly was eroded by the Anti-Social Behaviour Act 2003, which allows police and community officers to issue dispersal orders to groups of people in a designated area. A group was defined as more than two people. Refusal to leave or returning to an area once dispersed is a criminal offence. (Anti-Social Behaviour Act 2003)
41. Demonstrations within 1 kilometre of Parliament Square, without police permission,

▶

are forbidden. The police can decide the time and place of the demonstration and limit the number of participants as well as the size and number of banners.
(Serious Organised Crime and Police Act 2005)
42. A new definition of a 'rave' means that a gathering of 20 people, not 100, may be dispersed by police. (Anti-Social Behaviour Act 2003 amending the Criminal Justice and Public Order Act 1994)
43. The freedom to attend gatherings such as football matches and pop concerts was affected by the issue of section 27 forms. This allows police to tell an individual or a group to leave a locality for up to 48 hours to minimise the risk of alcohol-related disorder or crime. There is evidence that this law is already being abused to deprive innocent members of the public of their right to attend events. (Violent Crime Reduction Act 2006)

Freedom of Association, Article 11, ECHR
'Everyone has the right to freedom of peaceful assembly and to freedom of association with others, including the right to form and to join trade unions for the protection of his interests.'

Right to join and form organisations
44. The right to strike was taken away from prison officers.
(Criminal Justice and Immigration Act 2008)
45. Free speech and freedom of association were both reduced by terror laws. Any support for a proscribed organisation became illegal. (Terrorism Act 2000)
46. Certain clothing and the display of articles such as banners were outlawed if these aroused reasonable suspicion that they indicated support for a proscribed organisation. A person commits an offence if he/she belongs, professes to belong to, or supports a proscribed organisation. (Terrorism Act 2000)

Marriage, Article 12, ECHR
'Men and women of marriageable age have the right to marry and to found a family, according to the national laws governing the exercise of this right.'

Right to marry
47. The right to marry and found a family is affected by a new law that requires immigrants to obtain permission to marry from the Secretary of State.
(Asylum and Immigration (Treatment of Claimants) Act 2004)

Property, Protocol 1, Article 1, ECHR
'Every natural or legal person is entitled to the peaceful enjoyment of his possessions. No one shall be deprived of his possessions except in the public interest and subject to the conditions provided for by law and by the general principles of international law.'

Protection of property

48. The Englishman's home is no longer his castle. For the first time since 1604, bailiffs may enter a home to seize goods in the recovery of a fine owed as result of a magistrate's court conviction, and use reasonable force to restrain or pin down those present. Bailiffs may also enter on a High Court or County Court warrant for unpaid taxes and social security contributions. (Tribunals Courts and Enforcement Act 2007)

49. New laws allow police or local authorities to apply to magistrates to close privately-owned or rented property or local authority premises believed to be the centre of serious and persistent disorder or nuisance. The order for three to six months may be granted at short notice on extremely low standards of proof; hearsay and evidence from anonymous witnesses is accepted. (Criminal Justice and Immigration Act 2008 /Anti-Social Behaviour Act 2003)

50. Terror laws can be used to freeze assets as in the case of the stricken National Bank of Iceland. (Anti-Terrorism, Crime and Security Act 2001 & the Landsbanki Freezing Order 2008/2668)

51. Asylum seekers have no property rights while in detention. A detainee is not entitled to hold cash; the manager or Secretary of State can object to the holding of possessions if they are likely to be objectionable to others, are contrary to health and safety or are incompatible with storage in the facility. Any individual may, upon entering, or at sporadic times throughout his detention, be searched.
(Nationality, Immigration and Asylum Act 2002 & the Detention Centre Rules 2001/238)

Emergency Powers - Derogating from ECHR Rights, Article 15, ECHR
'In time of war or other public emergency threatening the life of the nation any High Contracting Party may take measures derogating from its obligations under this Convention to the extent strictly required by the exigencies of the situation.'

52. The Civil Contingencies Act 2004 allows that, in an emergency, a senior minister will issue emergency regulations by means of an Order in Council to protect human life, communications, property, supplies of money, food, water or fuel. The powers include the confiscation of property without compensation, the destruction of property, animal life or plant life without compensation, enforced movement from a specified place, the prohibition of travel, the deployment of the armed forces, the creation of new offences, conferring jurisdiction on new courts and tribunals and forced labour. 'The Civil Contingencies Act is the most powerful and extensive peacetime legislation ever enacted', wrote Clive Walker and James Broderick in their study of this little noticed Act. 'Indeed, it contains within it the tools for dismantling civil society.'
The safeguards against misuse of the Act are thought to be weak because there is no requirement of objectivity in the tests for invoking emergency powers. The minister must merely satisfy him or herself that an emergency has taken place, or is about to. The Act specifies that emergency regulations may be issued by the Prime Minister, the principle Secretaries of State, or the Commissioners of Her Majesty's Treasury, one of which is the Government's chief Whip. During its passage through Parliament, the bill was attacked by

Lord Lucas who said, '(t)he government have so many powers and sources of information that they are capable of creating the illusion of a serious threat to the country. Indeed one does not have to look back many months to see them do exactly that. We have just been to war (in Iraq) as a result of an illusion created by this government.' (The Civil Contingencies Act 2004)

SECTION 2: UNCODIFIED RIGHTS AND CONSTITUTIONAL SAFEGUARDS

Our human rights are not limited to those listed in the ECHR and the HRA. There is, in fact, a wider category of civil liberties and fundamental freedoms which are protected by the UK constitution, including rights to citizenship, freedom of movement and jury trial. Further, constitutional safeguards, such as public inquiries, provide essential accountability channels and therefore act as a check and balance on abusive executives. Equally, however, the attack on liberty has not been limited to the ECHR, but has encroached upon the UK's cherished constitutional foundations.

Freedom of movement
53. Freedom of movement without surveillance came to an end in the UK in 2007 when the Automatic Number Recognition Camera Network went live to track and record all journeys on major roads and through town centres. The system stores data for five years and allows real time surveillance of target vehicles. (See e-Borders data collection above. Immigration, Asylum and Nationality Act 2006)

Citizenship
54. The Home Secretary may remove British citizenship from dual nationals if 'conducive to the public good'. (Immigration, Asylum and Nationality Act 2006)
55. The Home Secretary may deny a person his/her British citizenship if he/she is satisfied that the person has done something seriously prejudicial to the vital interests of the UK. (Nationality, Immigration and Asylum Act 2002)

Jury trial
56. The Domestic Violence, Crime and Victims Act extends the slow erosion of the principle that every defendant has the right to be tried by a jury of his/her peers. The prosecution can now apply for a trial on indictment when some, but not all, of the counts included on the indictment may be conducted without a jury. Trial without jury is permissible if the number of indictable accounts makes it impracticable; and it is in the interests of justice to disallow jury trial.
(Domestic Violence, Crime and Victims Act 2004)
57. Trial by jury is set to be further undermined by a new bill which gives the Secretary of State the power to demand that an inquest be held (including one where a person has died in state custody or at the hands of the state) without a jury.

(Coroners and Justice Bill 2009)

Public inquiries
58. A grave reduction in scrutiny and public accountability was brought about by the Inquiries Act 2005, which also allowed a transfer of power from Parliament to the Executive with little public debate. Public inquiries are essential for maintaining transparent and accountable government. They provide necessary information for voters and the opportunity to exercise civil liberties such as expression and protest. However, the Executive now has the power to choose and appoint the chairman and panel members of any public inquiry, set the inquiry's terms of reference and alter them at any point without Parliamentary consent. The inquiry can be suspended at any point subject to the Minister's discretion. The Minister may also restrict public access to the inquiry and any inquiry documents for reasons of cost, delay or inefficiency and has the power to censor the content of the report, removing any information they consider would harm the economic and security interests of state. The Act was barely noticed at the time of its passage through the House of Commons. (Inquiries Act 2005)

19 FEBRUARY, 2009

AUTHORS:

HENRY PORTER (EDITOR)
UMAR AZMEH
JONATHAN BUTTERWORTH
TONY DALY
MICHAEL MOHALLEM
NAUREEN SHAMEEN
QUDSI RASHEED
EMILY RAYNER
RICHARD WALKER
KAI ZHANG

THE ORIGINAL VERSION OF THIS DOCUMENT (AS ABOVE) WAS PUBLISHED FOR AND DISTRIBUTED IN THE **CONVENTION ON MODERN LIBERTY**. FOR A REVISED AND UPDATED EDITION, PLEASE VISIT HTTP://WWW.UCLSHRP.COM

Are such things done on Albion's shore?
PHILIP PULLMAN

The image of this nation that haunts me most powerfully is that of the sleeping giant Albion in William Blake's prophetic books. Sleep, profound and inveterate slumber: that is the condition of Britain today. We do not know what is happening to us. In the world outside great events take place, great figures move and act, great matters unfold, and this nation of Albion murmurs and stirs while malevolent voices whisper in the darkness – the voices of the new laws that are silently strangling the old freedoms the nation still dreams it enjoys.

We are so fast asleep that we don't know who we are any more. Are we English? Scottish? Welsh? British? More than one of them? One but not another? Are we a Christian nation – after all we have an Established Church – or are we something post-Christian? Are we a secular state? Are we a multi-faith state? Are we anything we can all agree on and feel proud of?

The new laws whisper:

You don't know who you are;
You're mistaken about yourself.
We know better than you do what you consist of, what labels apply to you, which facts about you are important and which are worthless.
We do not believe you can be trusted to know these things, so we shall know them for you.
And if we take against you, we shall remove from your possession the only proof we shall allow to be recognised.

The sleeping nation dreams it has the freedom to speak its mind. It fantasises about making tyrants cringe with the bluff bold vigour of its ancient right to express its opinions in the street. This is what the new laws say about that:

Expressing an opinion is a dangerous activity.
Whatever your opinions are, we don't want to hear them.

So if you threaten us or our friends with your opinions we shall treat you like the rabble you are.
And we do not want to hear you arguing about it,
So hold your tongue and forget about protesting.
What we want from you is acquiescence.

The nation dreams it is a democratic state where the laws were made by freely elected representatives who were answerable to the people. It used to be such a nation once, it dreams, so it must be that nation still. It is a sweet dream.

You are not to be trusted with laws,
So we shall put ourselves out of your reach.
We shall put ourselves beyond your amendment or abolition.
You do not need to argue about any changes we make, or to debate them, or to send your representatives to vote against them.
You do not need to hold us to account.
You think you will get what you want from an inquiry?
Who do you think you are?
What sort of fools do you think we are?

The nation's dreams are troubled, sometimes; dim rumours reach our sleeping ears, rumours that all is not well in the administration of justice; but an ancient spell murmurs through our somnolence, and we remember that the courts are bound to seek the truth, the whole truth, and nothing but the truth, and we turn over and sleep soundly again.

And the new laws whisper:

We do not want to hear you talking about truth;
Truth is a friend of yours, not a friend of ours.
We have a better friend called hearsay, who is a witness we can always rely on.
We do not want to hear you talking about innocence;
Innocent means guilty of things not yet done.
We do not want to hear you talking about the right to silence;
You need to be told what silence means: it means guilt.

> *We do not want to hear you talking about justice;*
> *Justice is whatever we want to do to you.*
> *And nothing else.*

Are we conscious of being watched, as we sleep? Are we aware of an ever-open eye at the corner of every street, of a watching presence in the very keyboards we type our messages on? The new laws don't mind if we are. They don't think we care about it.

> *We want to watch you day and night.*
> *We think you are abject enough to feel safe when we watch you.*
> *We can see you have lost all sense of what is proper to a free people.*
> *We can see you have abandoned modesty;*
> *Some of our friends have seen to that.*
> *They have arranged for you to find modesty contemptible.*
> *In a thousand ways they have led you to think that whoever does not want to be watched must have something shameful to hide.*
> *We want you to feel that solitude is frightening and unnatural.*
> *We want you to feel that being watched is the natural state of things.*

One of the pleasant fantasies that consoles us in our sleep is that we are a sovereign nation, and safe within our borders. This is what the new laws say about that:

> *We know who our friends are,*
> *And when our friends want to have words with one of you,*
> *We shall make it easy for them to take you away to a country where you will learn that you have more fingernails than you need.*
> *It will be no use bleating that you know of no offence you have committed under British law;*
> *It is for us to know what your offence is.*
> *Angering our friends is an offence.*

It is inconceivable to me that a waking nation in the full consciousness of its freedom would have allowed its government to pass such laws as the Protection from Harassment Act (1997), the Crime and Disorder Act

(1998), the Regulation of Investigatory Powers Act (2000), the Terrorism Act (2000), the Criminal Justice and Police Act

> "We are so fast asleep that we don't know who we are any more."

(2001), the Anti-Terrorism, Crime and Security Act (2001), the Regulation of Investigatory Powers Extension Act (2002), the Criminal Justice Act (2003), the Extradition Act (2003), the Anti-Social Behaviour Act (2003), the Domestic Violence, Crime and Victims Act (2004), the Civil Contingencies Act (2004), the Prevention of Terrorism Act (2005), the Inquiries Act (2005), the Serious Organised Crime and Police Act (2005), not to mention a host of pending legislation such as the Identity Cards Bill, the Coroners and Justice Bill, and the Legislative and Regulatory Reform Bill.

Inconceivable.

And those laws say:

Sleep, you stinking cowards;
Sweating as you dream of rights and freedoms.
Freedom is too hard for you;
We shall decide what freedom is.
Sleep, you vermin.
Sleep, you scum.

SOURCE: THE TIMES, 27 FEBRUARY 2009

MORNING SESSIONS

Photo courtesy of Oliver Lamford

Opening Plenary
Citizens and the state: the crisis of liberty

British democracy is in crisis and it now seems likely that the constitutional rights that we all believed were our birthright, will not be our children's. Certain questions arise which go to the heart of the way we allow ourselves to be governed. Are Parliament and the parties failing in their duty? If that is the case, and the government is the source of the problem, where do we look to protect our liberties?

The state is here at our behest
HELENA KENNEDY QC

I became involved in doing cases around civil liberties in the 1970s when I was a young lawyer. Having seen law in the courts and then law being made as a member of the House of Lords, one of the things that has happened increasingly over the last 20 years, is the politicization of criminal justice, and of issues like liberty. We have been seeing a sort of Dutch auction between the political parties, as to who can be tougher. But while we may all be very cross with this particular government, if you look back to the period when I was first practising in the courts – and it was not Labour who was in government – there were pretty awful things happening then too in relation to liberty.

Why has this been happening? The reality is, liberty is never given to people. People have always had to fight for liberty. Liberty is an accretion of battles in order for people to claim what should rightfully be theirs. When you want to talk about liberty, you have to talk about power. Who has power? What happens when people have power? The common law in this country has taught us that you have to be very sceptical about power, because once people have it, the temptation to abuse it is very, very great.

Someone once said that power can turn even the gentlest of souls into a Nero. Well let me tell you, we have managed to see some Neros emerging in contemporary government. I always say there must be something in the drinking water at the Home Office. People who seem perfectly decent, who don't have staring eyes, who don't seem mad, go in there and are suddenly overwhelmed with the need to reduce our liberty. We saw it from the very beginning of New Labour in government. But the Dutch auction began before that. Let's not forget Michael Howard, Anne Widdecombe: let's not forget some of the people who were in that office prior to these who have followed.

What has happened in recent times is that this business of showing who can be tougher has become one of the ways of winning *Daily Mail* or populist approval for a government. I'm afraid that Labour was very susceptible to this. It came into government saying, 'we have to prove that, like the Conservatives, we can run the economy and be as tough with money and show that we can be liberal marketeers like the next guy'. By God did they too, and now we are paying the price! And they, too, wanted to show that the defence of the nation was safe in their hands and they could go to war like the next guy, and by God did they prove it! And they, too, wanted to show that they could be tough on crime. And, unfortunately, this business of being tough on crime very often involves erosions of liberty.

The trade-off is always sold to the citizen as being a deal that will only involve the liberties of other folk, almost invariably people whose skin colour is different from ours – but not always. The trade-off always says 'we're going to do this to deal with criminals, to deal with immigrants, to deal with bogus asylum seekers, to deal with terrorists'. The idea is that the rest of us are all to feel safer as a result. And in writing a blank cheque for the Government to look after us, we are actually signing away something very precious, because liberty is indivisible.

The trade-off is always a trade-off of something that belongs to us too.

Not everything is to do with terrorism. One of the shocking things for me occurred before 9/11, when I went into the House of Lords. One of the first things I fell out with the Government over, was the attempt to reduce trial by jury, one of the very precious and important features of our legal system. If I have learned anything about being a lawyer in the courts, it is that my point of entry into understanding civil liberties and why they matter, or understanding human rights and why they matter, is the pain of my clients - the number of times I have represented people who were wrongly convicted, based on the abuse of power.

But, interestingly, attacks on jury trial have very much been motored by people involved in the criminal justice system in Northern Ireland, who say, 'well, we did away with jury trial to deal with terrorism in the Diplock courts. It worked perfectly well for us. Why are you guys still insisting on it in terrorism trials here now?' There is an argument being made amongst judges that we shouldn't have jury trials for terrorism cases here. This is pernicious. But people, I think, actually don't fully appreciate how this erosion of liberties works.

It is a real fantasy that laws in relation to terrorism can be vacuum sealed, and that somehow they will only relate to terrorism and only for as long as the terrorist threat exists. The reality is, that you can't vacuum seal law like that.

It seeps into the culture of policing, for example. When one analysed what was happening in the courts in Irish trials, one saw that the same police forces that were responsible for the miscarriages of justice on those cases were also responsible for miscarriages of justice in other areas of crime, because there had been an erosion of standards around interrogation, and so you got false confessions and so forth.

We also saw standards being lowered on the right to silence and jury trial in the Diplock courts, which in turn have fed into attitudes to those things in the system as a whole. Now the right to silence has been eroded in relation to all crime. That followed within five years of a change taking place, first of all, in Northern Ireland, in response solely to terrorism.

So be very clear that what we are here trying to deal with today is the abuse of power. Of course, perfectly decent people don't realise that they are doing it. They, too, are like the frogs that go into the water. When the heat is turned up, they don't realise that they are becoming authoritarian. They think they are the good guys. And so when you say to ministers and government, 'do you realise what is happening?' they will often say 'no', because they have not been able to look collectively at the accretion of erosions that has taken place, and what they are actually going to mean.

I am very concerned about a number of things. Take civil liberties, that great long historic list that we have built up by battling as ordinary people. We seem to have lost our collective memories about having to struggle for these liberties. Tony Blair was the great man for saying, 'you know, it is all old-fashioned stuff'. Everything had to be 'new-new-new', and 'we shouldn't have 19th century systems to deal with 21st century society'. But in fact, many of these things are as true today as they ever were. When I started practising, it was young Afro-Caribbeans who knew what civil liberties meant because they were being arrested under the Stop-and-Search (or 'Sus') laws. Do you remember Sus laws, where you could be arrested for doing nothing on the say-so of a police officer who would say he saw your hand going out to a car door handle? Or your hand going into a woman's handbag and you were arrested, for being a 'suspected' person?

The Irish suffered all of this because they felt that being Irish during the Northern Irish troubles, or even speaking aloud with an Irish accent would draw down ignominy on their heads, that they might be arrested, or that

morning sessions

"I always say there must be something in the drinking water at the Home Office."

suspicion would fall upon them. The people who usually understood about civil liberties were the Jews within our midst, because they knew that power is abused and that people will be scapegoated: it had been so much a part of their historic experience. But that collective memory is being lost, and we have stopped telling the stories of why liberty has to be protected for all of us.

A false dichotomy that I am concerned about, however, is between civil liberties, on the one hand, and on the other, human rights. Human rights – modern human rights – are an evolution of civil liberties which were basically about liberty being in the hands of citizens. But human rights actually developed that premise to say, 'these rights have to be there for people because they are human, and not just gifted to you because you are British'. And so, I do not want us to be beguiled by the idea that somehow civil liberties have to be protected, but that the Human Rights Act does not, because - as Shami Chakrabarti says - we are talking about something that comes as one piece and has to be guarded by us all.

Finally I wanted to say, modern liberty is hopefully not about something that's modern or 'new' as in 'New Labour'. But there are new challenges that society presents to us, and we do have to have careful discussions about the extent to which surveillance of any kind is something that people are prepared to trade in, and if so, what level of it they would be prepared to accept. I am particularly concerned about the whole business of there being an incredible database in which our souls are sold by being told that it's about our own protection and security.

Because once you start having to give information to the police, where the police say to you, 'where are you going? Why are you here? What's your name? What is your address?' And you are required to answer them, and the police need give you no reason as to why they are asking those questions, there is a transfer: a transfer of power is taking place. Under the common law, we have always said that the state has to prove things, that there's a presumption of innocence, that the state has to prove its case in the courts, that if the state turns up at your door you can say to them, 'where's your warrant? Why are you wanting to search my home?' That if you're stopped in the street you can say, 'why are you stopping me?' But we are doing away with all of that. And once you do away with all of that, you are changing the nature of that relationship, the paradigm of the relationship between citizen and state. I want us to remember that the state is here at our behest and we are not here at the behest of the state.

Now, this is one glorious day on which all of you have come here caring about this and joining with the many organisations that deal with aspects of this. I hope that it won't just be a joyous day of us coming together and celebrating liberty, but that we will also be decrying the things that have happened and learning from each other. But I also see a window of opportunity. There is going to be an election next year. In that window of opportunity between now and then, I would like us to put a brake on the erosions that the government has in place currently and those it intends to proceed with. I would like to see commitments in the manifestos of political parties that they are going to do something about returning some of that liberty to us that has been taken away. I want us to make a decision today that we will prepare a document that each one of us as citizens will be able to take with us to challenge those who will be standing in our constituencies and to say, 'where do you stand on the following things: on a DNA database? Where do you stand on ID cards? Where do you stand on jury trial? Where do you stand on habeas corpus?' And I want those questions put to every single candidate: so that it is clear to them that your vote will depend on the way that they answer those questions.

The delivery of public services
SIR DAVID VARNEY

I was asked to look at the delivery of public services, which is changing in almost all of the major countries; each of them seeing whether they can modernise public services. In our current system, that involves providing services down individual stove pipes: somebody who's getting a pension typically would deal with the pension agency, housing benefit, and with council tax benefit - a long process where they were required to deal with each of those bodies separately. And I tried to address in my report, 'how can we make that an easier transaction for the citizen, more enjoyable for the staff and more effective for the taxpayer?'

I am not a champion of a great single database. Technically, one single database is unlikely to be used as efficiently as several. When you think about a database, you tend to think about what you can put on a computer. But given the sheer number of aspects we have to address, I think it will have all the disadvantages of corroding public liberties and very little to offer in terms of managerial efficiency, that is, in managing the complex problems that many of our services face...

So we're seeing bits of the state which need to be modernised, partly in order to be more effective in delivering those services. It is also partly to respond to the new series of reports that there have been on public tragedies. If you look at the Soham murders, at Victoria Climbié, at Baby P, the one common feature is the failure of public services to share information about the people they were dealing with.

Now, when I talk about bringing services together, I am saying that the sort of information we as a society need to share is name, national insurance number, date of birth and address. There needs to be a big discussion about whether that's the right information to share: but I believe that the public have a right to know what information is being held by public services, what use it is being put to, and what the safeguards are for protecting the integrity of that information.

That is a challenge which is going to come back to us, the state. But we also need to look a bit outside the state. Take the *Guardian*, who are sponsoring this event. If you want to subscribe to *Public* magazine, (the *Guardian's* online magazine for senior managers in the public sector) it asks for your name, your address, the company you work for, it asks about which sector you are in, it asks about what your area of responsibility is, how much budget spend you've got, and then it says at the end, 'do you want to receive *Public* magazine?' So that's all fairly straightforward.

In much smaller print is a statement that reads, 'if you specifically do not wish your details to be passed on please tick here'. This is the opt-out model of sharing data.

I am arguing that for most data, it should be an opt-in process. We need that process of information management, and this is a challenge which we will face not just in the public sector but in the private sector, too. I decided about two years ago that one of the things I would do is ask one of the internet agencies that monitors credit standing to monitor *my* credit standing. The thing that amazed me was that, at the end of the first month, they reported back what was known on the internet about me, and the first piece of information they got was my credit card debit balance. Not the details, but what the balance was – the account details, thank God, it kept to itself. But what amazed me was how much information is on the internet. We need a consistent policy line both in the public and private sector, because it would be mad if we imposed constraints on the public sector, and then just turned a blind eye to the private sector. So that's part of the challenge. Thank you.

> "We need that process of information management, and this is a challenge which we will face not just in the public sector but in the private sector, too."

Member of the audience: I'd like to ask Sir David Varney why, if he believes that only four items of information are necessary for the database, we are being asked for 53?

David Varney: I was talking about information which is required for service delivery. If more information than the four items I have identified is required, then I believe we need the service organisation seeking that information to get the consent of the citizen to provide it.

I think the 52 comes from security issues and you will have to ask these organisations because I certainly don't know why they need that amount of information… In my report, I worked out that, on average, a citizen has to reveal and prove their identity to the state 11 times a year. But of course if you're a vulnerable member of society, economically not very successful, maybe with housing difficulties, a number of dependencies, maybe health problems, you probably do that many, many times more.

And most of us will be carrying forms of identity around which other people, not the state, use, whether it's a credit card, a mobile phone - even in countries with written constitutions. It's quite striking if you look at Facebook and Twitter, the most amazing things that people are prepared to share with other people. Well, you have a choice and they've made that choice, which means there is a growing sector of information becoming publicly available from those sorts of sites alone.

I think we need a big debate... If you ask how to get to *Sun* readers, Obama has shown that one of the great advantages of the internet is the way in which you can communicate and raise collective pressure in unorthodox and quite forceful ways.

SOURCE: EXCERPTS FROM THE CML SPEECH AND FOLLOW-UP DISCUSSION

The Mega Snooper State
KEN MACDONALD QC

Helena has raised the question of what's in the water in the Home Office. Let me tell you something which is probably very obvious to all of you. When your every day begins with security briefings and threat assessments – and believe me, I've been there – and when you feel responsible for other people's safety, it is very easy to fall into a way of thinking that places security above absolutely everything else. It's a simple psychology to slip into. You start to develop a form of protective zeal. It's re-enforcing and very comforting when you are doing those jobs. You begin to believe that you have to do your best to abolish risk altogether and that you can legislate it away: that you can create a society where people are always safe. But as Dominic has said, the idea of total security is nothing more than a paranoid fantasy which would destroy everything that makes living worthwhile. And it is for citizens to make plain to their government that they understand this. We, as citizens, have to make this clear, that we are consciously prepared as adults to accept some element of risk in order to be free.

Now, Jack Straw, writing in the *Guardian* this week, has declared that Britain is not a police state, and there is nothing like a statement of the bleeding obvious to lubricate an article in a newspaper. I may have been guilty of that myself in recent days, but I want to concentrate on one particular threat which I do perceive.

There was another story in the *Guardian* last week, a front page story about a paper written by Sir David Omand, who was Security and Intelligence Coordinator in the Cabinet Office for some years. I know and admire David Omand. He produced a very thoughtful paper for the Institute for Public Policy Research (ippr) on, amongst other things, communications data surveillance. This too is a thoughtful paper which I think gives a glimpse of the scale of ambition in some parts of Whitehall, and he maps out a future that we would do very well to examine and consider with very great care.

Actually, I don't believe there is unanimity about any of this in government yet, and not even in the security services. There are arguments and disputes going on, and I am not sure that the position of the main opposition party is entirely clear yet. But essentially what is proposed, is that we might move away from a system in which only those suspected of involvement in, or association with, crime can be subjected to intrusive inspection and examination - to a world in which people suspected of nothing, the wholly innocent, may be dealt with by the state in precisely the same way, so that everybody's communications data, everybody's phone records, everybody's text messages, everybody's internet use, airline bookings, financial records, biometric data – all of it – may be integrated by the state.

As David Omand says, and I quote, 'such sources have always been accessible to traditional law enforcement seeking evidence against the named suspect, already justified by reasonable suspicion of having committed a crime. However,' he goes on, 'the application of modern data mining and processing techniques does involve examination of the innocent as well as the suspect to identify patterns of interest for further investigation. The realm of intelligence operations,' he says, 'is of course a zone to which the normal ethical rules we might hope to govern private conduct cannot apply. Finding out other people's secrets is going to mean breaking everyday moral rules.' And he concludes, 'so public trust in the essential reasonableness of UK police, security and intelligence agency activity will continue to be essential if we are to move into that world.'

Now, what the paper completely fails to address is how that precondition, that essential public trust, could possibly survive a system under which the security services were empowered by law to routinely trawl

> "...we should take very great care indeed to imagine the world we're creating before we build it. We might otherwise end up living with something that we can't bear."

through the private communications data of vast numbers of citizens suspected of no crime, simply in order, as Sir David puts it, 'to identify patterns of interest for further investigation'.

How would the public regard their security services in that world? Of course, such a world would change the relationship between the state and its citizens in the most fundamental and, I believe, dangerous ways. In all probability, it would tend to recast all of us as subservient and unworthy of autonomy. It would destroy accountability and it would destroy trust.

This is for one very simple reason: because to abolish the distinction between suspects and those suspected of nothing, to place them entirely in the same category in the eyes of the state, is a clear hallmark of authoritarianism. None of this is to argue against the rights of suspects – these are absolutely sacrosanct. But it is to take a stand against any government that might understand no distinction at all, so that everyone, each one of us, becomes a suspect.

You only have to imagine where the security services are positioning themselves. If they go down this road, what is going to be the view of the average citizen towards the security services and their remit? David Omand talks about a generally beneficent attitude that people have of the security services, in spite of current controversies – and we don't know where those will end – but a general feeling on the part of people that - you know - they do what has to be done. Now that may be shared in this room or not, but it's probably a broad view in the country. What's the view of them going to be if they become the kind of mega snooper into everybody's private life? What are people going to think about the security service and secret intelligence service in that world? And what is their relationship going to be with a state that controls those organs, in that world? This is, to put it in marketing terms if in no other, extraordinarily bad positioning for these people.

The threat that all of this could represent is only exacerbated, only underlined and highlighted, by any idea that all this private personal material might in future be held on a giant, central database, accessible to the government and its agencies. As I have said before, it is for these reasons that we should take very great care indeed to imagine the world we're creating before we build it. We might otherwise end up living with something that we can't bear.

In recent years, the issues we're considering today have interestingly cut across some traditional lines. On a couple of occasions when I have made interventions in the area of liberties, I have had approving responses in particular from two newspapers, the *Guardian* and the *Daily Mail*, often on the same day. The *Daily Mail* and *Daily Telegraph* have taken quite an interesting line on some of these issues. They were highly sceptical about 42 days, opposed it, in fact; they're highly sceptical about the rhetoric around the War on Terror and they are, to a greater or lesser extent, concerned about issues of torture. The position of the Conservative party - although we might have issues here and there around the edges - is very different from where it would have been 15 or 20 years ago.

This rather unpleasant place
DOMINIC GRIEVE QC MP

Thank you very much, and thank you for the opportunity to be here today at what is clearly, as we've seen in the build-up, a very important event. The road to hell is paved with good intentions, and I think that if we need to start with an overview about what's going so wrong in the field of civil liberties, we have to take a long look at ourselves, at how we have succeeded – forgive my saying this but – collectively succeeded in creating this state monster that is threatening to gobble freedom up. Under pressure from media, individuals, the electorate, politicians have been ratcheting along a road of greater regulation in the deluded belief that, by doing it, we all end up safer, better protected, better able to relate to each other. Whereas, in fact, the end product is going to be a state and society where we are vastly regulated, but where this makes no difference to our security and where individuals feel disempowered and demoralised because the things which come naturally to them, in terms of their relations with others, are fettered at every turn.

The idea that the criminal or the extremist - be it the BNP or mad Islamist - is in some way going to be deterred by these structures, is laughable. But we as politicians seem so often to lack the courage to just come forward and say, 'none of this will work. You have to accept that society and life carries risk. Death is an inevitability for us all, and whilst it is the duty of the state to do its best to moderate and prevent what is wrong, nevertheless there are finite limits on what we should be doing, because the moment you go beyond it, you start creating that monster.'

For me, as a Conservative politician coming in in 1997, and watching with increasing astonishment and horror what we have been creating for ourselves in the last ten years, that seems to be the source of the problem. And I say this at the outset of this discussion because we will, in the course of the discussion, have lots to say on 42 days and data sharing and DNA databases and ID cards. But actually, we have to get behind all that to understand the drivers that are forcing us down this crazed road, uniquely in Western society. I don't think there is any other European country, even the United States, that has gone completely hell-for-leather in this fashion – and which is transforming us into this rather unpleasant place. The whole episode concerning Binyam Mohamed fills me with utmost shame. Here we are, a country which outlawed torture in the middle of the 17th century, and yet we appear pretty clearly to have colluded with it in the course of the last few years, for issues of state expediency. We've got to change the philosophy, because, unless we change the philosophy, this is going to continue.

Conservatives can get things wrong. We don't have a monopoly on wisdom. But the one thing that keeps me on the straight and narrow – and I actually think helps us – is that, if we are about to consider something that is authoritarian, somewhere in the back of our consciences as Conservatives, somebody says, 'your grandfather wouldn't have approved'. It works quite well.

So what we need to do is to ally that spirit with the modernity and the social justice that many of you have come to this meeting fired with, and try to see how we can find a way forward which means that governments are no longer inclined down this road of constantly appealing to every knee-jerk reaction of the electorate in trying to strive for a totally mythical state of absolute security that can never exist and will destroy the quality of our lives if we let it continue…

It's entirely true that parties in opposition say that they are going to do things, and then they get into government and wonderful permanent officials come along and say, oh that's very brave, Minister. But just to make the position quite clear: we are going to get rid of identity cards! It's going. Finished. Done. And on top of that, we will also review the DNA database. It's got to be a database of those who have been convicted of criminal offences. There are other perfectly good models in the United Kingdom which can be used. And finally, we are going to look at repealing a lot of legislation. I would like to have a repeal bill in the first year of a Conservative government. There's all sorts of things I want to chuck into it, including much of the criminal justice legislation I spent hours looking at in committee, which we've introduced and subsequently never used and is now completely redundant…

> "But just to make the position quite clear: we are going to get rid of identity cards! It's going. Finished. Done."

Your average *Sun* reader is a person of strong views, but also, I have to say, a person of common sense. People are fed up with rules which appear to obstruct them or preach at them. They are concerned about their freedom in their daily lives, the freedom to go about their business. And one of the great challenges for us, particularly in the context of the European Convention on Human Rights, is translating that legal document in a way that makes it relevant to people, something which matters to them. That is how we can build a more cohesive society: one where people start recognising and respecting fundamental rights as something belonging to everyone.

Session 1
Judges and Politicians
SUPPORTED BY MISHCON DE REYA, SOLICITORS

For most of human history, the interests of the communities in which we live have been dominant and have thus determined the content of the rules we live by. Those rules, relating mainly to family, property and physical injury, were designed to promote social stability - something of prime importance to community members and those that led them. The rules were known and openly applied; the origin of what we call 'the rule of law'.

More recently, the acceptance that social stability is also dependent on recognition of the rights of individuals (and their enforceability against the community as such), has spawned intense political debate centred on three questions:

- Who decides what is in the interest of the community?

- Who decides what the rights of individuals are?

- Who decides when those rights should be suspended in the interests of the community?

"Close on 35 years ago, Leslie Scarman, already a greatly respected judge, said, with astonishing prescience, that he foresaw a situation in which our rights and liberties would depend on, and be defined by, not the law but complex governmental machinery subject only to administrative and political controls.

Such a system, he said, could, no doubt, be made to work in an age of computer devices and rapid communications: but where would be the safeguards against power? The men who pressed the buttons would be the very same men as those manipulating Parliament – the only safeguard left. Should we be content that the acute problems that would arise between the citizen and such a system were to be resolved by the men who operated the system?

Had Leslie Scarman been a member of this panel he would have said 'not the politicians'. But he would have said also, 'nor should it be the judges'. He would have thought that the question should not even be put.

He believed that we needed a new, democratically created, constitutional settlement that would limit the powers of both Parliament and Government and, as the highest law – unchangeable by government or judges, would entrench the rights of citizens and provide the framework and context within which conflicts between citizens and the state would be resolved.

He would have been intensely interested to hear whether his view was shared by any of us here today."

JOHN JACKSON, PANEL CHAIR AND CHAIRMAN OF MISHCON DE REYA

Relight the candle
LORD BINGHAM

We have heard much discussion in recent years of 'British values'. Questions have been asked, whether such values exist, and, if so, what they are.

To our forebears of one – two – three centuries ago, the answers to these questions would have been obvious.

What distinguishes Britain, they would have said – proudly and without hesitation – is that personal liberty flourishes here as nowhere else on the face of the earth.

And they would, at that time, have been right.

It is not necessary to go back to Magna Carta, although that is not a bad place to start.

It is over four centuries since the Court of the Star Chamber, not remembered as a source of subversive jurisprudence, declared that the air of England is too pure for any slave to breathe – a phrase heavily relied on when, in due course, the battle against slavery in this country was finally fought and won.

It is over two centuries since the Earl of Chatham declared –

The poorest man may in his cottage bid defiance to all the forces of the Crown. It may be frail – its roof may shake – the wind may blow through it – the rain may enter – but the King of England cannot enter – all his forces dare not cross the threshold of the ruined tenement.

Even the victorious American colonists, having thrown off the imperial yoke, acknowledged their birthright –

We are descended from a people whose government was founded on liberty; our glorious forefathers of Great Britain made liberty the foundation of everything. That country is a great, mighty, and splendid nation; not because their government is strong and energetic, but, sir, because liberty is its direct end and foundation
(Patrick Henry, 1788).

It may be said that this is all a long time ago. None the worse for that. Nor does it matter that the perception may not match the historical record. As Ernest Renan famously observed, 'getting its history wrong is part of being a nation'. But let me move closer to the present.

During the Second World War, when the survival of the nation was really on the line, a committee chaired by Lord Sankey, a very distinguished former Lord Chancellor, set out to answer the questions raised by HG Wells in 1939: 'what are we fighting for?' The committee's answer was a declaration of rights published in 1947. Advice was taken from many sources, including President Roosevelt, the Archbishop of York and AA Milne. Here was a modern, home-grown, British declaration of rights described as fundamental and inalienable.

Article 9 was entitled 'Personal Liberty'. It read:

Unless a man is declared by a competent authority to be a danger to himself or to others through mental abnormality, a declaration which must be confirmed within 7 days and thereafter reviewed at least annually, he shall not be restrained for more than 24 hours without being charged with a definite offence, nor shall he be remanded for a longer period than 8 days without his consent, nor imprisoned for more than 3 months without a trial. At a reasonable time before his trial, he shall be furnished with a copy of the evidence which it is proposed to use against him. At the end of the three month period, if he has not been tried and sentenced by due process of the law, he shall be acquitted and released. No man shall be charged more than once for the same offence ... Secret evidence is not permissible. Statements recorded in administrative dossiers shall not be used to justify the slightest infringement of personal liberty. A dossier is merely a memorandum for administrative use; it shall not be used without proper confirmation in open court.

The committee made no reference to the databases, the cameras, the gathering of huge quantities of personal and biometric material, the empowering of over 650 public bodies (including 474 local authorities) to obtain communications data, the introduction of an ID card rich in personal information, and so on. It made no reference because, doubtless, it failed to foresee these developments. Orwell's *1984* had yet to be written. But we cannot doubt how, if blessed with the gift of prophecy, the committee would have reacted.

So what has changed over the past 60 years, a short period in the life of a nation? There have, I suggest, been two catalysts of change.

> "It seems clear that the last half century has seen an erosion of values once held dear. It is not the work of one party or one government..."

The first catalyst is technological advance: it is now technically possible to observe, to record, to track, to measure, to analyse, to retrieve in a way which could never be done before. These new technological methods have, of course, many benign applications. A Luddite approach to them would be absurd. But the possession of great powers by the state, is not a reason for using them. We have, after all, enjoyed for many years, the power to destroy the world, but have wisely refrained from doing so. The possession of great powers by the state should rather prompt a principled determination to ensure that the permissible exercise of such powers is strictly defined, regulated and monitored so as to guarantee that any intrusion into the liberty and privacy of the individual is fully justified by an obviously superior community interest. It is an old but true saying that the condition upon which liberty has been given to man is eternal vigilance.

The second catalyst of change has been security: security against terrorist attack; security against the commission of crime. These are not considerations which any rational person would dismiss. But nor are they considerations the mere invocation of which trumps any other. Eternal vigilance must again be the watchword: to ensure that intrusive powers are limited to what is demonstrably necessary; to ensure that powers conferred for one purpose are not used for another; to detect and eradicate abuses. It is worth recalling Benjamin Franklin's observation that 'he who would put security before liberty deserves neither'. It is also worth recalling John Locke's even more salutary warning:

> *As soon as men decide that all means are permitted to fight an evil, then their good becomes indistinguishable from the evil that they set out to destroy.*

It seems clear that the last half century has seen an erosion of values once held dear. It is not the work of one party or one government, certainly not of the present government which, in enacting the Human Rights Act on coming into office, took the single most powerful step in the other direction. But, overall, an erosion nonetheless.

Can we stem or reverse this trend? Yes, to coin a phrase, we can.

How?

The first thing is to inform and arouse public opinion. On the whole, people do not much mind what is going on, because they have not been brought up to cherish the tradition of liberty, they do not in large measure know what is happening and they think of infringement of liberty as something that only happens to others. The responsibility of the media to inform, explain and warn is paramount, notably discharged by Henry Porter, week in, week out, and, we must hope, greatly reinforced by this Convention. But there must also be a determined, long-term educational ambition. For the last few months the great constitutional building blocks of our liberty have been modestly but movingly displayed in the British Library – Magna Carta, the Declaration of Arbroath, the Petition of Right, the Bill of Rights 1689 and many others. Some understanding of the significance of these documents should be imparted to every future citizen as part of his or her understanding of the country to which they belong.

Responsibility for protecting the liberty of the citizen must also rest upon Parliament, and particularly the House of Commons, traditionally regarded as the watchdog which would resist any unwarranted extension of ministerial power. But the watchdog has lacked ferocity of late. If that is because a government with a reasonable majority can impose its will on its own members, almost regardless of their private reservations, and thus on the House of Commons as a whole, and so legislate without effective restraint, then that is a defect in our constitution, compounded by an increased willingness to bypass the House of Lords, which calls for attention. The Commons should be a bastion and defender of our freedoms, not an accomplice in their unjustified erosion.

And then, thirdly, there is a responsibility on the courts. From their development of habeas corpus onwards, the courts have, on notable occasions but not always, proved staunch defenders of personal liberty.

'The law favours liberty', said Sir Edward Coke, and so it should. But the courts have been fairly described as the weakest department of government:

they can initiate nothing; they cannot annul legislation, even when it is incompatible with the Human Rights Convention; they acknowledge, as they have always done, the sovereignty of Parliament. They can check executive lawlessness, but they cannot dictate executive policy.

The Prime Minister said in June 2008 that 'these issues … how we maintain our security and advance our freedoms, are some of the biggest questions governments have to face'. They are some of the biggest questions we all have to face. That is why this Convention is so timely and so important: a candle may today be lit, or re-lit, in Britain which, we may hope, shall never be put out.

Can there be liberty without legal aid?
SIR GEOFFREY BINDMAN

I am looking for a much more principled approach to endorsing the need for public values that explicitly faces down the marketisation of government. That has been the tragic hallmark of New Labour. After a lifetime of support, I have witnessed this process at first hand, as the legacy of 1945 is systematically undone. We need the new generation to condemn the dominance of the market culture and pledge to reverse it.

There cannot be democracy, let alone social democracy, without the rule of law. The rule of law is meaningful only if there is equal access to the courts. Justice demands a level playing field. That is only possible if everyone has equal access to legal advice and representation. That means legal aid – public funding to provide necessary help for those who cannot afford the cost of legal services.

The Legal Aid and Advice Act 1949 was a striking achievement of the post-war Labour government, parallel to the National Health Service and just as remarkable. It put those too poor to pay lawyers on a par with those who could. By so doing, it made everyone more equal before the law. It did so by using legal aid to pay fees out of public funds. As a monopoly funder, the government could keep rates to a minimum and did so.

Now, however, the drive to cut costs has undermined the effectiveness of legal aid. It has restricted its scope to the extremely poor – those eligible for welfare benefits and a small number of others. It has excluded many lawyers from offering their services by making legal aid practice no longer economically viable.

Yet, at the same time, the need for legal advice and help has grown directly as a result of government policies. As more and more legislation pours out of Westminster and Whitehall, so the demand for interpretation and explanation extends among the population. Public authorities and private corporations have ready access to legal advice. They are expanding the resources they employ on them, as can be seen by the growth in the income and profits of the law firms which represent them. But this greatly increases the need for ordinary citizens to be able to defend themselves, challenge actions and interpretations, and pursue reasonable claims. Legal aid is no longer available to those in regular employment, however poorly paid.

Citizens can no longer afford to pay for vital professional help and advice. The government has failed to provide the resources to enable these needs to be met. Instead, it has tried to find ways of trimming the legal aid budget. Following a standard New Labour technique, it appointed a businessman, Lord Carter of Coles, to solve the problem. His main qualification seems to be that he made his fortune in the private health care industry.

But what is happening with legal aid is much worse than a misconceived initiative. For all the talk about empowering the individual and expanding choice, the fundamental obligation of progressive government is to assist the weak, when their case is just, against the strong. No one disputes that legal aid must be managed efficiently and economically, but the Government has pursued economy at the expense of justice. Its priorities must be reversed. Without effective legal aid, the rule of law does not exist and our system of justice is a mockery.

SOURCE: THE CML PROGRAMME

Session 2
Human Rights and Global Responses
SUPPORTED BY HUMAN RIGHTS WATCH, INDEX ON CENSORSHIP

Aryeh Neier has set out how, as the legal instruments designed to prevent war crimes against civilians have grown over 150 years, from the first Geneva Convention of 1864, to the ratifications of 1949 and now to the creation of an International Court, so, at the same time, the scale and frequency of violations against civilians has grown just as much. Are we now witnessing a similar bleak process, with respect to fundamental human rights and freedoms? UN proclamations and the deployment of military force to defend and expand democracy seem to coincide with a parallel increase in international surveillance, restrictions on speech and inhuman security measures in the name of counter-terrorism.

'Let me start by emphasising my view and the view of Human Rights Watch that we have actively made considerable progress in the last fifty years... In the past few years, as we have seen, times have been tougher, and corners have been cut and rights have been abused in the name of national security. Since 9/11, counter-terrorism has been an excuse for serious human rights abuses just about everywhere, including on the part of the US which, in connivance with the UK Government, has perpetrated abuses such as the torture and disappearance of terrorism suspects and has prosecuted wars using tactics which cause unacceptably high rates of civilian casualties. These policies and tactics are not just wrong: they are also counterproductive even on their own counter-terrorism terms.

In the immediate future, I think there are signs that the global economic recession or depression is likely to provide the context and pretext for a new round of human rights failings. In fact, I have a strong fear that the single greatest immediate threat to human rights in the world today, is the economic situation. Why? Because it will exacerbate existing social and political conflicts, and because states will seek to deal with unemployment, economic protest, political instability, and mass migration through repression and through alliances of economic convenience with repressive states. For similar reasons, I suspect that in the medium to longer term future, states' responses to the threat of climate change will present further threats to human rights…"

TOM PORTEOUS, PANEL CHAIR AND LONDON DIRECTOR, HUMAN RIGHTS WATCH

Calmly pulling down our eternal rights
TIMOTHY GARTON ASH

Friedrich Schiller's play, *William Tell*, which is about the Swiss rising up for their freedom quite a long time ago, has a great speech by one of the insurgents, a guy called Stauffacher, who says, I translate: 'When the oppressed cannot find justice, when the burden becomes intolerable, then he reaches calmly up into the heavens and pulls down his eternal rights, which hang there inalienable and unbreakable like the stars themselves'. That is a wonderful image of pulling down your eternal rights from the heavens. When the Swiss set about doing that, and indeed when Schiller wrote, those rights were not codified in any international treaties. There were no United Nations (UN) Conventions, let alone European Conventions on Human Rights. In the meantime, the heavens have come much closer.

We have, as it were, ladders down from heaven and, in the case of this country, that is not just the UN Conventions, but in particular the European Convention on Human Rights and the European Court of Human Rights. I think it is very striking that, when the Convention on Modern Liberty organisers commissioned this document which you can download from the website, *The Abolition of Freedom Act 2009*, with its royal crest, which documents all the liberties that we have lost - it starts in every category from the European Convention on Human Rights. That is the benchmark. This is what we have lost.

I have spent much of my life on what Shami Chakrabarti rather wonderfully called, 'continental people with memories of Nazis and Stasis' – so this is an important rebuttal to the narrative of the *Daily Mail*, which counterposes Europe to freedom: British liberty versus European bureaucratic despotism. The truth is that, in this respect, Europe, in the form of the European Court of Human Rights and the European Convention, has been one of the bulwarks of our defence of our liberties against our own state. I remember when I was working on my book on the Stasi, I actually got to see the Head of MI5 with a couple of his people. And they kept on talking with extreme irritation about people who had insisted on taking cases to the European Court of Human Rights. All sorts of unusual people go to the European Court of Human Rights, including Scottish opponents of the hunting ban, not perhaps the greatest enthusiasts for Europe normally. This was very tiresome indeed for MI5 and I realised what an important bulwark of our liberties it was.

We have had in that external framework, UN, international, but particularly European, a bulwark of rights that we ourselves have neglected.

But it only works if people and states are prepared to pull down those rights and translate them into their own reality – prepared and able. So in some places, such as Bosnia and Kosova, Zimbabwe, Tibet, they may be willing but they are unable, because of the coercive power of the state. Then it needs other people from outside and other states to take a stand. I think these last twenty years have been good for the spread of international standards of human rights - the years since the worldwide velvet revolutions of 1989. I am not sure that the next twenty years are going to be anything like as good – partly because of the national security rhetoric and other agendas which will curb civil liberties, but also because sovereignty is back big time.

Make no mistake. All the emerging powers of the world today have an old-fashioned view of sovereignty. The United States has always had an old-fashioned view of sovereignty. China, Russia, India too – all of them will put the defence of national sovereignty before international standards or universal standards of human rights and civil liberties. So we have a fight on our hands, internationally in my view, to protect the standards we already have achieved because of the return of sovereignty.

In talking about sovereignty, I have in mind the attitude of states towards their own citizens. In other words, it is not a question of what China does outside its own frontiers. It is states saying, 'you don't even have the right to raise the issue of how we are treating our own citizens by reference to international human rights'. China is pretty close to that position. Putin's Russia holds that position absolutely. That is different from what European countries say. They say, 'yes, in principle we recognise that right, but for the following special reasons, national security or whatever it may be, we are going to ignore them anyway'. At least that is the tribute that vice pays to virtue.

But on the European question, I see a huge danger here: populism which takes the form of ethnic scapegoating, a very old European pastime. All our countries have lots of migrant workers – *Gastarbeiter* – and the temptation

> "The truth is that, Europe has been one of the bulwarks of our defence of our liberties against our own state."

when everybody is losing their jobs and times are getting tough, is to say, 'blame it on the bloody Poles. Blame it on the bloody Ukrainians. Blame it on the gypsies, on the Jews, whoever'. And I see that as a very, very large and real and present danger not just in Eastern Europe but also in our own countries.

The last thing I want to say is about Britain. Britain is a very strange case. We have one of the greatest traditions of liberty in the world. I am always irritated when Americans talk about liberty as if they invented it, which they do all the time. Don't they realise that we invented it? They got it from us – maybe the Ancient Greeks had something to do with it too, but mainly us! Anyway a great tradition of liberty and all the legal and treaty supports and scaffolding you could possibly want – all the conventions and the Human Rights Act. Yet precisely in the ten years since we wrote the European Convention of Human Rights into law, we have gone backwards. That again shows that all that international framework is no use at all unless the people and the state they are in translate it into their own reality.

I think we got an interesting answer in the plenary session to the question how it is that we have got to this point under the new Labour Government: a curious mixture of a sort of nanny-state protective zeal, and an exaggerated and hysterical reaction to the real terrorist threat. That came out clearly in the group-think of people behind the doors of government getting the security briefings. Add to this, above all, the competition for the *Daily Mail* and *Sun* reader: 'We will show that we are tougher on crime, if not on the causes of crime, and that indeed we are tougher on everything else'. Those elements very simply created the particular dynamic under this Government.

That is why I think we need a British Bill of Rights as well as the European Convention - not instead of, as some Tories propose, but as well as - a written constitution and the movement that I hope we are starting, or at least developing, here. Because none of these international frameworks will be worth anything at all unless we follow Mr Stauffacher's example: reach up into the skies, and pull those rights into our own reality.

A proper British Bill of Rights would allow everybody to say, 'I know my rights', and everybody would then be able to feel that they could go to a British court and demand those rights. The road to the European Court of Human Rights is a long and slow road with a backlog of cases, and it is quite difficult for the ordinary citizen. So I believe that a British Bill of Rights would be complementary. What is wrong with the Human Rights Act is simply that there hasn't been a process of active debate by British citizens, saying, these are our rights and we want them. As long as they aren't in contradiction with the European Convention – I think that's fine.

What can Britain do? One thing we could do, is to stop colluding in torture. That would be a pretty good start. The other thing is this: no government can simply behave like Human Rights Watch: even Tom Porteous our chair would accept that. That is to say, it can't be: "human rights über alles". That is especially true if, for example, you are dealing with China – we all have a huge interest in getting China on board on the issue of climate change. The massive growth in carbon emissions is going to come from China and other places. So that is an interest we have and we can't simply sacrifice that entirely to human rights. But one thing we can do is get our act together. At the moment, China, Russia and the United States can simply divide and rule in Europe, because every European country comes to them with a different pitch and then says privately, 'Well we don't really mean it about human rights. So just give us that big contract for Russian gas, or the export contract to China'. So, speaking the same language in Europe and having the same standards would itself be a big step in the right direction.

> "…all that international framework is no use at all unless the people and the state they are in translate it into their own reality."

Standing up for repugnant views
JO GLANVILLE

I am going to focus on just one human right which is freedom of speech. Perhaps the most vulnerable, partly because it is not absolute, and because, of all the human rights, it is most likely to become hostage to political fortune. Over the last year there have been a couple of events that have marked a turning point in our attitudes to free speech, not only here in the UK but also globally. In March 2008, the United Nations Human Rights Council redefined the role of its special rapporteur on freedom of expression, declaring that he should now monitor abuses of the right to free expression when 'they form an act of racial or religious discrimination'. Now this has somewhat insidiously turned the rapporteur into a potential enemy of the very human right he is supposed to be defending – into someone whose job is no longer simply to monitor abuses to free speech, but to consider that human right as potentially a form of abuse. At the same time the Council passed a resolution condemning what it called 'a campaign of defamation of religions' and calling on governments to take action.

That very same month – in fact just the day before the resolution on the special rapporteur, the Dutch politician Geert Wilders released his film called *Fitna* online. If there is anyone here who hasn't come across him, Wilders is a platinum blond provocateur who has made quite a reputation for himself attacking Islam. He wants Muslim immigration to the Netherlands to be stopped: and in 2007 he told the Dutch Parliament that, 'Islam is the Trojan horse in Europe. If we do not stop Islamification now, Eurabia and Netherabia will just be a matter of time'. His film, *Fitna*, was a very crude piece of propaganda equating Islam with violence. No Dutch public broadcaster screened it, although the Dutch Muslim Broadcasting Association did in fact offer to show it (though they wanted to view it first for illegal content and they also wanted Wilders to take part in a debate and he declined both). The Dutch Press Centre also offered, but they wanted some money for their security costs and, once again, he didn't take up the offer. At the time, there were apocalyptic predictions of another outcry of Danish cartoon proportions. But that scenario failed to happen. The film, in fact, was a damp squib.

But the Secretary General of the United Nations, Ban Ki-Moon, decided to weigh into the row, describing the film as 'offensively anti-Islamic', adding for clarity, 'the right of free expression is not at stake here'. This was made all the more pointed by its timing, because last year was the 60th anniversary of the UN Declaration of Human Rights. But here was the global guardian of those rights undermining them. So entrenched has the notion become that there is a right not to be offended, that neither the Secretary General nor the Council seem to feel any need to argue for, or to justify, their position.

Just two weeks ago, our Government reinforced that position when they banned Geert Wilders from coming into the country, although I was quite puzzled by Lord Pearson's decision to invite Geert Wilders now, a year after the event. (I wondered how well he knew how to use YouTube.) The UK Government reason for keeping Geert Wilders out – that his opinions threatened community security and therefore public security – is becoming a common refrain when it comes to critics of religion and a justification for limiting free speech and a powerful argument for censorship. We saw exactly the same argument being used last year when Random House dropped a novel they were going to publish by an American journalist, *The Jewel of Medina* - a historical romance about Mohamed's relationship with his wife Ayesha. The publisher's statement said: 'The publication of this book might be offensive to some in the Muslim community. Also it could incite acts of violence by a small, radical segment'. They said they wouldn't be publishing this book for the safety of the author, employees of Random House, booksellers and anyone else who would be involved in the distribution and sale of the novel.

Now I wouldn't of course dispute the fact that these are serious considerations that have to be taken into account. But the irony is, in this case and I think in other cases, that it is actually the pre-emptive censorship – whether it is to decide not to publish or to ban someone from coming into the country – that enflames those situations. Without that, you wouldn't get the level of feeling that has been generated in both cases.

It is the Random House and United Nations Human Rights Council view that now prevails. Potentially offensive speech is so dangerous that it cannot be given a platform and our liberty is better served by censorship, rather than protecting the right to free speech. This is the 'Alice in Wonderland' world of human rights where the best way to exercise your rights is by having them denied. One of the most astute commentators, Kenan Malik, has observed that a profound shift has taken place in our attitude to free speech: 'It is no longer seen as an inherent good, necessary for expressing our moral autonomy, maintaining social progress, and safeguarding our other freedoms. It has to be seen as damaging, even as a problem'. I would add that it is the voices who want to limit free speech that are now occupying the moral high ground, not the human rights defenders.

> "This is the 'Alice in Wonderland' world of human rights where the best way to exercise your rights is by having them denied."

We published a special issue of *Index* last year, marking the 60th Anniversary of the UN Declaration of Human Rights, and we asked one of the most distinguished international defenders of free speech to write a piece for us. Aryeh Neier was for many years Executive Director of Human Rights Watch, and is now President of George Soros' Open Society Institute. He was a refugee from Nazi Germany as a child, but as head of the American civil liberties union in the 1970's, he took a controversial stand on what remains one of the most famous free speech battles of the past sixty years when he defended the right of a group of neo-nazis to march through a Jewish neighbourhood in Skokie, Illinois that contained a number of Holocaust survivors. He stood up for their right to freedom of expression. Looking back at that storm of controversy, he wrote for *Index* in 2008: 'Ensuring that all may speak freely no matter how repugnant their views, prevents the authorities from using the pretext that they are blocking hate speech as a means to censor expression that actually disturbs them for other reasons.'

Standing up for repugnant views can put you in a very uncomfortable position. At *Index* over the past year, we have had to stand up for racists and Holocaust-deniers. A colleague was very disturbed to receive a Christmas card from one of this country's leading Holocaust deniers with a delightful photograph of one of Hitler's leading apologists at the conference on the Holocaust in Teheran a few years ago, as well as a free DVD of David Irvine in handcuffs. I have been described as 'charming' by the BNP. They think we are their friends. We are not their friends. But we believe in the principle of giving them the place for their views – views that we know many people in this room find repugnant. We know that the discomfort this entails is the price that we have to pay if we want to live in a free and open society – a society that acknowledges the universal right to free speech and doesn't cut the cloth of human rights to fit the preoccupation and politics of the day.

Incidents in Fallujah
PAUL ROGERS

About a year after the start of the war in Iraq, there were incidents in Fallujah which led to a particular incident that I want to start by considering. This was several months before the major assault on Fallujah in November 2004. This was actually in April. Shortly after four contractors with the Blackwater Company had been killed, their bodies mutilated and hung from a bridge, the US Marine Corps tried to gain control of the city. On one particular occasion, they sent a convoy into one part of the city which ran into very serious trouble, and it took three to four hours to rescue the troops. None of them were actually killed, but some were injured. There was an American correspondent from the *Washington Post*, Pamela Constable, who was embedded with that marine group and she wrote in the paper what happened next:

> *Just before dawn, Wednesday, AC 130 Spectre Gunships launched a devastating punitive raid over a six-block area around the spot where the convoy was attacked firing dozens of artillery shells that shook the city and lit up the sky. Marine officials said the area was virtually destroyed and that no further insurgent activity had been seen there.*

Note the term, 'a devastating punitive raid'. This was actually a retaliation for what had happened. Nobody knows how many civilians were killed in that particular raid. Shortly afterwards, in a very bitter fire fight along the banks of the Tigris near Baqubah, a small army platoon was able to kill the people who were opposing them, although they took injuries. The platoon had experienced very grievous injuries among their own comrades in the previous weeks and what they then did was to tie the corpses of those they had killed to the bonnets of their humvees and parade them through the streets of the city rather like deer being killed in the hunt. Again there was someone embedded with that particular group who spoke of the antagonism and bitterness which was visible on the faces of the people who lined the route.

Those are incidents which will be paralleled by any army in any war, and I don't mean that it reflects particularly on the American army. Prince Harry's famous use of the term Terry-Taliban in Afghanistan is another demonstration of that same idea, and the nature of modern war. But if you look at it more widely, remembering that the war in Iraq is about to go into its seventh year, and that in October, the war in Afghanistan will enter its ninth year – what we have seen is so different from what was expected. I remember a column Mary Kaldor did for openDemocracy just a few months after the war opened, when she had just returned from a visit to the Green Zone, reporting on the way in which the Coalition Provisional Authority had this belief that everything would be magically transformed. The young staffers taking charge of quite large parts of the Iraqi economy believed that Iraq would make a transfer to a pro-western, liberal democracy with an absolute free market, flat rate tax, no financial regulation and investment from everybody including the Israelis; just as there was a belief at the start of the termination of the Taliban regime in Afghanistan that that also would make a rapid and immediate transition.

That's instead of what we do have: on the last direct count, 98 thousand people killed in Iraq, (the World Health Organisation surveys show many more than that); 120 thousand people detained without trial, many for years at a time; four and a half million people as refugees and all the problems of prisoner abuse, torture, rendition and the rest. It is so different from what was anticipated.

Part of that anticipation no doubt goes back to the nature of the Bush administration eight years ago and to the Project for the New American Century which saw the new 21st century world as one which would very much follow one particular issue led by the ideas and maybe political ideals of a rather narrow group within the United States. But this is very reminiscent of 1890s

Victorian London and the belief in a Pax Britannica which was going to bring civilisation to the world. I am always reminded of a comment made to me by a Ghanaian student – a very common West African saying in colonial times: 'There was a very good reason why the sun never set on the British Empire. It was because God didn't trust the British in the dark.'

What I am trying to get at is that the experience we have had over the last eight years is one expression of what I refer to as the 'control paradigm' in international security, or *liddism* - the one word I have ever invented in my life, to evoke the way you keep the lid on things while not looking at the underlying problems. In a sense the very failure of the 'War on Terror' to deliver what was intended, opens up the real possibility of a much wider debate on what should be the true nature of a genuine, human-oriented, sustainable security, which implicitly recognises from the start the significance of human rights.

> "...four and a half million people as refugees and all the problems of prisoner abuse, torture, rendition and the rest. It is so different from what was anticipated."

But if you take this broader view, leaving aside the 'War on Terror' for the moment, and taking into account climate change, certainly – the kind of world that we seem to be moving towards will probably be determined by three very large trends: one is the very strong development of a deep socio-economic division across the world, in which about 1.2 – 1.25 billion people, including more or less all of us here, have actually done very well. Over the last thirty or forty years, it has been a very good period for us, but not for the majority of people. And the gap between that large group and a much larger group has actually widened year on year. Read *The Economist* special supplement on the middle class: read it very carefully and see how they define middle class. It's very interesting.

At the same time, one of the very welcome trends in that period has been the immense improvement, normally by people's own efforts, in their education and literacy, and also in communications. But this means that the majority of the world is much more aware of its own marginalisation. Then factor in the developing risk over the next ten, twenty or thirty years of climate change

▶

impacting on human abilities to develop and that could be an incredibly insecure and very fragile world in every sense.

Those are the big issues for the future, and what will happen very much depends on whether we, the elite, continue to use the 'control paradigm', or whether we go much deeper to address these challenges. What was originally a financial crisis is now, I believe, a worldwide manufacturing crisis – the changes in Japan alone over the last year are quite astonishing – and that means we will be faced by a strong requirement to maintain security at a time that many, many people will get extremely bitter and resentful. You may have noticed a small item in the *Financial Times* about the experience of the Indian equivalent of the Lidl supermarket. This was a chain which started four or five years ago, trebled its number of branches in the last two years, and then more or less went bust overnight. It had sixteen hundred branches across India. As it went bust it was no longer able to pay for the security staff who guarded these stores, and during the weekend on which it went bust, six hundred of these stores were looted by people who were desperate for food. The Chinese, to give another example, are currently introducing a whole range of new, public order riot control outfits across virtually every major city in China because they fear that the economic downturn is going to lead to much greater violence.

So in one sense, while we have hugely better opportunities for addressing this core problem of trying to keep things under control, and time if we really act to alter these huge problems of socio-economic division and climate change – what we are going to see over the next two or three years will be a kind of marker for how things might happen in the future. It is really important that group initiatives like the one here today and many others are active now. What we have to move against is this idea that we maintain the status quo. We cannot do it in a globalising, communicating world. It seems to me to be hugely important to have this kind of event as part of the process in preventing that from happening.

> "...what will happen very much depends on whether we, the elite, continue to use the 'control paradigm', or whether we go much deeper to address these challenges."

The problem at root is that there is an assumption of superiority in the North Atlantic community. It is very deep: it has been cultural for many years and has many echoes right back to the colonial era. It makes it much more important to be well aware of how the global issues are viewed in different parts of the world. There are some good websites like Focus on the Global South – which are very good at doing this – giving the view from the 'Other' if you like. It makes it difficult for people who are campaigning on human rights and other issues from within that community, but in no way can that stop them. You will be criticised by others for being part of that community, but you still have your own voice. Living in West Yorkshire at the time of the miners' strike, I remember vividly a hotel keeper from Manchester loading up his car with food to take down to the striking miners and being turned back at a police roadblock. Western governments can get very heavy if they think there are threats to their own security. But, at root, we are still all in it together. And in spite of the way in which the West has conducted itself, it doesn't mean that those living in the West don't have the right to speak up, embarrassing their own governments and, on occasion, embarrassing the governments of others.

A single human community, arms and oil
MARY KALDOR

In the aftermath of the Israeli conflict in Gaza, we have seen on television Israeli soldiers saying, 'well if I have to risk the lives of civilians in order to save my soldiers, of course I am going to save my soldiers'. For most of us, that is a rather shocking statement. But from the Israeli point of view, they were thinking in war terms. That is what was so striking about this war: most of us saw it in human terms, and people being killed in Gaza as human beings - whereas, for Israelis, they were enemies. That represents, I think, a profound change since the Second World War in the way we think about human beings.

If you ask me what globalisation means, it means that we are much more conscious of a single human community than we ever were in previous eras. Think of the numbers of people killed in the Second

morning sessions

> **"**...because you cannot distinguish between combatants and non-combatants nowadays, the victims are nearly always civilians."

World War by us – civilians in Dresden, Tokyo, Hamburg – we thought of them as enemies. We didn't actually think of them as human beings. And that is a profound change. While this may seem obvious to the younger generation, it is not obvious to mine and to an older generation.

Nowadays, moreover, all wars are massive human rights violations. When we use the word, 'terror', we tend to think of non-state actors blowing up a bus or a suicide bomber and that is how it tends to be defined. But actually, all **contemporary wars are 'terror' wars**. They are 'terror wars' in two senses. One is the kind of sectarian wars we see in Iraq and we saw in Bosnia. A typical tactic was violence deliberately inflicted on civilians. The aim of these wars was usually population displacement - shifting people - and the typical tactic for achieving this is terror. You go into a town, you frighten people and you do some very public atrocity. Maybe you don't kill that many people, but your aim is to make everybody else panic and run away. The same is true of what is called counter-insurgency, the kind of war that Israel inflicted on Gaza, the kind of war that the Americans were fighting in Iraq and are still fighting in Afghanistan. It is very terrifying being killed from the air. Indeed, the very terms they use, like 'shock and awe' give you a sense of how terrifying it is, and of course, because you cannot distinguish between combatants and non-combatants nowadays, the victims are nearly always civilians.

This type of war which is most wars we see, is a consequence of the fact that technology has reached such enormous proportions, that we simply cannot repeat traditional wars where two sides engaged in a battle because those battles are so destructive. The only way you can gain any kind of advantage is by killing unarmed civilians.

Interestingly, if you look at the statistics on war, there has, over the last few decades, been a dramatic decline in the number of wars in the world, and not only that, but a dramatic decline in the number of people killed in wars. But what has increased first of all, is the proportion of civilians killed in wars and secondly, the number of displaced people – that is characteristic of our time. If we are talking about climate change, economic crisis, war - the characteristic of our time is people forced out of their houses. There has been a dramatic rise in refugees and displaced people.

The problem about war is that it is now very difficult to distinguish its parameters. There is a sort of blurring between war, human rights violations, crime, because, in many wars, there are lots of crimes. So, in a sense, what you see in big cities – the drug wars going on now in Mexico, or what's happening in the big cities of Brazil – is not so very different from what we mean now by war. Above all, we are all much more conscious of wars, so that we feel a sense of insecurity even if fewer people are being killed in them.

The implications of all that is that we are increasingly moving towards a world in which the coming together of international humanitarian law, the laws of war, and human rights law have become the way we deal with war. Instead of saying, 'we have got to go to war with our enemies' – although that is exactly what is happening in the 'war on terror', despite the fact that it simply results in more and more civilian deaths, and more and more terror - the move at least among people like us is to say, 'we have got to move towards a law-based paradigm. The way to deal with wars is actually through dealing with human rights violations and through applying the laws of war and international human rights law. What we really need, is better enforcement of international law. That is what we lack. And what we really need is for soldiers to stop seeing their primary role as killing their enemies, and start seeing their primary role as enforcing human rights. They have to learn to protect people, to be more like policemen and to learn that actually the lives of civilians do matter, in the way that policemen and fire fighters are trained to put their lives at risk for the sake of ordinary people'. That is the way we have to change.

Thinking about human rights and war today, the big problem, especially with these new risks of climate change and economic crisis, is that our security capabilities and our way of thinking about security is basically designed for war and aimed at war of a traditional kind. We have nearly two million soldiers in Europe, which, in the past, were meant to meet a Soviet invasion. The US has all these incredibly sophisticated weapons, and we know from Iraq and Afghanistan, that all that this does is to kill more civilians resulting in human rights violations. I find it absolutely extraordinary that in the cluster munitions and landmines conventions, we see these kinds of weapons as human rights violations, but we still talk about the need for nuclear weapons, and we are

morning sessions

> "The reason why we collude in torture is because we are so worried about our arms links with the United States, whether it's Trident we are talking about or BAE."

still going ahead in the UK with another generation of Trident. If you think about nuclear weapons in human rights terms, there is no question: they are a massive violation of the laws of war, of human rights – and they are completely in contradiction with the ways in which our Government, among others, insist that they are committed to human rights.

It comes down to the requirement for a very fundamental rethink of what we mean by security. Nowadays security has to mean human rights, rather than the defence of our island. Even though I agree with what Tim Garton Ash said about sovereignty, the meaning of sovereignty has changed. I don't think strengthening sovereignty in China, India and Russia means that they are going to seek military solutions on a large scale. They may acquire weapons as a symbol of their sovereignty, but there's a real change in the way we think about the world. Countries like China and Russia are also thinking in multilateral terms.

And following on from Paul Rogers' point about the financial crisis: my view is that it was never just a financial crisis. Money is an expression of power in the world, and there has been an underlying structural crisis brewing for the last twenty years. The financial crisis is just an expression of that. We tried to hide it by making riskier and riskier investments in order to keep up the rate of profit. But the crisis is only going to be solved if we start thinking really seriously about a new global deal on climate change and redistribution. I am not quite as pessimistic as Paul. I do think there is terrible danger here: but I do believe that this is also an incredible opportunity. The fact that this coincides with the coming to power of Obama – and this is very unusual in history, that coincidence – means that there are real opportunities to move towards a more multilateral, more human rights-based world, rather than the opposite.

One of the structural factors that I think gave rise to the financial crisis is our over-dependence on oil. It has led to huge imbalances, with us having huge deficits and these very, very rich countries in the Middle East. Similarly our economy has become incredibly dependent on arms production which is integrated into American arms production. The reason why we collude in torture is because we are so worried about our arms links with the United States, whether it's Trident we are talking about or BAE. This is something that nobody is really looking at, but it is incredibly important that we restructure our economy away from this dependence on arms and oil, as this will then give us a real capacity to act in support of human rights.

One of the problems with intervention is that it has been posed as the question of human rights versus sovereignty, rather than the question of how to reinforce human rights? So there has been no focus on what we need to be able to do to protect civilians, whether it is in Rwanda or Afghanistan. We should be protecting Afghans at the moment, not simply killing Al-Quaeda. My view is that one of the big problems we have, whether it was Bosnia or Rwanda, is that we simply don't have that capacity. Actually we should be transforming our soldiers and others into a new kind of capacity that can protect people from desecrations of their human rights.

Session 3
Business gets Personal – Can Privacy have a Future?
SUPPORTED BY THE OPEN RIGHTS GROUP

The web has revolutionised commerce and advertising. The companies we as consumers choose to do business with online (as well as some we don't) know more about us than ever before. How safe is our data in the hands of these corporations? What choices do we have about who collects data about us and where that data ends up? Is privacy dead? Or is there another way?

> "There remains an underlying question as to whether this distinction between private and public is valid. Lots of public services are contracted out now to private organisations. You heard already today about the Communications Database, where private communications data is collected by private service providers and communications providers, but is available to the government essentially for policing and law enforcement purposes. A huge amount of information, you know, can be tracked on the internet which could well be of interest to the state. So is the distinction valid? Where should we be concentrating our efforts? Your views, you know, are very much welcome."
>
> DAVID SMITH, PANEL SPEAKER AND DEPUTY INFORMATION COMMISSIONER (DATA PROTECTION), INFORMATION COMMISSIONER'S OFFICE (ICO)

A tempting honey pot
CASPAR BOWDEN

I am Chief Privacy Adviser for Microsoft in Europe, Middle East and Africa. But, up until 2002, I was director of a small think tank called the Foundation for Information Policy Research (FIPR). And during that time, I did a great deal of analysis, campaigning and legislative advocacy, for example to try and curb the worst excesses of the Regulation of Investigatory Powers Act. So, this means that I've had quite an interesting experience of both sides of the fence, as a privacy advocate and also as somebody now working in a very large company where these issues are much to the fore. While I'm talking here you should assume that I am not speaking for Microsoft unless I specifically say so.

Advertising is the fundamental business model of the Web. It does seem that most people won't subscribe to a service if there is a free service on offer paid for by advertising. We have a deep cultural expectation that when we borrow a library book or watch a television programme, for example, there's nobody actually tracking what we read, page by page, or which channel we flip. But that is pretty much the situation now on the web. That information is being recorded as you visit each website. It is recorded because, if advertising is placed according to a profile that's been built up which comprehends your interests, then that advertising slot is much more valuable to the advertiser than if that advertising is presented blindly.

The trouble is that once one has accumulated this kind of profile information with the consent of the user to fulfil this business purpose, it becomes a tempting honey pot for the interests of state surveillance to move in and try and use that data for other purposes. That is precisely what has happened over the years with the situation of mandatory systematic data retention by internet service providers (ISPs).

With respect to Microsoft, my position is 'no' to identity (ID) cards, but we do need forms of secure authentication online, because these services that we access online hold stockpiles of very private information. Particularly online, we're all going to need ways to manage

> "We have a deep cultural expectation that when we borrow a library book or watch a television programme, for example, there's nobody actually tracking what we read, page by page…"

that information in a way that excludes others that we don't want accessing that information, whether they're hackers or whatever. So, there is a field of technology which is called 'privacy enhancing technology', that has been pretty active now for 10 or 20 years and it really is the application of methods of cryptography, way, way more sophisticated than simple encryption to this task. It tries to square the circle, to enable people to personalise services and to access services securely without needing to reveal more information than they strictly have to. So for example, it is technically possible to prove that one is a member of some group of entitlement, whether that's somebody who has paid a subscription to use a service or enrolled to use some online service, without actually revealing who you are.

Now, the cryptographic methods underlying those sorts of capabilities are profoundly counterintuitive and they can be pretty disruptive. But there is a particular strand of work here, which normally goes by the name of 'private credentials', that goes back about 10 years and so far has frankly failed to find a place in the market. So, I'm very pleased indeed, having carried a torch for this kind of technology for about 10 years going back to my time in FIPR, that Microsoft is now introducing this technology (under the brand name U-Prove). We're building it into the fabric of Windows infrastructure, so that any programmer or any business that wants to introduce the state of the art in cryptographic privacy protection, will be able to do so, I hope, in about a year's time.

Now, of course, whether data controllers in government or business will actually take up and, as it were, bear the costs of innovation in a new and complex area, is not something that will necessarily happen through market forces, unless Data Protection regulation is strengthened. This would then create a presumption that privacy enhancing technologies such as I've described, must be introduced. (To date, frankly, the evidence that we've seen from market forces is that organisations don't bother.)

Realising the value of your personal information
IAIN HENDERSON

Mydex is a social enterprise that we only set up three or four months back. As a social enterprise, we need to have a charter. So our charter is 'to help the individual realise the value of their personal information'. That means 'realise' in both senses.

The first task we hope to tackle is to help people just figure out what the hell is going on, specific to their situation, rather than generically. If we succeed in that, we then move forward to realising in the other sense: 'You help me get a return on my information, whether that be to save me time, save me money, or save me hassle'. We're doing that because we believe that the current ways of working around personal information are structurally broken.

Organisations like Facebook, or the Government, or BT, or whoever, have to behave the way they behave. They have shareholders and they have stakeholders. They have to make a profit. The best way that they can do that is to gather up as much information as they possibly can, regard it as their asset and turn it back against the individuals that they deal with.

We believe that we need to establish a different type of model, a more balanced and more respectful model that effectively puts the individual in charge of their information and allows them to selectively disclose it to the organisations that they deal with. That model won't replace the current model overnight. Frankly I would still expect to be doing this in 15 - 20 years time, before we can expect to see a much more balanced viewpoint.

But roughly what we're saying is, my view of me is vastly superior to any other person's or any organisation's view of me. Customer Relationship Management (CRM) is the set of tools that you deal with every day, day in, day out, when you phone up the call centre for British Telecom, hang on for half an hour to get your service issues dealt with and they're trying to sell you five or six more things that are probably irrelevant because you bought them last week from British Gas! I worked in CRM for 20 odd years and believe me, I realise how broken this system is. All that they know is that this person bought that thing at that time, for that price at that outlet. That information is used to guess what they're going to do next and to try and get a relevant message in front of them.

My view of me is, 'I'm going to buy a new car in six months time. I pretty much know the process I'm going to follow. I know where I'm going for advice'. I hold back on that information, because if I give all that information upfront, that reduces my bargaining position. So, my view of me is better than anyone else's. Sometimes, I *will* need to prove who I am or how much money I've got or whatever. But I can just as easily get that proof as any organisation can, given the right tools and processes.

Currently you spend, say, £3 per year to access what is really a poor quality record. That's pretty toxic because it carries all sorts of liabilities and data protection problems - when you could spend £2 per year to access records in a different way, in a more respectful way through the tools Mydex and plenty of other organisations use. Mydex uses the kind of technologies that Casper mentioned. We call our concept, 'volunteered personal information'. It is literally volunteered by you of your own free will and it will come with a contract that the organisation signs. These will be your terms and conditions rather than the 25-page privacy policy that - at the moment - you can't do anything about. To design those contracts, we use very high-end lawyers that tell us it's perfectly feasible. We use very high-end and secure technologies. And we won't do anything radical, because this approach needs to be worked out carefully and slowly. That's where we are.

> "But roughly what we're saying is, my view of me is vastly superior to any other person's or any organisation's view of me."

Acknowledge the commercial imperatives!
PETER BAZALGETTE

As you said in your kind introduction, I have a couple of angles that I come from. I have spent a life creating television content; and I'm currently very concerned about where the revenue is coming from to create the content that people would want to watch in the future. Second, I personally invested in two or three digital start-up companies that are trying to create the new online economy, and who are on the forefront of trying to turn the online world into business. They are struggling with what people's privacy and personal rights should be. Very quickly, I would like to point out three contradictions or paradoxes that I see at the moment.

First, Gordon Brown and Lord Carter are working on something they call Digital Britain at the moment. Their bet is that they have a collapsing income from the financial sector and services - for reasons we all understand - and that there has to be that digital dividend they are hoping to establish. They hope to get lots of revenue from the online world in the future to replace what's been lost. That's their dream or their vision.

> "...no media company at the moment knows what its business model is going to be in ten years' time, so great is the level of digital disruption."

And yet the truth is that there is a hell of a lot of activity online at the moment, yet not a lot of revenue. From the business point of view, this concerns me a lot. Facebook is, on the face of it, a rather marvellous service, something that millions of people enjoy using and taking part in. But it has no financial model. And it isn't a charity. In addition, it was sold for a lot of money a few years ago, but it is not making money, and has not yet found a way of making money. In the end, things like Facebook have to function and find a financial model, not one that abuses people's rights, but it has to find one. And that's something we have to grapple with. In fact, no media company at the moment knows what its business model is going to be in ten years' time, so great is the level of digital disruption.

A second little paradox is that I have watched Facebook users quite rightly get very concerned about Beacon which was going to do 'me-too-marketing' using their personal data; and also, more recently, getting annoyed about Facebook's alleged ownership of their personal data and the retention of their data. But at the same time, the paradox is that many of the users of Facebook are completely profligate with their own private data, and wild and mad about it; they are not media-sensible. And they are pretty wild about other people's personal data. Individuals abuse the net, and abuse online social networking, and so on. The paradox there is that people worry about the system but are actually abusing the system at the same time.

> "...you have got some commercial organisations trying to be more responsible, while the government is tugging in completely the opposite direction. Between those two points is a complete public policy vacuum."

My third paradox of the morning would be that Google is allegedly sensitive to data retention. Over the last few years, it has actually reduced considerably the time span for which it is holding personal data. Meanwhile, you've got the Home Secretary wanting mobile phone companies to hold personal data for much, much longer. So you have got some commercial organisations trying to be more responsible, while the government is tugging in completely the opposite direction. Between those two points is a complete public policy vacuum. Privacy is only one issue and I'd like to hear people in the debate this morning acknowledge the fact that developing new revenue flows to fund content and services online - that we all enjoy - is also important.

We have to acknowledge the commercial imperatives. In the future, we will very often pay for content and services that we want, with the following two commodities. One is our personal attention. 'I will give you my attention for thirty seconds watching an advertisement if you'll give me that download of that movie'. And secondly, we'll pay with our personal data, i.e. 'my personal data is valuable including what I'm interested in, if reported consensually with my permission. It is valuable because you can target advertising towards me and that targeted advertising could well be to my benefit'.

I was asked to mention PHORM very quickly. PHORM is a way of tracking your online activities and then delivering you targeted advertising. Compared to some other services online, it is not a bad system. Please see the significance of it. If you don't like the system of PHORM, nevertheless there have to be systems like that if we're going to get content and services in the future. That's my argument. We'll debate it!

So, in the future, there may well also be a new definition of intellectual property (IP). We know the music companies have not been able to protect their intellectual property online and this has somewhat destroyed their model. In the future, perhaps, the definition of intellectual property, owning IP, will be 'not being able to control who accesses your content, but having a right to know who saw it'. That way you'll still derive flows of revenue from your IP and believe me, the online economy does need a method of deriving revenue flows from IP ownership. Otherwise you don't get an economy; you don't get economic growth; you don't get all the pieces of entertainment and other things that you enjoy. So overall I'd say, a bit less privacy please and more practicality; a bit less outrage, a bit more cooperation, a little less posturing. And better public policy. Thank you.

Session 4
Faiths and Freedoms
SUPPORTED BY EKKLESIA

The centralising, technocratic impulse behind the 'database state' is a challenge to citizenship. But citizenship is itself much more than a legal status; it is a way of being in society, that all the major faiths also address. Fundamental human rights have been supported by many faiths but does their secular character strike at the particularity of belief however powerful its humanism? Just as the Church of England opposed '42 Days' and may have contributed to the shift of opinion on that issue, the major religions can have an influential role to play in defending, as well as defining, freedom in the 21st century.

"What we all need, is dialogue and persuasion within a framework that seeks space for all: believers and non-believers, Christians and Muslims, Jews, Hindus, Sikhs, and people from a whole range of backgrounds. Privilege for a few will not work, and neither will exclusion. That is the basis of what could be a different kind of conversation about faiths and freedoms. Negotiating what that means in practice isn't easy, but where a real commonality can emerge, is in the recognition that overbearing state or corporate power is not what makes for a healthy society or for a meaningful exchange amongst people. We need to challenge those trends together, which is what the assumption behind a people's convention, a civil convention like this, is all about.

Then we need to use that possibility of togetherness as the spirit with which to address disagreements, and there are disagreements. We now live in a mixed belief society rather than one that is dominated by institutional Christianity, and I say that as a

Christian, a member, as it happens, of the Church of England. That may question assumptions and patterns of ways of doing things that have existed in the past. But my conviction as a Christian is that that isn't a negative thing. There is a lot of talk at the moment among some Christian circles about persecution and marginalisation. There are victim discourses growing in other belief communities, you'll find, and indeed in non-religious communities. We need to recognise that there are hurts and wounds that need to be addressed, but that they can't be addressed by just assuming that the benign dominating Christian context is one that will continue. And indeed its replacement opens up new possibilities, not least radical possibilities for Christians.

So, for people of faith from all backgrounds, there is - in a sense - a choice to be made. Will we turn in upon ourselves, resort perhaps to aggressive forms of populism and shy away from sharing public space with others? Or can we develop global understandings of citizenship and shared responsibility which are rooted not just in some abstract discourse – secular or otherwise – but also in the specifics of our own traditions of reasoning and belief, in ways that open doors and expose abuses of power both within our own communities and elsewhere. It's of course much easier to address abuses elsewhere, but not within your own midst."

SIMON BARROW, PANEL CHAIR AND CO-DIRECTOR, EKKLESIA

It has begun to get serious
VAUGHAN JONES

If you come to the civil liberties agenda from a faith perspective, you have got an awful lot of baggage hidden which you might not want to own. But there is an authoritarian tradition somewhere in the background that must be acknowledged. This country has a bizarre set of settlements around church and state, and the relationship between them is defined by old battles. I come from the Christian tradition which won the English civil war but then lost the peace! I am quite proud of the contribution of Christian tradition to liberal democracy, to the rights of the individual, the rights of freedom of worship and association and so on. My starting point is that democracy in both church and state is a crucial and fundamental cornerstone value in my beliefs. Freedom of worship, freedom of association have to be somehow enshrined within basic statutes, balanced by an obligation to obey the law, and the right and responsibility to oppose unjust laws.

But I don't think, having said that, that faith communities have any requirement for special privilege and they should not claim special privilege. The fundamental rights that a faith community needs to be a faith community, to be itself, are actually no different from the rights that all citizens need. So, any constitutional reform, it seems to me, must take away the establishment of any one particular faith group. That would do an enormous amount of good for the relationships between people of faith, relationships within the Christian church, and it would fundamentally change the nature of the British state for the better. Most people put disestablishment on the shelf as not very important, but it is fundamental.

I arrive at this position as someone who has worked within the area of social justice for a long time, especially in the areas of migration, poverty and anti-racism. Over the last years the area of migration particularly has been the front line of the erosion of human rights in this country. Major infringements such as detention without trial have been brought to public attention for the first time through other issues, but they have been longstanding features of the treatment of immigrants. Most mainstream religious traditions have these two parallel themes within them. The one is 'care for the stranger in your midst'; hospitality and openness and seeing the person who is different from yourself as a person nevertheless, who is worthy of respect. The other is the requirement to care for our brothers and sisters of faith, for the community, the *umma* or the church or however that is defined.

I was shown around Colnbrook Detention Centre and Harmondsworth at Heathrow – both maximum security prisons designed to keep these terrible people off our shores and to throw them out of the country. We went into a maximum security cell where there was a young African man, probably 19 or 20 years old. He was sitting in his cell, reading his bible. From the perspective of faith – which tradition then do I have to apply? - is this the stranger in our midst who requires decent treatment, or is this my brother of faith who should expect my solidarity?

> "The water is boiling in the pot, slowly but surely, and it seems to me that unlike the frog, you have to keep an eye on it."

The *how* and the *why* of our moral and religious duty to defend the rights of others has reached an interesting stage. One of the shameful episodes, the bits of baggage, I am reminded of in church history was when the Spanish conquistadores went to Latin America and this huge debate took place within Catholic church circles: did the indigenous people of the Americas have a soul? And once you had agreed that they had a soul, you had a different set of relationships, and a different set of moral obligations. Admittedly, evangelisation was a part of that.

But we are almost back in the same debate. Does the migrant worker who has slipped into the country through unofficial channels have a human right? And if they don't have a human right - which is what it seems to me our country is saying, so that you can put a child in a detention centre for more than 42 days, you can round people up in their workplaces with police raids, and you can enter into someone's front room at 4am in the morning and hold children down while you pull their parents away - we are surely in the same debate. If they haven't got a human right, then they won't be treated as human beings. And that is equally wrong.

All faith communities have something to hold onto here. Any community that, at any point in its history, has experienced persecution or genocide – and all faith communities have in some way or another – has an institutional memory that ought to alert you to the dangers of pursuing this kind of path. It may not be that we have got to that terrible place of being a police state. It may not be. But there are sufficient signs of that process going on to alert people whose community memory is one of persecution, and all of us have that somewhere in our history.

Last weekend in our project we had an event for groups – mostly Christian groups although it isn't only them who are doing this – who are offering accommodation in their own homes to failed asylum seekers, because people with no recourse to public funds for whatever reason, not only failed asylum seekers but other undocumented workers also, are very vulnerable. We were bringing those groups together to look at how we could develop strategies. One of the Christian groups said we had to think very carefully: was this legal or not? Having decided that it probably was legal, they had decided to go ahead. But, they said, if they had found out that it wasn't legal, they would still have had to go ahead with it. That obligation is at a sort of cutting point. At this point in time, we are still on the right side of the law. But if we are effective in protecting the rights of the most vulnerable migrants in this country, then I suspect that it will very quickly become illegal.

Asylum seekers are not given cash, but supermarket vouchers. We buy them from them and sell them off to good people. I'll sell you one later! If that became illegal, we would still have to do that and if it was being truly effective, then you can be sure that the government would make it illegal. The water is boiling in the pot, slowly but surely, and it seems to me that unlike the frog, you have to keep an eye on it.

There is another issue that is really important for communities of faith in the area of freedom of movement and freedom of association. Faith communities are, by definition, international communities. Our solidarity, our relationship, crosses national boundaries and the idea of the nation state has always been a problem for a faith community whose loyalties cross national boundaries. This is why all sorts of strange settlements take place.

But it seems to me that it is increasingly impossible for faith communities to function as international organisations because of the restrictions on freedom of movement. Our churches' national assembly invited several people to come and speak on climate change, development and so on from sister churches in other parts of the world. They were not given visas. They were told that their sponsor didn't have sufficient assets: we own a thousand church buildings across the country and have approximately £15 million in our reserves, but apparently that wasn't sufficient. We have disbanded our missionary societies. We don't have that legacy of colonialism any more. But we do have church exchanges of personnel. The head of that organisation had to go personally to Jamaica to be interrogated in order for a Jamaican minister to come here. That is bad enough for Christians, but Muslims must be finding the situation a hundred times worse.

The UK Borders Agency – this dreadful, dreadful organisation – is imposing its restrictions and its own paranoia on the every day life of faith communities. Make Poverty History, the environmental movement, all of these initiatives have grown from faith communities because we have that direct, immediate contact with people who are in other parts of the world.

Some of the discussion around the public space is tiresome. Keep Sunday Special was a big Christian thing, but I am happy to experience Sunday in the same way that Jewish people experience Saturday and a Muslim, Friday. We all have to find our ways of being. If a funky opera uses Christian imagery in a way that might make me wince a little – well that is part and parcel of being in a liberal and an open society.

> "The UK Borders Agency – this dreadful, dreadful organisation – is imposing its restrictions and its own paranoia on the every day life of faith communities."

But if my brother is deported to his death in Zimbabwe, then that is a completely different order of relationship between my community and the state. We are in that sort of relationship now: it has begun to get serious. Remember that under apartheid and in Nazi Germany, the church could hold itself up as being very strong and of course it wasn't persecuted. It was individuals on the margins of faith who, driven by their faith motivation then joined in the wider struggle. They were the people who suffered. That may be where we are heading at the moment.

Session 5
The Conservatives and Civil Liberties

The Right is traditionally strong on issues of personal liberty. But conservative thinkers and policy makers are much less certain when it comes to rights and whether to support universal human rights. With the Tory Party, the favourites to form the next government, this session will host a debate between conservative panelists about the aspirations and principles of their views and thinking about fundamental rights and freedoms.

"One of the things that comes with being a Member of Parliament is that you are forced, whether you like it or not, to talk to people and to hear their views. Sometimes it is the view of the man in the saloon bar, who tells you that, if you have nothing to hide, you have nothing to fear. Sometimes it's the views of others who realise that even if you have nothing to hide, you have plenty to fear. I am afraid that I am persuaded by that second category of person, and not because I don't like going into saloon bars. But I happen to agree with the way in which that describes the proper relationship between the citizen, the subject, whoever it is, the individual and the state…

Someone this morning drew the contrast between being a citizen who could travel, and a Soviet subject who could not. In 2005-6, I led in committee for my party on the Identity Cards Bill, which is just the sort of regime which we were warned about. The problem that we faced in that committee in dealing with that Bill is that the concerns that I expressed - concerns very similar to those expressed in the main hall this morning - were not taken seriously. 'You are exaggerating', it was said. 'you are simply making these points in order to undermine the Government's policy which is to introduce an Identity Cards system'. Of course if you go to my friend in the saloon bar and tell him about the Identity Cards Bill, he'd say 'well, look, I've got hundreds of ways of my identity being verified, what is the problem?' But the poverty of the imagination of the back bencher and of the saloon bar man who doesn't understand the implications of the policy is precisely what I have concerns about.

We all have in our pockets, I dare say, methods of identifying ourselves. But I dare say none of us has in our pocket an electric key which allows the Government to access information which is private to us, that they can then trade among other Government agencies, but also, according to the Government Business Case published in 2005/6, to 40,000 independent, private operators."

EDWARD GARNIER QC, PANEL SPEAKER AND THE SHADOW MINISTER FOR JUSTICE

The liberal conservative case for human rights
DOMINIC RAAB

It was Churchill who said that if you're not a liberal at 20, you've no heart, and if you're not a conservative by 40, you've no head. I'm rather attached to both, so I'd like to make the 'liberal conservative' case for human rights. That draws on a strong tradition that we have here, the legacy of great thinkers like Burke, Locke, Mill's 'harm to others' principle. And I would add Isaiah Berlin, both because of his strong emphasis on the freedom that shields us from abuse of power by the state, but also his acknowledgement that liberty is not the most important - nor necessarily the only thing - in life. Zealous campaigners might just from time to time reflect on his plea for moderation, and I'm quoting: 'everything is what it is. Liberty is liberty, not equality or fairness or justice, or culture or human happiness'.

That's fine as far as first principles go, but what, practically, would this involve? In my view, we have to navigate the path between two principal hazards. The first is to avoid throwing the baby out with the bathwater. What we see time and time again from ministers when they make a call for greater powers, is that it's said to be based on 'unprecedented' threats – 90 days, 42 days, ID cards, and now again with the giant new communications database. Of course, we face new challenges. But that's no reason to suspend all critical judgement and junk the basic freedoms that we've nurtured and defended for centuries, without properly scrutinising the case. That is part of what has been so wrong in what has happened over the last decade. It might not sound particularly earth-shattering, but one practical way to avoid the 'baby bathwater' syndrome, if I can call it that, is to provoke and prolong debate. 42 days is a classic example of a policy that crumbled in Parliament and in the polls, the longer the debate went on. And it keeps on crumbling. It has not been necessary to hold someone for longer than 14 days, let alone 28, in over a year and a half.

The second hazard is a slightly more subtle one: the risk of stretching, to breaking point, the credibility of the basic idea behind what human rights stand for. I support the European Convention. I wouldn't support withdrawal. It's a sensible list of core freedoms. But there has been massive judicial legislation from Strasbourg, especially since the Golder case in the 1970s. One consequence has been to increase what the Court calls the 'positive' obligations on the state, rather than just shielding the individual from abuse of power. And that has inflated rather than checked the role of the state. The Human Rights Act has exacerbated this and, on top of that, we're now hearing the Government talking about economic and social rights. For those who see in expanded definitions of freedom and human rights, a redemption of the state, beware the warning first attributed to Thomas Jefferson: 'Government big enough to supply everything you need is big enough to take everything you have'.

> "What we see time and time again from ministers when they make a call for greater powers, is that it's said to be based on 'unprecedented' threats..."

This phenomenon of ever-expanding rights has long been criticised on the centre-right for undermining democratic checks, undermining social responsibility, and fuelling the compensation culture. But there are flickers of concern on the left now as well, with one human rights lawyer who's speaking here today slamming the Human Rights Act as a 'villain's charter' in the *Guardian*, of all places, because it was arming hedge funds in their claim for compensation after the nationalisation of Northern Rock. And again, you have BAA's attempt to deploy the Act to trump the ruling that found it in abuse of its market position as an airport operator. It's surely only a matter of time before we see the bankers brandishing the Act to claim a human right to bonuses.

But on the whole, those flickers aside, the left still retains its crusading zeal, relishing the conquest of new territory. It's a sort of human rights imperialism - whether it's Mary Robinson arguing for human rights to tackle global warming, or Francesca Klug's 'building up' from a charter of rights approach.

What do the public think about all this?

Well, the good news from a 2008 Ministry of Justice survey is that the public associate human rights - at least in a positive way - with the core fundamental freedoms in the ECHR.

The bad news is that they're sceptical about the Human Rights Act and human rights that, in the words of the survey, 'burden public service providers and encourage unscrupulous individuals to seek unjustified compensation'. It's very easy to blame all of this on tabloid hysteria. In truth, the rapid inflation of rights beyond core freedoms risks devaluing the currency - and credibility - of all human rights, at a time when British liberty has never been more important, or more under threat. That is one of the 'risks of rights' today.

So, those are the two hazards that I believe we need to chart a course between. We need a Bill of Rights, both to protect our fundamental freedoms, but also to define them with greater clarity – and to avoid the temptation to keep over-selling human rights, as all things to all people.

> "...the left still retains its crusading zeal, relishing the conquest of new territory. It's a sort of human rights imperialism..."

Liberty doesn't come from liberalism
PHILLIP BLOND

If I may, I'd like to suggest a distinctly conservative contribution to the debate. But before I do, I want to make it very clear that, when we have individuals versus the state, I always favour the rights of individuals over those of the state.

Let's be clear. There's something wrong with our language of rights; there's something wrong with our present political settlement. More or less, it is distilled down to an authoritarian, absolutist, bureaucratic, and dysfunctional state versus a series of isolated individuals - individuals who claim rights against the state, but rarely associate with each other to articulate an alternative social settlement. As a result, individuals always lose.

The history of the liberal legacy of the state which produces an authoritarian state and atomised individuals is that the rights of individuals were always overridden, always derogated, abrogated or even dispensed with. There's something insufficient about a purely liberal language about rights and there's something that always loses.

Now what I want to suggest is a distinctive conservative contribution to this debate, which tries to dissolve this opposition.

For conservatives, you are always born a free individual in free association with others. You're born into families; you're born into a human community. There's never a point at which you're an isolated individual, separate from culture, society, tradition, time, culture, whatever you may say. So conservatives have never believed in the isolated, abstracted individual of liberal contractualist political theory. Liberal contractualist political theory, by way of contrast, always says that the original state of entry is horrible, it's horrific, people are isolated, alone, and at war with one another. Therefore, you need a state to manage their conflict.

Conservatives have never been like that. Conservatives are the society of the civic society; of you and I and each other. As such, conservatives have a huge amount to contribute to the present debate, because they can dissolve this false and disempowering opposition. Conservatives can talk about free association, an association around common goals, around the nature of locality, and around civic institutions.

As such, I want to argue that liberty doesn't come from liberalism. In fact, its true origin rests with this conservative discernment. Let's be very clear, habeas corpus happened before any liberal settlements.

You can think rights through the plurality of a diverse and civic associational society. Paradoxically this does two things. It dissolves the liberal idea of isolated individuals competing and warring with one another, and subsequently needing an absolutist state to police them. If, instead, we put first that primary conservative intuition, the Burkean intuition that we are first born into little platoons, then you're no longer trapped in the language of absolutist states versus individual rights. This, I believe, is a distinctly conservative contribution to the debate. We have somehow got to introduce notions of a plurality of groups rather than a plurality of individuals.

What I would argue for is a proper historical understanding of English laws and English rights which runs alongside the social and which we don't need to import from the Continent. The trouble with continental models of the

> "The history of the liberal legacy of the state which produces an authoritarian state and atomised individuals is that the rights of individuals were always overridden..."

Enlightenment is that they say, if you're not like me you're a savage; if you're not like me you're not reasonable. That French revolutionary universalism delegated to itself the ability to legislate to all peoples: you have to be like us if you are going to be free. But actually, since I am a Conservative and I believe in history and freedom, I think there are different formal models of what constitutes personhood in different traditions, and the key for Conservatives is to have a plural society. That may mean plural in terms of different cultures debating with each other what good is. English liberty has far more to offer than the continental versions.

If you look at British appeals to liberty, they are always historical. They are always talking about the rights we have lost, the times when freedoms have been taken away from us. You have a traditional account of what is being removed. So many of the debates are about 'we had these rights – an absolute power has formed and has taken them from us'. And those rights in English history have almost always been social and economic: they're about use of the land, the claims we have on common land, your rights of tenure and so forth. Looking at social and economic history, what actually happened in Britain is that gradually, all of these rights were indeed taken away from people and assigned to a centralised State. The centralised state was essentially engaged in several acts of dispossession. The rights that were removed, were rights that were concomitant with social and political responsibilities.

So what I would say is that the British notion of remedy already includes the notions of the social and economic. It already includes what is due to an Englishman - the notion of self-sufficiency, property, the ability to exercise your rights and to be free. We don't need the continental tradition to do that, because all rights are based on concepts of personhood and especially in England, all notions of personhood are associated with property. Conservative politics are all about, for instance, creating a property-owning democracy: a society where people are self-sufficient and have the conditions to be so.

Session 6
Press Freedom
SUPPORTED BY THE OBSERVER

Ever since John Milton published *Areopagitica* in 1644, freedom of the press has been a cornerstone of English democracy. Yet lately those foundations appear to have been crumbling... As yet, Britain is a long way from suffering the lack of free speech experienced in countries such as Pakistan. But thanks to apathy and a failure to find a new model of local and national journalism, the threat is growing...

"The point I want to make and indeed rather urge on you is that we need to have a change in the way we think, and indeed write, about freedom of speech and freedom of the press. To generalise perhaps wildly, since the 1980s, campaigns for liberty have centred on the law and the emphasis on human rights in the Helsinki accords. If I am being honest, this was underpinned by the defeatism of the left in my generation who just saw Thatcher win one election victory after another.

We thought we could not win democratically, but perhaps we can win by changing the law so that the judges do our work for us. I don't want to get into the rights and wrongs of that, but one problem is that the judiciary cannot be relied upon to defend freedom of speech. Like the ruling classes in a lot of Europe, they still have an aristocratic element in their thinking - which you don't get in America – that freedom of speech for the masses is dangerous. It is not something you can teach in law school. You have either got an instinctive belief that it is wrong to ban books or you haven't. The lack of that instinct for liberty in the judiciary is being seen now in our courts and is causing something of an international scandal."

NICK COHEN, PANEL SPEAKER AND JOURNALIST

The Prevention of Electronic Crimes Act
FATIMA BHUTTO

Pakistan is a new country - 61 years young - and its history of resisting press censorship is already a very brave one. The last dictator we had in the 1980s, General Zia ul Haq, enforced strict censorship across the board with provincial censorship boards set up across the four provinces. Every article to be printed - whether it was in the sports or the comment page - had to go to a censor board. Under this dictatorship, the censor boards became very strict and they would block out entire articles. So what the broadsheets did was that they started to print empty space in Pakistani newspapers. You would open up Monday's paper and there would be three stories and the rest, empty boxes. The censorship boards caught onto this and said, 'OK, not funny. You have got to fill space.' What they started to do then was to fill the space with pictures of donkeys, or dogs or farm animals. So we come from quite a subversive history of resisting press censorship.

Two civilian governments and another dictator later, with a so-called democratic government now, and that vigilance has effectively been dropped. In Pakistan we not only have blanket press censorship in terms of what is discussable and what is not discussable, but in our newspapers, we censor based on languages. What you can say in English is more flexible because only 14,000 people read the English papers. But what you can say in the Urdu press, which 4 million people read, is very different. Of course, there is a degree of self-censorship as well that is practiced.

But I want to speak about this new law which is being introduced in Pakistan and which is currently before Parliament. It is going to be passed. We don't have an opposition. It is one of the great things about our democracy! And it is called the Prevention of Electronic Crimes Act. It extends throughout Pakistan and applies to any person of any nationality or citizenship. The definition of what constitutes an electronic crime doesn't follow any international recognised standards. It consists of, but is not limited to, 'electrical, digital, analogue, magnetic, optical, biochemical, electro-chemical, electro-mechanical, electro-magnetic, radioelectric or wireless technology.' So that means anything that you have transmitted via email, the internet, your mobile phone, or indeed via your toaster! – they all fall under this law.

This idea of cyber crimes came out several months ago under this new government, and first the Federal Investigative Authority was charged with 'hunting down anti-democratic forces'. This is the other feature of our democracy: it is incredibly vindictive. The authorities were charged with hunting down those who sought to character-assassinate our country's politicians.

> "...'investigative officers' – and we don't know if this is the army, intelligence forces, or the police, it doesn't specify – are given access to all and any electronic systems..."

In text messaging, really, how much can you do? What they are really interested in is people who transmit information. For example, the recent story about drones flying out from air bases in the Baluchistan province started life as a ticker that exploded in the international press, and then it had to be covered. So, everything from basic news and information trading aggravates the Federal Investigative Authority, including a popular joke that can only be described as silly: *three countries are sitting around talking about how to deal with their criminals; America says we put them to death, England says we give them clemency for now, and Pakistan says, oh, well we make them President!* This constitutes 'character assassination'...

This law enforces prison sentences for such crimes: anything from three years to death for vague crimes such as 'spoofing' which could mean satire, jokes, who knows; spamming which – apart from spamming – also includes the passing of information to large groups, such as if I send out information to my 200-strong mailing list; the crime of having a fake email account sends people to jail for three months; 'investigative officers' – and we don't know if this is the army, intelligence forces, or the police, it doesn't specify – are given access to all and any electronic systems, any and all data banks, and are given the power to coerce service providers, not only to give forth information from people's Google searches and so forth, but they are also required to keep it confidential that the government has access to their files.

This is as scary as it sounds and even more so when you look at the fact that part of Pakistan now is going to be ruled by Taliban law, after this government made a peace deal with militants in the Swat valley. The fact that the government has switched to Sharia law in one section of the country unilaterally without a vote or a referendum is not discussed. It just slid by.

The press needs to start getting angry
ANDREW GILLIGAN

The threat to press freedom is more complicated than some of the others. It comes not just from the state, from judges, from the increasingly precarious economics of the industry, but actually from the press itself. One of the biggest state threats is the database that has been proposed where literally everybody's transactions with any internet provider, Google search, email, telephone records, movements in your car as tracked by number plate recognition cameras will be stored which clearly marks the end of privacy for all of us, and also the end of journalism. A lot of journalism relies on confidential sources and no source will want to come forward if they know that their confidentiality is no longer assured. Did the media make a fuss about that? I have read a few articles and written one, but no.

There is a policy to crack down on whistle blowers. They are doing a great deal to be aggressive towards whistle blowers already, even without those powers. For example, two men called David Key and Leo Connor were recently jailed for leaking to the *Mirror* a story which, I believe, completely fits the definition of a public interest story – which is that George Bush and Tony Blair discussed the bombing of a TV station, Al Jazeera, during the war on Iraq. Did anyone make any fuss about that? The media was almost silent about that major attack on press freedom. Even the journalists they have leaked to have been arrested and searched. The journalist on the *Milton Keynes Citizen*, Sally Murrer was arrested, strip-searched and spent two nights in the cells. She got off, but again, it was almost eighteen months before anyone in the mainstream media even mentioned her name.

In the case of Jean Charles de Menezes, one of the key details, as is often the case in this very secretive country, came out from the media. This was the leaked Independent Police Complaints' Commission (IPCC) report revealing that Menezes was not in fact running away, and that he had not been wearing a heavy coat, as well as a number of other incriminating details that raised very serious questions about the police decision to shoot him. All those details came out first from a leak to ITV news. The IPCC Secretary and the ITN journalist who received the leak from the Secretary were arrested. To this day, those two journalists are the only people to have been arrested for the shooting of Jean Charles de Menezes!

> "To this day, those two journalists are the only people to have been arrested for the shooting of Jean Charles de Menezes!"

The police have those enhanced powers of search and they use them. They have even started branching out into TV criticism. Do you remember the extraordinary decision taken by the West Midlands Police to report *Dispatches* – the programme I work on though not that particular edition – to OFCOM, the broadcasting legislator, for a programme that they said was a distortion? Now it wasn't of course: OFCOM ruled entirely in its favour and I believe the police settled a libel action brought by the programme makers. But it is the responsibility of the police to investigate crime, not editorial standards in TV journalism.

As for economics and journalism, we already appear to be witnessing the disappearance of local newspapers, and that upsets the whole ecosystem. A lot of stories that eventually became big national stories started out in the local newspapers. Major newspapers in America are closing down. My own paper, the *Evening Standard*, was sold for a pound to a Russian oligarch and transferred today. We will see what happens. We have to start thinking seriously about the way in which commercial pressures are preventing journalists from having the time to make basic phone calls, let alone go out and do some of the impressive investigative journalism we have seen in the past.

Probably though, the hardest thing of all is to make people understand why a free press is needed. The press, I think unfairly, is often seen in the wider public as an abuser of human rights as much as a protector of them. It is unfair because that is largely the legacy of past misbehaviour by a fairly small number of red-top tabloids. There is no question that they did abuse human rights: they did smear and slander innocent people who could not answer back. There was a very interesting case I wrote about of a perfectly ordinary woman in Scotland living on a council estate who had an autistic child. *The Sun* wrote up that this child was the most disruptive child in the town, named the child, picture of the child, and the child's life was destroyed. He couldn't go to school any more; lost a lot of confidence; started crying at night; told his mother to 'fuck off'. She didn't have any redress. She didn't have any money and couldn't sue. This was in the 1980s.

They have cleaned up their act a bit now. Nevertheless, the clarion call to defend the freedom of the British press is not one that is always shared. But I do believe that we are a state with relatively weak democratic institutions. Not as weak as Pakistan's, but weak by comparison with most other advanced democracies. Power in this country is heavily centralised. A very few people take all the key decisions to an extent quite unknown in any other democracy. And a lot of the institutions of state that are supposed to protect us have failed to protect us. On the other hand, we have a very strong democratic culture. That's what makes up for it. You are probably very bored with me banging on about Iraq by now, but the fact is that over the dossier story and the case that was made for war - all the institutions of state that were supposed to protect us - failed: the civil service in the person of John Scarlett became Alistair Campbell's accomplice; the courts in the person of Lord Hutton failed rather spectacularly; the legislature in the form of Parliament's Foreign Affairs Committee seemed to be more concerned with attacking me and David Kelly than trying to get to the bottom of the dossier story. The only estate of the realm which did its job in the end, and brought out the truth more quickly and comprehensively than anything else, was the fourth estate.

That's one of the reasons why we are pretty important and that is part of the case we have to be making. The press themselves need to start getting angry about press persecution, the persecution of journalists, of sources, and they need to start getting angry about attacks on them by the state. The press still has

> *...over the dossier story and the case that was made for war – all the institutions of state that were supposed to protect us – failed..."*

a great deal of power in this country. Whatever they may tell you, they listen to the *Daily Mail* and even occasionally to the *Evening Standard* and the *Guardian*. Journalists are going to have to learn new techniques, including encryption techniques, in order to be able to communicate secretly and safely with their contacts and conceal their activities from the state. Because whether we defeat this latest Big Brother thing or not, it is going to come back, and it is probably happening already in some form, secretly.

Journalists, meanwhile, are going to have to start making a case for their own work, partly by doing that work. We have to start making the case to a wider public for our role as a key voice in society, the importance of a free press to a society with weak democratic institutions, but a strong democratic culture. Civil society, including a free press, is probably the most important safeguard that we have. But we need to make that case more widely.

When matters become undiscussable
ALAN RUSBRIDGER

Libel is a difficult subject to speak about: it seems like a small subject of interest to journalists. But I hope to convince you that it is something you all ought to be interested in, especially against the background where the established media in the western world is in crisis. A lot of them are about to be obliterated by a combination of technology, the recession and the economy. For the first time since the Enlightenment, we are going to have societies, cities, communities, regions, countries, which don't have a verifiable source of information because the old economic model for what we do is dramatically threatened. However much we dislike newspapers and disapprove of what journalists do, we have to bear in mind what society is going to be like without them.

You could begin almost anywhere, with the laws on confidence, data protection, privacy, contempt and their impact on free speech. I personally am wondering about state surveillance and what impact that will have on whistleblowers, other sources and that confidential interaction between people who want to tell journalists things and the receipt of information. If every phone call and email can be traced, then we are going to see an awful lot of whistle blowers and journalists in the dock for doing things that seemed unremarkable in the past.

But today I want to talk about two aspects of libel: libel tourism and cost. The libel industry in this country is a bit like the investment banking industry before the bubble burst. London has become the centre for this industry, like banking. It has become so well-established now, that anyone with a dodgy reputation wanting to stifle free speech not only in their own countries but in Britain and the rest of the world, will come and sue in London. They do that because the laws and the costs of suing in London are so favourable to those who want to silence free speech. The press itself has some borderlines to draw, like the ones between what is private and what is public. But there is insignificant protection for journalists who are writing about things that do matter, and we should ask ourselves why it is that the US Congress, in a country with such a reputation for free speech, is currently passing a bill through Congress which would make British libel judgments unenforceable in America, so alarmed are they by the developments going on here. Something is wrong, and this teaches us that the British libel laws have an impact far beyond these shores.

> "...anyone with a dodgy reputation wanting to stifle free speech not only in their own countries but in Britain and the rest of the world, will come and sue in London."

The other way it all resembles the bankers before the collapse, is the fees that lawyers are paying themselves in order to suppress free speech. There was a well-intentioned piece of law that allowed conditional fee arrangements, no-win-no-fee, so that people could have more access to libel law, that has enabled lawyers to double fees that were, in my opinion, grotesquely large to start with.

morning sessions

> "Libel is no longer as it was once, a battle between Davids and Goliaths. There are very few Goliaths left. There is the BBC and Rupert Murdoch."

A fascinating study done by the Comparative Media Law Centre in Oxford compared the cost of libel in the UK to the other European states. It won't surprise you to know that England and Wales come top of the league. Fees here and in Wales were four times as large as the next country on the list, Ireland, which, in turn, is ten times more expensive than the next. England and Wales are 140 times more costly than anywhere else in Europe – that's right – 140 times.

Most of this is hidden from public view. We have a few well-publicised cases, such as Tesco versus the *Guardian* in which the *Guardian* was wrong in essence, or at any rate we got some facts wrong, which we apologised for twice and corrected twice and used the swiftest, cheapest, easiest route in which to settle the case, and we have just received the bill for £800,000 pounds. This includes a staggering £350,000 which was for Tesco's own accountants to explain to their own lawyers about the tax avoidance schemes which we got muddled. So that is a staggering amount of money and it leads on to the chill factor.

The predictable consequence of this is that almost nobody will write about tax avoidance in future, because they look at that and they think, 'If we get it wrong, it's so complicated - it's almost impossible to understand anyway and we probably will get something wrong and if we do, it's just so forbidding: we are not even going to try'. I thought it was important that we at the *Guardian* did go back and write something else about tax avoidance. We recently did so. The cost of getting that series legally approved over two weeks in order to get us to the point where the lawyers and the accountants agreed that this was 'probably right' – the most you can hope for in that area - was £100,000. No news organisation is going to spend that amount of money. Which means that this terribly complicated subject isn't going to be written about or discussed in this country. Parliamentarians across the board do not understand it, and if they don't have journalists to explain it to them, they are not going to discuss it and there will be very little pressure to change those laws. If you believe in tax avoidance then it is highly rational and sensible to invest in that amount of money to suppress that subject, and just get it out of the public eye.

We can't blame the litigants: we have to change the law. This is urgent because, as I have said, the press is in a dire financial state. It has been hit by revolutions in advertising and technology. Libel is no longer as it was once, a battle between Davids and Goliaths. There are very few Goliaths left. There is the BBC and Rupert Murdoch. That's about it. In a few years time, we won't be asking why newspapers made mistakes in digging into complex matters, we will be marvelling that they ever tried reporting on this stuff, because they simply won't be able to take the risk under the laws that we have. That is what should worry us. At its heart, this is not a debate about the perhaps arcane subject of libel law – usually people switch off and journalists neither expect nor receive much sympathy for bleating on about libel – but whatever it is that you care passionately about, that will become 'undiscussable' with the laws that we have at the moment. This is about what is discussable in society and what happens when a matter becomes undiscussable.

Session 7
The Police
SUPPORTED BY RED PEPPER, THE FOOTBALL SUPPORTERS' FEDERATION

There are numerous examples of their questionable conduct:
- Damian Green;
- Jean Charles de Menezes;
- The abuse of Form 27 to disperse legitimate assembly – especially football supporters;
- The building of the FIT database;
- The unscrutinised roll-out of automated number-plate recognition (ANPR) without debate in Parliament;
- Cash for peerages;
- The routinely oppressive policing of demonstrations;
- The routine mistreatment of suspects;
- The lack of accountability of the Association of Chief Police Officers (ACPO) (it sets policy and pursues goals but is immune to scrutiny and freedom of information (FoI) requests).

Who are the police working for – themselves or us? Who are they answerable to? Have they become politicised?

"It is now illegal, as of very recently, to photograph police. It's an offence. It seems ironic that in one of the most surveyed societies on the planet - everybody and everything is taking photographs of us, from today's *Guardian* to different agencies that have acquired or misused powers of surveillance - they're all photographing us and the only people who can't take photographs, are us. For some of us in the protest movement, being able to photograph the police is really rather important. Being able to have your own independent record of an event saves you from getting seven shades of shit kicked out of you when they go to break up a squat, or evict a camp. It's really disturbing if you're no longer allowed to photograph what the police are up to. For us, it's a real safety issue...

For suggestions or provocations to finish with, policing is becoming more oppressive in my kind of non-violent activist career. It is becoming more oppressive and I suggest it's going to further develop that way. I feel policing is not merely protecting the old political and state interests of the past, but that it is protecting the business interests of today more and more. The idea that oppressive or aggressive policing is done by the police force is so last century. It's done by private companies who can buy their own laws through injunctions and enforce them through private security companies. Finally, that leads to a change in thinking about direct action. I've just done it as an expression, a wish to try and protect the planet for our future generations. It's also an affirmation of what existing civil liberties we've got left. Now, I think it is becoming an imperative. We need to be taking peaceful direct action, because in that way, maybe we can start recreating our modern civil liberties."

MALCOLM CARROLL, PANEL SPEAKER AND SPOKESMAN FOR PLANE STUPID morning sessions

Where it all went wrong
STEVEN POWELL

Well, Madam Chair, ladies and gentlemen, it's a privilege and a pleasure for the Football Supporters' Federation (FSF) to have been invited to speak to the convention today. I hope that what we have to report to you this morning will strike you not as the trivial concerns of people pursuing what - after all in the last analysis - is a hobby, but that there's another aspect to it, as we have already heard from speakers telling us about the shooting at Stockwell tube station of a Brazilian citizen happily going about his business; the repression of legitimate dissent and protest over environmental issues; and the disquiet of many rank-and-file police officers. My father was a police officer for most of his working life and the reason that he took early retirement was how disturbed he was at the way policing was going, from policing by consent to more and more repressive measures.

I want to pay public tribute to Liberty, the human rights organisation, and particularly the legal officer, Anna Fairclough, and her colleagues, for coming to the defence of those football supporters who have been made subject to a recent law called Section 27 of the Violent Crime Reduction Act, 2006. Liberty's swift response left us with a debt of gratitude - both from my Federation and from those football supporters concerned - that we're going to find difficult to repay. I am pleased to tell you that the FSF decided at its national council meeting last Sunday to affiliate to Liberty. Many national council members and other FSF activists have joined as individual members, many more intend to do so over the coming weeks.

So, what is section 27 of the Violent Crime Reduction Act? This is a relatively new law. It gives power to a police officer of any rank to require any person that they believe is likely to participate in the proximate future in 'alcohol-related' - and those specific words are in clause 27 – 'alcohol-related disorder', to leave a locality by a route that the officer can specify, for a period not exceeding 48 hours. Now, I don't suppose there's any citizen sitting in this room today who won't accept

105

that we have a problem as a society with alcohol-related crime. Violent crime as we've heard, particularly knife crime affecting black and minority ethnic communities in London, is reaching plague proportions. So, it would appear on the face of it that this is just a 'new tool in the toolbox' as modern police management like to call it, and it isn't too burdensome or disproportionate. If only that were the case.

I can briefly cite two cases. In one of these, papers have been served on the Greater Manchester police by Liberty on behalf of the individuals concerned, to seek a judicial review of the actions of their officers. On 15 November 2008, around eighty supporters of Stoke City were peaceably gathered in a pub in Earlham on the outskirts of Greater Manchester prior to their club's game against Manchester United. Now, those of you who know your football will know that Stoke City has spent a long time in the lower divisions of English football, having been relegated in 1977. So this was the first occasion in thirty years that Stoke City have played at Old Trafford against Manchester United: a very special day for those supporters.

Unfortunately, the day turned out to be special for all the wrong reasons. For reasons still unclear to us, the police surrounded the pub, refusing to allow any of those Stoke City supporters inside to leave. All of them were issued with notices under Section 27, which I remind you requires individual assessments. Every single Stoke City fan in the pub was issued with a notice. One of them refused to sign a copy of the notice because he believed that the statements being made about him being involved in disorder were factually incorrect. He was told that if he refused to sign, he would be arrested. The police organised buses outside the pub and all those eighty or so Stoke City fans were processed onto the buses.

Now, clearly because these people had been in the pub, some of them required the toilet. The police refused to allow those fans to go back into the pub to use same. They were told to urinate in empty containers. I ask you, how dignified is that for people who are quite happily minding their own business, bothering nobody? And we've got a written statement from the publican to say that all of the fans were peaceable. None of them was drunk. They weren't even singing. Every one of them, he said, is welcome to go back to his pub anytime they like.

Eighty people didn't get to see the match; match tickets worth over thirty

> "...taken down the motorway surrounded by police cars with a helicopter above them – these are nine football fans, including an 11-year-old boy..."

pounds were worth nothing. All of them were bussed from Manchester back to Stoke, including one Stoke City fan that lives in Manchester! He then had to take himself to the railway station at his own expense and buy a railway ticket back home. He made that clear to the officers at the time and they essentially said, 'you're confusing us with people who care'.

An even more bizarre case surrounds nine Plymouth Argyle fans who travelled by minibus up the motorway from Devon to south Yorkshire for their game at Doncaster Rovers in December last year. So far, so normal, - something that thousands of football fans, tens of thousands of football fans do every weekend. Amongst this group were the son of a recently retired senior police officer and a company director. After arriving in Doncaster at midday, they headed for a pub where they knew that a lot of Plymouth Argyle fans would be gathering before the game, to have some lunch. Discovering that the pub didn't serve food, they attempted to leave. This is where it all went wrong. The pub had been surrounded by police officers and they were refused permission to leave. One of them who tried to explain was told, 'Don't bother, you're not leaving the pub. Go back in and have a drink.'

Now, let's remind ourselves that Section 27 is designed to deal with alcohol-related disorder. Is it really a good idea to tell somebody to have a drink on an empty stomach when all they want to do is eat? But it gets more serious. They were marched back to their minivan, escorted to the motorway where they were picked up by police cars in South Yorkshire, taken down the motorway surrounded by police cars with a helicopter above them - these are nine football fans, including an eleven-year-old boy – and at the Derbyshire boundary, they were met by officers of the Derbyshire Constabulary, likewise at the boundary between Derbyshire and Leicester.

When they needed petrol, they were refused permission until it was pointed out to the police that an internal combustion engine doesn't function very well when there's no fuel in the tank. They pulled into a service station, and asked to be allowed to leave the van to use the toilet facilities. They were told 'no'.

Reluctantly, the police finally agreed to take each of the people on the minibus under escort to the toilet, with baying police dogs which were terrifying to both the occupants of the van and bystanders. Now, I ask you, do you really think that a) that's a proportional and sensible use of police powers; and b) those police officers in cars and a helicopter could have been doing something more useful in detecting and deterring crime?

Well, I know what my answer to that is. Let me be clear: the FSF doesn't support and never has and never will, condone violent crime. An often ignored fact is that the single biggest group that are affected by football-related disorder and violence are football supporters themselves. We've got no interest in promoting violence. In cases such as these however, the police have massively overstepped the mark. The abuse of a dangerous power that Parliament in its lack of wisdom, has seen fit to grant, should concern all of us who care about civil liberties and human rights. Simón Bolivar, one of the historic liberators of South America, celebrated to this day in the title of that continent's international football tournament, the equivalent to the UEFA Champions League, the *Copa Libertadores de América*, or American Liberators' Cup, in his famous letter from Jamaica nearly two hundred years ago said that, 'a state too extensive in itself is transformed into a tyranny. It disregards the principles which it should preserve and finally degenerates into despotism'. How right he was. A lesson that we appear to have forgotten in the supposed cradle of democracy. Thank you.

"All for two good holidays a year..."
HARRIET SERGEANT

I'm going to talk about your bread and butter, day-to-day policing and how that's affecting our individual liberties. I was asked by the Police Federation - the 'trade union' that represents the rank and file of policemen - to write this report because the police themselves are so concerned about what's going on (see *The Public and the Police*, London: Civitas, 2008). I went all over the country interviewing different police forces, and all my interviews were characterised by a high level

> "...police are judged by the numbers of arrests made, while we the public, judge the police in a completely different way. We judge the police by the absence of crime."

of frustration and bitterness. The police felt they were not giving the public the kind of policing they want. As one superintendent said to me, 'The police have become an extension of the Government'. Another remarked that 'politics currently control the police'. This is a very worrying development for our liberties. In Sir Robert Peel's *Nine Principles of Policing* (1829), seven - seven! - are devoted to the relationship between the public and the police. Only one is on the relationship of the police with the state. He knew where police priorities should be. Number two, for example, states that the power of the police is dependent on public approval for their existence, actions and behaviour, and on their ability to secure and maintain public respect.

Government's actions are directly affecting that relationship. Law and order is a hot political issue. The government cannot be seen to fail. They're trying to get good crime figures. That's their number one priority. And they're trying to do this by controlling the police with targets. Targets are no bad thing, but these targets, as the police pointed out, are badly thought out. They force ethical public servants to behave unethically. Also they don't give the public the kind of policing that we want.

What are these targets? A policeman has to perform to get a certain number of 'sanction detections' every month. There are a number of problems with this; the first is that a murder gets the same number of 'sanction detections' as a child stealing a Mars bar. So, serious crime is ignored and minor crime is elevated to equal the serious. Then, some crime just doesn't count. A policeman will get a 'sanction detection' for arresting a child scribbling on a pavement with a piece of chalk, but he won't get one for tracking down a missing child, which takes hours of work, and is very painstaking and time-consuming.

This is failing to give the public what we want. The police are judged by the numbers of arrests made, while we the public, judge the police in a completely different way. We judge the police by the absence of crime. Survey after survey shows the public does not want crime happening in the first place. However, prevention of crime is not a police target. One policeman said sadly to me, 'I remember when you were judged about how quiet you kept your patch and policing was about problem-solving. Now it is all about, "well how many have you locked up then?"'

The government says, 'Look, we're bringing more and more people to justice'. But the police say, 'it's the wrong people, and in the process we're criminalising a generation'. Rather than address persistent and violent offenders, the police complain that they are just creating crime to government order. And they're usually arresting previously law-abiding citizens. One policeman said to me that, at the end of the month, if he hadn't got his sanction detections, he went down to the local university, because he knew that if he stopped a student or two, he'd probably find drugs in their pockets. He said, 'You know, really I should be going into the university and explaining to them the problems about drugs'. And his partner looked at him and replied, 'Are you mad? Do you want to get rid of an easy supply of sanction detections? We're not going to be doing that!'

How all this is affecting our civil liberties is clear from what happened to the son of a friend of mine. He's about 19, and he was on his way home from an evening out and going to catch the tube lift. The lift doors were closing, and he put his foot in the lift doors just to hold them open. The next thing he knew, he's being arrested by the transport police, handed over to three policemen from the Met, handcuffed, and his friend wasn't allowed to come with him in the van. The custody suite at the local station was full, so he and three policemen sat in that van for an hour. Finally, he was led through the criminal entrance to the custody desk, had his rights read to him, his shoelaces and other personal things removed and he was put in a cell with a toilet and a camera. About five in the morning, he was told what he was guilty of: breaking a community bylaw. 'Apparently', he said, 'you're not allowed to stop a lift from moving'. He added, well actually he wasn't doing that, he was trying to stop the doors from closing. That was the point: the lift wasn't moving. But they said, 'No, you've done this'. They said, 'Look, you can stay in prison all night and go to court, or you can just accept a caution'.

Well, here we have the bizarre effects of a target culture. The first question is, what do we want? In a city where knife crime has doubled in the last few years, and young, mostly black, men are being routinely murdered and not much being done about it, do we really want three policemen tied up for a night arresting a young man for putting his foot in a lift door? Why are they doing this? They're doing this because a caution earns a sanction detection and it's an easy option. But as the policeman said to me, saying to someone, 'You're just going to get a caution!' is actually unethical. Because a caution can stop you getting jobs for example. It stops you working for the police. One woman who is training to be a nurse recently found that she can't work for the NHS, because she has received a caution for something equally trivial.

> "British police were not intended to be servants of the state, but servants of the communities that they serve."

Also, everyone arrested has to give a DNA sample which automatically generates a criminal record number on the police national computer. And with a criminal record, you can't get a visa to the States, for example. I was told by police that there are two senior policemen from ACPO currently employed in explaining to American immigration that a lot of people who have British criminal records aren't exactly criminals: they're simply the victims of targets.

What all this has made us realise is that our police do have massive powers. They've always had these powers. But, before, it was up to them whether to haul you in or not. Now it's at the Government's whim. One of the biggest complaints of the police is exactly this: the loss of their discretion. Over and over again, they emphasise the point that they cannot police without the consent of the public, and their loss of discretion is alienating the public, and if you alienate the public, you are policing in a police state. As Sir Robert Peel said, the police are the public and the public are the police.

Many officers felt their senior officers had abandoned them, because they're getting bonuses of £5-10,000 a year which depend on them securing a certain number of sanction detections. They accused their superior officers of turning the force upside down, undermining the ethos of policing and jeopardising relations with the public 'all for two good holidays a year'.

Police officers, we should remember, swear an oath of allegiance to the Queen and not to the Prime Minister, unlike many other police forces. British police were not intended to be servants of the state, but servants of the communities that they serve. Their powers are personal, used at their own discretion and derived from the Crown. This essential feature of British policing, policing by consent, which guarantees our individual liberty, is now in jeopardy.

Session 8
Liberty and the National Question
SUPPORTED BY CAMPAIGN FOR AN ENGLISH PARLIAMENT; INSTITUTE FOR PUBLIC POLICY RESEARCH

By a majority of 19, English MPs voted against 42 days. If the national parliaments across the UK could have voted on the question, they would almost certainly all (including Stormont) have rejected a further extension of detention without trial. ID cards can be seen as an attempt to bind the devolved nations into an all-British 'Union database'. So, are British institutions a source of danger and would national parliaments make us all freer? Or would they undermine the framework of universal, justiciable rights?

SOURCE: HTTP://MODERNLIBERTY.BLIP.TV/FILE/2014480/

"Since we are talking about rights and liberties, an interesting place to start might be the nationwide British Bill of Rights, and Responsibilities, which Gordon Brown's Government is looking into at the moment. I hear now that the Conservative Party wants to look into a similar kind of thing for if and when they become a government. I think the Conservative Party wants it to replace the Human Rights Act and the Labour Party doesn't. But either way, it looks like we will get some form of legislation giving us - apparently - a code of rights.

One thing that interests me in the reporting of the way the Government's Bill of Rights would work, is that, assuming that it is passed in the British Parliament, it seems it would then go to the devolved parliament in Scotland and the assemblies in Northern Ireland and Wales. They will be allowed to tinker around with it if they want to. It seems possible, if not likely, that they will be able to add their own rights on if they want to, according to their own national traditions. – to alter it in some way to make it, perhaps, culturally or politically more appropriate for those countries.

Now what happens in England will be entirely different. In England, the people will get what the British Government gives them, whereas the people in the other countries of the UK will get what they want, or at least what is expressed in their own, elected legislatures. It seems to me, based on that and many other similar instances that Gareth Young of the Campaign for an English Parliament can probably cover better than me in this session – that 'the national question' at the moment in the UK is: why aren't all nations in the UK equal? Because it's clear that England is getting a rough deal at the moment. Now there may be some Scottish and Welsh nationalists who find that quite amusing and who are having a bit of a good time with some Schadenfreude, which I can entirely understand.

But it's not a good idea. Because, around 80 – 85% of all the people of Britain live in England, including plenty of Scottish and Welsh people, including most of Britain's ethnic minority population. If we have got a deal on liberty, on our rights, on the constitution, that makes the people of England unhappy, then we've got a problem for the whole of the United Kingdom. And we've got a problem with the idea of equality of rights and equality of liberties as well."

PAUL KINGSNORTH, PANEL SPEAKER AND AUTHOR OF 'REAL ENGLAND'

Some thoughts on sovereignty, voice and power
GERRY HASSAN

What is the UK? British political science says that the UK is a unitary state. But it is not: it is what's called a 'union state'. A union state is shaped by national and regional differentiation beginning with 1707 and the negotiation of Scottish autonomy, the retention of pre-union rights, and so on. These are political concepts known across the world, yet the political centre has increasingly understood the UK as a regimented unitary state. It has forgotten the evolving unionisms that have held us together. It has increasingly become a neo-liberal space, polity, and state, dedicated to the furtherance of neo-liberalism, which prioritises a certain kind of narrow, dogmatic set of economic relationships.

What was 'Britishness' in the past? It was a popular project. It wasn't just a Tory project. There was a progressive version of it, a Labour story about working people getting a fairer deal, and income redistributed across the isles to areas that needed it. This Britain would take us out of feudalism and the Dark Ages to a better opportunity for all. There was an emotional strand to that and there was also a spiritual and metaphysical strand. People saw the 1953 coronation as a national communion, and there were a set of stories surrounding it that meant something at a popular level, linking a political and an everyday discourse.

It was thirty years ago that Tom Nairn wrote about the break-up of Britain and we are obviously still living through that long 'end' phase in the UK. But something major has happened to it quite recently. Britishness still exists at a governmental and an elite level. But a gut emotional unionism is no longer there. The stories and narratives told about Britishness are increasingly threadbare and problematic, often to the point of being laughable – as in the 'golden thread of liberty'. The Brown project seems to be straight out of the Ladybird books, and has some essential lacunae – it does not talk about London, the world city; it never talks about Ireland; and there is no mention that we are still living with the defeat of British imperialism in 1921.

The laughable nature of this only crept in with the failure of the 'new Britishness' project which initially held out some hope in 1997, around the time of New Labour. Maybe we were kidding ourselves, because a lot of it was risible even then: 'Britain TM', 'Creative Britain', 'Cool Britannia'. How we laughed. But there was seriousness about a political project. There was Charter 88, which hadn't quite won over New Labour to a different model of popular sovereignty. But there was a programme around decentralism and a sense that a different kind of country and political culture was possible.

Why didn't it happen? It is too easy to say that Tony Blair didn't understand constitutional reform. Or even that the 'War on Terror' got in the way. Some things much deeper were at work, and I think they go to the heart of what the UK is. There had been an erosion of the old gentlemanly checks and balances as the state got larger, and those fell into abeyance at the same time as the gentlemanly model of capitalism, with all its problems, was taken to a level of utter grotesqueness. In the gap created, this misunderstanding of the UK as a unitary state arose - with both politicians and civil servants and most of the UK's media. This gives us an over-reaching, unreformed centre which misunderstands the set of relationships that it has with the rest of us – and then, as I mentioned, to cap it all, there is the neo-liberal state.

> "The stories and narratives told about Britishness are increasingly threadbare and problematic, often to the point of being laughable..."

So – some thoughts on sovereignty, voice and power. I am generalising and summarising here, but the majority public opinion and the political elites of Scotland and Wales generally know they are living in a union, the United Kingdom. They have that union state view, and they have a shared post-nationalist idea of sovereignty, such that, even if Scotland becomes independent, its sovereignty wouldn't be absolute. But in England, certainly at the level of the political class, they are still obsessed with old-fashioned notions of sovereignty. They have no idea that they are living in a union. The union the English political class live in, of course, is the European Union, and they see that as a threat, to precisely that absolutist view of sovereignty. They are right to do so. Some of us would see that very threat as an opportunity for something better. The Scots, Welsh and Northern Irish have our own active ideas and embodiments of popular sovereignty in our national, devolved bodies. England has neither voice nor power.

This makes for a very confused picture and it looks unsustainable. Yet one answer would be to say: 'The English question only needs to be answered if the English want to answer it'. As Robert Hazell said: 'It's not an exam test: you don't have to sit it'. And even if you wanted to answer it, you don't have to go down the same route as the devolved Scotland, Wales and Northern Ireland. You can express it, instead of in devolved institutions, in terms of culture and identity. But the relationship of Englishness and Britishness is crucial.

The Tories were once brilliant at managing that balancing act between the two, at least until Thatcher came to power. Labour, historically, have tried to subsume all identities into this British project of which Brown's is just the latest version. But the status quo - the unitary state on a neo-liberal model - isn't sustainable in the long-term. The challenge, the hope, as Raphael Samuel put it, is to 'invent a new set of island stories' that can evolve a level of Britishness in which there is some kind of political cooperation and cultural areas, but could also put in place all sorts of different sets of governmental and democratic relationships – four separate nations; Scotland being independent and England finding a new identity with other nations and a new name if 'the United Kingdom' is abolished. Whatever it is, the old model clearly needs to be killed off and a stake driven through its heart.

There are many different Englands out there, and we have to hope that, whatever happens, we are not left with the Rupert Murdoch playground. There are many different Scotlands and Wales' and Northern Irelands too. It is true that in Scotland, for all its faults, the Scottish National Party (SNP) Government has given voice to a much more social democratic set of values and policies than New Labour has advanced north or south of the border. This can be seen in its progressive social justice and public health policies, in its opposition to PFI-PPP, and a host of populist measures.

Herein lies a complexity. For the SNP's social democracy also masks an underlying duality in the party, rather similar to New Labour. While the party has a social democratic 'heart' on social policy this is combined with a neo-

> "Gordon Brown is a majority British nationalist and majority nationalisms very rarely understand what they are when they say, 'Grow up and join the real world!'"

liberal 'mind' on economic policy.

Within the limitations of the Scottish settlement and the limitations of the SNP, it has broadly developed a more centre-left and progressive politics than New Labour would ever have dared to advance post-1997, while at the same time not transcending the limits of progressive politics found across the globe.

There are other problems. There is a homogenising project in Scotland, advanced by the SNP which involves piling everything into one Scottish identity basket. This seems to me, as someone sympathetic to Scottish nationalism, to be taking one problem area, the British project, and putting it into another one. So the SNP will take one of our most successful plays – *Blackwatch* – a play about the Iraq war and a regiment of Scottish soldiers who were involved in the attack on Fallujah and disbanded by the Blair Government - and use it to invoke one, over-prioritising Scottish identity. Those of us who want a different Scotland, one that is self-determining and that challenges Westminster, will have to resist those absolutist tendencies within the SNP too.

Meanwhile, there is a fundamental problem about how the left think of England, which isn't just a fear of xenophobia and racism. It is a fear that England is an innately Conservative country and that, if Scotland and Wales are not somehow kept on board, you will be left high and dry. It isn't true – England voted only once in post-war times by a majority for the Conservatives. That was in 1955 and in that year a Scottish majority voted the same way because the Tories were just very popular in that year. As did Northern Ireland (with only Wales proving immune to Tory charm!).

At the heart of the small nation project is a set of conflicts between minority nationalisms and majority nationalism. Gordon Brown is a majority British nationalist and majority nationalisms very rarely understand what they are when they say, 'Grow up and join the real world!' or 'You're all separatists and you want divorce!' We have got to recognise the problematic impact of that kind of majority nationalism around the world.

Session 9
Xenophobia
SUPPORTED BY MUSLIM SAFETY FORUM

Some advocates of the database state and counter-terror agenda exploit xenophobia and fear of foreigners while there are also strong pressures to restrict legislative human rights protections to UK citizens only. In the past, racism was indiscriminate, targeting entire ethnic groups or skin colours. Today it can take more insidious forms, identifying groups and individuals while nonetheless drawing upon the old wellspring of prejudice. What can be done to ensure that fundamental rights and freedoms are extended to Muslims and other minorities while they too embrace the principles of human rights that are part of modern liberty?

"You have to look at the impact of certain measures that the government is pursuing, such as anti-terror raids on communities. This is having a huge, huge impact on the community. It's generally accepted by civil liberties groups and British Muslims that the sensational manner in which these raids and arrests are carried out with extensive media reporting, all have a huge impact on the individuals involved, their families and the local Muslim community as well as much further afield. And there is an equally devastating impact on the wider community, once an individual is arrested in such a situation. In most cases, the individuals will have been released without charge after a period of detention. The information from the Muslim Safety Forum is that 32% of all arrested are released within 12 hours, 46% within 24 hours and

93% released within 10 days and only 6% are held for more than 10 days. This is not as widely reported as the arrests when they first take place. However the impact the arrest has on the lives of the individuals involved is devastating. They find themselves, together with their families, ostracised by the wider Muslim community, who are afraid to be seen, to be connected with those involved, for fear of being labelled as sympathisers or terrorists themselves."

EDIE FRIEDMAN, PANEL SPEAKER AND DIRECTOR, JEWISH COUNCIL FOR RACIAL EQUALITY

"I'm a commercial lawyer in terms of my day job. Ten years ago, the approach to Islamic banking, to a murabaha transaction was so often, 'That's a very strange thing, we don't recognize that here. Is it indeed a genuine financing transaction?' Today, it is valued and respected and encouraged in the city, such that it may even be one of the preferred forms of financing transactions in the years to come. You can do it! And what did it was simply a process of a few lawyers sharing a meal together, sometimes literally, and making sure that they didn't just talk with the people it was easiest to bring together, but that they sat down with some of those who knew about Islamic banking and that they learned about it, and that the fear of something foreign receded."

ROBIN KNOWLES QC, PANEL SPEAKER AND SOUTH SQUARE CHAMBERS

The backlash against Macpherson
TUFYAL CHOUDHURY

Thank you very much for the opportunity to speak today about the very important issue of how current debates both on counterterrorism and on community cohesion and integration have the potential danger of reinforcing or exacerbating xenophobia and racism. My particular focus is on how the debates around integration and cohesion have been used in public policy and the impact that this may have. The debate around social cohesion - community cohesion - was set off by the riots that took place in northern England in 2001. But part of that debate relates back to an earlier discussion in the period running up to 2001 as a result of the Macpherson Report with its findings on institutional racism and discrimination. This was the first time there was a focus on institutions rather than communities, and the responsibilities that they shared for racism and discrimination.

My reading of the community cohesion agenda is that it was part of a backlash against Macpherson. This was an attempt to say, 'Well, no. You should focus back on communities and what they're doing'. Although the community cohesion focus can open up a useful way of discussing race issues between communities, and how we build positive relationships, what we've seen is that there is a danger that the focus is not on the obstacles or barriers to integration. In fact, the debate has pathologised the way that some communities, particularly Muslim communities, are perceived and understood, so that, rather than focusing on the social barriers to economic integration and political participation, much of the focus has been on issues of culture and cultural integration and values. And the way that debate has taken place has created a sense in which Muslim communities are somehow different and 'Other'. They're seen as the problem.

Last year, an interesting piece of work was done by Cardiff University looking at the coverage of Muslim communities in the press and the media since 9/11. What was really telling is that 2008 was the first time in which the majority of stories in the press about Muslims was no longer about counterterrorism, but about identifying cultural differences as a threat to British society and to our shared values. Within the context of that discussion about culture, there is, moreover, a failure amongst non-Muslims and in the wider public debate sometimes to understand the role and importance of religion to the Muslim identity. I am a trustee of an organisation called the Muslim Youth Helpline which was established by and works with young Muslims, and this is one of the things that I have seen: a failure to understand exactly why religious identity is an important aspect of the lives of young Muslims. Non-Muslims fail to see that, as part of their British identity, it can be an important tool for integration for a lot of these people. It is an important way of debating with their parents, arguing for greater participation, education and employment; because they know that their parents will find those arguments much more persuasive. It's also seen as empowering. So there's a lot of research in the field of education which shows how religious identity is almost a form of 'ethnic social capital' which positively supports educational advancement and social participation.

Recently, we have had leaks in the *Guardian* suggesting that there might be a shift in antiterrorism strategy, in which the dividing line between a good Muslim and a bad Muslim, whom we must guard against, shifts, to put it crudely, to whether they support things like Sharia law. That's very dangerous, because while the idea of Sharia law is contested (in a way that is also poorly understood), it is also something that is valued greatly by Muslims. For so many Muslims, Sharia law is about what they eat, how they pray, all the things that are personal to them. The wider public construction of Sharia law as 'criminal punishment' is not what is at issue. That needs to be understood.

Several false notes have crept into the community cohesion debate: firstly, the notion that Muslims live parallel lives to other people. Social science research evidence and even the Government's Home Office citizenship surveys show that the evidence is not there to support that contention. Even in somewhere like Bradford, there is no evidence of the greater ethnic segregation of communities. There is evidence of areas where an ethnic concentration is growing, mainly due to normal population growth. At the same time, there is evidence of people moving into the leafier suburbs of Bradford. But even outside Bradford, there is no support for the contention that people want to live in segregated communities. The debate has suggested that, because Muslims are different,

> "…while the idea of Sharia law is contested (in a way that is also poorly understood), it is also something that is valued greatly by Muslims."

they do not have a sense of loyalty and belonging to the UK, but again, all the evidence suggests that there simply is no conflict or tension between being British and being Muslim. The vast majority of Muslim people have a sense of belonging to Britain. They have a sense of loyalty to Britain. All too often, any difficulty that occurs arises from the way that the questions are posed in the first place, as if being British and being Muslim are necessarily in competition with each other.

As regards our civil liberties, the counterterrorism debate tends to link antiterrorism to community cohesion and to say that the radicalisation of extremists is a process related to the failure of integration. I think these are two distinct challenges. I'm not sure whether you can argue that the link is there at all. But one thing is clear: if there is a focus on integration because of concerns about radicalisation and counterterrorism, then the signal being sent out to communities is that this is the sole reason why you are concerned about their economic, social and political participation in our society. You're not concerned about it otherwise. That seems to me to be a counterproductive and dangerous signal to send out. Surely there should be a concern for the economic and social integration of all communities, irrespective of problems of counterterrorism and radicalisation.

Racialising rubbish collection
STUART WILKS-HEEG

As I came off the train today from Liverpool, arriving at Eastern Station and walked through Bloomsbury, usually I get a lovely warm feeling because I was a student here and it reminds me of that time. But today I felt a bit of a chill, to be honest, not because it's cold, but because I knew what I had to talk about. I thought about the sceptics out there, and the complacent, who will probably mock us for being here, and talk about the chattering classes meeting in Bloomsbury, this historically liberal, bohemian part of London. We'll all be sitting there discussing this stuff about rights and liberties while everybody else will be ignoring us.

I don't know if I am a member of the chattering classes or not, or if you are, but what I want to try to do is to take you far away from Bloomsbury to talk about the nature of xenophobia in Britain today. To understand that xenophobia, we also need to understand what has been happening in relation to inequality in Britain in the last decade.

So, I'm going to talk partly about economics, social divisions, the demise of political parties and local government, if there's time. Why do we need to take the British National Party (BNP) seriously under all these headings? I'm sure you don't need persuading, but you might be surprised at some of the reasons I'm going to offer. We need to take the BNP especially seriously when they start talking about speed bumps, rubbish collections, who gets weekly rubbish collections and who doesn't, housing allocations, local government issues; this is when we really need to take notice of what the BNP are up to.

Something happened two weeks ago on the M65, near Preston. News bulletins began to come in, saying that on 13 February, two vans had been stopped, emblazoned with Palestinian flags and with slogans like, 'From Blackburn to Gaza'. The drivers and the passengers told the police that stopped them that they were joining the aid convoy to Gaza. The police obviously thought otherwise. They detained six men from Blackburn in the back of a police van for seven hours. Three men from Burnley were arrested and taken to a secure detention centre in Manchester for questioning under the anti-terror legislation. The media reports told us this was an intelligence-led operation by Lancashire police and the North West counterterrorism unit resulting from a couple of months of surveillance of the individuals concerned. We learnt subsequently that five properties in Burnley had been raided and searched. Forensic teams went in, computers were taken out and this was in the predominantly Muslim areas of Daneshouse and Stoneyhome in Burnley.

Now as we've just heard, in cases like this - and there are many cases like this - there was rather less coverage when these people were released without charge, six days later. But there are, as my former university colleague and now Respect Party councillor in Preston, Michael Lavalette pointed out, some

> "...in cases like this – and there are many cases like this – there was rather less coverage when these people were released without charge, six days later."

serious questions that need to be raised here. I don't know the answer to them, I don't know the ins and outs of this. But we do need to know why these arrests were made, on what basis, and, if the evidence and the intelligence was flawed, why was it flawed? Perhaps most importantly, as Michael has asked, where are the Labour ministers on television or in the press defending the arrests, and explaining the actions that were taken?

I'm sure people on this panel could come up with many more stories like this. But there's an editorial in the *Guardian* today arguing that the people who highlight the erosion of liberties sometimes need to spell out the context in which these erosions take place. So, in my last three minutes, I will explain why context is particularly important in a place like Burnley.

I don't know how many of you have been there, probably very few. It's definitely one of Britain's forgotten places, one of the places that has not shared in the boom of the last 10 years. We almost forget that debt-driven, consumer-driven boom these days. Apparently there was one.

Now, we used to get figures all the time of jobs created under New Labour. 'Four million nationally since 1997: half a million of those in the north-west'. How many of those jobs are in Burnley? Zero. In fact, there are no new jobs in Burnley, but 2000 less than in 1997. I can't find many places that have had a similar decline in employment over the last decade, but, after a long search, I managed to find two more. I searched a lot. One was Stoke, and another was Barking and Dagenham. You might already be thinking what I'm thinking: these are the three main centres of BNP activism in the country. These are the places where the BNP has managed to get party groupings of eight or more representatives since 2002. In Burnley, the percentage of the working age population on state benefits has not changed since 1997. It is absolutely rigid at 21%. So all those claims about how poverty is being tackled in these places? Well, it's not true in Burnley. Instead, there has been a dramatic decline in manufacturing employment, in all three areas, where it has gone from about a third of the local economy down to a fifth.

Now all this matters. It's all connected. We might want to discuss the civil liberties issues around leaking membership lists, but as you might know, the BNP membership list was leaked, and it's told us where its members are. It did reveal that some of them were police officers and some of them were ballerinas and some of them were retired army officers and so on. But we do know that most BNP supporters are semiskilled and skilled working-class voters, predominately in the types of areas where there is a high scale of job loss. Of course, we sometimes forget that where those BNP voters have lost their jobs, jobs were also lost by others in the same communities - in Burnley for example, Pakistani and Bangladeshi immigrants were brought in to do those jobs in the same mills and factories.

It is classic. Those people have been thrown into conflict. We know that's the formula, and that's what's breeding xenophobia. All the BNP has done is to have found a way of localising this even more. They've got into its micro-politics. What they have started to highlight is – 'There's a regeneration scheme here and you've drawn a line on a map, and you've got some spending on that side and not on that side'. They've racialised the issues. They've even done it around issues such as rubbish collection. You might not believe it, but they have. Why has a weekly collection of food waste been started in this area first, before this area over here? The implication is always that a predominately British Asian group is gaining at the expense of a neighbouring white working-class one – no matter how apparently mundane the issue.

> "Why has a weekly collection of food waste been started in this area first, before this area over here?"

It is in places like Burnley that xenophobia breeds – though Burnley is not the only one: there are others like it. It's where the implementation of anti-terror legislation on a daily basis coincides with the activities of the British National Party - to produce as we know, a really very explosive, very damaging mix.

Session 10
Democracy and Liberty
SUPPORTED BY IMPRINT ACADEMIC

Democracy originated as a champion of liberty for ordinary people against oppression, but it seems to have lost its way. The systematic erosion of rights and freedoms in recent years has occurred alongside a steady decline in political participation – both point to a crisis in our democratic institutions. But is it a crisis specific to Britain's antiquated and over-centralised state or a failure of **representative democracy more broadly**? Should we remember Aristotle, who stated that electoral representation is not a form of democracy, but of oligarchy? The Power Inquiry showed why citizens must claim an active role in the political process if our democracy is to possess any kind of legitimacy and trust. But is it also the case, as republicans from Machiavelli onwards have suggested, that we can only truly protect our freedom through an active and assertive citizenship?

> "My name is Pam Giddy. I am Director of the Power Inquiry. We were charged by the Joseph Rowntree Reform Trust and Charitable Trust to look at democratic participation in the UK and we published a book called Power of the People. I have many left, if anyone is interested just see me afterwards. Today's discussion has been broadly about liberty. But it is crucial – and I would say this wouldn't I, given my background and my heritage - that for both the protection of our liberty and our ability to express our freedoms, we do also need a strong, fundamental democracy. The erosion of our rights and freedoms over the past twenty years especially, has gone alongside a decline of both trust and belief in our democratic institutions. In my view this seems to be going along in tandem, one affecting the other…"
>
> PAM GIDDY, PANEL CHAIR AND DIRECTOR OF POWER 2010

Democracy is an untried adventure in the modern history of the west
IVO MOSLEY

Sortition had a much easier name for two thousand years up to 1800 – its name was democracy. The method of government that we adopted instead is called electoral representation. In the whole tradition leading up to 1800, electoral representation was regarded as an oligarchic, aristocratic or elitist form of government. Democracy was a participatory form of government.

I want to ask the question: how have governments in the western world got away with calling themselves democracies for so long? If you feel our system isn't very democratic, you have two thousand years of tradition on your side. Before 1800, democracy meant that political assemblies and political officials were chosen by lot from among the citizens, much as juries are chosen today. Government in a democracy consisted of citizens giving up their everyday lives for fixed periods to do their duty; just like jury service, except they decided on law and policy too. The difference between democracy and electoral representation is significant. Electoral representation brings with it professional politicians and political parties whose interests and objectives are bound to be partial, favouring one interest or another. Democracy means that government is conducted directly by the people, presumably in their common interests.

So how did it happen around 1800 that people began to think that electoral representation was a form of democracy? My story begins with the revolutionists who liberated the United States from British rule: Washington, Adams, Madison, Hamilton, Jefferson to name the most prominent. Having won the War of Independence, they designed a self-consciously elitist system of government that effectively entrusted power to themselves. Four of those five names became President and the fifth was killed in a duel. The Founding Fathers made no bones about it. They did not think ordinary people should be given power. In fact they were very rude about democracy, which like everyone else they

morning sessions

> "...how have governments in the western world got away with calling themselves democracies for so long?"

understood to mean assemblies chosen by lot. Here are some sample sentences from their published writings:

Madison wrote: 'Democracies have ever been spectacles of turbulence and contention and have in general been as short in their lives as they have been violent in their deaths'.

John Adams wrote, 'Democracy wastes, exhausts and murders itself. There was never a democracy that did not commit suicide'.

Jefferson thought democracy was 'impractical at any rate beyond the limits of a town.'

Benjamin Franklin is credited, perhaps wrongly, though it is not out of character, with the sentence, 'Democracy is two wolves and a sheep deciding what's for dinner'.

So the system that the Founding Fathers wanted and designed was republican. In Jefferson's words, 'Power will be entrusted to a natural aristocracy, the most talented and virtuous, replacing the old artificial aristocracy founded on wealth and birth'.

What elections would grant was the right to choose who those natural aristocrats should be. In Madison's words, 'Public opinion would be refined and enlarged by passing it through the medium of a chosen body of citizens whose wisdom may best discern the true interest of their country'. To the disappointment of many after the ratification of the US constitution, politics was dominated, not so much by superior individuals as by strong political parties representing not the shared interests of citizens so much as powerful embodied interests. The fault lines were already apparent that would result in the civil war: one party representing the industrial north, and the other party the agricultural, slave-owning south.

The significant crisis during which democracy changed from being a dirty word to a badge worn with pride, came just after the 1800 presidential elections. The electoral college was in deadlock over who would be the next president, and rival state militias were converging on Washington to claim the presidency for their party. Jefferson, the republican candidate had the larger

▶

share of the popular vote, and his supporters claimed that the will of the people should prevail even though a lot of his votes were based on slaves who had no vote, but whose masters voted for them. Jefferson became president and civil war was averted.

Meanwhile, it had become apparent that there was a strong, potentially overwhelming demand among Americans for democracy, although not as a system as such. They were ignorant of the political system because only the educated elite knew the history of democracy. But they had a feeling that the people should be in charge of their own destiny. Jefferson referred to his victory as 'the revolution of 1800'. In his words, 'the nation had declared its will by dismissing functionaries of one principle and electing those of another'. The new democratic principle was recognised when Jefferson's party changed its name to the Democratic Republican Party. In 1809 Elias Smith proclaimed, 'My friends, let us never be ashamed of democracy!'

So, the reinvention of electoral representation as a form of democracy took place not in theory, but in the sphere of practical politics. Jacob Burckhardt put it best: 'The experience of revolution was that public opinion forms and transforms the world. The traditional powers, too weak to prevent it, began making deals with individual currents in the stream of public opinion'. And that, as Rudyard Kipling might say, was how democracy came to mean its opposite; as if by shaving a dog and feeding it oats, you could believe it was a horse.

Now this new and powerful reality has never been justified in theory for one very good reason - it is impossible. To argue that rule by elected party officials was a form of democracy when there was a perfectly good form of democracy and participation to hand, was a non-starter. According to historian Bernard Manning, the best anyone has done to justify this absurdity is to summon up the old aristocratic theory of consent and maintain that by voting in elections once every few years, the people signify its consent to be so governed'. Well, true democracy of course needs no such theory. Citizens are rulers on one day and ruled over by their fellow citizens the next.

After all this, you may say history is irrelevant, and so what? Today when we say 'democracy' we mean electoral representation! I think it is important to recognise that electoral representation is essentially undemocratic. First, it helps us understand the world we live in today. It explains how power becomes unaccountable. Suddenly we can understand why western governments are pursuing policies that could destroy the planet such as, unpopular wars; why governments give bankers free range to bankrupt their nation; why welfare is deflected away from the truly needy towards those who might vote; and how things get transformed into the opposite of what they should be. But secondly it gives us hope for the future. Democracy is an untried adventure in the modern history of the west. How many British people know that democracy has worked in a variety of ways and at different levels, often alongside electoral representation, as it has at different times in Athens, Florence and Venice?

Government is imposed willy-nilly on us, and lives off us. It is inherently parasitical. However, by taking over responsibility for health, education, welfare, business and a host of other functions that used to be a matter for society, government has now become something different and worse. It has invaded the organs of society, swelling them into huge state apparatuses in which it is harder and harder for professionals to carry out their duties. Guidelines, constant supervision, form-filling,

> "...it is important to recognise that electoral representation is essentially undemocratic."

quota and target-meeting and so on, mean that administrators, consultants and state employees make good livings while people's needs are not met. Government has become a cancer. Democracy and freedom are candles in our darkness. If we recover their meanings we can begin to recover their practice. It is time to reintroduce some true democracy into our perilously top-heavy civilisation.

Organise!
NEIL JAMESON

One of the negative things about community organising is that, when you ask people on the streets what they are worried about, the answer tends not to be the threat to their liberties. It tends to be the dirty street or the street lights that don't work. And that is where we start with community organising – where people are at. Then you can get more and more ambitious. London Citizens is also very keen on democracy, at least the real interpretation of the Greek word *democrazia* which means people power. Our experience is that the least successful way of changing things is voting. Voting is alright: it has its place. But frankly if that's all they offer us, what is the point? We think it is very important to get involved on a daily basis and to try and shape the communities you are in, which is why our community organising actually offers people a daily invitation for action – a daily invitation for meaning – a daily invitation for 'voice'. All of that is possible if you organise in a sophisticated way.

On April 9 last year, there was an assembly in Methodist Central Hall, Westminster – a hall with a great tradition of bringing people together. We organised two and a half thousand people into that hall that night. It took us six months of democratic activity starting with a listening exercise amongst our members. The question was: what do you want to say to the next mayor of London? We organise what sociologists call, 'anchor institutions'. If you want to organise London, look at where people gather. We go to places which people respect and also pay money to go to. That's very important, and whether you like it or not today this means faith institutions, perhaps trade unions although they are not very strong these days, student unions if they want to be included, schools and community associations. We are now an alliance of these, and that alliance allows us to be powerful.

A mantra of community organising with which Barack Obama would concur is 'Power before programme.' It has taken me twenty years to understand that this is very important: if you haven't got any power, why start the programme? Build power first. We have spent several years building this power base which is now a hundred and twenty institutions strong across London. This power base is the democratic machine which allows us, by consent, to develop the campaigns. When there is an election coming along, we take that very seriously, because we know we can influence it. Not just by voting, but by gathering large numbers of people into a room with their own agenda, to put to the candidates, with the media there. We ask the politicians to respond to the people's agenda. That's what politics used to be. We have slipped back, and now think that it is all about the candidates coming with their agenda to get our vote. What London Citizens has managed to do now on a fairly consistent basis is to fill rooms. Whoever fills a room, wins the debate in many cases. It's slightly dangerous, but that is our experience. Providing these people are organised together using democracy, and as long as the Muslims are there, the trade unionists are there, the Christians are there and the secular folk are there – that's what people power is.

> "Our experience is that the least successful way of changing things is voting. Voting is alright: it has its place. But frankly if that's all they offer us, what is the point?"

The night in question started with a fantastic headline in *The Independent* for us, which said, 'Amnesty Now!' All four mayoral candidates agreed to support our campaign called 'Strangers into Citizens' which would allow long-term irregular migrants an amnesty to stay there. Fantastic. Boris Johnson signed up. Ken Livingstone already supported our campaign. That issue of what to do about the long-term irregular migrants is one that we feel passionate about, because they are in our communities. We know them. They are our members and we fight for them. And it's very important that the media covered this. The other significant thing about that night was that the room was packed with ordinary folk from North, East, South and West London. And they all knew why they were there - because they owned the agenda, an agenda that had been put together very carefully over a long process of voting, negotiating and bartering over the issues to end up with five issues for the candidates to respond to, all of which were winnable.

Some were ambitious, one or two really small. We had lots of young people there, who really enjoy this form of democracy, because they can get their hands on the process and they can see it happening. The panel was made up not of celebrities or media people, but ordinary people who are able to do this, who called forward the candidates and said to them, 'If elected, Ken Livingstone, will you do a,b,c,and d'. He has had the issues to look at beforehand. There are no surprises on the night, no unprepared questions from the floor, no eccentrics leaping up on their own hobby horse issue, because two and half thousand people have already agreed the agenda beforehand and all the questions and discussion have already happened elsewhere.

Then we called for Boris Johnson and we said, 'Mr Johnson, if elected, will you set a living wage for London, will you pay the living wage for London, will you be the champion for the living wage, will you only put people into hotels that have the living wage? You have one minute to answer this, Mr Johnson and you should primarily say, yes, no or maybe'. And Mr Johnson said, 'yes'. In July, the Conservative mayor announced his new living wage for London, set at 7.45. You will have read about that. What is not normally told is the story of how that happened, and that's the problem. People who interpret history all too often ignore us – the dockers, the workers, the fighters, the suffragettes, the women who made this happen - who throughout history eventually get to Westminster. So don't put your faith in Westminster, Strasbourg or wherever – we have the power to make things happen. Is Boris Johnson only using the hotels that pay a living wage? No, he's not. That doesn't mean to say that the whole process is flawed. We then just increase the pressure and step up the campaign outside his office to remind him of these promises.

You may remember that we have the Olympics coming to London in 2012, which felt like a good idea at the time! It is interesting how these things go pear-shaped. As an organisation, London Citizens were well-organised in 2004 and ready for this opportunity. The International Olympic Committee (IOC) were sending people to check out whether London was enthusiastic. The Parisians were very keen, but Londoners were very cynical about the Olympics. So we worked out in our power analysis that the powers-that-be really needed East Londoners to do some flag-waving. The only thing we had in our power in East London was the ability to look negative. And we agreed to do this on certain conditions. We said, 'We won't wave any flags unless we get living wage

> "the room was packed with ordinary folk from North, East, South and West London. And they all knew why they were there – because they owned the agenda..."

jobs on the Olympic site, a construction training academy immediately, money going into hospitals and the health service through Section 106 agreements'. We managed to withhold our consent to the point of having big assemblies, lobbying Seb Coe and Ken Livingstone, until two weeks before the decision, we had a letter signed saying that this would be the first ethical Olympics – living wage jobs and so forth, and that the land for housing that would be allocated after the Olympics would be for family housing for the five boroughs putting up with the building damage that was going on. That was signed, and we were in Trafalgar Square when it was announced, much to our surprise, that London was going to host the Olympics! With the help of our students we had been practising our congratulations in French, and how to say how pleased we were for Paris: but we had won. We cheered more than anybody because we knew we had a deal.

Has that deal been met? It has in most cases. The Olympic Delivery Authority deserve some applause instead of the constant rubbishing they seem to get. All the jobs are paid a living wage and we monitor that. The construction training academy has opened. The Section 106 agreement will go into schools. Will the housing be there? It's looking very doubtful. There is a consultation process going on now in which we are lobbying constantly for them to stick to the original promise: considering the state of the markets at the moment, it doesn't look good. But that isn't an argument against organising and we will just continue to organise. If you organise you can occupy, start petitions, lobby and fill rooms. This is a long way of saying – organise!

Session 11
Freedom and working people
SUPPORTED BY THE TUC, ACCOUNTABILITY

Faster than legislation can keep up, technological advances - from cameras and multi-directional hidden microphones to database-driven identity systems - are being rolled out in the workplace. Some working people must now operate these technologies on behalf of the government, with draconian controls imposed on their own lives as a result: in the legislation, anyone working on the new Identity Cards scheme who goes on strike could face up to 10 years' imprisonment, and their homes may be searched by the authorities for up to 25 years following their employment. Others are simply being watched themselves, under new powers, which leave the old controls of democratic debate and consensus standing, and call into question the hard-won freedoms of collective action.

The machinery is everywhere. Where consent to being watched is not required, and the use of surveillance technology can't be controlled, is it possible to have a free and consensual workplace at all? What can we do to protect workers' rights and their autonomy, while making appropriate use of powerful technologies that were never intended to control people, but were meant to empower them?

Imagine CCTV in the boardroom
JERRY HICKS

There are parallel CML conventions today in cities up and down the country including Bristol, where I live. In the former church in Trinity Road, there are going to be some fantastic discussions taking place today. This church is in the shadow of Trinity Road Police Station - a police station recently built that's like a fortress. For my journey here I booked a ticket on the internet, walked down to the station with a few CCTV cameras watching me – there was definitely one at the bus station – and when I got off in Victoria, there was a camera there and then I used my Oyster card – actually my mate's Oyster card, so that might confuse somebody - and here I am. The point is I have been monitored during every stretch of my journey here. We have gone from being the oldest democracy to being the most watched and monitored of people.

I'm very interested in words, and 'Employment Law' is an interesting phrase. Almost anyone in a trade union would class that as 'anti-union legislation'. We have been criminalised. Nowadays, you can't meet in a meeting like this and have a discussion and then take a decision. There are hoops and hurdles. Addresses must all be correct, and then everyone has to be able to take part in the ballot. You have to straddle weeks, as well as giving the employer seven days notice, and by that time, all the work has gone or the matter is over and done with. Even when you have jumped through all those hoops and gone through all those legalities, if you occasionally take matters into your own hands, you are limited to six pickets. It is no longer legal to take solidarity action. If that hospital closes, if that school closes, if that post office closes - all of which you might want to use in some stage in your lives - you can't go along to the demonstration against closure and take a photograph of a policeman, as I now know. Of course, they can sack you at one hour's notice, as they did with a whole shift of Cowley's agency workers, hundreds of them not needed any more. Yet it takes us weeks and weeks and weeks, if we are to comply with all of the laws, to do anything about it.

The European Union (EU) Posted Workers' Directive that was cobbled together to give even more power to business said that there would be freedom of movement for workers. You might think: 'that is fantastic! I'll have a bit of that freedom to move about'. It was watered down by our government to weaken pay and conditions, and the terms of employment. That 'freedom of movement' means that an employer can just uproot the whole workforce from its own country, or

> "Of course, they can sack you at one hour's notice…Yet it takes us weeks and weeks and weeks…to do anything about it."

another country, and it can supplant them, not on the wages and conditions of the country that they are in, but the worse conditions and pay of the country they come from. So it is worse exploitation. And sometimes this does not even happen voluntarily. The new workforce are segregated and accommodated in such a way that they are not allowed to meet, greet, or speak. So I believe these directives are designed not for the working people involved, but for business, and that they are there to weaken the trade unions.

The Posted Workers Directive was in the news a couple of weeks ago in connection with the Lindsey Oil Refinery in Humberside. You would think that it had come out of the blue: 'Blimey, where did that come from?' But this volcano has been rumbling for years since the EU Posted Workers Directive was first put together. That volcano erupted two weeks ago, and gave us a fantastic glimpse of what is possible. Awful things happened - the awful slogan 'British jobs for British workers!' came out of the mouth of a Labour Prime Minister, a year, by the way, after it came out of the mouth of my General Secretary, who I'm standing against in the next election. He might lose and I might win – wouldn't that be a fantastic world? But the point that I am making is that this was five days that shook the world, not even ten. The miners' strike lasted for twelve months and people are politicised during struggle. It doesn't always start off pure. I was relieved, you know, that the slogan wasn't 'British jobs for British workers and piss off Itis or Poles!' But the only reason the people shouting that were at the fore, was that the union banners weren't being waved: red Unite and Amicus banners. Why not? Because the union was afraid that their money would be sequestrated. So this was an unofficial strike. These members

▶

had taken part in a democracy. They had put their hands up and said 'Enough is enough: all these people are being exploited!' and 'Jobs for all available to all' – even translated into Italian to make those links. They had said, 'Let's contact these Italian workers' - who had been shipped in, by the way. But it was unofficial and the union only tacitly, not visibly, supported it. And politics abhors a vacuum. It gets filled up.

But by the end of the week, there was an agreement and there were jobs available! I think that there was an agreement from the highest level. Because I know that the next wave of strikes would have been in the oil field. That is where this dispute was going: workers deciding that something is wrong and something has got to be done. There were twenty solidarity walk-outs for the people in this Lindsey Oil Refinery dispute, all across the country - because construction workers are nomadic - including Polish workers in Plymouth taking solidarity action, which blew the myth that it was a racist dispute.

> "...politics abhors a vacuum. It gets filled up."

I was assaulted at one of these demonstrations, on January 19, – remember, not an official strike so we couldn't have the pickets and couldn't talk to people and all those things – and had my fibia broken. I was always going to get around to making a complaint, just so that it was logged. But two weeks after the assault on me, I was rung up by Nottinghamshire Criminal Investigation Department (CID)– I had to apologise for not getting it right and calling him PC (Police Constable) – who said that there was 'a rumour going around that you are alleging that you've been assaulted'. Well, of course it was more than an allegation. I've got X-rays and a doctor's report. So I said, 'What do you mean "rumour"?' 'Well we have seen it on a few websites'. Well, you know what I think. Why would the police worry themselves about my fractured leg? No, the message they were sending is: 'We know who you are and where you are and we've got your mobile phone number'. I hadn't given my number to the Nottinghamshire police.

In a way, it doesn't bother me. I will do what I do. But years ago, they used to be a little more subtle than that. There was the famous occasion of a Campaign for Nuclear Disarmament (CND) village fete, raising money for nuclear disarmament, where they had a couple of blokes in plain clothes just wandering up and down and taking down car numbers. It was really weird. So this woman

> "No, the message they were sending is: 'We know who you are and where you are and we've got your mobile phone number'."

came out - probably Neighbourhood Watch – and said, 'Excuse me, excuse me, what are you doing?' 'Well, we're just taking numbers down. You know, there's a CND fundraiser in there'. It was just making a point more than anything else. I remember talking to a chaplain for the National Union of Mineworkers who said that he was being followed for the whole year of the miners' strike in 1984. Bizarre stuff. It gets more bizarre. His car wouldn't start one day, so he went down his drive and said, 'Listen, I know you are going to the same place as me because you are following me, so could you give me a lift?' And he did! So perhaps that was a 'good cop' – I don't know. But when he got there, I suppose he smashed him over the head with a truncheon.

What is the difference between a well-organised trade unionised work place and a non-unionised workplace? Well, I'm not going to bombard you with facts and figures: but basically it means better pay, better terms and conditions, fairer systems. In a non-unionised workplace, you very much know that you are on your own, and defenceless. But even in a well-organised workplace there is a constant battle of ideas and control: a relentless to-ing and fro-ing of monitoring and tracking by the employer. Clocking in and clocking out was one thing. We would argue, 'Why? Don't you trust us? Surely, if the work is done, what's your beef…?' And we won the argument eventually and they dispensed with that. Then they brought in swipe cards and you go through these arguments all over again. But the swipe cards then get extended to doors which used to work on a punch key where you got entrusted with a code. But they couldn't track you on that I guess, so the swipe cards and turnstiles would proliferate. By the way, who gets the contracts on making doors for workplaces? They must make a small fortune.

But in a well-organised workplace you have those arguments. Sometimes you win and beat them back, and sometimes you don't. A good outcome might be an agreement that no matter what the swipe cards say, this won't be used against you as evidence in disciplinary matters, for example. But these tracking and watching devices are precisely for that, to restrict your movements, to make you feel oppressed, intimidated and isolated. And I guess, in their system,

▶

it is to increase the profits. But it is all one way, you know. Just imagine our Close Circuit Television (CCTV) in the boardroom, especially in the bank boardrooms over the last couple of years while they have been taking on these toxic debts and 125% mortgages and then taking your houses off you! Then, we would have known. But we don't get that. It is all one way. So you might ask, why is it that we can't just believe them when they say that all this is for our own good and for our national security?

The reason is that we have got experience. That's why we don't believe them. I am not paranoid – not that that stops them talking about me! But we have got experience. Take the 'War on Terror'. This was supposed to usher in all these restrictions that would ultimately protect us. My view is that a decent foreign policy would make us all an awful lot safer. But the biggest danger working people would say, anybody would say, kids in school would say, is global warming or recession. None of our making. If we had had CCTV cameras in bank boardrooms, we may have been able to avert that. But it is the 'War on Terror' that is the going thing: ID cards and billions of pounds. I tried to work out on the coach coming up how they could put fifty pieces of information about me on that ID card. I could only think of twelve things anyone might want to know about me. I must be one of the most uninteresting people in the world – actually I lie, I ran out after ten! But this is serious. If we are going to spend money, let's spend it on schools, hospitals. Let's decide where they should be and that they are publicly owned. I don't mean to trivialise this. The catastrophic mistakes they make with all the information that they have! The worst case so far, in terms of lives lost, must be the weapons of mass destruction. 'We know', they said, 'they're there. Believe us – by the way – because we've seen the evidence. You can't. But we have'. They didn't even show the evidence to many of the Members of Parliament (MPs), I think, but they were all too easily persuaded in my view. But there weren't any. They weren't there.

There are two conclusions we might draw from this. Either we say, they were

> "So you might ask, why is it that we can't just believe them when they say that all this is for our own good and for our national security?"

lying through their teeth to get the oil and do what they do in the name of imperialism. That's one theory and it might be right. But if that one is wrong, then for all the information-gathering, that was a pretty poor outcome

> "When have we ever heard the slogan, 'What do we want? More surveillance! When do we want it? Now!'"

wasn't it? Then there's nuclear energy. We are just about to build an awful lot more nuclear power stations. My union says that is being done in my name. I would argue against that, if I became General Secretary. But the point is that we were told this would be cheap, clean and safe. One of the slogans was, 'You wouldn't ever want to turn the lights off, it would be so cheap by comparison. You would want to turn your heating up and run around in flip-flops'. Cheap? My goodness no. Clean and safe? No. A thousand years of toxic waste.

There is an almost relentless one-way process of legislation, both in the workplace and in society at large. Any attack on the trade union movement weakens our chance of beating back the attacks on our civil liberties. And I think this is very much a class-based conflict. Who controls, who has access, and who is ever held accountable for all this information that is gathered about us? Jean Charles de Menezes was an electrician and might very well have been a member of our union. He was going about his every-day business, and the wrong information led to a tragic consequence: an innocent man was shot, killed, murdered. What followed that? With all the information? You would think to yourself, well at least the truth will out! But there was no CCTV – surprise, surprise. There was a pack of lies – a puffer jacket when they want one, and leaping over one of the turnstiles when it didn't happen. A pack of lies and a cover-up. It is one way, all this legislation and all this control of information. Even the Israeli troops had their mobile phones confiscated in the last invasion and slaughter in Gaza.

When have we ever heard the slogan, 'What do we want? More surveillance! When do we want it? Now!' We never have, have we? But our strength is their weakness. And the counterbalance is there. It is available. All this information needs to be gathered and processed. And that means people, lots of people. And when we say 'No' in whatever way it takes, it stops dead for them. We have to open our minds: all things are possible. What a strong trade union means, even though there are less of us - but there are millions - is that individuals like ourselves have come together, participated collectively in debates and come to a decision which enables us to win rights through struggle. None of the rights I believe were ever given us by philanthropists who said, 'Hmm. You have got a pretty rum deal, you lot. Here, have some rights!' They were all fought for by the trade union movement and ultimately won: the freedom to associate in the first place - the Tolpuddle Martyrs made that sacrifice and were deported for it, the right to vote, the right not to be racially or sexually abused, the right to equal pay, the woman's right to choose. The trade union organisation is the backbone – not the whole skeleton and not the flesh - but the backbone of the struggle to cling onto in order to add that skeleton and flesh, and bring about the change to a society based on our civil rights.

> "None of the rights I believe were ever given us by philanthropists who said, 'Hmm. You have got a pretty rum deal, you lot. Here, have some rights!'"

Attacks on civil liberties, in my view, may require civil disobedience. Over thirty-two years as a trade unionist, I have taken part in both official and unofficial solidarity action and I will do it again with pride. I have called for unofficial action and got denounced by my union leaders for it: but when the law's an ass - civil or employment law - you break it. I might be faced with a lawsuit for some of the things I have said in my election address, but I'll say them. That's my position. I know that there are millions of people who want to say them, and hundreds of thousands who do say them. And when we get together, anything's possible. I've seen some fabulous things: the Berlin wall come down, the end of apartheid, Thatcher leaving Downing Street with a tear in her eye, the poll tax smashed by civil disobedience when the Labour Party was telling us, 'Pay the poll tax. We'll sort it out when we get in!'

I'm a great advocate of talking nice. I can do that, not without some difficulty. But I also know that, when the chips are down, you have got to do what you have got to do. When determined people get together, anything is possible. It isn't easy. But is it impossible? Absolutely not. As an activist, I was one of the people who were organised in coaches to take part in a fantastic demonstration in the streets of London, with millions of people protesting against going to war in Iraq. The biggest demonstration in history. That was only a few years ago. And I believe this is an even bigger challenge to us now, because it strikes at the heart of our civic liberties. Freedom is a right we have to fight for, over and over again. Our union's founding statement is organise, agitate and educate. Thank you very much.

Captions for photos on pages 147-156 (top to bottom):

147	Henry Porter; Anthony Barnett; Helena Kennedy (courtesy of Mike Goldwater)
148	Philip Pullman; Lord Bingham (courtesy of Mike Goldwater)
149	Shami Chakrabarti (courtesy of Mike Goldwater); Anthony Barnett chairs the second plenary (courtesy of Miki Yamanouchi); Phil Booth (courtesy of Mike Goldwater)
150	First plenary: Ken Macdonald QC; Dominic Grieve QC MP and Helena Kennedy QC (courtesy of Mike Goldwater); Sir David Varney and Ken Macdonald (courtesy of Miki Yamanouchi)
151	Jonathan Butterworth speaks to the 'Abolition of Freedom Act 2009'; CML participants reading (courtesy of Miki Yamanouchi)
152	Clare Coatman (courtesy of Miki Yamanouchi); question from the audience (courtesy of Mike Goldwater); Phoebe Dickerson and Guy Aitchison (courtesy of Georgia Haseldine)
153	Busy lobby; lunch (courtesy of Mike Goldwater)
154	CML participants in plenary (courtesy of Mike Goldwater); and in the green room (courtesy of Mike Goldwater)
155	Question from the floor (courtesy of Mike Goldwater); thanks to all the stewards in Logan Hall (courtesy of Mike Goldwater)
156	Press Freedom Session speaker panel; and audience (courtesy of Miki Yamanouchi)

in photos

convention on modern liberty

in photos

convention on modern liberty

in photos

The Abolition of Freedom Act 2009

convention on modern liberty

in photos

convention on modern liberty

in photos

convention on modern liberty

in photos

convention on modern liberty

in photos

convention on modern liberty

in photos

convention on modern liberty

in photos

in photos

convention on modern liberty

Captions for photos on pages 157-166 (top to bottom):

157 Love and Liberty Session speakers: Marina Warner: Michael Edwards listens to Satish Kumar (Editor, Resurgence) (courtesy of Mike Goldwater)

158 Xenophobia Session speaker panel; and The Police Session speaker panel (courtesy of Miki Yamanouchi)

159 Freedom and Working People Session speakers (courtesy of Miki Yamanouchi): Jerry Hicks listens to Pete Murray (Vice president, NUJ); Child's play? Session speaker panel (courtesy of Miki Yamanouchi)

160 Torture Session audience (courtesy of Mike Goldwater); speaker panel (courtesy of Miki Yamanouchi); and Moazzam Begg in the press room (courtesy of Mike Goldwater)

161 Human Rights and Global Responses Session speakers, Mary Kaldor and Timothy Garton Ash; audience listens (courtesy of Georgia Haseldine)

162 Vince Cable MP and Kate Hoey MP (courtesy of Miki Yamanouchi); Brian Eno (courtesy of Mike Goldwater)

163 Chris Huhne MP, Will Hutton; David Edgar, Suzanne Moore (courtesy of Miki Yamanouchi)

164 David Davis (courtesy of Mike Goldwater); his audience (courtesy of Mike Goldwater)

165 Anthony Barnett applauds (courtesy of Miki Yamanouchi)

166 Six thumbnails of the Cambridge Student Union debate – David Howarth MP proposes, Andrew Watson chairs, Bill Rammell MP opposes (courtesy of Richard Neill); blogging during bloggers' summit (courtesy of Mike Goldwater)

AFTERNOON SESSIONS

Photo courtesy of Miki Yamanouch

Digging for victory
SUNNY HUNDAL

So you're angry about the growing database state – government and corporate – and you despair at the loss of our civil liberties. You're frustrated at the way the government ducks and hides its information while trying to pretend that it is being as honest and transparent as it can. What do you do about it?

For an increasing number of people, using online tools, blogs and other social networks to hunt for information and then spread it for good use is the front line of the fightback. But will it have any impact?

I hosted a lunchtime event at the Convention on Modern Liberty today - the bloggers' summit with Liberal Conspiracy and Comment is Free - where we wanted to explore this fightback. Joining me were Sam Smith from My Society, who briefly described some of the excellent tools their organisation has developed and warned that while some campaigns were very successful online (most notably the recent one on MPs' expenses), others could fail quickly if not executed properly. Starting a Facebook group or launching a petition were not the be all and end all of campaigning.

Heather Brooke, who runs Your Right To Know, and has written a book of the same name, then spoke about how she used Freedom of Information (FOI) requests to dig up information around crime and related issues. She mentioned that while newspapers had cut down on such reporting, and even paid freelancers pitifully for investigations compared to comment pieces, there was a lot of opportunity to use online tools to make information requests and try to hold authorities to account. Heather's blog, intriguingly, also has a section where she outsources her requests and open issues. That attempt at sharing information and outsourcing work is a way forward, I think.

Ben Goldacre of Bad Science infamy followed with examples of how many bloggers, academics, statisticians and even accountants have collaborated online to expose vital information on how medical companies were releasing wrong information or trying to fool consumers. He offered some excellent examples illustrating how people afternoon sessions

working together online, each using their own specialisms, had exposed big pharmaceutical companies. The medical community is, no doubt, ahead of political bloggers in evidence-based work that various people pick up and run with, to devastating effect for 'the quacks'.

> "There are some brilliant people out there burrowing away at data and trying to dig out information to create a better democracy. What we need is a more collaborative environment..."

Phil Booth from NO2ID then finished with the point that his campaign had started simply with a straightforward blog and a small joint event. And now it is a huge grassroots organisation that, through diligent attention to detail and wading through tons of material, has forced the government to backtrack on some of its plans or admit to facts it had earlier denied. In other words, once again, group work and digging can lead to results.

The discussion that followed was interesting...

The general consensus, though, was much more heartening than I thought it would be. There are some brilliant people out there burrowing away at data and trying to dig out information to create a better democracy. What we need is a more collaborative environment where people share information and work together to achieve results. We also need action as well as complaints – and there are plenty of examples across the internet where this has delivered excellent results. If you want to challenge this assault on our civil liberties, it's time to get involved.

Sunny Hundal also linked to the video of the bloggers' summit on Liberal Conspiracy:
http://www.liberalconspiracy.org/2009/03/21/watch-bloggers-summit-at-coml/

SOURCE: COMMENT IS FREE, GUARDIAN.CO.UK, MODERN LIBERTY SERIES, 28 FEBRUARY 2009

Session 1
The Database State
SUPPORTED BY NO2ID, CENTRE FOR POLICY STUDIES

The UK government is embarking on a massive electronic unification of all the departments of state in a programme that will 'transform' - in its own words - the relationship between the state, the citizen and private enterprise.

This programme has never been debated in the House of Commons or in a select committee. It goes much further than the national information register, a major intrusion into privacy in its own right, which lies at the heart of the ID card programme. What are the implications if it works - and if it doesn't?

> "So, what is the Database State? Well the phrase, which was kindly credited to me by Shami in this morning's keynote address, was first applied in this sense around 2004. Before that, it was a technical term from computing. Its reference to political science is new and it means, essentially, the use of computers to govern us: the centralisation of information; the management of government services; and 'hard government', as it was described to me during the lunch break - government regulation, oversight, control, discipline of the population through the collection and dissemination of information; either information to be monitored for intelligence's sake, or information to be acted upon in one of any numbers of ways. It's that pro-active management of information that's new. Just as communism was projected in one Leninist tag to be 'Soviet power plus the electrification of the Soviet Union', so the new Jerusalem is supposed to be created by 'networked computing applied to British government power', and increasingly world government power."
>
> GUY HERBERT, PANEL CHAIR AND GENERAL SECRETARY, NO2ID

"Let me just dispense with what's going on, straight off. I believe what's going on works at three distinct levels. It's not just the technological; the creation of networks of networks - of links between networks which we might call data sharing, interoperability, however you want to describe it. The two other strategies at work here are the manipulation of language and imagery, and the destabilisation and sometimes destruction of due process. Put those three together and you've got real trouble. The problem is, it determines public consciousness…

If we put to government as we have done, countless times: 'Hey where's your justification, where's your business case, where's your evidence, where's your statistical work, where's your quantification of results?' - it's not available. But a series of assertions are made that manipulate language to achieve their goals. 'Modernisation', what's that? When someone says 'modernisation' to me, I think they're going to screw me. When they talk about 'review', that means to rip apart. So what does the 'data protection act review' do? It takes out the consent principle: it's not a review, it's a slash and burn policy."

SIMON DAVIES, PANEL SPEAKER AND DIRECTOR OF PRIVACY INTERNATIONAL

Tell us everything
SAM TALBOT RICE

Transformational government is a subject which we at the Centre for Policy Studies (CPS) think is belatedly coming out of the shadows. It has been a key area of focus at the CPS since we published *Who Do They Think We Are* by Jill Kirby just over a year ago (I've got a limited number of copies here and it is also available on our website.)

The concept itself has been around for at least a decade. Originally, it belonged under the guise of e-government and was designed for cost efficiency (saving government back office costs), and so forth. But it's worth saying at the outset that this agenda isn't a post-9/11 security agenda.

Let me quote from the canonical text which is Sir David Varney's report for the Treasury in 2006, on the process of collecting personal data and this idea of identity management. By 2020 it envisages, and I quote: 'Older people, children and young people, workless people and other customer groups can choose packages of public services tailored to their needs. Public, private and third sector partners collaborate across the delivery chain in a way that is invisible to the public. The partners pool their intelligence about the needs and preferences of local people and this informs the design of public services and the tailoring of packages for individuals and groups. Measured benefits, services and facilities are shared between all tiers of central and local government and other public bodies. The public do not see this process, they experience only public services packaged for their needs.'

What's striking is how this process is supposed to be invisible and out of the sight of the public. In most areas of public policy, the Government has talked a lot, but arguably achieved little. In this case there's not much talk at all, very little public scrutiny or parliamentary debate, but a huge amount going on behind the scenes. Now it seems very clear to us at the CPS, that transformational government is wrong both in principle and in practice. The philosophy that lies behind it is one of centralisation, using technology to achieve better state planning and by doing so, to set the balance between the state and individual far too much towards the state. The programme is equally flawed in terms of costs. We know the track record of government IT projects. The Convention researchers produced a very useful briefing on the estimated cost of state-run databases over the next ten years, which they put at £30 billion, just when we need to cut government costs. And secondly, of course, there are the security concerns associated with gathering large amounts of personal data and storing it in databases. Again, the University College London (UCL) student research team have put together an excellent briefing on the sheer number of data losses that we've seen from the state in recent months. So if you take this idea of 'a single source of truth' - a phrase used by Lord Carter in another review in 2002 - or the aim as the Varney report puts it, 'to develop a deep truth about the citizen based on their behaviour, experiences, beliefs, needs and rights', I'd ask, who would trust government to undertake this kind of programme efficiently and securely?

> "The public do not see this process, they experience only public services packaged for their needs.'"

Let me deal with the justifications that are used for transformational government briefly. Normally they hinge on the Tell Us Once argument that people don't want to have to notify different agencies when, for example, a member of their family dies. Government should be able to share that information out appropriately. This is the central justification for Jack Straw's provision for greater data-sharing powers in the Coroners and Justice Bill. But NO2ID have pointed out that you could rectify this simply by seeking people's consent to share information when a death is registered. Tell Us Once is better described as Tell Us Everything, in which we become customers of the government as a whole, rather than users of a single service. But it's worth saying that the scope of this programme is much more ambitious than simply collecting names and addresses. It involves a kind of 'predict and provide' mindset, where we are the passive recipients of a package of public services, formulated from our personal data and yet unseen by us. In fact, the Varney report takes us into a whole other world of behaviour management. As a 2005 Cabinet Office document made clear, this leads inexorably towards the biometric identity card and the national identity register. So that's the Tell Us

> "What we like to say is that we want to move towards an information society rather than a database state."

Once argument.

The other argument is the Tesco Clubcard argument. In the same way that Tesco gathers information about customer purchases to plan their stock and target advertising, so government says it needs to collect this personal data in order to plan public services more efficiently. Now of course, this is another spurious justification, because as dominant in the market as Tesco is, none of us are forced to shop there, and even if we do feel forced to shop there by the lack of choice, we're not forced to use a Clubcard when we go there. The Tesco model only works in a system where there's choice and competition and an absence of compulsion. But in public services, there is exactly that element of compulsion and an inadequate supply of choice and competition.

Another justification for data collection and sharing on this kind of scale focuses on its 'inevitability'. The challenges of the 21st century, whether in fighting terrorism or delivering public services mean that technology simply has to be used this way. One Cabinet Office report said that the whole process ought to be irreversible by 2011. In this way opponents can be labelled as Luddites: 'you don't really understand technology, you are in some way resisting innovation and progress'. Yet, the more I look into this and talk to IT experts, the more I realise that the Government is behind the technology curve on this, because technology itself should be moving us away from the Database State model.

To quote one Microsoft expert: 'putting a comprehensive set of personal data in one place produces a honey pot effect, a highly attractive and richly rewarding target for criminals'. Now it's fashionable, at public sector or public policy conferences, to attack silo governments. The demand is always for more joined up public services. But the definition of a silo could be 'a place of safe-keeping'. In the case of personal data, that could hardly be more important. Meanwhile 'joining up' is not at all the automatic panacea and guarantee of good services it is made out to be. You just have to look at the tax credit regime within the Revenue and Custom Service to see that.

We would argue that an alternative path should take us down the track of data minimalisation. Rather than amassing sensitive personal data and storing it in one place where it's insecure, the retention and use of data should be strictly limited to the minimum amount required for the minimum time required. Allied to this, a key principle for us is that individuals should have greater control over the storage and use of their data. Talk of 'personalising public services', while a laudable principle, is contradictory if you're gathering more power and information at the centre. True, personalisation would mean decentralising power, giving more choice and control to individuals and breaking up the centralised structures in Whitehall.

Over the coming months, we need to look at specific alternatives to the Database State. We know what we're against, but we need to really look at how we can take back ownership of our personal data. We want to look at how other countries take privacy much more seriously at the higher levels of government, and we want a far greater distinction to be made between access to, and control of, data. Our fundamental principle is this: that it's our data and not the Government's. The policies that we put forward hinge on the idea that we need to give greater power and choice to the individual rather than use technology to empower and extend the arms of the State. What we like to say is that we want to move towards an information society rather than a database state.

The Stockholm Programme
TONY BUNYAN

Statewatch monitors civil liberties in the European Union (EU) and has been doing so since 1991. It's a sad reflection on our politics generally in this country that even at a conference like this, the word 'Europe' hardly appears. Europe is important. Data retention of all communications started in the EU, while fingerprinting people for passports came up in the G8 before it came to the EU under policy laundering. We really need to get rid of the idea that the debates we have here are disconnected from the outside world.

The EU is going to put in place a new five-year programme from 2010 onwards called the Stockholm Programme, which I have been working on. One of the key themes is the need to harness the 'digital tsunami', as they call it, to be used by the state. Another piece of work done for Statewatch by Ben Hayes is called *Arming Big Brother*. This is about how the EU took a decision, five years ago, to create a 'security industrial complex' in the EU to compete with the United States' (US) military industrial complex.

Most of you probably don't even know that this is happening. But the 2004 report talked about the tracking of movements of all goods, vehicles and people, and the need to apply technology and science to achieve that end. It's now coming onto the streets and looking at the European level, I can see that one card - which is a passport, ID card, driving licence, health card and e-government services all in one - is not a hundred years away. These documents and possible linkages are being discussed. Our debates here in the UK need to take this into account and understand where these ideas are coming from.

Let us remember that when a Directive or Regulation is adopted in Brussels, a Regulation applies everywhere and a directive has to be transposed into national law. If you oppose the tracking of internet usage, you have to realise that that decision was taken in Brussels three and a half years ago. If we are to fight those decisions, we have to get our local and national work to understand the struggles at the European level as well - because the United Kingdom (UK) plays a major role. Mass data retention, a fingerprint passport - the UK was running around Brussels mobilising all its officials, whether permanent people in Brussels or people who were brought over especially, to say what good ideas these were. There was to be no opt-out here. Britain wanted our multinationals, our Home Office, our summit, to be part of that decision-making. Of course Britain wants to be part of it. We are talking about megabucks being made out of this system.

> "If you oppose the tracking of internet usage, you have to realise that that decision was taken in Brussels three and a half years ago."

Why is it happening? A lot of people think that it started after 11 September 2001. It didn't: it was there before. Technologically, capitalism had already reached that point where it had a global reach that needed translating into action. Capitalism had the capacity to do it and 9/11 gave it the green light to go ahead. In 1998, mass data retention had been kicked off the agenda by the campaigning activities of groups like Statewatch, Privacy International and

▶

others. 14 days after 9/11, on 25 September 2001, it went straight back on the agenda again as one of the four priorities in the EU's response to the attacks.

Our governments are trying to sell us this system as exceptional power for exceptional times - implying a time limitation. But what we are finding now is that the exceptional is being used to define the whole law. Say you park your car and it gets lost. They say: 'Don't you want to know where your car is? If it has been stolen, then we need to track every car'. You might say, 'Hang on, I want some privacy as well'. They say, 'You might get ill, so your health card with this chip on it which can be used across Europe, that's going to help you'. What they're doing in each of these cases - and it's the same with the children's database – is that they're choosing exceptional situations to define the norm and make compliance compulsory. Compulsory compliance is critical, not just for the state. It's critical for the multinationals, and for making all these technological solutions available to the law enforcement agencies. Universal application is not only going to make them a lot of money; it's going to let them go about their own business better. It's so that they can say, 'Show us your passport. Show us your ID card. Tell us who you are'.

> "In Europe we need to have a political debate before they start developing the technology and bunging our money into it."

There's this idea that Europe is somehow value-free. But we're talking about a Europe which, in 1999, at the time of the European Parliamentary elections, had 15 member states, 12 of which were broadly social democratic. Three were on the centre-right. Now, in the European Union there are 27 member states, 21 on the centre-right or far right, and six are on the so-called social democratic left, including the government of this country. There has been a massive shift to the right in the EU that means that the people running the Council of the European Union – it makes all the final decisions over what comes out of 40 working parties in our area of civil liberties alone - is being run by predominantly centre-right and far right governments from the national level. The far right and even worse still, racists and fascists, are a growing presence in the European Parliament. In 1999, the count came to 66 racists and fascists elected into the European Parliament. These are challenges which affect all of our work.

Governments tell us that this terrorism we're confronting - they say it in Brussels and they say it in London - will destroy our way of life, destroy our democracy. Quite the reverse. This form of terrorism will never destroy our way of life and our democracy. What will destroy our way of life and our democracy is the reaction of our respective governments to that terrorism.

The emergent system is also about social control. Think about the shift that has happened between the 1970s and 1980s and now, and measures that they would never have dared introduce in the Cold War – measures the Soviet Union would be proud of. Here's David Omand, the former Cabinet Office advisor, talking about his national security strategy report in the *Guardian* three days ago. It is an amazing quote. I hope I'm quoting correctly. He is talking about how 'access' to the personal information that resides in databases, 'and in some cases the ability to apply data mining and pattern recognition software to databases, might well be the key to effective pre-emption in future terrorist cases'. And then he says, basically, it is vital that public trust be maintained in the 'essential reasonableness of UK police, security and intelligence agency activity'. What?! Has nobody got a sense of history? Was the British Empire benevolent? But they are telling us what we should think. They say, go away and trust us. This sort of thing makes us what we are of course: subjects rather than citizens.

This is not just about the collection of data. It's not just about privacy. It is also about how that data is going to be used. The people who know this well are migrants who are trying to get into the EU, fleeing from poverty or persecution. They are facing that surveillance system. They're enduring the tracking, the fingerprinting, the misinformation, the intelligence reports that they can't see, the police reports that they can't see. The Muslim communities around Europe, not just in Britain, are facing extraordinary surveillance of their social and political lives. We have cases from all across Europe. Also all across Europe, protests have been policed differently, more aggressively. Now we have a conflation of security in policing. The policing of big international events against terrorist attacks is now equated with protests, cross-border demonstrations. The EU now has one manual to cover both.

We must not cut ourselves off from other struggles. Yes. We've got to campaign on our own issues, but we must not become single issue campaigns. We have got to work in context, within this country and in Europe and internationally. We must follow what is happening here and what is happening there, in order to best combat it.

The last point I want to make is about technological determinism as a driver. We heard Tony Blair say it: 'If it is technically possible, why shouldn't we use it, if it makes people's lives better?' That is a sort of mantra. But in Europe, they're throwing bundles of money at these projects. They're developing the technological ideas long before there has been any political debate. The ideas emerge from sitting down with the multinationals, with their researchers, with law enforcement and security people - and this is unseen. Having developed that technology, they then construct a legitimation for it. And when they construct that legitimation, the last thing that happens is the thought, 'Oh, we'd better genuflect to privacy and civil liberties: we've got to mention them'.

In Europe we need to have a political debate before they start developing the technology and bunging our money into it. That space exists to some extent, but it needs to be pulled together, so that a political decision is taken before we get the technological development, and not the other way around. If we don't watch it, that old scenario of the death of civil liberties by a thousand cuts, will become a reality. We are a long way down that road now, and - if we don't watch it - when they come for us, there will be nobody left.

Session 2
Parliament's Role
SUPPORTED BY DEMOCRATIC AUDIT

Why can't Parliament protect our liberties against the executive? Parliament has failed to stand up to the government on counter-terrorism laws, ID cards and the database state. Why does it evade debate on crucial violations? How does the Home Office manage to impose an authoritarian agenda on Government *and* Parliament, by introducing requirements without Parliament debating them?

Human rights and liberty
STUART WEIR

I was one of those who argued and campaigned for a Bill of Rights to underwrite civil and political rights in the United Kingdom (UK) when we started Charter 88 twenty years ago. We demonstrated that the 'three pillars' that were supposed to provide the traditional protections of our liberty - Parliament, the judiciary and public opinion – were all failing to do so. Adverse judgments against the UK were piling up in the European Court of Human Rights (ECHR).

We did not get a Bill of Rights. Instead Labour introduced the Human Rights Act 1998, incorporating the European Convention into British law. After ten years, the Act itself is under political siege and the erosion of freedoms is intensifying. The root cause of the Act's failure is that it and other constitutional measures were simply added to existing structures of political power that left the dominance of the executive essentially unchanged. Further, the law may have changed, but our political and judicial culture did not.

We live under a determined state that is pursuing two dynamic courses that are eroding liberty. Most obviously, the government uses the fear of terrorism, organised crime, extremism and other forms of anti-social conduct to justify severe measures that remove and restrict traditional civil and political rights. Secondly, and more insidiously, the government is creating almost out of sight a 'transformative state' that it intends to build around huge, linked databases – and it is doing so for 'our own good'! The ID card scheme is only the tip of this bureaucratic iceberg. Long ago, the idea that our homes were 'castles' became obsolete; very soon people will be unable even to protect their personal privacy and identities from arbitrary access by officialdom at all levels.

Parliament has largely been powerless. The House of Commons failed even to vote down the proposal to hold terrorist suspects for up to 42 days without charge. It was left to the unelected second chamber to hold the line. The creation of the Database State continues almost unscrutinised. The judiciary is failing too. Even the apparently landmark rulings on detention without trial have failed in practice to end the protracted incarceration of terrorist suspects. Court rulings on control orders have, in effect, legitimised house arrest in this country.

But the general public has also been all too complacent. We need the Convention on Modern Liberty to act as a catalyst for an informed and wide-ranging movement of resistance to the encroachments on rights and liberty; one that links the currently disparate issues and strengthens existing organisations, many of which inevitably compete for support. Just how any such coalition of the willing is to be assembled and sustained has yet to be resolved. One key issue will be how we do more than just protect the Human Rights Act but campaign to strengthen it, perhaps in the form of, at last, a constitutional Bill of Rights.

While the Act itself does not command popular support, the rights and freedoms that it protects do. A campaign to save and strengthen it needs to concentrate on those rights and freedoms; to argue for its extension to protect trial by jury; to assert social and economic rights in the face of the slump and to wake people up to the oppressive dangers of the Database State.

> "...more insidiously, the government is creating almost out of sight a 'transformative state' that it intends to build around huge, linked databases – for 'our own good'!"

SOURCE: CML PROGRAMME, FEBRUARY 2009

"Parliamentary difficulties"
ANDREW BLICK

In November 1882, Eddie Hamilton, Private Secretary to the then Prime Minister, William Gladstone, was sent what he described in his diary as 'some extremely interesting papers about the secret societies'. They suggested the existence of two separate assassination committees in Dublin, to which 900 members belonged. The groups were believed to have long lists of prominent targets and 'some sort of blow was expected to be struck ere long' was how Hamilton put it. While he felt the discovery of this threat was an achievement, Hamilton noted that, 'breaking up these horrible societies is a difficult matter'. One option was what he called 'renewing the power of arresting on suspicion' but the previous suspension of Habeas Corpus was not judged an encouraging experience by Hamilton and, as he said, 'any appeal to Parliament for further powers, which would have to be ostensibly for the purpose of breaking up these societies, would probably put an entire stop to the flow of information, to say nothing of the Parliamentary difficulties which such an appeal would involve'. Hamilton concluded, 'It seems best to work out in secrecy with the present powers'.

I open with this quote because it is relevant to what I want to consider today; the performance of Parliament in protecting our liberties in a number of ways. First, it shows that some of the security problems we face today are not as novel as is sometimes made out. Second, government has long considered resorting to a similar menu of responses often involving the suspension of due process in some way. Third, governments have in the past at least been able to learn from earlier experiences that certain methods are not effective. Fourth, governments are reluctant to reveal security-sensitive information to Parliament. And finally, the threat of what Hamilton called, 'parliamentary difficulties' can dissuade a government from even bringing forward proposals in the first place. This last point is pertinent because we do not always know when Parliament has been successful in averting stringent security measures. It may be that Government wants to introduce them but concludes that parliamentary resistance would be too great, and therefore does not do so. Equally, it could be argued that if a government brings forward these measures at all, Parliament has, in a sense, failed, whether or not it ultimately agrees to the measures, and history suggests, it unfortunately usually does.

One obstacle to Parliament's successful protection of our freedom is the multiple roles it is required to perform. As Michael Wills, the Minister

> "Parliament is a body over which the Executive enjoys a high degree of leverage, both with a power of patronage, and through normally possessing a majority in the Commons."

responsible for democratic reform put it last year, 'Parliament exercises power on behalf of the people who elect it; passes laws for the courts to apply; provides the authority for the Government to govern and holds the Government to account'. I could add a number of other functions to this list, like being the pool from which ministers are drawn and traditionally including within it the highest court in the land. This list suggests various conflicts of interest. Very importantly for the subject we are looking at today, Parliament is a body over which the Executive enjoys a high degree of leverage, both with a power of patronage, and through normally possessing a majority in the Commons. A body like this cannot necessarily be expected to prove effective at holding the Executive to account, including in restraining any threats to our freedom.

We should not therefore be surprised that, on many occasions in the past, governments have introduced major internment programmes, in Ireland, in both world wars, and - as is often forgotten - during the first Gulf War in the early 1990s, with little parliamentary resistance.

There has been a high degree of concern over the infringement of human rights that has been contained in counter-terrorism legislation and policies pursued in recent years. A central obstacle to Parliament properly overseeing the Government in this area, is the taboo surrounding the public discussion of intelligence and security policy. Increasingly, stringent measures are justified on the basis of a threat which is said to be growing, but about which little meaningful detail is provided. In October last year, the parliamentary Joint Committee on Human Rights (JCHR) was moved to state that, 'We do not underestimate the threat this country faces from terrorism, but when the Government seeks more extensive counter-terrorism powers on the basis of broad assertions about the growing threat, it is vital that it produces to Parliament the evidence on which those assertions are based'. The Government has yet to produce this kind of evidence, or even an account of what this kind of evidence might be. Even measuring Government performance against its own security targets – and this after all is a target-obsessed Government – is impossible for Parliament, because Public Service Agreement 26, entitled, 'Reduce the Risk to the UK and its Interests' states, 'The text of the Public Service Delivery Agreement (PSA) on countering terrorism is not being published. By its nature, the PSA contains information about the UK counter-terrorism effort that could potentially be useful to those who threaten the

UK and its interests'. So it is very hard for Parliament to hold Government accountable.

Furthermore the main body responsible for scrutiny of security and intelligence agencies is the Intelligence and Security Committee (ISC). Traditionally, it is not a full parliamentary Committee. There has been talk about changing this but it has not happened yet. The ISC is appointed in consultation with the Opposition by the Prime Minister to whom it reports. Its meetings are held in secret. Often passages from its reports are deleted on security grounds before they are published. It uses Cabinet Office premises and staff. From 1999 to 2004, the ISC had an investigator to help it in its work, but after he made comments on the BBC about the use of intelligence prior to the invasion of Iraq, his contract was allowed to lapse and he wasn't replaced. For all these reasons, the ISC has proved to be insufficiently autonomous from the Executive in both symbolic and practical terms, to be a satisfactory component in the democratic oversight of security policy.

Finally, I would like to make a more general point about whether parliamentary scrutiny has adapted sufficiently to take account of the changing nature of legislation. While the number of full Acts of Parliament being passed is possibly in long-term decline – although the length of individual acts has tended to grow – there has been, over the decades, a steady increase in the quantity of secondary legislation. The Merits of Statutory Instruments Committee - a good innovation - set up to deal with this in the House of Lords, had to consider over 1,154 instruments during just 33 meetings in 2007-8. It is quite hard for Parliament to really keep a handle on what is going through the system.

This secondary legislation can have severe consequences for liberty, amongst many other things. For instance the Identity Cards Act 2006 is largely enabling legislation with the details to be filled in later by secondary legislation. And the same applies to the Children Act 2004, regarding the parts dealing with the maintenance of data on children. Often, parliamentary scrutiny on secondary legislation is severely circumscribed or non-existent, and secondary legislation usually can't be amended. The control orders and 28 days pre-trial detention regimes are both renewed by secondary legislation and the JCHR has complained repeatedly about the way the Government has handled the renewal processes for both measures including not making important material available in time for it to be debated.

Earlier this month, in its report on surveillance, the House of Lords Constitutional Committee argued that, if possible, Government's powers should be set out in primary legislation. It also argued that in the event that secondary legislation is necessary, it should be subject to robust parliamentary scrutiny. A particular problem to be avoided which was identified by the Committee is 'function creep' where the scope of the Bill is gradually expanded beyond what Parliament envisaged. Examples of where 'function creep' has taken place include the National Pupil Database, originally contained in the Education Act 1997, and - famously - Local Authority use of powers granted to them under Regulation of the Investigatory Powers Act 2000. The use of secondary legislation can be a way of expanding primary legislation far beyond what Parliament originally envisaged it would be used for when it passed that primary legislation.

> "Improving parliamentary oversight therefore, including of intelligence and security policy and secondary legislation, is a task we need to take really seriously."

To conclude, given the nature of Parliament, its past record in this area, and current trends, it is fair to conclude that we cannot always rely on Parliament to protect our freedoms. I would argue that, in the event of a major terrorist attack in the UK, it would be unlikely to provide an effective break on a government which wanted to introduce far-reaching security measures using secondary legislation under the Civil Contingencies Act 2004. Improving parliamentary oversight therefore, including of intelligence and security policy and secondary legislation, is a task we need to take really seriously. Thank you.

Towards a culture of justification
MURRAY HUNT
LEGAL ADVISER, JOINT COMMITTEE ON HUMAN RIGHTS [1]

I want to take a step back to consider what the nature of our Parliament's role is under the current arrangements. We have heard quite a lot of calls this morning for a new constitutional settlement, a new dispensation. And those of you who were in the session on Judges and Politicians this morning, will have heard Lord Bingham quite rightly warning us that that might mean we would be going for a model of judicial supremacy, making the judges the supreme interpreters of our human rights protections. At the same time, we had Keith Ewing in that session saying that what we need is Parliament - and not the courts - to protect our human rights. Keith Ewing is probably one of the last defenders of a pure legislative model of human rights protection, in which it is for Parliament - to the exclusion of the courts - to be the authoritative interpreter of human rights protections and to have the final say on all matters to do with human rights. There is a lot in what he has to say about mechanisms which could improve Parliament's role.

But I wanted to start by counterposing those two extremes – a judicial supremacy model of human rights protection and a legislative model. What we have under the Human Rights Act is something very different from either of those extremes. It is a quite unusual hybrid model and it is worth thinking about what that means. Under our system and under the Human Rights Act as it currently is, it is for both courts and Parliament to interpret what the human rights standards mean and to take a view on them. We then have a role for courts to look at Parliament's interpretation in the way that they have drawn up their legislation, to see if it is compatible. In the institutional mechanisms set up in the Act, it can come back to Parliament if there is a declaration of incompatibility for Parliament to look at it again and

---

[1] *The views expressed here are personal to the author and do not purport to represent the views of the Joint Committee on Human Rights, Parliament, or any Officer of Parliament.*

consider, in the light of how the court interprets those fundamentals.

So, we have got this very interesting and different type of human rights mechanism set up in our Human Rights Act, and I just want to think for a moment what that means for what Parliament does. Because, what it commits us to, is a distinctively democratic culture of human rights. The Human Rights Act has at its core a meaningful role for politicians and accountable decision-makers to debate and discuss and disagree, within certain parameters, about what human rights mean in practice, in particular contexts. This is a culture of justification. What I mean is that all the major constitutional actors in every branch – legislative, executive and the judiciary – operate on the assumption that any exercise of power or any omission of the exercise of power by the powerful, which affects anyone's fundamental values and interests, has to be justified by reference to publicly stated reasons. There have to be institutional mechanisms for those reasons to be scrutinised, and for the givers of the reasons to be held to account for the adequacy of those reasons to see whether they are good enough justifications for the interference with a right, or for the failure to act to protect a right.

> "The Human Rights Act has at its core a meaningful role for politicians and accountable decision-makers to debate and discuss and disagree, within certain parameters, about what human rights mean in practice..."

This idea of a culture of justification, for which the Human Rights Act sets up the mechanisms, is a useful way of thinking about what it is that Parliament should do under a system of human rights protection, such as the one that we have. One very important role that Parliament then has in that system, is to subject to scrutiny everything which the Government does which has human rights implications. That will include a very large - and what we might call a negative - dimension to that activity. It will involve looking at the adequacy of the justifications given by the Government for – let's say - passing a measure which interferes with privacy, such as a data-sharing measure – and subjecting these to a very rigorous independent and sceptical scrutiny starting from a standpoint which asks why the measure is necessary, demanding the evidence that this will not have a disproportionate impact on those affected, and so on. That is a very important aspect of Parliament's function, that scrutiny for compliance, where a measure is going to interfere with human rights.

But an equally important aspect and one we have heard much less of today, is a positive dimension to that function of scrutinising for justification. An awful lot of human rights standards require the state not only not to interfere with things, but they also require the state actively to do things. An awful lot of human rights law imposes positive duties and obligations on the state to do something. That is where Parliament also has a very important role, to identify where those duties and obligations require the state to do something, and where more often than not it requires the Government to take some action. It is a much more difficult part for Parliament to play than one where it reacts to measures which have been brought before it by the Executive, but it is vital. We see this in a whole range of issues. The JCHR has held inquiries into the rights of older people in health care, which have identified the need for the Government to take positive steps to protect the dignity of people in those settings. In the current controversy about torture, there is an obligation on the state imposed by human rights law to carry out positive, adequate investigations. The Government has to do something. And it is for Parliament to put the pressure on the Government when human rights standards actually require the Government to do something.

It is in that area, in particular, that we can identify quite a lot of institutional obstacles to Parliament being able to fulfil that positive role of scrutiny for justification for inaction or omission. What the JCHR does to try and facilitate that parliamentary role is not to perform that task itself, but to facilitate well-informed Parliamentary debate so that Parliament can play its role of holding the Government to account. The way the JCHR has interpreted its remit in comparison to other human rights committees in other countries, is rather more extensive than these, most of which are confined to scrutinising legislation for compatibility. The JCHR has developed a much wider range of activity, including importantly – looking at court judgments, where the courts are given a role under the Human Rights Act, finding violations of human rights, and scrutinising the Government's response to those judgments. There is often a role for Parliament to decide what should be done. There may be a whole range of options, and the JCHR looks very carefully at how it can best provoke debate in Parliament and promote other human rights obligations. It examines the extent of the

> "...there is possibly even scope for a national human rights action plan."

UK's compliance with other human rights treaties, looking at the most recent recommendations from the various monitoring bodies. It has a whole series of thematic inquiries on at any one time: it is currently examining policing and protest for example. And it looks very carefully at how the Government is implementing the Human Rights Act. So, for example, whether it has responded swiftly enough to restrictive judicial interpretations such as the House of Lords interpretation of the meaning of public authority in the Human Rights Act. It brings all those together and tries in its legislative scrutiny work to suggest amendments to Bills in its reports which members of the Committee can put down in their own name – to try and implement the recommendations it has made in these various multiple strands of its work. So it is much broader than a mere scrutiny committee.

Now whether it has been effective is a matter for you to form your own view about. Unfortunately, very little research has been done. There is obviously much scope for improvement. But I wanted to finish by identifying a few examples of the sorts of institutional mechanisms within our current arrangements, which could be adopted without requiring a constitutional resettlement – which would help Parliament to more effectively fulfil this scrutiny role in a culture of justification. One would be to extend the coverage of scrutiny of legislation as Andrew Blick identified. Statutory instruments go relatively unscrutinised for human rights compatibility. The JCHR would like to see the reasoning which accompanies Government Bills; reasoned statements of compatibility. I would like to see the adoption by the Government of a human rights impact assessment methodology – a much more thorough, systematic approach to assessing the compatibility of a measure with human rights standards. There ought, in my view, to be more positive statutory duties to implement rights where those rights impose positive duties and obligation on the state and those should be accompanied by various reporting mechanisms to Parliament - independent review mechanisms, and so on. Parliament could be the body to which the national human rights institutions report and there could be, for example, departmental plans which include express consideration of human rights and there is possibly even scope for a national human rights action plan.

All these are measures which would enhance Parliament's role and give it a much more central role in debating and discussing what being committed to a fundamental set of human rights actually means in practice.

Parliament's role in the Abolition of Freedom
JONATHAN BUTTERWORTH

You should all have the report in front of you that is entitled, the *Abolition of Freedom Act, 2009*, produced by myself and eleven other members of the UCL Students Human Rights Programme. Essentially what it looks to do is to answer the question: why and how is Parliament incapable of protecting our liberties against the executive? Particularly when it comes to the database state – the interception, collection, storage and sharing of private information – what we have since 1997 is a stream of legislation which has eroded our privacy to such a degree that it is shocking. If this is the best that Parliament can do, then we will have to ask where accountability is going to come from on this, if not from Parliament? In some cases, the House of Lords is doing a good job, and the Joint Committee on Human Rights (JCHR) is doing good work. But we should expect more from our democratically elected legislature, the House of Commons.

There are six main problems with the House of Commons as I see it. One of the main problems is the programming and scheduling of bills: they fly through the House of Commons so quickly that MPs are unable to take account of what is passing through. The Anti-Terrorism Crime and Security Act of 2001, that came out just after 9/11, went through the Commons within about three days, and it was this Act that allowed the executive to detain non-UK nationals in Belmarsh without trial. Many MPs were simply unaware of what was in that legislation. You have another example now in the Counter-Terrorism Act 2008 which means that photographers find themselves committing an offence if they take pictures of the police or armed forces which could then be used by other individuals for the purposes of terrorism: they have to give their film up and can be imprisoned for up to ten years.

> "You have Parliament, the courts and the executive role – but most importantly to my mind, you have our role. What is the role of the public?"

The codification of prerogative powers needs to be addressed urgently. The fact that the government can still go to war without a democratic vote, the ratification of treaties and appointment of judges – all these executive powers are being examined at the moment and they should be parliamentary powers. Select Committees need increased power to be able to command civil servants and ministers to appear before them and then provide evidence. This is mainly reliant on political conventions and Codes of Practice which as a general rule – with exceptions for certain committees including the committee on standards and privileges – mean that these committees have insufficient powers to fully scrutinise. Keith Ewing MP has recently made a bold proposal concerning the powers of committees. He suggests that we should look to the Swedish model where the Constitutional Committee of the Swedish Riksdag have the power to veto legislation. It may not be the answer for the UK, but it is in this direction which we need to look.

Because if you look at the figures prepared by the previous special adviser to the Joint Committee on Human Rights, Professor Klug, it seems that the JCHR, though it may get a polite hearing in the House of Commons, is much better listened to by the House of Lords, and its work is hampered as a result. From its inception to 2007, 500 bills were examined by the JCHR, but only 18 were actually repealed by Parliament on the basis of the JCHR's recommendation. That is better than none, but it isn't very good.

Whipping within the House of Commons is another major problem. While some votes are free for the backbenchers to dissent from, too often there are implicit pressures placed upon MPs, especially those who would like to make a political career in the future. For them to be able to vote against a bill is almost impossible.

Finally, a major problem is our first-past-the-post electoral system and the disproportionate majorities that we have in the House of Commons. Moving towards a model of proportionate representation, such as single transferable vote or additional member system, would make for a stronger and more democratic House of Commons.

Due to these failings, the House of Lords and the courts have become our constitutional watchdogs because the House of Commons is doing an embarrassingly bad job. Currently, the House of Commons claims to be sovereign. But I feel that we have executive, not parliamentary or popular sovereignty within our legislature. If, in the case of Jackson versus the Attorney General over the hunting ban, the courts have gone so far as to threaten to remove parliamentary sovereignty, effectively making the courts themselves the supreme branch within the UK – this is a regrettable reaction to what has happened in Parliament over a long period of time.

I would like to add that the role Parliament can play shouldn't be looked at in isolation. It needs to be looked at within a web of accountability: you have Parliament, the courts and the executive role – but most importantly to my mind, you have our role. What is the role of the public? Parliament should be receptive to the public. Events like this, where we have Dominic Grieve, Michael Wills, the ex-Attorney General, are essential to pass the message forward that civil liberties are something to be cared about. I would like to throw a gauntlet down to the Convention on Modern Liberty. I would like it to become an annual conference where we meet and discuss what has happened in the previous year: what has been gained so that we advance our civil liberties – so, for example will Dominic Grieve stick to his promise to pass a repeal bill which pulls back all of this legislation? – and what hasn't, thereby holding people to account.

I would also like to see even more cooperation in civil society to this end. The CML is a very positive development, and the UCL Students Human Rights Programme would certainly like to reach out and collaborate more with organisations such as Democratic Audit, Liberty and Justice, who are doing such fantastic work. Through collaboration, the sort of pressure directed at Parliament will ensure that MPs feel that they are actually voting on behalf of the people, and that we, the people, demand that they protect our civil liberties.

Session 3
Protecting rights
SUPPORTED BY UNLOCK DEMOCRACY

How do we stop rights and freedoms being a political football? Unlock Democracy brings together the Justice Minister and an exciting line-up of leading thinkers to debate and discuss whether civil liberties should be given constitutional protection and how this might be brought about. As progressive steps forward in defence of civil liberties such as the Human Rights Act are continually brought into question, could having civil liberties enshrined in a UK constitution help safeguard citizens' fundamental rights and liberties? Do we need a fundamental shift in attitudes?

> "This country has got a proud record of human rights, and this Government is proud that it brought in the Human Rights Act to entrench those fundamental rights in British courts. We are proud of it. Sometimes it is uncomfortable for us: the courts have found against us. We abide by the judgment of those courts. But the most fundamental right of all is the right to life, and Government has got to fulfil its duty to the people that it serves by protecting that right as best it can, for everybody. How you strike that balance between the need to protect the public from a real threat such as terrorism - and terrorism is a real threat - and the need to protect the civil liberties of every individual, that is a problem that confronts Government every single day. Now we can and should argue over where that balance should be struck case by case, but we can't credibly deny that there is a balance to be struck, and it runs throughout our public life....
>
> The argument that Anti-Social Behaviour Orders (ASBOs) should be scrapped as an erosion of civil liberties, I can assure you, does not carry any weight at all on the Pinehurst estate in Swindon, and if all of you who have reacted so vocally to what I have just said today, sought to advance that argument there, you would be howled down in the way you have just howled me down. This is a balance that has got to be struck and we need to respect all sides in this."
>
> *MICHAEL WILLS MP, PANEL SPEAKER AND MINISTER OF STATE, MINISTRY OF JUSTICE*

They are our servants
AC GRAYLING

Our session is about protecting rights. Immediately, of course, that entails protecting the rights of individuals against sources of power, mainly state power. But one has to bear it in mind that there are other sources of power in society too – economic power, and the influence of certain lobbies like the media. But the primary focus here is state power: the power of government over individuals. Peter Facey (Chair) began by quoting James Madison, who was not only President of the United States but one of the authors of the Federalist Papers. It was from him we get the quotation - the first time it is mentioned really - about how liberties at home are always reduced in the supposed interests of protection against threats from abroad, which is very pertinent to our concerns today.

I am speaking as - at first a reluctant and, as time has gone by, a more passionate - convert to the idea that we need a new constitutional settlement in this country. The term 'constitutional settlement' is a little bit broader as a concept than a new constitution. We may need a new, and indeed written, constitution, but there may be steps prior to that which might help to remedy some of the difficulties that we are currently experiencing.

We are all familiar with the erosions of liberties that have taken place in this country over the last several decades. The present crisis really began in the early 1990s when Michael Howard was Home Secretary - for various reasons. One is that it was then that we started to become one of the most watched countries in the world with CCTV cameras everywhere. Things have got worse since then. Before 9/11 there were already measures introduced by the post-1997 Labour Government which constituted depredations on our civil liberties. But that has been accelerated by our security situation from 9/11 onwards. I assume that most of us agree that we are in a perilous situation. This is the time that we have got to do something about it.

The first step that could be taken to preserve our liberties in this

> " A long time ago, Quentin Hogg – Lord Hailsham as was – wrote that this was an elective oligarchy, an elective tyranny in effect, and it's true."

country is for individual members of Parliament to go back to being what they once – and for a very long time – were, and that is more or less independent members of Parliament, able to vote and to take action independently of the line whipped by their party. When Voltaire said of England that the reason why it was the home of liberty was not because of the constitution of the country but the constitution of the people, he had in mind the ruddy-faced farmer who happened to represent a constituency of two voters, who could be very independent-minded and sometimes take a line quite different from the other members of more or less the same political persuasion. That doesn't happen any longer. Back in 2006, when the Identity Card Bill was being discussed in the House of Commons, I wrote a pamphlet on behalf of Liberty, which was sent to all MPs, and I received scores of replies from Labour MPs, all saying that they agreed with the argument against having an ID card scheme and a National Identity Register, but saying that they were going be whipped into voting for it and that they couldn't do otherwise.

The question arises, why not if they didn't agree with it? And they also said something which I found even more dismaying: that the argument against an ID card scheme would not be won on principle – the principle of individual autonomy and being a private citizen or private member of this society - but only on grounds of cost. If it was too expensive, then that would be the reason why it would not happen. Money replaces principle: that is what we have come to.

So the first step would be to get our MPs to be more independent-minded and to stand up against things that they believe to be damaging to our civil liberties and our polity, because our traditional polity very much turns on the idea that as responsible adult members of this society, we are all players in the decisions about what happens in our lives.

But that is not likely to happen soon. The next step would be to do something about our system of representation. As the centrepiece of any kind of new constitutional settlement in this country, we have to have a new and better system of representation. Apart from anything else, it is just a matter of principle: that a very unjust electoral system which militates against smaller parties and smaller interests in society, and which delivers power – sometimes very considerable power, for example when you have a very large majority in the House of Commons which you may well have on a minority of actual votes cast, and certainly on people enfranchised to vote – allows certain people to do whatever they like. A long time ago, Quentin Hogg - Lord Hailsham as was - wrote that this was an elective oligarchy, an elective tyranny in effect, and it's true. All our rights, all our entitlements, or practically all of them, are held at the discretion of the House of Commons and if the majority in the House of Commons wished to change them, it could do it. That is a very unsatisfactory situation. One way to defend against it therefore would be to have a system of representation which makes it more difficult for any one party to have a big enough majority in the House of Commons to do that. The standard argument against it is that the result is 'weak government'. Well, great! I'm all for that. I think that as a rule, the weaker the Government, the better for the rest of us. It would be a bulwark, in fact, against things happening that we all find disagreeable.

But if you are going to alter the system of representation in this country that dramatically, it would involve certain knock-on effects, because you can't just take one tile out of the line of dominoes – even though that one thing would have a very positive effect on our society. It must tie in to a lot of other needed constitutional changes too. And the reason why I have become a convert to the idea of a written constitution, is the comparison with the experience that people interested in civil liberties are having in the United States of America (US). One of the major concerns in the US has been the warrantless wire-tapping under the auspices of the George W Bush administration. You can trace online in the History of Commons, in fact, everything that has been done by the two Bush administrations and, opposing them, by civil liberties groups and others affected by eavesdropping on their communications, and see the actions that the latter have taken in the US courts. This is because they have constitutional protections for their liberties and they can appeal to amendments to the constitution to take action against or to call into question what the administration is doing. And even though, when the administration has tried to introduce some measure and been knocked back by the courts, it has introduced a law afterwards that makes it legal to do that same thing - there has been a kind of waltz or three-step procedure going on there, such that defenders of civil liberties in the US recognise that, in some ways, they have themselves been the agents of more draconian laws as a result of challenging the Executive. Nevertheless there is that resource. And in a fresh new-minted constitutional settlement in any advanced country like our own, something could be built in to protect us from that tendency of an administration to change the law retrospectively in its own interests when it has been challenged on some constitutional matter.

What we need I believe, now that we have had this experience over the last couple of decades and seen what effect it has had on the fabric of our freedoms as citizens, is a clearly carefully thought out, properly debated and finally - we hope - nationally adopted set of provisions that would really genuinely entrench our liberties. That phrase is just shorthand for saying, 'put genuine brakes on what the executive can do, the legislative can do, and what the arms of the state can do in dealing with private citizens and in their relationships with those private citizens.'

> "We want our liberties, and if the only way of getting them is to have a written constitution, then I'm for it."

The argument is a very familiar one - and has been put any number of times: that we live in dangerous times. I think the threat is, at times, very serious and has to be taken very seriously. For this reason, the argument put by people like Lord Acton and John Stuart Mill in the 19th century, and all the way back to Locke, about the relationship of the individual to the state, involves individual members of society in recognising that, because it is so important to be a possessor of liberties, without which we cannot be constructors of good lives for ourselves that we have chosen for ourselves, we have to be prepared to take the risks that come along with it.

The first duty of Government, said Acton, is to protect the liberties of the subjects, the citizens. The first duty is not to protect our security; it is not to keep us safe. This latter is a high duty of the state, certainly, but not the first duty. The first duty is to protect our liberties. The logical conclusion of trying to protect our security is to lock us all up in our homes. That is impractical. Therefore we all have to recognise that we must take some risk, some responsibility for enjoying our freedoms. A mature government in a mature society ought to be saying to citizens, 'This is the fact of the matter: we cannot make you 100% secure. You are going to have to take the risks associated with living freely. You therefore have to keep your eyes open and be party to protecting yourself and everybody else. But you do that because it is worth it in order to be free'. And if, little by little, we are being turned into servants of the state, because the state thinks we can't look after ourselves and they must look after us, then we have to remind the state that actually things are the other way around. They are our servants. We want our liberties, and if the only way of getting them is to have a written constitution, then I'm for it.

The quango state
DOUGLAS CARSWELL MP

Four years ago, when I was first elected to the House of Commons, I was conservative both in name and outlook when it came to constitutional matters. I have changed my mind though, and now come to the conclusion that we need far-reaching and very radical reform. We have an over-bearing technocratic state that is encroaching on our freedoms and liberties. We need to do something about it. The question I face - and I think this is where the division between myself and Francesca Klug will be - is that I believe that our liberties are best guarded by empowering the legislature and the people against the executive. I am very wary of those who suggest we should allow the judiciary and unelected judges and lawyers to safeguard our liberties and I want to explain that a bit more later.

We need to radically change the relationship between Parliament and the executive, by empowering the people directly against the executive in ways that weren't possible until the age of YouTube. We need far-reaching electoral reform to achieve the independent-minded legislature that Professor Grayling spoke about – and I'll say how I think we can do that. We need direct democracy. Traditionally, conventionally, we are taught that there is a balance between liberty and democracy: too much of one and you lose a bit of the other. I actually think the biggest threat to our liberty comes from a lack of democracy. What is the cause of our lack of liberty? It is a lack of democracy, not too much democracy. executive power is overbearing and encroaching upon the nooks and crannies of our lives, because executive power is now exercised by institutions that are not answerable to anyone one can vote for.

In the old days, when I was studying politics at A-level, I was taught that executive power was wielded by those accountable to ministers. The one thing I have learnt in Westminster is that ministers are the spokespeople, the puppets for those who wield real executive power. Forgive me, but whichever clown in SW1 happens to be the Home Secretary, they are following the agenda of the technocrats in the Home Office. The quango state explains why executive power is so overbearing, whoever is in office.

Let me give you a few examples. Customs and Revenue a few years ago seized people's private property, why? Because they had decided they wanted to. They had no legal basis for doing so. The BBC Licence Fee collectors make legal threats against people but have absolutely no basis for that in any law passed by Parliament. On ID Cards: perennially, whichever government is in office and then runs out of steam, a civil servant, the Sir Humphrey Applebee of the day, suggests ID Cards as some sort of solution to some problem. It is a solution in search of a rationale. In education, the nappy curriculum is imposed upon perfectly good schools that just teach children slightly quirkily – like the Steiner Academies. We see central government intruding on nooks and crannies. Primary Care Trusts in my constituency pay for people to go and frighten young toddlers on what will happen to Mum and Dad if they don't do what the Primary Care Trust thinks they should when it comes to smoking. The Financial Service Authority (FSA), when I worked in fund management, used to impose lots of utterly ridiculous regulations on us, but failed to do the pretty obvious stuff – i.e. make sure that banks weren't going to go bankrupt. We see the technocratic quango state failing to do what it should do, but deciding for itself to tell us what it suits them to do. It is the quango state that explains the loss of liberty and the extension of executive power. As an aside, I just want to point out that it is good that those on the centre left now talk in terms of small government and safeguarding our liberties. But I think we cannot be selective about which liberties we safeguard. If you believe, as I do, in a free society, you cannot - if you are on the centre left - also suggest that we can have safeguarded liberty, but we will still, nonetheless, impose our agenda on your classrooms. Small government means getting the Executive off people's backs whether or not we think we have the right solution for other people's children when it comes to the National Curriculum.

And I think there are basically two solutions to the problem. Do we give some judges the power to basically do the job of guarding liberty for us? Do we put it above party politics? Whenever I listen to *Question Time*, you get a cheer from the audience whenever anyone says such and such an issue is too important for party politics. The National Health Service (NHS) – let's leave it for the technocrats at the National Institute for Health and Clinical Excellence (NICE) to decide who gets the medicine. Banking is pretty important: let's leave it to those technocrats at the FSA to decide. Exams and tests: let's leave it to the Qualifications and Curriculum Authority (QCA)! The trouble is, if you leave something to the technocrats and bureaucrats, as Max Weber understood, they do what suits them, and often they are monumentally useless. It's the QCA who messed up SATS (National Curriculum assessments). It is the FSA who fails to regulate effectively. If we give our liberties to unelected judges and leave it to them to do the job of safeguarding our liberties, they will not safeguard our liberties.

I grew up in a country which had a wonderful constitution, but unfortunately President Amin paid little attention to it. Executive power cannot be constrained by leaving it to unelected judges to do the work for you. That's what they do in Teheran: it doesn't work. It is also the solution that Rousseau came up with: we should leave it to the experts to decide what is in the public interest. I don't think that is the answer. Judges are not disinterested experts: they are people; they have subjective opinions. Twenty, thirty years ago their ideas may have been more Colonel Blimp than they are now: they are still subjective and biased opinions. Serving on the Joint Committee on Human Rights, I came to the view that we needed to withdraw from the European

> "We need to radically change the relationship between parliament and the executive, by empowering the people directly against the executive in ways that weren't possible until the age of YouTube."

> " Executive power cannot be constrained by leaving it to unelected judges to do the work for you. That's what they do in Teheran."

Convention on Human Rights and scrap the Human Rights Act. It is the wrong solution to this problem. It might make us feel good, but it will do nothing to get the executive off our backs.

Instead, I think we need radical change in our democracy. The judiciary has only stepped in to try to constrain the executive because the democratic process and the legislature are not doing the job properly, because basically elected politicians are useless. You can't take the balance between individual rights and security out of the equation: it is a profoundly political issue and it is right that you can vote for the people who will safeguard your liberties. We need radical reform to make sure that the supine and spineless institution that is the House of Commons is doing its job effectively. At the moment it is monumentally useless at holding the executive in check. Here are some ideas of how to do this.

- I have come around to the idea of electoral reform: we need multi-member constituencies, because the fact is 60-70% of MPs in the House of Commons stand zero realistic chance of ever losing their seats. So guess what: the whips have a lot of power; the voters don't. If we had a system of multi-member constituencies, I think we would start to see MPs behave in a way that represented what their constituents felt and they would be more willing to play a critical role vis-a-vis the Executive than they are at the moment. At the moment, the fact is that most MPs in the House of Commons are there to support the agenda of the Executive. Until we have electoral reform, big intrusive Executive power is going to become even more intrusive.

- We also need open primary selection so that we decide democratically who actually stands for public office in this country. The idea of one-party fiefdoms where a few people happen to be in with the trade unions, or - on my side of the house - in with their local Women's Institute – is not the way to decide who sits in the democratically elected legislature.

- We need secret ballots to choose a Speaker. He's nice as a person but I am on record saying the incumbent is not up to the job. Until we can choose who is in the Chair, the legislature is not going to be able to do its job.

- We also need the House of Commons to choose who chairs the Select Committees and then we need to give the Select Committees the power to ratify executive appointments of ministers and quangocrats, and for each Select Committee to ratify the budgets of their departments – that will constrain the quango state.

- We also need direct democracy. Instead of contracting the process of holding the executive to account out to elected politicians and the SW1 tribe, we need the power to do that ourselves. That means negative vetoes, to reject the absurdities and the follies of the political classes when they try to impose ID cards, or the Maastricht Treaty or the Dangerous Dogs Act on us.

- I wouldn't rule out the idea of a formalised Bill of Rights. I wouldn't rule out the idea of formally redefining the relationship between the tiers of government. I personally would like to see quite a federal system: a devolution of power – not a European federal system, a domestic federal solution.

But the trick to this is not giving it to the judges and the human rights lobby to solve the problem for us. They will make it worse. What we need is radical reform to ensure that those we actually elect on elections day hold the Executive to account rather than simply seek to become part of it.

Scoring Points
FRANCESCA KLUG

Sometimes it feels like the current climate is more like a wrestling, than a football match!

As all academics tend to do, I will try to deconstruct this question and address it in two parts.

First, how do we stop rights and freedoms being political? If this were the whole question, it would be a misguided one. Rights and freedoms come from political struggle, of course. As Helena Kennedy said this morning, human rights values may endure, but you will never end the **debate about the appropriate balance between liberty and security** or privacy and free speech. Nor should that kind of debate ever end. I think politics always has a role when it comes to protecting rights and freedoms: I'm with Douglas Carswell on that. That is why I was part of the group that fought very hard for the Human Rights Act (HRA) not to give judges the final say, but to leave the final say with Parliament. (There are people who want a new Bill of Rights precisely because they oppose that approach.)

The issue that confronts us is not how to take rights out of politics, but how to enable all to participate equally in politics – and society as a whole – by ensuring that everyone can fulfil their potential through the guarantee of certain fundamental rights; some of which inevitably tread on other people's freedoms, by the way.

This is the whole point of bills of rights, of course; in particular, to protect individuals and minorities whose views and aspirations are not necessarily represented by a system based on majority rule.

Any bills of rights worthy of the name, whilst protecting everyone's liberties, gives most succour to the marginalised and unpopular – or controversial causes and questions – precisely because these are the people and issues with least protection from other legislation and policy. When this happens, you will never eradicate negative headlines – they can still dog the Canadian Charter of Rights, more than 25 years after it was enacted.

convention on modern liberty

> "Rights and freedoms are not a game, of course. Least of all one whose rules should change to suit political leaders – across the political spectrum – or respond to newspaper headlines."

What bills of rights cannot do – of course – is create Nirvana, or Shangri-La.

Think of the Patriot Act, Homeland Security Act, Real ID Act 2005, Detainee Treatment Act and the removal of habeas corpus from detainees the (former) US President designated as unlawful enemy combatants.

The American Bill of Rights stopped none of these being passed and nor can any bill of rights based on post-legislative judicial review, if politics does not come into play to ensure that the rights it upholds are respected and protected by governments and courts alike.

As the famous US Justice Learned Hand memorably said, 'liberty lies in the hearts of men and women; when it dies there no constitution, no law, no court can save it'. But politics is only one side of the equation we are asked to consider. The second part of this question, football, is altogether another issue. It is a game which ignites passion, without doubt. A game in which scoring points is the whole point, and backing your side against the other team is the whole pleasure. Point scoring in the current debate about a bill of rights and the HRA is evident, although sometimes the race seems to be to the bottom rather than the top (of the division).

The irony is that, whilst giving an appearance of being two opposing teams, the two main political parties have, at times, been strikingly close on this issue. Both have resented the sometimes significant incursions on state power brought about by the HRA. Both have stated their support for a bill of rights which underlines the responsibilities of the individual. The leader of the Opposition, David Cameron, has gone further and called for the repeal of the HRA and the introduction of a specifically British Bill of Rights, in part to *increase* the power of the executive (to deport people and fight terrorism and crime) and *reduce* the power of the judges. These are perfectly legitimate reasons to dislike the HRA, of course, but they are also legitimate reasons to *oppose any* bill of rights worth its salt – *not* to *support* one!

Rights and freedoms are not a game, of course. Least of all one whose rules should change to suit political leaders – across the political spectrum – or respond to newspaper headlines.

People who call for a new bill of rights have got to make up their mind exactly what vision they are conjuring! If they are seeking enduring values which are constitutionalised, they will have to accept that, although we might be the lucky ones to have a say in what these fundamental rights and freedoms should be, we will deprive future generations of this pleasure. It will inevitably fall to unelected judges, not 'the people,' to interpret their application, and flesh out their meaning, as the years go by.

The post-war human rights framework – which emerged through the ashes of Second World War and the Holocaust, building on the Magna Carta, the 1689 English Bill of Rights and the US Bill of Rights – has been adopted by every country in the world; specifically through the values and standards in the Universal Declaration of Human Rights and the Geneva, Torture and Genocide Conventions.

When other countries argue that these treaties do not, or should not, apply to them – be it the U.S.A after 9/11; Zimbabwe after a sham election; or Israel following rocket attacks – we call this exceptionalism, a breach of common values and disregard for basic decency. When democracies try and find loopholes to avoid these established standards, or court judgments which uphold them, we see the path to extraordinary rendition and Guantanamo Bay.

If we want to stop rights and freedoms being a political football, I would respectfully suggest that the post war human rights framework – kicked off by Winston Churchill and FD Roosevelt – is a pretty good starting point.

Every country in Europe (except Belarus) has not just signed and ratified Churchill's charter – the European Convention on Human Rights – but has, through one means or another, incorporated it into their law. This is what we did ten years ago through the HRA. Other countries have bills of rights that stand alongside the European Court of Human Rights (ECHR) or build on it, as we could, of course. But all modern bills of rights are based on the post-war human rights framework.

No other country in Europe , besides us, is contemplating de-incorporating the ECHR from their law. Why? Because it is there precisely to stop governments from turning rights and freedoms into a weather vane or political football; depending on who is in power or in favour.

If we turn our back on these common values and say we want to start again, make them up, reflect what the majority want rather than what minorities need, then don't be surprised if these enduring rights and freedoms are up for grabs again when the next generation wants to consult on them. Don't be surprised if the goalposts in this game of football forever change.

Don't be shocked if 20 years from now, some of you are here listening to young people spit outrage at the travesties of the next government and your failure to prevent them. Just as some of us did twenty years ago when this book – *Decade of Decline* – was produced by Liberty to trace the trashing of civil liberties under the Thatcher government.

Only then, there was no HRA or equivalent bill of rights to provide any protections against a system based entirely on the sovereignty of government (let's not kid ourselves it's the sovereignty of Parliament). Decisions by public officials could only be overturned if they were so irrational, the official should probably have been locked up anyway. Banning Sinn Fein politicians from the airwaves or gays and lesbians from the army were deemed perfectly reasonable. And Acts of Parliament were protected from judicial review altogether.

> "If you would believe the tabloids, only terrorist suspects, asylum seekers and Gypsies and Travellers have benefited from the HRA. Even a cursory analysis of the case law suggests otherwise"

I have a little list here of some of the differences the HRA has made. Just imagine if these had been the headlines in the *Daily Mail* in the last ten years instead of 'human rights for scoundrels and villains!' If you would believe the tabloids, only terrorist suspects, asylum seekers and Gypsies and Travellers have benefited from the HRA. Even a cursory analysis of the case law suggests otherwise with landmark rulings giving same-sex partners 'nearest relative' status, changing cell-sharing policies following a racist murder in prison, ensuring lifting policies consider the dignity of disabled people as well as the health and safety of care workers, naming deceased fathers on birth certificates, requiring independent investigations of deaths in custody, and enhancing the freedom of assembly for protestors.

This is in addition to cases in which the HRA has protected British soldiers serving in Iraq, banned evidence procured by torture from being admitted in our courts, held that 'control orders' and indefinite detention breach fundamental rights, reduced the destitution of asylum seekers and enhanced due process safeguards for mental health detainees.

Football ignites passion and is fun. Defending common values from those who would destabilise them in order to score points and win games – or elections – is much less exciting; but all the more essential.

A balance has got to be struck
MICHAEL WILLS MP

Perhaps unsurprisingly, there is a huge amount of agreement between what I will say and a lot of what has already been said. But there are some fundamental differences and I would like to spend my ten minutes talking about what I think is profoundly important in this debate. In answer to the question, how do we stop rights and freedoms becoming a political football, I agree that we can't. But I also agree with Douglas Carswell that we shouldn't, because rights and freedoms are at the very heart of our politics. Some of them, rightly, as Francesca Klug has said, are non-negotiable, profound human rights; but rights and freedoms go much further than that and the reason that they are the stuff of our politics is because, at their very heart, the battle of the individual to protect their individual liberties from being eroded by a careless or a malign state is actually a reflection of an even more profound issue which is always going to be at the core of our political debate - and that is power.

Individual rights and freedoms protect us, all of us, individually against the arbitrary exercise of power over us. Where power is located in our society, how it is distributed, how it should be exercised – these are fundamental issues for all of us. They are the stuff of politics. That is what political debate is about in a democracy, always has been and always will be. And, of course, that struggle for power is often with the state. But that isn't always the case. Enormously wealthy individuals can manipulate and cow a complex modern state, which is sometimes conflicted by competing interests. This is one reason why I take profound issue with Douglas on this issue of direct democracy. It sounds great until you look at the history of referendums, and you look at the way that direct democracy can be manipulated by the wealthy and the powerful against the interests of the less articulate and most vulnerable members of society. Our system of representative democracy is not perfect by any means, but it is a protection for the weak and the vulnerable in a way that direct democracy is not. So I do disagree with him on that.

But equally, a benign state, and sometimes the state can be benign – the National Health Service was a creation of the state – can use its power to advance and protect the interests of the weakest and most vulnerable individuals who would otherwise be exploited and disadvantaged by wealthy, powerful individuals. In a healthy society, power is never concentrated. It is never in the hands of the few. It is always diffused as widely as possible and it should flow freely, because societies change and the distribution of power must reflect those changes. But inevitably, chemically, it tends to concentrate around the already powerful: rigorous, vigorous activity and debate is always needed to keep the powerful in check, so that the rights and freedoms of all of us can be upheld. And that is not football: that's politics.

There aren't easy answers. I have read a lot of the documents produced in the run-up to today and the Anti-Social Behaviour Order (ASBO) features quite frequently, cited as an example of the erosion of liberty under this Government. But on the estates where vulnerable pensioners are being terrorised by gangs of thugs, and I can take every single one of you here to several such estates in Swindon now – I had an email just before I came out from one of my constituents saying exactly what had happened to her last night at the hands of one of these gangs of thugs – those ASBOs have not destroyed the liberty of pensioners. They have secured it. We can debate the mechanism and we can debate the balance of proof, but in the end this is a question of power. How should the power of those gangs on the ground in those estates to destroy the fundamental rights of those pensioners to live in peace, be contained? Sometimes the power of the state, properly accountable, properly scrutinised, is the only answer.

Now I often hear the charge that this Government and other governments as well, have used the cloak of security as a way of eroding civil liberties, and of course there is always a risk that might happen. But in making this charge, we should not forget that there is always an inherent tension between those imperatives of security and liberty. There is a balance that has to be struck. Professor Grayling has talked about this today, but there is an argument about this, about what the first duty of a government should be. It is an argument on which people will take different views. Neither side is axiomatically right: neither side is axiomatically wrong. There is an argument to be had, and, in democratic societies, we resolve that democratically. How you strike that balance best between those two imperatives is a constant and enduring struggle for any government and actually for any people.

The liberty that has represented the best of our history has never been a crude libertarianism. If you remove the power of government, you remove its power to protect the weak and vulnerable, and this is not an easy balance to strike. We have heard a lot about data sharing today, and in the run-up to today. But that data sharing by public bodies which is already in place, some of which is already in place, some of which we are proposing to put in place – that data sharing which so many here today say is an unacceptable intrusion on privacy by the state, actually can help thousands and thousands of children who are eligible for free school meals, but don't get them at the moment, to get those free school meals. *Response to audience protest*: Well, it's all very well for you to sit here complaining – you've probably all had a hot meal in the last week. I'm just telling you that one in five in my poorest wards have not had a hot meal in the last week. We will come to the questions afterwards. I am just saying that we have a problem. We have to deal with it, and these powers help us to deal with it.

There are three million people who are not registered to vote. The right to vote is the best guarantee of our liberty. Data sharing will help us get those people onto the electoral register so that they can exercise their democratic right to vote, and those people who are not on the electoral register to vote by and large are some of the weakest, most defenceless and vulnerable people in this country. You may not like these answers, but we have a responsibility in government to address them as best we can. Data sharing is an answer. It is not an unfettered power. It has to be properly scrutinised and it has to be properly accountable and no doubt we can make the provisions better than they currently are. But we turn our backs on these measures at our peril because, when you turn your back on them, you are turning your back on a remedy for wrongs that exist today in our society.

Now, reconciling these different goods - security, liberty, the empowerment of the least powerful in our society - is never easy. Language is crucial, and I know that I have been talking about the importance and inevitability of argument and debate. But we really have to be careful about anyone on any side of the argument being dogmatic that they have all the answers. Such dogmatism is dangerous wherever it comes from and it undermines the cause that it seeks to espouse. I want to give you some examples of this. To argue that the collective security of all must always override the rights and liberties of the individual is to embark on a path that 20th century totalitarianism trod with such terrible consequences. And because those memories are so fresh, those who advance such arguments weaken the essential case that needs to be made for measures that protect the people of this country from the real threats that they face. But equally, to ignore the conflicts and hard choices that governments and parliamentarians have to make in striking this balance between liberty and security, is to risk losing the democratic support of the democratic majority who want their individual rights protected in the way that the state has to protect them, if it is to protect their security.

> "Where power is located in our society, how it is distributed, how it should be exercised – these are fundamental issues for all of us. They are the stuff of politics."

I just want to stress one thing. This is not an argument for avoiding unpopular positions. And I absolutely agree with what Francesca was saying about majority rule. Our constitutional arrangements are largely unwritten. They strike a careful balance between the areas of responsibility of the courts and parliament and the executive. These balances are very precious and they are deliberately and wisely not majoritarian. The lonely advocate of the unpopular

▶

> "'Tories are proposing to bring in a Bill to restore British freedoms'. What this actually means, is that they are planning to repeal the Human Rights Act."

can be a hero and I certainly don't want to suggest otherwise. But we do have to be careful to respect all those who take a different view. If you show disrespect to your opponents in this crucial area of public debate, you actually polarise an issue which only can be resolved effectively and sustainably through democratic dialogue and debate. When believers only talk to believers, nobody else listens. I can assure you that the Labour Party learnt that lesson bitterly in the 1970s and 1980s.

Government doesn't always get this right, but neither do those who criticise it. And I'm going to say something that I suspect won't get much support here. But the years since 1997 have not been, and I quote, 'a crisis of liberty'. This is the government that brought in the Human Rights Act: it gave individuals the right to enforce their fundamental freedoms in a British court. It is the government that brought in the Freedom of Information Act. It is the government that brought in the Data Protection Act and established the office of the Information Commissioner, which have given us quite a lot of trouble as a government, but rightly so. That is what we set them up to do. This is the government that has presided over the radical devolution of power away from the centre. Now, of course, people argue over the extent to which these reforms should go, and they call for them to go further. But that's fine. That's democracy. But you can't deny the fact that this government has brought them in and that they are significant enhancements of individual liberty. Not to weight them in the balance is to manipulate the fact.

And the tone of all this debate matters. Now Francesca quoted from the *Abolition of Freedom Act, 2009*. This is a very interesting and controversial document. And it is polemic. But look at this line from it, 'Children are being groomed for life in the database state'. Now this is a description of ContactPoint – a project that the Department of Children, Schools and Families have developed in relation to the inquiry into the tragic death of Victoria Climbié. It is a measure designed to enable professionals who work with children who are vulnerable, to keep in touch with each other, so that they know who is working with which child. It is a measure designed to protect vulnerable children and keep them safe. Quite apart from the melodramatic description of modern life - because after all, Google and Tesco and telephone companies – all of whom need to be accountable and scrutinised as well – are all hugely powerful component parts of the database state! - this is language that is derived from an analysis of paedophile strategies. This doesn't help sensible, rational discourse of these important matters at all. The removal of nuance destroys meaning. That was the goal of newspeak in *1984* where it was an instrument of the totalitarian state. Here, in the real world, language matters. Francesca quoted the *Guardian* piece with its headline saying, 'Tories are proposing to bring in a Bill to restore British freedoms'. What this actually means, is that they are planning to repeal the Human Rights Act. They say that their new bill of rights would 'better tailor but also strengthen the protection of our core rights.' But we need to know what our core rights are, and which of these fundamental rights and freedoms - which are currently included in the Human Rights Act – would potentially be removed under this new bill.

Mutual respect and honest dialogue are the only sustainable ways in which we resolve these difficult issues in the defence of liberty. If vigilance is the price of liberty, then honest debate keeps vigilance alive and muscular. And that *is* why today can be so important.

Session 4
The Left and Liberty
SUPPORTED BY COMPASS, SOUNDINGS, THE FABIAN SOCIETY

Historically, the Left has always been stronger on equality than liberty, seeking immunity from the law rather than freedom under it, which it has regarded as competitive and individualist rather than collective. In office, it has been largely statist in its approach rather than pluralist. New Labour has embraced a market version of choice in the public sector rather than enabling citizens. While it has embraced human rights, it still has difficulties with empowering citizens to fulfill their free emancipation. Can this change?

> "We've had a long period of Labour Government. The Labour Party is not well-represented at this event today... Part of the charge sheet is that the left doesn't care about liberty; that the Labour Government has been authoritarian and the Labour Party is authoritarian. That is often part of how Henry Porter, co-director of today's events, puts the charge. Other people may agree with that. I think that's rather one-sided, myself. But a more telling critique is that the left has a rather benign view of the state because the left has been involved in this country's proudest achievements: using the state for progressive purposes; creating universal healthcare through the National Health Service; creating the Beveridge welfare settlement...
> So when the left is running the state, does it have too benign a view of it, because it's in charge?"
>
> SUNDER KATWALA, PANEL CHAIR AND GENERAL SECRETARY OF THE FABIAN SOCIETY

"We wanted to do this session because we wanted to fly the flag for the left and liberty. It isn't flown very high or very much by the left and I think that's a real mistake, a central mistake. The advertising guru, Maurice Saatchi used to say that every organisation needs its single universal recognisable truth (or SURT) to distinguish what it is about. And he said the SURT for the right was always freedom. That should be the one word that encapsulates what they are And the left, I think, has just abandoned that term, to its political peril, and we need to grab it back…

There are two problems around the issue of liberty for the left – the first is market fundamentalism and the second is state fundamentalism, and the two things are tied together. The politics of market fundamentalism has ruled our world for almost exactly thirty years, since Thatcher came to power in 1979. Market fundamentalism means that the route to freedom is as individualised, atomised consumers. You go and buy freedom in the shops every day. Freedom in the words of Zygmunt Bauman is to be found 'under the knife of the plastic surgeon'! Now that's quite alluring in some respects. But it has its limits… The problem with the politics of the free market, as Andrew Gamble says, is that it always requires a strong state. If you don't regulate the market, you end up regulating society. That's effectively what we've been doing. The state didn't shrink under Mrs Thatcher. It just shifted from welfare through to policing and surveillance. And unfortunately, to a large extent, that has continued under New Labour. That doesn't mean to say that the last twelve years have been wasted. They were absolutely not. State spending in lots of areas has gone up, and we welcome that in terms of public services, minimum wage, tax credits and all the rest of it. But the notion that actually what dominates our lives and our politics is the philosophy, process, institutions and culture of the free market, means that the state has had to come in and pick up the pieces."

NEAL LAWSON, PANEL SPEAKER AND CHAIR OF COMPASS

Embracing the collective
MICHAEL RUSTIN

I agreed with most of the things that were being said on the platform this morning about the advance of surveillance, the intrusive state, 'terror' laws, and so on. But I have quite a lot of misgivings about the framing of liberty in these terms as the primary issue that we should be talking about now. I ask myself who, ideologically and politically, are going to be the beneficiaries of that campaign and why do they favour that agenda? That is where Neal Lawson's words earlier today about the wider social and economic environment that we are currently living in, come in: there are wild animals out there called market forces, corporations, banks, global capital who are just producing a colossal smash-up of our system. That is going to lose us millions of jobs, pensions, income and possibly lead to damage to social order as well. That regime came about in 1980 with Thatcher and Reagan and has continued more or less unbroken, although with a slightly different inflection in the last few years in Britain. It is the idea that market forces know best and that global market forces know better than anybody else, and that it is the job of governments to try to accommodate and make sense of that kind of system. That was an idea of freedom. The word 'neoliberalism' encapsulates precisely that ideology of the freedom of property, of ownership, as the driver of the system. There is the idea in the neoconservative programme that if those forces are allowed free play in a reaction against the welfare state, the trade unions and so on, everyone will be better off in the end.

And of course, it is true to say that in the last twenty years in countries such as ours, quite a lot of benefits have derived from this system, both in terms of prosperity in Europe (not so much for most people in the United States) and, more importantly, in the rapid economic growth in China, India and Brazil. The market is fundamentally important. However, the question is: what kind of relationship should the modern, democratic state have to that market? The growth of the modern state was, historically, an attempt to regulate the power of property and ownership. If you left markets as they were, people would have no protection (therefore you had to have Factory Acts, for example); they would have no security in old age (therefore you had to have an old age pensions system); you would have enormous levels of inequality and no healthcare (which is why we have the National Health system). State power in most countries in Western Europe and in the United States grew as a means of redressing and offsetting the disadvantage of the market. That was its primary function.

> "The Labour Party is in no position to say 'we stand for the regulation of markets just like Obama', because they have been responsible for the deregulation of markets..."

You have to ask: is that function obsolete? Should we not be talking about that anymore? Well, there is a big argument going on about that at the moment in the United States. Obama has produced a stimulus package to try to deal with the excesses of deregulation in the American market economy which proposes increases in taxation on the very rich; large amounts of public expenditure and a great deal of regulation. And the Conservatives there, the Republicans, basically oppose that legislation on the principle that it is an offence against liberty and free market ideology. That argument is ongoing.

Here, the argument is much more confused and that is part of the problem. The Labour Party is in no position to say 'we stand for the regulation of markets just like Obama', because they have been responsible for the deregulation of markets; they have presided over the development of a quasi-feudal system of inequalities in terms of what people feel entitled to have in relation to others, and are in a state of total confusion about whether the job of Government is to regulate markets in the interest of the majority of people, or whether the job of Government is to favour and support market freedoms. They have been doing both quite vigorously at the same time, which is confusing both for them and for us. Here is a government which claims that it wants to improve equality and public services, and to a degree does this, but which also says, 'Well, actually, without free markets, without corporations, with globalisation and without the City – we are doomed'.

So they have created a monster hybrid state which is neither a democratic state, nor simply a servant of the corporations, but something in between the two. In this process many state institutions have become rather corporate in their methods of management and control, and also somewhat authoritarian. There has been a kind of socialism of losses and a capitalism of profits, whereby private organisations get a guaranteed way of making a living – the Private Finance Initiative is one example, the bail-out of the banks is another, the large subsidies to the privatised railway companies – much larger than to BR in the old days – is another – whereby British capitalism, it seems, can only function if the Government provides massive underpinning and support for it. Now the system is in serious trouble and we have to ask what Government should do about it?

Our Government says it is committed to reflation and stimulus and so on, so they are in that sense, like the Americans, trying to do something about the situation. But they can't articulate a clear purpose for government, in my opinion, because they have muddled the sphere and function of government between that of the protector of a democratic public, and as the supporter and enabler of market forces and corporations. That ambiguity of purpose now leaves them very vulnerable.

Now, in this predicament, the Conservatives come along and say, 'Civil rights are really important. Liberties are extremely important'. No doubt men like Dominic Grieve really believe this. But when you look at their economic programme, what do they favour? They seem to favour the state doing less rather than more. They are certainly not espousing a programme like that of Obama in the United States. I would say their programme is: 'Let's have the markets more in control and let the state try to do less'. We are likely to end up, given that programme, with a weak-state version of neoliberalism as contrasted with a strong-state version of neoliberalism. What kind of system will that be? And, in the end, will it do much for civil liberties?

When you have states that don't look after the majority of people and produce high levels of discontent, it creates disorder. And if you have disorder, as we have had with trade unions in the past, and in Northern Ireland, you have security problems and alarms. I am not confident that an initial commitment of the Conservatives to support individual rights against the state wouldn't melt away with the first fracas, if social conflicts and tensions grow as a consequence of their economic and social policies, which I think is likely.

This isn't a very optimistic picture, and indeed we might be heading for something like the 1930s. But let us hope that the concerted action of governments, and – let it be noted – the intervention of the state in opposition to unfettered financial market forces, will produce some kind of stabilisation and a return to quasi-normality.

But what do we need in this kind of situation? Well we certainly do need an entrenchment of individual rights. But I think that what we need even more is the regeneration of democratic institutions. The principal problem we have is the way the state has become so isolated and cut off from representative processes: the hollowing out of the Labour Party is one part of this; the castration of local government such that it depends on central government for 75% of its financial resources is another; the unrepresentative parliamentary system which means hack majorities are often wheeled into line to endorse whatever deal the government has hatched with private companies (the third Heathrow runway is one example of this) is yet another. You have a system in which democratic representation is very attenuated, and I think it is a great pity that the organisers of this conference – Unlock Democracy, Anthony Barnett and so on – didn't stay more fully with the full agenda of Charter 88 itself, which was committed to democratic regeneration, constitutional reform and democratisation, as well as individual human rights, and instead moved into what I think is a more conservative, right-wing territory of individual liberty and freedom as the primary goals. Individual liberties must of course be part of the picture, but if it is allowed to become the whole of it, we are in difficulty.

> "I am not confident that an initial commitment of the Conservatives to support individual rights against the state wouldn't melt away with the first fracas..."

I believe that the left must campaign for a pluralisation of our political system. This may come about one day (maybe soon) as a result of a hung parliament. The Lib Dems, the Scots and the Greens then might get some leverage on this political system. This is necessary in order to open up a space in which a more honest exposure of the differences of function between a commitment to democracy and to the market, to the protection of people versus the protection of property, can take place. That choice seems to me to be the primary issue. So I would like to see the debate about modern liberty being extended to embrace what you might think of as collective as well as individualised forms of freedom and expression. I don't think we will make much political progress, even with the agenda of individual liberties, unless that happens.

Session 5
Liberty, Sovereignty and Republicanism: Can the Leveller Tradition be Revived in the 21st Century?
SUPPORTED BY HISTORY TODAY, OUR KINGDOM

The British Library's magnificent 'Taking Liberties' exhibition provides a vivid refutation of the establishment narrative which says that British liberty has been gradually and consensually achieved without the need for popular struggle or the kind of written constitutional document found in Europe. Liberty was not a gift from on high; it had to be fought for, taken and written down as a reminder to the ruling elite.

For centuries, the establishment myth of British liberty managed to suppress the radical tradition of the English Levellers. But here, in all their glory, are the Agreement of the People of 1647 and a transcript of the Putney Debates at which Colonel Rainsborough declared that 'the poorest he that is in England hath a life to live as the greatest he...that every man that is to live under a Government ought first by his own consent to put himself under that Government'.

The Levellers understood that the freedom of the people was too precious to be left in the hands of parliamentarians, however well-intentioned. Today, as an executive-dominated Parliament threatens our freedoms anew, what can be learnt from the Levellers and their appeal to republicanism and popular sovereignty?

convention on modern liberty

The elephant in the room
EXCERPT FROM GEOFFREY ROBERTSON'S SPEECH

It is an abiding irony that a country that historically has done more for liberty than any other, should be so reluctant to acknowledge that fact – to put Republican heroes and liberty heroes on coins and statues and plinths to teach our children about their birth rights. For all the complaining and handwringing that we have heard today – proposals for British Bills of Rights and written constitutions – I don't think that we are going to get anywhere until we work out how to instil in our children a fierce pride in the achievements of their forebears in what has been, for eight centuries almost, a struggle (and continues to be a struggle) for liberty.

The Government announced last week, in answer to a parliamentary question, that it had no plans at all to celebrate the 800th anniversary of Magna Carta. That's typical of the ignorance and the lack of pride and the inability to understand British liberty. Here is a document revered around the world. Eleanor Roosevelt introducing the Universal Declaration of Human Rights said that it would be 'the Magna Carta for mankind'. The impact of Clause 29 - 'To no man will we deny or delay justice and right' – has been extraordinary in terms of habeas corpus and the history of liberty. Of course, we don't want to be anachronistic. Magna Carta in 1215 was a squalid deal between a feudal king and feuding barons. It was immediately dishonoured by the king, and it did not in fact begin to become the iconic document it is until it was revived in 1628 by Sir Edward Coke, (the former Chief Justice sacked by the king when a judgment displeased him), when it was rewritten as the Petition of Right.

That was the beginning of the crucible years for liberty in this country, and indeed in the world. We all have our favourite moment: mine I think goes back to 1618, when Eliot, Pym and Hampden sat around the gallows listening to Sir Walter Raleigh's gallows speech and realised that they could never live free under an absolute monarch who put that man to death so brutally through a corrupt Lord Chancellor.

afternoon sessions

> "We should be enormously proud of our abolition of Star Chamber in 1641, which marked the end of torture."

But there it is. The years of the 1630s with the ship-money case and the death of John Eliot in the Tower leading to the civil war, but first, in 1641, to the Act that ensured the independence of the judiciary; one of the most important principles, that the judges should hold office subject to good behaviour rather than at the king's pleasure. 1641 also saw the last torture warrant issued in England. Thereafter, as one historian said, 'Torture was something that's done by the French'. And indeed, it was! Throughout Europe for centuries, torture was part of the official legal process. If you remember the second act of Tosca where the judge has a non-singing role, he leads the revolutionary painter downstairs to the cells, to have formal torture, which was part of that process. We should be enormously proud of our abolition of Star Chamber in 1641, which marked the end of torture.

In addition, comparative religious tolerance (for everyone except Catholics), the return of the Jews and so on – yes, partly influenced by religious preoccupations of the time, but also by ideas about religious freedom. The *Areopagitica* (1644): the end of censorship and Milton's famous cry, about censorship being 'as absurd as the farmer who sought to keep out the crows by shutting his park gate'. Or the Levellers with their Bill of Rights, *The Agreement of the People*, in which the Preamble said that they wanted to make it appear to the world (this was in 1647) 'at how high a rate we value our freedom'.

Colonel Rainsborough – well we hear more about him in the *Devil's Whore* on Channel Four than in any school textbook. The end of impunity – the word comes into the English language in the Rump Parliament Statute which set up the court that tried the king, so that no great Officer of State or Chief Magistrate shall attack their own people henceforth 'and expect impunity for so doing' – impunity, the great struggle that we still have today to deny impunity to tyrants and torturers. The trial of King Charles I, the first war crimes trial of a head of state, where the evidence against him was that he organised and authorised the torture of prisoners of war – a crime even then.

Our children are taught nothing of this. They leave school at 16 knowing absolutely nothing of this whole period. I am currently going through the

GCSEs with my children. If they do history at all, they study the rise and fall of Hitler, the rise and rise of the United States, and their idea of liberty at 16, if they follow the school curriculum, is Little Rock and Mississippi and never, never Naseby and Putney. At 13, they are permitted to notice for one lesson the civil war, the year of 1649. According to the Government's curriculum, they must focus on Cromwell as 'a man of vengeance' – seriously! And the year of 1649 is to be studied as the year of vengeance, the universal Groan at the king's execution being the main subject. Of course it was thought of at the time as the first year of freedom, by God's blessing restored!

> "At 13, they are permitted to notice for one lesson the civil war. According to the Government's curriculum, they must focus on Cromwell as 'a man of vengeance' – seriously!"

But it is, I think, a serious indictment of those charged to teach our children well, that they fail to teach them at all about the struggle of what Quentin Skinner calls in his writing 'the democratic gentleman'; struggles that led to those democratic gentlemen having their bowels burned in front of their eyes in the real year of vengeance which was, of course, 1660.

But what is the reason, I wonder, for this inability to comprehend, let alone celebrate, the origins of English and indeed world, liberty. When Bernard Crick produced a booklet for the Home Office for migrants on the *History of Britain*, he left out the Civil War completely. And when taxed with that, he said, 'The wounds are still too fresh'.

Last night I read the latest paperback, published two weeks ago, called *The Assault on Liberty*, by someone called Dominic Raab, who is said to be the brains behind David Davis. His first chapter is a history of liberty and it is quite a competent history until a paragraph on 1628, and then it segues immediately into 1689. He doesn't mention the entire period between 1630 and 1660! It is astonishing that this country even today still cannot cope with the idea that anything good could come from cutting off the head of the only monarch who ever cared about culture.

When we talk about liberty, you know, republicanism is the elephant in the room. We have to square our belief in sex equality and religious equality and non-discrimination in a democratic or meritocratic society with the idea of a white Anglo-German Protestant monarchy, which, thanks to the genes of Sophie, the Electress of Hanover – winner in 1701 of Britain's top sperm competition – currently occupies the head of state of this country.

Secure freedom is the only freedom there is
QUENTIN SKINNER

Our topic is liberty in relation to republicanism and sovereignty. But I want to address this issue in general terms as well as historically, because I think it is worth making a contrast between what has come to be thought of, in our tradition, as a republican way of thinking about freedom, and consequently about sovereignty, and a view that can I think best be described as liberal in character.

Let me begin by going back to the crucible of these contrasting ideas in the English Revolution of the seventeenth century. The Levellers offer us one instance, although not the only one, of a political group who adopt what I am calling a republican theory of freedom. We need to start, however, by recognising that the republicans agree with their opponents in the 17th century, and with the liberal tradition as it has developed, that if we are focusing on freedom we are examining a concept which they already describe as a 'negative' one. The presence of freedom, they all agree, is always marked by an absence of something – hence 'negative'. So the question for all these theorists is --the absence of what makes the presence of freedom? And that's where our traditions have divided.

One answer, and the one that has become hegemonic in the modern liberal tradition, is that the absence which marks the presence of freedom must be absence of some interference with some power of yours to act in some determinate way. If your freedom has been taken away from you, then there must be something which you can do which you are being prevented from doing, and that element of interference is what marks your lack of freedom. The interference can be physical and bodily, but it is usual in the liberal tradition to argue that coercion of the will is what basically takes away your freedom. But whatever form of impediment is being discussed, the key assumption is always that, in the absence of some such act of interference, we cannot speak of any loss of liberty.

This analysis of freedom in terms of the absence of impediments is what the republican and Leveller traditions contest. There is a great moment in the Leveller tradition when John Lilburne emerges in the historical record as a petitioner for his rights. He has been falsely imprisoned on the order of the House of Lords and writes a tract about his right under Magna Carta to be released. He is sharply told by Richard Overton in the *Remonstrance of Many Thousand Citizens,* July, 1646 that 'Magna Carta is but a beggarly thing.' Overton's point is that Lilburne has not understood what really matters about freedom if he thinks that what matters is his rights.

There you have the moment of division: what matters for the Levellers and the republicans of the English Revolution is that that talk of rights misidentifies what it is that creates unfreedom. They regard loss of rights as a mere surface manifestation of a far deeper affront to liberty. The reason for this commitment is that, according to the republican theorists, the real affront to freedom arises not when you are subjected to interference, but when you are made dependent upon the will of arbitrary powers – the arbitrary powers of monarchy – or, in Lilburne's case, the arbitrary powers of arrest which have been taken over by the House of Lords. These theorists agree, of course, that if you are impeded in the exercise of your rights, that limits your liberty of action. But what fundamentally takes away freedom, they want to insist, is the mere existence of arbitrary power, and hence the entrenchment of relations of domination and dependence.

The crucial distinction between the two traditions - and this is really what I most want to say - arises at this precise point. According to the republican account, your freedom can be taken away from you even if there is no interference. That is something which, I think, people still have difficulty in understanding. How can my freedom have been taken away from me if there has been no interference with my powers? And specifically, no interference with my rights?

The answer given in the English Revolution was that there are two ways in which your freedom can be undermined even if there is no interference with your rights. One is that, if there is arbitrary power that goes beyond the law –

for example an arbitrary power of imprisonment – or any arbitrary power that is imposed where you haven't consented to the terms of that power, then you are not being treated as a free agent. You are not in a space of argument in which you are being offered reasons and are able to accept them as reasons (or not) for what is being

> "...the real affront to freedom arises not when you are subjected to interference, but when you are made dependent upon the will of arbitrary powers..."

done. So, crucially you do not freely consent or refuse to give your consent, because your consent is not sought. The reason why you have lost your freedom is, as they like to put it, that you are being treated not as a free person but a slave. That is why the vocabulary of slavery becomes so central to the Leveller and Republican case in the English Revolution. If there is arbitrary power, then our wills depend upon it, and if you depend on the will of somebody else, that is what it is to be a slave.

The second point – in which, in the English Revolution the Republicans were more interested than the Levellers is that, if you are subject to arbitrary power then you are very likely to self-censor. Self-censoring in the face of arbitrary power is a second way in which the mere existence of that power undermines your freedom. It is not that you know you are going to be interfered with if you do something challenging or subversive. It is that you don't know. And again, that is the position of the slave. You never know what is going to happen to you. But the problem, as Milton says in *The Ready and the Easy Way*, is that then there will be no speaking truth to power. There will only be the abjection of a defeated nation. There will be cringing and bending of the knee. People will cease, in other words, to speak and act freely.

So, there's the second point. No interference has taken place, but liberty has been undermined. By way of illustrating, let me be deliberately anachronistic for a moment. Suppose you are a journalist and you want to broadcast or write something challenging, but it's not clear what might happen to you if you did. It is not clear that anything bad will necessarily happen, but you are very likely to think – nevertheless, I'll play safe. The point that the 17th century writers I have been mentioning want to underline is that this is to behave as a slave.

If the very existence of arbitrary power takes away freedom, what should those who value freedom be doing about it? Surely the main thing we have to do is to abolish arbitrary powers which have not been consented to at least by the represented will of the purportedly sovereign people. So the monarchy has to go, the non-elected element in the House of Lords has to go, all ministerial discretion with respect to statute has to go. Furthermore, your most fundamental rights will have to be enshrined beyond the power even of the elected legislature to tamper with them. So there must be a written constitution. There you have four features of a constitutional revolution which were proposed at the time of the establishment of the English Republic in 1649, none of which we have yet managed to put in place.

> "...then there will be no speaking truth to power. There will only be the abjection of a defeated nation. There will be cringing and bending of the knee."

I want to finish with one word about something which is constantly reiterated by liberal critics of the republican claims I have tried to lay out. It is that, in circumstances of crisis, you must of course be willing to give up some of your freedom in the name of security. Notice that, according to republicans, by contrast with liberals, that is a false dichotomy. What the republican is telling you is that, unless you have security for your liberty, you don't have liberty. There isn't a dichotomy between liberty and security – secure freedom is the only freedom there is. So to be asked to give up the security of your freedom is to be asked to give up your freedom. And that's the Leveller case. Thanks very much.

Levellers and the good life
MELISSA LANE

I want to make three perhaps progressively less familiar points. The least unfamiliar develops Quentin Skinner's point about freedom requiring the control or the consent of the represented will. Not only the fact of control by elected representatives, but the nature of that control, is a major Leveller concern which has clear ramifications for politics today. For the Levellers, that wasn't just about controlling executive privilege. It wasn't just *any* represented will, but will represented in a very strictly controlled way. Characteristically, they were as much, perhaps even more, concerned with the method of electing parliament and controlling the legislative as they were with controlling the executive. Indeed, it was through control of the legislative that it was thought it would become impossible for the corruption and the temptation of power to take root. So, at various times they called for annual parliaments or biennial parliaments; for a quiver of classical models such as the rotation of offices; removal and scrutiny of ministers and officers designed to check 'corrupt interests'; a ban on term limits so that no MP could serve in successive Parliaments.

That might spark us today to think about the need to control the privileges and advantages of incumbency, for example: also to think about the importance of individual MP accountability, not shielding behind their party. I was very struck this morning when Helena Kennedy proposed that one mechanism to try and take this Convention forward is for people to ask searching questions in the processes of selection of MPs coming up before the next general election. That intervention in the legislative is a crucial opportunity and method of control.

Indeed, this again reminds us that we have become very accustomed in both this country and the United States, to thinking about liberty as nourished by the culture of opposition and the culture of civil society: we have tended to forget about the very important roots of electoral power. Electoral power is the fundamental source of power, and the electoral mechanism is therefore a fundamental means that needs to be exploited in order to defend liberty.

My second point will sound less familiar in relation to the Levellers, and perhaps a little anachronistic. But I hope to persuade you that this is not so. It is a thought about post-partisanship. Scholars, including David Wootton and Jonathan Scott, have pointed out that the Levellers did not constitute themselves as a distinct party, preparing for power, or even see themselves as a distinct ideology which might be set against rival ideologies contending for power. Scott comments (in England's Troubles: *Seventeenth-Century English Political Instability in European Context*, Cambridge University Press, p.270) that 'As a public phenomenon, "Levellerism" must be first understood as an activity' - the activities of petitioning, pamphleteering, publishing, agitating and mediating. They saw the principles they were defending as those of all like-minded (right-thinking) people, certainly of Parliament as a whole in the age of its innocence, before it tasted the temptation of arbitrary and absolutist power from 1642 onward. Their principles were not primarily a programme for using power (though they did agitate for the relief of the indigent and hard-pressed, and of course for specific benefits for the New Model Army). They rather sought to define the proper relation to power, the framework, the constitution of power and its limits.

What might this non- or post-partisanship suggest today? One's thoughts turn inevitably to President Obama and the aspiration and travails of his aim to transcend or tame partisanship in the United States. But there, the structural necessity of bipartisan negotiation within Congress and often between Congress and the Presidency, coupled (paradoxically? or for that very reason?) with the far more vitriolic and strident tone of partisanship in the public culture, makes the American example of only limited relevance. Indeed, whereas President Obama's call for post-partisanship at least makes sense in the American context, such a call might seem to be structural anathema in Britain, where partisanship itself plays an important and honoured role in structuring the division of power between Government and Opposition and also, to a great extent, in its responsible and accountable use in office. And yet one of the most striking aspects of today's Convention is its non- or post-partisanship: the fact that it is deliberately drawing on speakers and ideas from across the whole political spectrum.

By saying 'we', however, I also mean to indicate the limits of post-partisanship. It cannot (as President Obama too is discovering) be allowed to become an excuse for lack of principle, for softening or abandoning core values. As has been said today already: of course the defence of liberty is a much easier and a much more characteristic project to adopt in opposition. It is very difficult, however, not to succumb to the temptations to abandon it when in government. Here, we need to think of institutional devices, instances of what one philosopher would call 'self-binding'. We need to think of ways to get the parties to commit themselves while in Opposition in such a way that it can be made too costly and embarrassing for them to renege on those undertakings. There might be a variety of institutional forms of 'self-binding' to make their commitments more credible and also to give people more opportunity to hold them to account. I think that actually is a message from the Levellers.

> "That might spark us today to think about… the importance of individual MP accountability, not shielding behind their party."

The defence of liberty is best understood as an oblique axis in British politics, running through each of the parties and forcing each of them to take a stand on how they will reconfigure their ideologies and platforms to respect it. Not everyone is committed to that defence, however, and its friends must recognise that it has real enemies, even as they reach out to each other across party lines. As for the Levellers, the defence of liberty should be seen not as a partisan programme, but as a structuring principle, a presumption, an orientation: a commitment which rules certain possibilities absolutely out of bounds, while directing attention to the systematic effects of others on the universe of liberties which we value.

The notion of the 'we' brings me toward my final point. Here I want to respond to the Chair, Paul Lay's invitation in his introduction to us to think about religion and the Levellers. My final point is about the linking of the cause of liberty to wider social ideals, how the Levellers did that, and why I think it is important today. The 'we' of the Levellers was of course different from ours in very many ways : the 'we' of an overwhelmingly Christian society, a 'we' who argued passionately for freedom of worship from the standpoint of the recognised and ineradicable (except on pain of hypocrisy forced by compulsion) diversity of belief among the Christian churches and sects. That argument for religious freedom and pluralism is both tantalisingly parallel to our own concerns with pluralism today and tantalisingly far from it. But there is at least one respect in which I think we can learn from it, and this is the urgent need to embed the defence of liberty, as the Levellers did, within wider social ideals.

If the republican content and knowledge of the Levellers has only recently been fully recognised, it has long been known that all of them were serious and committed believing Christians, whose engagement in politics was structured by their grappling with the implications of the proper understanding of their faith: Walwyn began by writing on religion, Lilburne ended as a quietist Quaker. In their politically active period, theirs was a practical Christianity, which was, as Walwyn put it, a religion of love ('love makes you no longer your own but God's servant', quoted in Andrew Sharp, *The English Levellers*, Cambridge University Press, 1998, p.xix), and a fused Christian-classical notion of the 'public good' was the standard to which they repeatedly appealed: as Lilburne's broadsheet of 1645 argued – 'the letter [of the law] kills', whereas it is the spirit of equity, defined as 'the public good', which 'gives life to authority' (Sharp, pp.3-4). Leveller writers constantly invoked the public good: the purpose of consenting to government can only be the good, not the harm, of the people (Lilburne, *The Freeman's Freedom*, in Sharp, p.31). Liberty was justified by God's purposes and the nature of His creation, and it served those purposes, even as it was demarcated according to classical models.

> "...the liberty movement itself needs to celebrate... those who make use of their liberty to serve the welfare of others and to advance broad social ideals..."

Again, the Levellers' own broad social philosophy is not one that most of us can share today. But I want to close by saying why articulating some sort of broad social philosophy - one that can make sense of liberty as a shared social value - is so important if the movement to defend liberty is to succeed. As central to the Levellers as their defence of liberty, was their vision of how liberty could be best employed. They struck a chord in their own society because they were able to articulate what many people cared about, and why they cared about it: their many contemporaries who saw themselves as freeborn children of God could understand the value of religious toleration, for example, in the light of their own highest values.

In recent years, however, the defence of liberty has risked becoming - under pressure of circumstances - oppositional and isolated, involved in defending a bare list of rights, not a social outlook which connects with people's wider values. The Levellers' pluralist defence of liberty in defence of a broad and inclusive social good as they understood it, has been replaced in our day with a neutral defence of liberty, isolating it from any wider or deeper social values. Even the list of martyrs is telling: very often today the celebrated cases of **defending liberty are defending those with whom most people in society have little sympathy** - the rights of people who may sympathise with terrorism but not engage in it, for example. Now, of course, we all agree with Voltaire that we may disagree with people but we will defend to the death their right to say it. I don't at all mean to say that such cases are not important, or should be abandoned. But contrast such cases with the Levellers' most frequent martyrs for the cause, Sir John Maynard or John Lilburne, who was himself a hero of the ideas and values that they themselves believed in, using his liberty to argue for what he and his fellows understood as the social good. These were people who were actually living up to the very ideals that the movement itself was espousing. They were admired.

To win genuine popular resonance, the liberty movement itself needs to celebrate not just the liberty to do what others don't like, but also those who make use of their liberty to serve the welfare of others and to advance broad social ideals - to show that, while we will defend the liberty of everyone, we most value the liberty which is used to help others, not to harm them. Otherwise liberty risks becoming seen as a cause only of the marginal, the eccentric, the disagreeable. While it is indeed their cause, it is also everyone's cause, and in the service of everyone's good. The moral is not to defend only the freedom of those whom we admire, but it is to link the active defence of the liberty of all with a story of why liberty is to be valued and how it features in the good life and good society. One unsung lesson of reflecting on the Levellers is that, while liberty unused is at risk of being lost, liberty used (or seen publicly to be used) only for values which people do not respect or share, is at risk of being too easily devalued.

Session 6
Torture and the Decline in Fundamental Human Rights Standards
SUPPORTED BY CAGEPRISONERS

Prior to 9/11, the idea that the United Kingdom (UK) and its closest allies would be complicit in the rendition and torturing of detainees would have been unthinkable. But seven years on from the launch of the so-called 'War on Terror', that is where we find ourselves. The recent case of Binyam Mohamed has exposed a continued reluctance on the part of the United States (US) and the UK to face up to their professed commitments, with both states collaborating to suppress politically embarrassing information on the treatment of detainees, interrogation techniques and rendition.

How did we find ourselves in such murky territory? Is the wider decline in our human rights standards a result of crossing that boundary that was once thought absolute? How do we ensure we stay true to our ideals whilst defending ourselves against the threats we face?

Jacqui Smith vs. Mitting
VICTORIA BRITTAIN

I am very sorry that Dominic Grieve isn't here. Wasn't it terrific to hear him say how upset he was about Binyam Mohamed this morning? I wanted to ask him - but the chair didn't take my hand - how come this was news to him, when the question of torture in Guantanamo has been written about for seven years? Moazzam has written his book, and spoken in every town in England, dozens of times, and somehow we didn't quite get Dominic Grieve's attention. I chatted to him afterwards and he said it was very unfair for me to characterise him as not having been interested, he was very interested and he was sorry he hadn't come to any of our meetings at the House of Commons or elsewhere. I then said, 'Well, as you're so interested, I was also a bit disappointed that you didn't mention the other British resident who has been so badly tortured in Guantanamo and who has five British children and a British wife, Shaker Aamer' and he clapped his hand to his forehead and said 'I'm terribly sorry'. He has now agreed to take up his case: so one thing has been achieved today - we've got a Conservative on our side who wasn't before.

Anyway, the other very wonderful intervention this morning was Lord Bingham's speech. For those of you who weren't there, I'll just summarise one of the things he said that is so pertinent to this session. He talked about the 1947 committee led by Lord Sankey which took evidence from all the different parts of British society, asking what Second World War was about, what were we fighting for? Among the things that they came up with was that secret evidence is not ever permissible. And the second thing was that nobody can ever be held for more than three months without trial. Well I'm going to talk today about people who have been held in Britain for seven years without any trial, and who have no prospects of any trial.

You may have read a recent report from the International Commission of Jurists (ICJ) on terrorism, counter-terrorism and human rights. It's very detailed and it highlighted three things that immediately concern us here. The first is that cruel, inhuman and degrading treatment is illegal and unacceptable. Secondly, raw intelligence has started to be accepted as a substitute for evidence. And thirdly, the fact that the Executive has accrued power alongside a weakening of the legislature. I won't detain you on that one because it was extensively dealt with this morning.

What I want to underline is the final point of the ICJ report: a recommendation that there should be a complete review of counter-terrorism laws and practices and, in particular, our Secret Immigration Court (SIAC), and the question of secret evidence. In audiences like this, where you all have voices and some of you are in positions of great influence, I think we can really begin to put these very targeted things on the agenda of the Dominic Grieves of this world.

This very week there was a hearing in SIAC, in which Justice Mitting ruled against the Home Secretary, Jacqui Smith. She had requested the revoking of bail for five, what she calls, 'terrorist suspects'. Now, these are among the people I've talked about who have been held for seven years, never having known what they're accused of, never having been in court. Five of these men were in court to see if their bail was revoked. Justice Mitting, by the end of a very long day, including some long sessions of closed evidence, ruled against the Home Secretary. He laid out a timetable when he would hear these cases starting next week. In the meantime he refused her request that they should be immediately arrested, so we all left thinking - a great day. On the way home, those who had been in court were arrested, and those who hadn't been in court were arrested in their homes. Can anything more illustrate why we're here in this meeting?

The following day (yesterday), Mitting sat again in the same court, but rather brilliantly reconstituted himself. Instead of holding a SIAC hearing (because there's no appeal to SIAC), he sat as a High Court judge. And he ruled against the Home Secretary's overnight arrests in four out of the five cases. If you want to see the interplay between the Judiciary and the Executive in a nutshell, Jacqui Smith vs. Mitting sums it up for me. I wrote it up in the *Guardian's* Comment is Free and, instead of the abusive torrent I usually get, the first three comments all said, more or less, 'Home Secretary, you couldn't make it up, how could this have been happening in our country?' So I was very happy about that. But the deportation bail conditions that those five men were on - which are very similar to control orders - although everyone is devised slightly differently, put some people on 20 hour a day house arrest. One of those five men is on a 24 hour a day house arrest. I'll let that just sink in for a second.

These lives have everything squeezed out of them by rules of deportation and control orders which include wearing an electronic tag, not being allowed visitors who have not been vetted by the Home Office, and - in one case I know - only one visitor is allowed at a time. If a visitor speaks a different language to the detainee, a translator is not allowed. As far as children are concerned, they cannot have internet at home for schoolwork or any other purpose. And just to show you how cruel, inhuman, degrading and indeed petty these rules are, I want to mention one family, where there are five kids, all of whom are high achieving. Their father is a) illiterate and b) disabled. They live in a maisonette with a computer upstairs, but are not allowed internet on the computer in case this man should go upstairs and somehow use it to organise a terrorist plot.

> "This is cruel, inhuman and degrading treatment British-style, and if you're interested in knowing the texture of these people's lives, I've written a long report..."

Lastly, there are financial sanctions. This means that people have been designated, by this country, as terrorist suspects who might use their money for some nefarious purpose. They are never told what that purpose might be, but are immediately prevented from having any money of their own. Their wives have to take over all their financial responsibilities. If you could visit some of these families and see what a transformation this causes both in gender relations and in the children's situation, you would be shocked and ashamed that we allow this to go on. And again, they have no idea what it is that is being held against them or when or if ever anyone will tell them what they are supposed to have done wrong.

These regimes will never end, as far as these people know. They've been in and out of Belmarsh, Long Lartin, house arrest now, as I said, for seven years. The only exit open to them is to go back to the countries where they were originally tortured, so you won't be surprised when I tell you that, among these cases, there are three people who have repeatedly tried to commit suicide. There are two men who now, more or less, live in wheelchairs, and a third who lives permanently in a mental hospital.

This is cruel, inhuman and degrading treatment British-style, and if you're interested in knowing the texture of these people's lives, I've written a long report which can be obtained through the Institute of Race Relations website. I think they've made it free to download.

These people are important to all of us because they are iconic victims of the War on Terror: they are powerless, invisible, often known as Mr U, Mr X, Mr Y, apart from one whose case you probably know, who has been demonised by the media with the assistance of security services special briefings, and with the extremely helpful interventions of Jacqui Smith. Her interventions about how glad she is when this man loses a case and how unhappy she is when the court in Europe freezes his deportation are, I think, completely inappropriate for anybody in the position of Home Secretary.

A desire to seek justice
MOAZZAM BEGG

Good afternoon, everyone. It's been an amazing week. It began, for me, with news of the release of Binyam Mohamed whom I had the pleasure of spending several days with over the past week. At the same time, another man, from Qatar, came to the United Kingdom to seek legal representation from Gareth Peirce for his brother, who is the only enemy combatant held in the United States of America. He was held in a British detention centre for five days before being returned to Qatar. He was also a Guantanamo Bay detainee for six years and eight months. Last month, he took part with me and a former American soldier in a tour called *Two Sides - One Story*, when former Guantanamo detainees and an American soldier who guarded prisoners in Guantanamo toured together around the country. We did a House of Lords press conference when he first arrived, so he'd already been in the United Kingdom. Yet, bizarrely, he [the Qatari] was not allowed in a second time. The reason they gave for this was that they alleged that he hadn't told people that he had been in Guantanamo Bay, which was bizarre. So he was returned.

You may have heard on the BBC of the case of Ali al-Marri, who has now, after seven years, been charged.

Today, this event is called the Convention on Modern Liberty, but I want to tell you about a convention of ancient liberty called habeas corpus. Habeas corpus is enshrined in the Magna Carta, that great institution of Britishness, one of those British roots which we - Muslims especially - are urged to know all about in order to integrate ourselves into society properly. So, it is bizarre that on the day that I was taken, in front of my wife and children in Pakistan, with a gun to my head, by CIA agents and Pakistani intelligence agents, that within hours, my wife, through the courts in Pakistan, had had a habeas corpus writ issued in Pakistan. This great right of habeas corpus is no longer confined to people here in the United Kingdom or the United States of America, but reaches out to third world countries like Pakistan. It might not work very well, but at least theoretically, it's part of the several legal systems. It didn't amount to anything though, because I wasn't released as a result of any habeas corpus proceedings in Pakistan, the UK, or in Guantanamo Bay. It was only after the embarrassment caused by letting the British Government know, and the British people know, that British citizens were being tortured by the Americans with British intelligence's complicity, that I was released.

During his visit, Al-Marri was also hoping to see Binyam Mohamed. One of the things Binyam doesn't like to talk about, although it's been talked about a lot, is the torture that he had to undergo in Pakistan, in Morocco and in Guantanamo Bay, before he was returned to the United Kingdom. He's terribly emaciated and weak-looking, but he's strong of heart. That has been my experience and that of most of the people that I've seen that have passed through this great test. The system attempts to break them down, to remove all sense of hope. So it seems bizarre and shocking that they come out of all of this filled not with rage or bitterness, but with a sense of bewilderment, relief, and a desire to seek justice for those who remain behind. The only way to do

> "...if people are patting themselves on the back because they think Guantanamo is coming to a close, they should take a look at the secret detentions process."

that, sadly, is to broadcast what took place in your own case. They don't want to hear you talking about other people. They do want to hear you talking about yourself. So you can't let go. You can't put it behind you: it has to continue. The torture, both physical and mental, continues in that sense. It continues for a lot of us and will have to continue for Binyam if he wants his case brought out into the public arena which I think everybody realises and recognises is going to cause a great deal of embarrassment for the British government.

But Binyam Mohamed is a British resident, not a citizen and there's been all this argument: 'Why should these so-called "residents" be brought back to this country? Who are they?' Well, first of all, because they were given political asylum in the first place. The reason why the asylum cases have been reviewed is because, being held in detention, they were not able to be present for the reviews that took place. But I am a British citizen. So, there is no doubting my position. And I am here to tell you, and the press, and everybody else, and have done so for the past four years, that I was held with the full complicity and knowledge of members of the British intelligence services that I had encountered in the United Kingdom. They were from MI5, not MI6, which is an important distinction, because it shows that the people who were working on these issues at home, were ready to go abroad to learn lessons from what took place in the War on Terror, including the cruel, inhuman and degrading treatment of British citizens. That happened in Pakistan. It happened in Bagram. It happened in Kandahar and it happened in Guantanamo Bay.

As British citizens and British residents, even before the return of Binyam Mohamed, we have already brought a case to the courts accusing the British intelligence services, including the Attorney General, of complicity in our detention, false imprisonment and torture. If people are now jumping on the Guantanamo Bay bandwagon, that's welcome. But people like me have been campaigning for those held without charge or trial for years, and finding it hard to get an ear to listen to them. Now that it's the 'in' thing, the fashionable thing to talk about – perhaps Guantanamo's days are numbered. The most powerful man on earth has said, within the first two days of his presidency, that he will close it, before he spoke about anything else.

But I'm here to tell you that there is a whole process that one has to pass through before anyone ever gets to Guantanamo Bay. By the time I passed through this process, I was actually looking forward to going to Guantanamo! So if people are patting themselves on the back because they think Guantanamo is coming to a close, they should take a look at the secret detentions process. Extraordinary rendition has not been addressed by the American President. Military detention sites at Bagram, Kandahar, and Abu Ghraib have not been addressed by the American President. If we are to believe what we hear - that a significant increase of troops in Afghanistan is likely to take place - that means by definition that there will be more prisoners in the Bagram detention facility where I personally saw two people get killed, as was featured in last year's Oscar-winning documentary, *Taxi to the Dark Side*.

This is the reality. And if that is the case in Guantanamo Bay, and Bagram, and the other places, then imagine what it's like over here, the land of habeas corpus. That person who was still held after his deportation order was blocked, has been held in this country in fact for nine years, not seven years. And a lot of the evidence that's being used to hold these people has been justified by the use of secret courts.

Now, secret courts in the UK may be a relatively new thing, except perhaps for what happened during the period of the Irish 'Troubles'. But in Guantanamo Bay, Combatant Status Review Tribunals were held in a secret court which justified our continued detention in Guantanamo, with secret evidence. The finger has been pointed over there. But it's about time that we started looking over here, right in our own backyard, to see what is really happening in this great land that exported habeas corpus to the rest of the world as a civilising factor. Thank you.

Torture is absolutely wrong
EDWARD FITZGERALD QC

I wanted to talk on the phenomenon of deportation to torture regimes and deportation with assurances, but obviously, it's all part of the wider phenomenon Moazzam Begg has talked about: the doctrine that in the so-called 'War on Terror', 'the normal rules of the game', in the words of Tony Blair, 'have changed' - that the basic rules of justice don't apply; the Geneva Convention can be dismissed as quaint or obsolete; and that the European Court rulings and principles can be said to be out of touch leading to cause for amendment of the European Convention, or replacement of it by something else.

It is all part of this notion which has led to the degrading of international law, the degrading of human rights principles and then Bagram, Abu Ghraib, Guantanamo and the whole policy of extraordinary rendition - expounded on by Tony Blair in his 12 points of July 2005. He basically said: 'The rules of the game have changed, we're just going to tear up the obsolete old human rights principles and from now on start to deport to torture regimes. We'll get assurances and, if the judges object, if the European Court objects, we will amend the Human Rights Act and we will, if necessary, pull out of the Human Rights Convention.'

It's important that we resist that. It is still this issue - the issue of deporting terror suspects (because that's what they are; suspects) to torture regimes - which has led to the suggestion, from both sides of the House of Commons, from the Labour Party and also from Tories (indeed, from David Cameron at one stage), that the Human Rights Act should be amended or repealed, and that, instead, we should introduce some new Bill of Rights which balances national security on the one hand, against the rights of the terror suspect not to be tortured on the other. The suggestion is made whenever there's some ruling in favour of a terror suspect, and against deportation to a terror regime.

Why can't we just send the ideologues of hatred back, they ask. They represent a threat to us. Who cares if they go back and they're tortured in Syria, or Libya, or Jordan: that's not our business. And the only answer to that is, because they are human beings. Torture is absolutely wrong. We have signed up to the United Nations (UN) Convention against Torture which commits us in Article 3: not to extradite and not to deport where there is a real risk of torture. We cannot expel, we cannot extradite people who face a real risk of torture. If I could just trace the first three key steps, as it were, beginning with the Chahal vs. United Kingdom decision of the European Court of Human Rights, much condemned by politicians. That decision ruled that even if someone has been found to be a national security risk, you cannot deport them to a regime or a system where they face a real risk of torture. That has been denounced and the Government have tried to get around Chahal by arguing in a European Court case called Saadi vs. Italy, that Chahal was now obsolete after 9/11 and the July bombings, and that one had to balance the right not to be tortured against the duty to provide national security.

> "There is absolutely no doubt that Jordan practices torture. Even the Foreign Office…openly gave sworn evidence to that effect. But nonetheless, it said, we can accept the assurances."

The European Court rejected that. It said: no, this is an absolute principle; it's a principle that 154 countries have all signed up to in the UN Convention against Torture. The test is this: is there a real risk of torture? And if there is, it doesn't matter what you're suspected of, it doesn't matter what findings are made in secret tribunals or in hearsay evidence or whatever it is, you have the right to be protected against that.

The next attempt to get around Chahal, we all know, was Belmarsh. They said, 'Alright. We can't extradite or deport to torture regimes. But we will lock-up indefinitely, in this country, without trial, those who we would like to deport, but can't deport'. And that was the first step in this procedure of eroding the basic rule of law.

The House of Lords held that response to be disproportionate, arbitrary and contrary to Article 5 of the European Convention. So, after that ruling, the Government didn't seek to bring back Belmarsh. Instead, they have brought in

> "...if the judges object, if the European Court objects, we will amend the Human Rights Act and we will, if necessary, pull out of the Human Rights Convention."

control orders which, as Victoria Brittain said, can include detention in your house for up to 16 hours a day, plus effective internal exile and incredible restrictions on who you can see, who you can talk to, what you can do. Again, all this is on the basis, very often, of evidence that you haven't seen and that you have no opportunity to challenge.

But after the July bombings, one then had this new initiative: 'Alright. We're going to go back and look at the Chahal principle again. And this time we are going to deport to torture regimes: but we're going to deport with assurances.' The reasoning goes like this: we're now great friends with Colonel Gaddafi, we have Libyan suspects in this country, we will deport to Libya because Colonel Gaddafi has promised us that, when they get there, these suspects, who are sworn enemies of his, will not be killed or tortured. Moreover, he set up a human rights organisation to monitor that. That organisation is run by his son. That was the reasoning behind the argument that it is legitimate to deport which was put forward and defended by the Foreign Office.

Now again, when the courts said no, there were howls of protest from the Home Office and indeed from some sections of the press. There was this talk of, 'Well, if the courts won't let us send people back to Libya who we regard as terror suspects to torture if necessary, then we must amend the Human Rights Act'. All the Human Rights Act had done was to enshrine and enforce a principle which 154 countries have signed up to, and which we also signed up to, under a Tory government, when we committed ourselves to the Convention against Torture.

As you know, though the court stopped the deportation of the Libyan cases, in the case of Jordan and in the case of Algeria, a different conclusion has been reached. It is said that these assurances can be accepted, and therefore people can be deported to regimes which undoubtedly practice torture. There is absolutely no doubt that Jordan practices torture. Even the Foreign Office accepts that and openly gave sworn evidence to that effect. But nonetheless, it said, we can accept the assurances, we can accept a body, a human rights monitoring body which had never been heard of before but was created for that purpose, to ensure that the person being returned will not be tortured.

I just want to say three things about this policy of relying on assurances. Firstly, if there is a country which practices systematic torture, you cannot rely on that country saying: 'We'll carry on torturing everybody else, but we'll leave this person out of it'. The European Court, having failed abysmally in a case where they accepted assurances from Uzbekistan, is beginning to point to the principle of international law that, if there is systematic torture being practiced, you cannot accept assurances from that country. In a recent case called Ismoilov vs. Russia, this seems to have been recognised.

The second point is, proponents of this argue, 'We can monitor this. We can send in Foreign Office officials to see if the person is being tortured'. But the whole nature of the exercise is clandestine and frequently you have situations where monitors are being told: 'He doesn't want to see you today', or 'We have no desire to see you'. That happened in a case in Egypt, where, as a result, the Swedish diplomat simply failed to monitor that the no torture assurances were being kept. But because it's clandestine, deniable, and because they have control of those in the prison, you simply can't rely on those assurances.

The third point is, there's nothing you can do about it, once the person has been tortured. You can protest, but, in the end, the desirability of having good relations with a country will always be more important than any serious diplomatic sanctions if there is non-compliance. And so, my view is that the whole enterprise that started with Tony Blair's 12 points is completely wrong. But the European Court and Article 3 of the UN Convention provide some basic protection to which one can have appeal. And the idea that is being floated that, instead of clinging to the sheet anchor of international law principle and the Human Rights Act, we should get rid of the Human Rights Act and replace it with this Tory suggestion of some Bill of Rights which - God knows what it's going to include, but presumably it is going to allow for deportation to torture because that's why they're recommending it, to get around these kinds of decisions - is, I think, deeply flawed. Problematic as the European Convention still is (it probably would permit control orders for a certain period of time), it is at least a bedrock of principle to which we have signed up, underlined by the UN Convention. To abandon those principles and give way to security at any cost, over rights, would be a disaster.

So, this is a plea to continue to defend the principles that we have; in all situations to condemn torture as wrong; and to say that this isn't something that we should acquiesce in or connive at, or facilitate, by deporting people into those situations.

Session 7
Are Human Rights Universal or a Privilege of Citizenship?
SUPPORTED BY BRITISH INSTITUTE FOR HUMAN RIGHTS, JUSTICE

The Human Rights Act currently protects everyone living in the UK, be they citizen or refugee, asylum seeker or migrant. Would proposals for a British Bill of Rights add to or subtract from this protection? Would it contain rights that are universal? Asylum seekers, refugees and migrants are among the most vulnerable members of our society. Often victims of human rights violations or poor treatment, they have fewer alternative means of protection and often live in poverty. What would be the implications of an exclusive Bill of Rights restricted to British citizens only?

A second major issue is the content of a Bill of Rights: would any existing rights be taken away? A Bill of Rights opens the opportunity to discuss the protection of economic and social rights, such as the right to health, education or shelter, as well as traditional common law rights such as the right to trial by jury. And a British Bill of Rights would not happen in isolation: what would it mean in the context of the international human rights treaties that the UK has already agreed to and ratified, including the European Convention on Human Rights and the UN Convention on the Rights of the Child?

Is this an opportunity to take the international lead on human rights thinking or will it result in a weakened human rights framework, in which the vulnerable lose out?

Bringing socio-economic rights back home
GERALDINE VAN BUEREN

If we are going to prevent the formation of the surveillance state that we have all been talking about today, we really must make human rights more popular. We have to try and make them more familiar to everyone, recognising that some of them are very British indeed, including the forgotten socio-economic rights.

It is true that socio-economic rights are universal: the right to the highest attainable standard of healthcare, the right to an adequate standard of living, the right to work, interestingly. But what has been forgotten is that these are rights that we have had from the medieval ages. While the focus has been on the Magna Carta signed by King John, two years later, his son, King Henry II, signed the Charter of the Forests containing what nowadays are regarded as socio-economic rights: to food, to water, and to an adequate standard of living. The only reason why the Magna Carta was called the 'great charter' was because it was longer in length, not because civil and political rights were supposed to be of a greater value than these. To adapt a British Conservative party slogan, I would like to see a return to traditional British values!

Britain also contributed to socio-economic rights formulation. It was British government officials who helped draft the Universal Declaration of Human Rights that enshrined socio-economic rights. It was British government officials who helped draft the international Covenant on Economic, Social and Cultural Rights, and it is the British Government who are involved in the drafting of the European Social Charter. We need, as Jack Straw might say, to think of a way of bringing them 'back home', to the home of the Charter of the Forests.

How would a British Bill of Rights work if it enshrined socio-economic rights? It would act as a safety net. People would be able to hold government to account when they declared that child poverty can be halved. Child poverty could be tackled through the courts if enshrined in law. If living conditions fall below the adequate, they could also be challenged. At the moment, the only way to challenge this

> "If we are going to prevent the formation of the surveillance state that we have all been talking about today, we really must make human rights more popular."

under the Human Rights Act, is to allege that conditions amount to degrading treatment. What are we saying about British society if we suggest we are content to let people's standard of living, their dignity, fall to that level. 'Degrading' is not the benchmark of a civilised society. And these socio-economic rights would help. They would help the elderly in care homes. It would make it easier to receive life-saving drugs. For although these rights are recognised by the British Government, they have not been brought down into British law.

They are not only legal rights. Very importantly, they would operate as educational and preventative principles for a wide range of occupations, of people working in the public services, so that this really does help create a culture of rights, and crucially, prevent violations of rights. Many countries have found that widening the appeal of human rights in this way helps bolster democracy. I had the privilege of working in South Africa for five years from 2002 and have seen these rights used very effectively by the poorest and most vulnerable people in the community. This has had two effects: firstly, there has developed a great pride in and sense of ownership of the whole range of human rights. If an individual or a group claims rights of access to the highest attainable standard of health - access to a life-saving cancer drug, say – then it benefits everybody who is eligible, and instils a sense of community, because socio-economic rights are based on the principle that 'I am, because you are.' Secondly, it helps change the face of the judiciary. Serving on the bench are those who have experienced poverty issues directly and this widens those who are willing to sit on the bench because they can see a role in helping to alleviate poverty.

But socio-economic rights are not only for the poorest countries. According to the United Nations Committee on the Economic, Social and Cultural Rights (CESCR), the right to adequate housing, for example, includes a duty on the government to make mortgage finance available to those who wish to purchase their homes. What it does is to turn what is currently a political discretion into an effective legal right. Europe has its own socio-economic charter pertinent for

European countries. The revised European Social Charter is the sister-treaty of the European Convention on Human Rights and countries from Portugal to France, the Netherlands and Ireland have allowed collective complaints of their citizens to petition it for rights which have been denied to them. It has been very successfully used and implemented by these governments.

> "These are not idealistic goals. They are rights which have to be progressively implemented according to the maximum available resources."

These are not idealistic goals. They are rights which have to be progressively implemented according to the maximum available resources. 'Progressively' means less waste: funds being spent more efficiently.

So to better protect our human rights in this country, firstly, we have got to consult widely, as Jean Candler said, on what should be in a Bill of Rights. We are falling behind a growing number of countries who are protecting their socio-economic rights - rights that are particularly important as we enter a deep recession. Secondly, the United Kingdom should be lobbied to ratify all the provisions of the European Social Charter, to enable us to petition on a wide range of economic, social and cultural rights where British courts are unable to deal with them. That is a very simple and a very speedy procedure. Thirdly, we should enshrine socio-economic rights in our British Bill of Rights. What we are asking for here is both traditional in Britain, and universal. In other words, this is simply joined up human rights.

'Bringing Socio-Economic Rights Back Home' does not represent the views of the Equality and Human Rights Commission, which has not yet adopted a policy on the incorporation of socio-economic rights.

Liberties with teeth: lions parallel to the throne
ROGER SMITH

One of the great things about today is that it has brought together in coalition those who would say that they believed in and were advocates of human rights, with those who believe in and are advocates of civil liberties. That is a delicate manoeuvre and it is a rather good and unique thing to have done. There are all sorts of difficulties about keeping that coalition going, but for today, it is brilliant.

We have the question: 'Are human rights universal?' Yes they are, because that is how you define them. They come in various shapes and forms and the irreducible minimum, it seems to me, is the human rights which are internationally acknowledged, which your country has signed up to, and which anybody of any sense agrees you must follow, either if you want to, out of principle, or if you don't want principle as the basis – then just pragmatically. Those, for us, are in the European Convention of Human Rights.

We should begin by acknowledging that we wouldn't be having this debate about rights and civil liberties if we didn't have the Human Rights Act. It was an enormous achievement of Labour's first administration to bring this Act in, and as someone who has described himself as a rights lawyer since 1973, when I called myself a welfare rights lawyer, the difference the incorporation of the European Convention has made is huge. My view of what human rights are is that they are liberties with teeth. The teeth are due to the fact that you incorporate these rights in ways which judges (albeit with final authority only at the level of the European Court of Human Rights) will enforce.

> "We should begin by acknowledging that we wouldn't be having this debate about rights and civil liberties if we didn't have the Human Rights Act."

If you went to the session with the Conservative party politicians, it was rather interesting that they each, in a rather Marxist way, had a concept of the individual, the little person, against 'the state'. I wanted to scream, 'Hey, the state is a lot more complicated than that!' The crux of the matter is accountability and we must recognise that the state is not just one thing. Power in this society is held in various different places. I began with welfare rights cases, then judicial review cases in the 1980s, ending up with human rights cases. What I have seen as a practitioner and observed as a citizen in that time is that, if ever there was a coalition around a coherent 'state' under the water of politics in the UK, bits of it are now floating up to the surface. The state is rebalancing itself and one of the elements which is currently rebalancing itself is the judiciary.

> "...we can only have a British Bill of Rights that goes beyond the European Convention if there is political consensus on it. And in a parliamentary democracy, that means cross-party consensus."

One of the first social security cases I remember was when [Lord] Denning said, almost in these terms: 'If this case had been about anything other than social security, I would have insisted on a fair hearing. But hey, this was a tribunal and the standard of adjudication doesn't matter'. Time moved on swiftly and, by the early 1980s, the minute the Government began to use that disreputable argument, you knew you had won. We have moved on since then through a whole series of ways in which incrementally the judges held the executive - locally and centrally - to account and developed mechanisms of accountability. From that point of view, it was a seamless extension when the Human Rights Act came along.

Now the executive is being held to account by human rights norms. The judiciary used to be described historically as 'lions under the throne'. Now they are becoming 'lions parallel to the throne'. I think there is a real challenge here for anyone who is democratically engaged, including politicians, to get parliament up to the same level of equality with the powers of the executive, because the defect of the UK Constitution in the words of Lord Hailsham, is that it is an 'elective dictatorship'. How can you control an executive when, by definition, it is the element with the largest party in a still largely undemocratic parliament?

The state is mutating and changing, and it seems to me healthy that, in the past twenty or thirty years, the courts have played a leading part in accountability. I have three examples of why human rights are universal, why they are a good thing, and why the role of judges makes a difference. First, internment. In the 1940s we interned enemy aliens and someone wanted to challenge that on the grounds that he had been certified as an enemy alien by the Home Secretary and he just wanted an open process of certification. Judges sent him packing back to the Isle of Man. But this is a great contrast with the decision the judges took when they had to look recently at the position of people in Belmarsh: they took a different view. Knowing that the **European Court of Human Rights would agree with the domestic courts**, the Government changed the law.

Take the DNA database which went through Parliament. JUSTICE did briefing after briefing saying that this extension of the database to cover those who had not been charged with anything was outrageous. Did they get anywhere? No. What will make the difference is that the European Court of Human Rights has said that a test of proportionality must be applied to those who are placed on it. In principle, it should exclude the innocent.

Look at torture - a brilliant judgment of our own House of Lords. The common law position was that, in civil cases, you could look at torture-induced evidence. Judges said: 'No. On human rights grounds, we won't hear evidence that has arisen from torture in any event'.

Two points arise. Firstly, a very positive point. We need to keep together civil liberties and human rights. It seems to me that the assertion that there is a difference between them just comes down to the method of enforcement. At one level, that is really important: but we have to hold this coalition together for as long as we can. Secondly, I have a note of caution on the extension of human rights beyond the European Convention. Personally, I'm all for it. I want to be part of a discussion about a right to medical care which is enforceable by the judges, as best we can. But we can only have a British Bill of Rights that goes beyond the European Convention if there is political consensus on it. And in a parliamentary democracy, that means cross-party consensus.

For the present and foreseeable future, you can forget it. The issues are too over-politicised and there will not be consensus on what should be in a

British Bill of Rights. For that reason, I would fall back on the irreducible minimum, the defensible redoubt, the unassailable redoubt. I would hold to the European Convention and the Human Rights Act and celebrate, in a way that David Goodhart probably will not, the potential of the judiciary to assist in upholding what, in almost every other country, would be seen as constitutionally guaranteed rights.

Freedom from want
ANDREW DISMORE MP

Geraldine mentioned she had been in South Africa. As part of our inquiry into the question of a British Bill of Rights on the Joint Select Committee on Human Rights, we too visited South Africa, and Albie Sachs, the famous constitutional court judge, said to me: 'A country without social and economic rights is a country that has given up on aspiration'. I go back to Roosevelt's statement of the four freedoms before the war: the freedom of speech and the freedom of religion – the traditional ones, then the freedom from want and freedom against fear which ultimately became incorporated into the United Nations (UN) Charter, thanks in part to President Roosevelt's wife, and, since then, into a plethora of international conventions.

Today's debates have so far focused very much on negative rights: that is, the civil and political rights where it is the individual against the state, whether it is the right for freedom of expression that shouldn't be interfered with by the state, intrusions into privacy by the state or detention without trial – all very negative things. What we are talking about with socio-economic rights is a positive duty enjoined on the state to actually do something, rather than not do something: on health, education, housing, and an adequate standard of living.

These are very important issues. I was in my constituency surgery this morning, so I didn't get to hear the start of Convention. But when people come into my surgery and thump the table about their rights being infringed, this is usually not about their right to vote, but about

> "In Northern Ireland, they have just published their consultation on a Bill of Rights...All the opinion polling showed that the whole aspect of socio-economic rights... was very popular indeed."

wanting to have a decent council house, or 'I can't get my kids to school', or 'I can't get my kid's Special Needs Assessment done' or 'The National Health Service (NHS) isn't giving me my appointment on time' or 'My benefits have been cut'. These are all issues relating to socio-economic rights which touch everybody, and not just vulnerable people (although particularly vulnerable people), every day of their lives. We take the political and civil rights that today's event is highlighting for granted, since we live in an established democracy. But we also have to look at the more positive side, particularly in an economic downturn.

These rights are of very great importance to the middle classes too. A good example was the Horsham Property case, last autumn. The High Court ruled on a combination of the small print in the Mortgage Deed and the 1925 Property Act, saying that a mortgage company can sell your house over your head if you are just one payment in default of your mortgage, without an order in the court. That turns you into a trespasser in your own home, and you can be evicted without any inquiry into the circumstances. Now the Government has put an awful lot of effort into making housing repossession the last resort, for a court to order proper inquiry into the circumstances: could the mortgage be rescheduled, etc. All that is out of the window because of this case. If we had a basic right to housing that you can't be evicted without an order of court and a proper inquiry, the court would not have been able to come to that conclusion because it would not have been in accordance with the right to housing. On another issue, we are now seeing a lot of middle class people migrating into the state sector of education – I wonder why! – and again, these issues start to become very important.

When we talk about the universality of human rights, some of those who are criticising the whole discourse on the grounds that it favours the vulnerable, might see themselves benefiting from it as well. In Northern Ireland, they have just published their consultation on a Bill of Rights and their recommendations to government. They are ahead of us in the game. All the opinion polling showed that the whole aspect of socio-economic rights and raising that profile was very popular indeed.

To some extent, these rights are emerging already. The UK Government has said that in this current session of Parliament, we are going to have a Bill on Child Poverty. That is essentially putting into statute a social and economic right, and I think it should be incorporated into a Bill of Rights. We have seen the publication of the National Health Service (NHS) Constitution – again a social and economic right. There are arguments about its enforceability. If you look around our legal system you will see all sorts of rights and duties buried in all sorts of statutes. There is no over-arching view that pulls all those together. We have got lots of laws on housing and housing protection, education, and benefits, but no over-arching philosophical statement like a Bill of Rights which can pull the whole thing together in one framework to say: that's what it's all about.

The whole issue of socio-economic rights is on the agenda in a way that it probably wasn't eighteen months ago, despite the fact that - I will say it myself - my Committee has been nibbling away at this for some time. There have been some interesting comments from the Prime Minister which seem to confirm this. In his speech to the 60th anniversary of the UN Declaration to the Equality and Human Rights Commission, what he actually said, as opposed to the public text, was quite interesting: 'There is an indivisibility of civil and political rights and social and economic rights. They go together'. You won't find that in the published text, but that is what he said, and it might well be what he believes. You can see that we are swimming with the mainstream, in the Government's response to our own report on the British Bill of Rights and Freedoms, as we called it.

> "We don't have to have 'direct enforceability' because I think that encroaches on significant areas where elected politicians should be taking the decisions."

The real issue here is enforceability. And this may be where to an extent I part company with Geraldine, because I am a politician. The real question is this: to what extent should these rights be individually enforceable through the courts and to what extent should they be enforced through other means? We have tried in our report to square that circle. There is a real difficulty in giving the courts the role of politicians to decide on the allocation of resources. It is our job to decide how much tax you should pay and where the money should go. That is not to say that we can't have an indirect enforceability of these rights. The courts are public bodies and when interpreting the law - as in the Horsham Property case I just mentioned - they should be required to interpret that existing law to give effect to a basic, underpinning Bill of Rights. Had that happened, I don't think they could have come to that conclusion. We could also have what in all the international treaties is called a 'progressive realisation within available resources'. In other words, a duty on the Government to work towards expanding and improving the lot of the people in accordance with the money that is available. That is what I think we will see in the pledge on child poverty.

You can also have a bottom line which says, nobody should fall below this standard. Three examples of this from South Africa's Constitution Report show how it works: in one healthcare case, someone tried to jump the queue for a kidney transplant using their rights to healthcare in the Constitution and they were blown out; a group of women who were pregnant and had HIV Aids were being denied anti-retroviral drugs by a South African government, not on grounds of cost (it was being paid for by overseas donors), but because of President Mbeke's somewhat strange views on Aids, and here the constitutional court reversed that bad policy decision. Lastly, on the bottom line, a group of people were evicted and living on a football pitch with no shelter whatsoever, and in that case, the government was instructed by the courts to provide a basic minimum shelter.

There is no reason why we can't have these in a Bill of Rights. We don't have to have 'direct enforceability' because I think that encroaches on significant areas where elected politicians should be taking the decisions. But this provides a vital underpinning, and provides a way forward for making human rights understandable, popular and of relevance to everybody in this room.

Human rights fundamentalism
DAVID GOODHART

I want to draw the camera back a bit and challenge some of the things that have been said so far. It seems starkly obvious to me that human rights, at least in a non-technical sense, are neither universal nor innate. After all, most people in the world have none, as Geraldine Van Bueren reminded us. We didn't have any rights until a few hundred years ago and we now have a vast number of social and political ones as a result of all sorts of political battles of ideas and technology, but mainly institutions – criminal justice systems, courts, police forces, parliaments and so on. These struggles and institutions are mainly - but not entirely - national, and they declare and enforce rights.

Non-citizens of course, historically, have had rights too, albeit not the same rights as citizens. They now have, partly thanks to the Human Rights Act, a great many more rights. That is partly the result of what we might call the universalist shift of the 20th century. Following two world wars, the Holocaust and decolonisation, there was a general belief - at least among the Western political class - that we had to embrace the previously Utopian religious idea of the moral equality of all human beings. And we did embrace that idea: it was laid out in the UN Declaration of Human Rights, and via that, found its way into our laws and statute books. And we all sign up to that now and rightly so.

But I think that the great fallacy of liberal universalism - or what one might call human rights fundamentalism - is the claim that universal moral equality plus human rights legislation somehow makes the nation state and the national political community increasingly irrelevant. I was reading, as I always do with great interest, Shami Chakrabarti in the *Guardian* the other day. She wrote this sentence: 'In the modern world of transnational and multinational power, we must decide if we are all "people" or all "foreigners" now'. No, we mustn't decide that. We are both and obliterating the distinction in effect obliterates the nation-state and national citizenship. Why on earth would we want to do that when the nation-state has conjured up all the things that we

> **"It seems starkly obvious to me that human rights, at least in a non-technical sense, are neither universal nor innate. After all, most people in the world have none."**

hold most dear: the democratic accountability we have been talking about; the ability of a political community to debate with itself; the welfare state which has existed only in nation states; redistribution; inter-class, and inter-generational solidarity. These are things that might exist to a small extent outside the confines of the nation state, but not to any great extent.

So I would conclude that the moral equality of all human beings must be compatible with special obligations and commitments to fellow citizens. The analogy used to be with the family. Most people do not consider their family morally superior to other families; but they automatically put their interests first. To consider the political community as an extended family may seem rather old fashioned nowadays, and I think it probably is. But still, the idea of fellow-citizenship favouritism is still essential to the workings of the nation-state, and implicit in so many of our political actions. One of my favourite examples is that we spend 28 times as much on the National Health Service (NHS) as on development aid.

To recap so far, most rights are national in origin and they are also contractual and reciprocal and derive from membership of a political community. That seems pretty obvious in the case of social and welfare rights: you pay in through your taxes and you draw out when you need to. But it is also true, I think, of political and legal rights. Now of course, non-members have rights too. But they have rights because we extend those rights to them by signing up to the various European Union (EU) and international human rights norms. However, we must be free not to extend those rights to them, especially when their rights conflict with the rights and well-being of British citizens as they can do sometimes and have done in recent 'terror' cases. This obviously affects the whole tricky business of people's rights to come here and stay here. The Belmarsh case and related cases is a very good example of this dilemma: when there is decisive intelligence information which suggests that people are a serious danger to British citizens, but not sufficient evidence to prosecute them in a British court and they are not British citizens, it seems to me that in most circumstances you should remove these people from the country.

Now to sum up, it seems to me that there are at least three problems with human rights fundamentalism. First, if all humans have essentially the same rights regardless of political community membership, it breaks the bond of citizenship, it destroys something very precious. Second, the rights we claim, are also demands we make on each other. Some of those rights are very costly and therefore imply obligations on other people to pay their taxes and fund those rights. I think that the whole human rights debate presupposes the solidarity and sense of obligation and recognition that it imagines that it creates. The whole human rights discourse is in a sense parasitic on existing commitments and if rights are extended too indiscriminately, they will no longer connect to a felt obligation and the system will gradually unravel. Finally - and perhaps most important of all - I think we are labouring under a legalistic illusion. The idea that all these deeply, deeply political decisions - who gets what, when and where, or the abolition of poverty, or who is allowed to come to Britain and who isn't - can be 'legalised away', taken from the political community and handed to judges and human rights experts, seems to me deeply misguided and reactionary.

> "...if all humans have essentially the same rights regardless of political community membership, it breaks the bond of citizenship, it destroys something very precious."

Session 8
Love and Liberty
SUPPORTED BY RESURGENCE, OPENDEMOCRACY

Love is often seen as an expression of the ultimate personal freedom, as well as the most private personal fate. But does it end there? A body of work is growing in the United States on 'The Love that does Justice', a phrase of Martin Luther King's.

Standing up for sissies
MARINA WARNER

Edward Carpenter is a paradigm of some of the things I want to note today. I believe that the role of artists - in the broadest possible sense, including writers and thinkers - is to try and rebuild the world in the image of our hopes, our dreams, and our desires. As with Sheila Rowbotham, my background lies in the female emancipatory movement of the Sixties, when the underlying principle was that we were going to bring about sexual emancipation. It was a question of sexual liberty for women. That was my formation. So I want to take a few steps back, and look a little at some of the first principles involved in this cultural rethinking of love.

We have to distinguish between the different forms of love. Socrates and Plato after all were profoundly concerned with creating the idea of a polity by examining the connectedness of people in many different relationships, in order to harness the different motives and energies that come from them. Various languages have very different words meaning 'love'. Sheila has just used the phrase, 'beloved community' and this is *agape* in Greek, where it means 'communion', not only of the family, but also of like-minded people who come together to do something. At that point it had nothing to do with *eros*. Then there is the Latin word we are familiar with, *caritas*, which has an underlying tone of sympathy. This is where you experience fellow feelings, when you empathise, project into another, feel with the other, and become equal to them in your projected emotions. Then *amor* itself, which is often thought of as *eros*, includes in its meanings the 'love of children', and not only the love of children for their family and vice versa, but also the love between children. Children experience love, and not only at the erotic stage: we all know how children get very fond of someone and radiate very powerful energy towards them.

So the word which I think is key to the kind of love that we are talking about is 'kin' - not meaning blood kin - but the word which leads to 'kind', to 'kindness' and to 'loving-kindness.'

afternoon sessions

> **"** It is important, in the crisis of our times, that we look at precisely that: how inequality of means affects conditions and our ability to reciprocate."

Is it possible to join up this idea with structures of law and economics and so forth? I think if you look at the field that I work in - fairy tales - you can see how social and legal structures undermine this loving kindness. Sibling rivalry in fairy tales is often driven by poverty. Wicked stepmothers are often active and struggling with a paucity of resources in two rival families: the orphans who survive their dead mother fight with the children of the new families. Fairy tales record these lesions in the social body that is the family. It is important, in the crisis of our times, that we look at precisely that: how inequality of means affects conditions and our ability to reciprocate .

It is important to provide a critique, but we should also remind ourselves of the progress which we have made. One gain we have made in the area of loving emancipation is registered by a family card game I played as a child in the fifties called *Old Maid*. On these slides, you can see how sexualised the nurse and sailor are, but how obvious it is that the one thing not to become in life, and the bad card to get, is 'the old maid'. We have moved on. And the other great legal achievement of recent years is the introduction of civil partnerships. I would like to mention something that I as a Catholic and many other Catholics regard as very wrong, and we have petitioned against it: the idea that disabled people should not have children.

So there have been some gains in the current world. But there are many, many losses too.

In 2010, the Wellcome Institute, a medical foundation, will conduct a census of the United Kingdom's population's sexuality; the questionnaire shows that all affective and emotional experiences are left out of this enquiry. It is only an enquiry into acts; for example paying for sex through the internet will be noted, etc. It will contain nothing about all the other ways that sexuality manifests itself. I don't know how you would set about recording this in a census, but it seems wrong to me that a lot of people who are celibate are omitted from any record of sexual life. It seems to show the narrowing of the concepts of love and sympathy, and a failure to encompass fully human psychology.

There is another area where there have been no gains and that is the

▶

incredible increase in separate gender demarcation in marketing for children. It is really deplorable. Certainly, we feminists monitored this closely and fought against it. But if you go into any toyshop or look at the magazine rack for young people in any Tesco, you will see absolutely stereotypical gender marking, in which they are being trained: boys are being trained to be 'hard' and girls are being trained to be 'girly'. It is a disaster, perpetuated at the consumer end of the market. Again it has the effect of leaving out a whole range of ways in which people can express their emotions. A friend of mine, Carol Mavor, in her recent book, *Reading Boyishly*, explores the concept of being 'sissy'. She and I stand up for the sissies!

> "There is another area where there have been no gains and that is the incredible increase in separate gender demarcation in marketing for children. It is really deplorable."

Susan Sontag's diaries also show an extremely interesting trajectory in what we may have lost. Early on in her life, she wrote: 'Sexuality is the paradigm; the orgasm focuses. I lust to write. The coming of the orgasm is not just the salvation, but more the birth of my ego. I cannot write until I find my ego.' Later in her career, she was much criticised for not coming out, people said that she didn't speak up for the rights of the lesbian community to which she belonged. But I believe she perceived something that was happening, which was that people were being increasingly imprisoned in their sexual and gender definitions, and she wanted to retain a freedom not to be.

The other areas in which I think we have lost our liberty, in terms of flexibility and a sense of range, is in wider notions of sexualisation outside the sexual relationship. For example, fear and suspicion of siblings who have strong feelings for each other has increased. There are numerous stories in fiction and from the past where intense relationships between siblings resulted in an extremely productive relationship – whether sexually enacted or not, we don't know, and it is their right that we don't know. William and Dorothy Wordsworth are one example. Mary and Charles Lamb, whom Lisa Appignanesi has written about in her book *Mad, Sad, and Bad*, looked after each other all their lives, both of them with mental problems, in an incredibly intense personal relationship. And so forth.

This brings us to how the competitive model drives against these alliances and this sense of community. We are atomised, rather than united, and a lot of the market axioms are playing to that. In academia, collaboration is frowned upon. You don't get rewarded. The most unselfish members of university departments who work with other people, or those who collaborate on books, do not get the necessary Research Assessment Exercise (RAE) points and thus cannot advance. The idea is to fight with one another. And not only must academics become competitive with one another - even when they don't want to - but the competition for resources, rather like in a fairy tale, drives one university against another. Again, in a completely false model that is nothing to do with community or making common cause.

I will end with something that Daniel Barenboim has said in one of his Reith Lectures. He thinks that political community should be like an orchestra. You can have single individuals who might play a solo and might excel, but they are drawn back into the orchestra and the orchestra draws together. It moves together and it makes something together, listening out for one another.

Thank you.

The prison in which we have placed ourselves
MICHAEL EDWARDS

All my work is based on a simple assumption; that the health of our interior lives affects the success of our work for justice in the world, and conversely - and just as importantly - that the shape of social and political institutions and public policies deeply affects the health of our interior lives. This is a reflexive and reciprocal relationship. This probably sounds obvious, but it is the one thing that I think is missing from the way we often approach the problems of life - the kind of things that we are talking about today.

If one follows that assumption, then it seems obvious that the most effective path to the transformation of society lies in the integration of those two aspects of change. This means we can 'be the change we want to see in the world' as Gandhi put it, so that we can 'translate love into justice structures' which was Martin Luther King's phrase. In one of the speeches he made before he was assassinated he made the remark that our life's mission as human beings is to find ways of constantly translating love into justice structures, and finding structures – structures of justice – which nurture love inside of ourselves. These are powerful words which must be remembered.

If we apply that simple phrase to the analysis of problems in our current system which we are critiquing today, it is clear how that feedback loop is operating in a very destructive, negative and damaging way. As I understand it, the current system is based on a philosophy that if we have more information, we can predict and control the world. If we can predict and control the world, then bad things won't happen. But bad things will always happen, and many more bad things will happen when that desire to avoid bad things happening turns into a desire for domination and persecution, particularly against certain groups of people, and generates widespread mistrust that leads to the breakdown of social solidarity, and the whole cycle starts afresh.

> "...many more bad things will happen when that desire to avoid bad things happening turns into a desire for domination and persecution, particularly against certain groups of people..."

We are caught in a negative cycle where we have institutions and policies which deny our deepest feelings of love, sympathy and solidarity with each other. And we are not able to find expression for those deepest feelings in the real institutions and processes which drive society.

So how do we turn that fundamentally negative cycle into a fundamentally positive one? Well, ultimately, as Satish Kumar was hinting, the only way to be free from insecurity and the toxic influence it has over our actions is to become firmly and permanently established in a state that is free from fear. That is the only ultimate answer to the puzzle that we face. That state goes by many names and we probably all call it something different. I call it unconditional or unlimited love – the love that does justice – because that is what resonates most with me, but I realise that there are many other names. For me, unlimited love

> **"We are caught in a negative cycle where we have institutions and policies which deny our deepest feelings of love, sympathy and solidarity with each other."**

is the ultimate experience and expression of freedom from fear and rage and the urge to dominate: whether it is to dominate others, or dominate the natural world, or dominate those who are less powerful. It therefore provides the only potential basis for new and healthier forms of politics and public policy and international affairs.

What might society and security policy look like if you turned it on its head in the way that I am suggesting, and developed it from a radically different place; the place of unconditional love? The honest and obvious answer is that we don't know, because we haven't tried. But I suspect that we are going to have a lot of fun finding out. That is the challenge. If we issued that challenge to ourselves and to our leaders, what kinds of institutions and policies would we come up with, especially in contexts - since this is a real discussion - where there are limits to love or trust, in a context where there are people who are intent on causing serious physical harm to ourselves, and to each other?

It is better to approach that concrete question from the direction of unlimited love and see how far we can get in minimising intrusions into personal freedom, trust, solidarity and so on, rather than to start from the opposite perspective, which is what we do now. That perspective maximises those intrusions, because there is no limit, no boundary, no logic, no mechanism to stop us from gradually going further in that direction. So what will pull us back, I am quite convinced, is a renewed commitment to discuss this most difficult of issues in the public sphere constantly, and continuously, and honestly and rigorously. It is very difficult because it challenges pretty much everything that we are used to doing, and the basis on which we are used to doing it. But I think it is absolutely essential if we are to find a sustainable route out of the kind of prison in which we have placed ourselves.

Thanks very much.

Session 9
Who Rules? Is there a Media-Political Class?
SUPPORTED BY PRIVATE EYE

The close relationship between power and the media is fundamental to an understanding of how our civil liberties are framed. Politicians seek to manage the media, not least through dominating the news agenda. When the twin towers were attacked, all major news broadcasters in the UK fell in line, describing the response - in Afghanistan and Iraq - as a 'War on Terror'. Independent challenges to government positions need to be absolutely watertight to survive: Andrew Gilligan, Greg Dyke and Gavyn Davies were all forced out of the BBC when the Hutton Inquiry (despite manifest flaws) found gaps in their defence.

The lobby system reinforces this mutual dependency. The weakness of original journalism in the UK - as exposed by Nick Davies in his 'Flat Earth News' - makes the US press look good, despite the fierce financial pressures. Investigative reporting has largely disappeared from ITV. The concept of 'balance' mutes strong voices. Even in the BBC, the battle for Saturday night ratings takes precedence over the battle for breaking news.

Rupert Murdoch is not alone amongst newspaper executives in engaging with power, whether in pursuit of influence, profit, peerages or political preferences. In most of the West, news organisations have been co-opted into the structures of power. Truly independent voices are rare, and usually marginalised. Those who look to the media as the main bastion of our civil and political liberties, have never had stronger grounds for concern.

"If you were in this morning's session on press freedom, you will have heard the speakers mostly talking about the external threats to freedom and the press, the judges, the law, a casual House of Commons, the economics of the industry, etc. I hope that this session will concentrate more on what is wrong with our media anyway? How far have they been co-opted into the political structure? How reliable are they likely to be as a bastion in the defence of liberty? I was very struck by a phrase that Alan Rusbridger used in this morning's session where he talked about the press being a source of verifiable information – that being, in his terms, a key criterion. Those of you with a taste for Gilbert and Sullivan may recall that the Mikado song about 'making the punishment fit the crime' is actually called 'a source of innocent merriment.' I did quietly wonder to myself how long ago it was that I regarded the press as a source of verifiable information – a long time ago I suspect. Those of you who ever read the *New Yorker* may have picked up the 9 February edition, where there is an article about fact-checking that publication. Imagine that! Fact-checkers in the British press. That'll be the day."

DAVID ELSTEIN, PANEL CHAIR, COMMENTATOR AND CHAIR, BROADCASTING POLICY GROUP

Healthy bacteria
LIZ FORGAN

Lloyd George had breakfast, lunch, tea and supper with the great *Guardian* editor CP Scott throughout the time that he was prime minister. He told him absolutely everything: international negotiations, party in-fighting, military strategy during the Great War. The result was that Scott was fantastically well-informed, but arguably hopelessly compromised on key issues like Ireland and Palestine, and simply unable to see straight on the subject of Lloyd George's great rival, Asquith. I'm sorry to say this because CP Scott is a great hero to those of us who work on the *Guardian* or the *Observer*. But I must tell you that I think he went way past his duty as a chronicler and a journalist, acting on behalf of his readers. He had become a player. 'When shall you be in London again?', Lloyd George wrote to Scott in 1917, 'Come to see me when you can, just to keep me straight'. I can't say I get that sort of note from Gordon - maybe Simon does.

Every serious journalist worries about the balance of his relationship or hers to politicians. As Hugo Young, the great *Guardian* columnist who died in 2003, wrote: 'The columnist owes it to his readers to know as much as he can conceivably find out. The audience also needs to rely on us being outsiders ultimately'. But I must tell you that I think that clubbishness, cosiness and conspiracies between politicians and the media are the least of our worries. There are plenty of countervailing forces. The relationship between politics and media is a shifting and unstable one and there are plenty of media monsterings of politicians and cosy deals. There is a lot of evidence that for good or ill, politicians are basically afraid of the media. Sometimes that is a disaster. It makes them turn away from expert, evidence-based advice and their own principles, out of fear of a powerful partisan press on all sorts of issues from criminal justice to asylum seekers and the pricing of car and air travel. Some people would call that a blow for freedom: not I.

Politicians and all manner of powerful individuals and institutions also fear the media for better reasons. Now that the little policemen in our heads appear to be losing their power to terrify - notably among bankers, I think - it is equally clear that the freedoms that interest the citizen are often dependent on the little policeman in *Private Eye* or even the *Daily Mail*. Freedom of information, investigative journalism, daily acting upon iniquity, indolence or incompetence, are the healthy bacteria in our democratic digestive system. However cosy the relationship may get between media and politicians, the media are still well capable, when it suits them, of biting the hands they have been feeding with all those trips to Wimbledon or the Cup Final. For me, fears about undue cosiness are absolutely trivial by comparison with the continuing function of the serious media as vital guarantors of liberty.

The power of the media, misused though it often is, is the price of their irreplaceable, essential, infinitely precious ability to speak truth to power and do it in public. And what's more, to the extent that there ever was a cosy media-political class, it is undergoing rude shocks. The blogosphere means that such a comfortable structure is constantly being tipped over and kicked to pieces within seconds of its establishment. CP Scott never had to face the certainty that every word he wrote in the *Guardian* would be seized upon, analysed and subjected not only to a range of invective and criticism, but often to the most expert and abstruse knowledge, greater than anything he could bring to bear. In its way the internet contributes to the possibility of a more honest, better-informed, cleaner information system than we have ever had in history.

But a bigger danger looms, far more menacing than conspiracies at the Garrick. And it is that the economics of serious journalism are tottering. We absolutely require well-established media institutions, resourced, motivated and able to insist on an unpopular agenda of painstaking investigation, on challenging powerful interests and voices. But serious newspapers from the *Christian Science Monitor* to the *Rocky Mountains News* are closing every day all over the Western world. Free media doesn't buy you news-gathering, investigation, first-hand reporting, expert scrutiny of courts, legislation and global business. Liberty is not just the freedom to say or do what you like. It is the access to information about the way in which the society we live in really works: who pays whom, for what, where does power flow, who guards the guarders?

And this stuff is tough to get at. The *Guardian* has recently done a huge investigative series on the tax avoidance arrangements of many of Britain's

> "Freedom of information, investigative journalism, daily acting upon iniquity, indolence or incompetence, are the healthy bacteria in our democratic digestive system."

biggest corporations. It took weeks of work. It cost a small fortune in specialist technical advice and it risked consequences that very few media organisations could or would have been able to contemplate. It couldn't have been done in that way by a blogger - though incidentally the blogosphere comes very interestingly into its own in response to things like that; all manner of extra insider information appears. But with every day that passes, fewer media outlets are resourced or motivated to get stuck into such enterprises. They are by no means box office: they are often a daunting read without pictures; bad news for the ad department. But they are vitally important and the situation in which we find ourselves now is that more and more of those serious media outlets are desperately looking for help to survive, and some of them are contemplating some pretty devilish bargains.

Regional news is held to be a finished matter in our lives unless the Government can find some way to subsidise it. People ring me up every day to ask how they can reproduce the wonderful solution that the Scott Trust has found for the ownership of the *Guardian* and the *Observer*, to save their organisations from disaster. The situation of the Scott Trust is absolutely extraordinary. It is that a very wealthy Manchester family - partly out of idealism and partly out of a wish to avoid death duties - gave its entire fortune into trust to preserve the *Guardian* and the *Manchester Evening News* and liberal journalism. And the clever thing they did was to give the dowry to the idealistic entity. The idealistic entity, then, has created a commercial group around it to generate the money that is needed to subsidise this kind of journalism, because subsidy is necessary. The danger in all this is who you look to as your paymaster and who will condition what you do. The *Guardian's* paymaster is there to ensure freedom and the continuance of liberal journalism. Other paymasters have different considerations.

My other worry is that, even when the media do expose incursions into the liberty of the citizen such as the growing appetite of the state for information, for example, we don't rise up in the streets or sack our councillors and members

▶

of parliament. On the whole - and the organisers of today's event obviously represent honourable exceptions - we shrug our shoulders, mutter something about the threat of terrorism or organised crime, and we continue to pride ourselves that we live in such a free and stable society.

The real danger I think, is not villa holidays in Corfu, but a decimated media and cynicism and indifference on the part of a materially prosperous society to the erosion of liberty. Recently, Tom Bingham - who has incidentally just made the most wonderful speech in the other room - expressed his frustration with the reluctance of citizens to challenge infringements of liberty such as the retention of DNA samples of innocent people. Here is the pillar of the legal establishment, all ready with his sword of justice and liberty, but no one will ask him to wield it. He said, 'Judges are not legislators. They cannot rule on claims that litigants do not choose to bring'. Stability, prosperity and our long history of liberty are devoutly to be wished for, but they also bring real dangers. Listen to the 18th century English antiquarian - a person I really like - Thomas Hollis. He was a fervent supporter of the American revolution and a great patron of intellectual and cultural life. He gave the British Museum all kinds of bits of classical antiquity, but his gift to Harvard University was a collection of the works of John Milton and it bore an interesting inscription coming from a scholar of the old empire to the firebrands of the new republic: 'People of Massachusetts, when your country shall be cultivated and adorned like this country, and your shore becomes elegant and refined in civil life, then, if not before, beware your liberties'.

> "In its way the internet contributes to the possibility of a more honest, better-informed, cleaner information system than we have ever had in history."

Recession is waking us all up from some very easy assumptions about stability and prosperity. Maybe it will teach us not to take liberty for granted either. There is something in the wind at the moment and this extraordinary event has captured the time. Something is happening when you hear judges talking as they have been talking this morning and when you see people queuing up to get into something like this. Something is happening. When Tom Bingham says, 'A candle lit today may never be put out, we may fervently hope', he is saying something that I think isn't just rhetoric. I very much hope that it's not.

A conspiracy against society
PETER OBORNE

That was tremendous, Liz. Completely wrong, but tremendous. On the subject of Hugo Young - almost as sanctified as CP Scott - and his characteristically solemn remark about the duties of a journalist, there is a little anecdote here which nobody yet knows, but it needs to come out! This concerns the Hugo Young Diaries, that luminous, incredibly boring and unreadable piece of sycophancy to worthy politicians. Almost all politicians are allowed these worthy and very solemn remarks to be written about them, with one exception as far as we understand: Peter Mandelson. According to this volume, Peter Mandelson and Hugo Young never had lunch: an extraordinary omission by the great man as well! Except that they did, frequently. A friend of mine acquired the dates on which all of those lunches took place. The actual lunches and the accounts of the subjects raised in them remain veiled in top secrecy, a matter for the Cabinet Office to release in about thirty years' time. However, if you trace the dates of these lunches and the column that follows, the independence of Hugo Young becomes clear for all to see. Almost without exception, the column that follows the lunch is a vicious and vile attack on none other than the current prime minister himself, Gordon Brown. I recommend that you do this: it's a wonderful example of the independence of thought of *Guardian* journalists.

Now, what I am going to do is to address the subject, which is: is there a political-media class? I'm going to show that it exists and I'm going to connect that to the theme of this conference by demonstrating that the new political-media class represents a profound and direct threat to liberty and the rule of law. It is a novel phenomenon: such a close and incestuous relationship. The common metropolitan, urban status of this political-media class is a relatively new phenomenon and very under-analysed in political science. I would recommend two very short works of academic literature (all on the left by the way – only the left has become aware of the significance of this development): firstly, the Katz/Mair thesis on the emergence of cartel politics,

convention on modern liberty

Changing Models of Party Organization and Party Democracy written in 1994. They anticipated this development and showed that it already existed on the continent; but made the false assumption that conventional, traditional politics continued to exist in Britain. That has been overridden in the last few years in ways I am going to explain very briefly. The other core text is the brilliant essay by Colin Crouch, *Coping with Post-Democracy*. I found them utterly shattering when I started to read them because, what these two texts brought back to me brilliantly, was my own experience as a junior reporter going into the House of Commons in 1992, trying to make sense of the politics and failing to do so because it failed to conform to the tradition of what we used to be taught about the way politics worked, i.e. that there was an opposition which held the executive to account and that, what went on in the House of Commons reflected the needs and concerns of a wider society.

What these two short essays reveal is that what we have now is a cartel politics in which the politicians on either side of the House have far more in common with each other than they do with the voters, and that they form a conspiracy against that wider society.

> "...the new political–media class represents a profound and direct threat to liberty and the rule of law. It is a novel phenomenon: such a close and incestuous relationship."

There are endless examples that manifest this from the Tory-Labour conspiracy against the voters over the Iraq war, to Jacqui Smith's thievery of public money through her expenses claims. She comes in after it having just been revealed that she is stealing £25,000 a year from the taxpayer. She goes into the House of Commons, nobody complains, nobody raises it in Home Office questions. There is a deadly conspiracy of silence between the state-funded political class against ordinary taxpayers. It's a scandal. Torture is another example. On Thursday, we had John Hutton come to the House of Commons to make a fundamental statement admitting that the Government has been lying about its collaboration in the torture of terror suspects over the last ten years. He admitted this. Has anyone heard what Liam Fox, the shadow Secretary of State had to say about that? [*louder*]Any word from Dr Fox, the

> "...what we have now is a cartel politics in which the politicians on either side of the House have far more in common with each other than they do with the voters..."

shadow Secretary of State for Defence in response to this stunning admission about the shameful involvement of the British state in extraordinary rendition? Not a word. And that is because both the main political parties are clients of the United States of America and dare not threaten that particular relationship. I am fascinated that Dr Fox remains in power actually. The only manifestation of his political utility was the shameful contacts he maintained with the now discredited Bush regime. I suppose he has that much in common with David Miliband…

So, what this new cartel politics has, something that the major political parties all have in common, - and, of course, the Liberals made a historical mistake in sticking to that coalition rather than going against it - is a hostility to the mainstream institutions of the British state, to Parliament and the rule of law, as well as a desire to appropriate public space from other independent institutions, whether these are the universities or the monarchy. There is a case study of this which would stretch into volumes. Instead, they seek a direct relationship with the voter, and this is where the media becomes so important. They have sought to govern through the media, rather than through conventional, traditional methods such as Parliament and the rule of law.

This is a very important, novel form of governance. And it is very menacing. And this is where we come to the hideous threat that this poses to liberty and to the rule of law. The endless attacks on judges that we have seen; the hatred of the judicial process manifested by successive Home Secretaries - always in collaboration with the press - is a conscious process. Do you remember Peter Hain - who has recently discovered his roots in liberal democracy, but who had forgotten them for a long time - talking about how Labour would make the security agenda a vote-winning process ahead of the 2005 general election? That was a very explicit plan to fight on 90 days, abolish habeas corpus, in alliance with a populist press against the judges, against the rule of law, and against liberal democracy. John Reid – another horrible, grim, dirty, foul example. If you ever want to know why the great totalitarian movements of the 20th century emerged on the left – whether it was national socialism, or Mussolini –

▶

look at somebody like Reid, fundamentally authoritarian and totalitarian. The nastiest thing of all he did, I think, was to make an appeal to Muslim mothers to hand over their children to the police if they suspected them to be engaged in terrorist activity. He did this using a classic new Labour strategy, a speech in a town hall in North London, which was announced in that morning's *Sun*, and which was clearly meant to appeal to white working class voters rather than making this very sensitive and difficult appeal directly to the people for whom it was intended. I can tell that I'm being told to shut up!

Thank you very much.

Are they all devious, venal liars?
SIMON JENKINS

A fascinating thing happened in Norway at the end of the last century, believe it or not. They decide to celebrate the Millennium, not by building a dome, but by asking the five wisest people in Norway to tell them what Norway would be like a hundred years hence. These five people went away and spent a fantastic amount of money. They were given unlimited resources, which is a very stupid thing to do to an academic. And they wrote fifty books – this is a totally true story – all in Norwegian, and came to a very alarming conclusion. They said that in the year 2100, Norway will no longer be a democracy. The reason they gave is fascinating. The constitution in Norway, they said, is such, that the way it was going meant that by 2100, Norway would be ruled by quite a small elite, an oligarchy in Oslo composed of a stage army of politicians never quite out of power because their system of proportional representation meant endless coalition government, shifting nuance in each general election, but not substantially, so that you never really lost your job. They rule through a coalition of bankers, corporate executives, senior civil servants, 'in' academics and journalists. At no point could they see how this oligarchy could be broken.

> "...when you read daily now in our newspapers about what the organisers of this conference call 'the surveillance society'...you are left thinking, 'What on earth is there to stop it?'"

There would eventually be an underclass of about 30% of the people who had no electoral power at all, and yet most people were perfectly happy with the way things were and would vote these same politicians back in with a nuance change in each election. The only way they saw this system breaking down was either literally by a revolution, or by breaking Norway up into its component regions, localities, townships and so on, such that local democracy in effect smashed national democracy. But they couldn't really see how the latter was going to happen because the constitution couldn't be changed without the permission of the oligarchs.

I think anyone looking at any community in Europe at the moment can sort of see the same things developing. And when you read daily now in our newspapers about what the organisers of this conference call 'the surveillance society', every week another step down a particular road, you are left thinking, 'What on earth is there to stop it?' Literally, what will stop it? There is always an argument for doing it: there will be another terrorist attack if you don't. But there is no good argument for not doing it, other than some wishy-washy libertarian one.

Now most people gathered at this conference, I have a sneaking suspicion, all agree. I wonder how many people were invited from the manufacturers of surveillance equipment? The problem, I believe, is not the argument. We can all agree on the argument. The problem is the way in which you structure government such that interest groups, lobbyists, special interests will always win their way. It is exactly what Dwight Eisenhower, back in the 1950s, said in an extraordinary speech for a man who lived his entire life either in the military-industrial complex or in presidency and is a huge hero of right-wing Americans. He said, 'I warn America. You will find that America will be perpetually at war if you don't curb the military-industrial complex which is now more powerful than the Pentagon'. This was a hugely perceptive remark. And I personally, for what it is worth, think that you can make the same speech today about the security-industrial complex.

We now apparently spend more money on surveillance equipment of all sorts than on arms. We are getting to the stage where there is a huge interest out there simply demanding that we spend money on this kit. Why has it proved so difficult to stop ID cards? Why has it been so difficult to stop the National Health Service computer - a huge intrusion on personal liberty? Why can you never have fewer CCTV cameras anywhere? The answer is that it is worth an awful lot of people's money to make absolutely sure that you don't.

When asked what you can really do about this, I go back to a 'commencement speech' – as they were called – at the Columbia School of Journalism about ten years ago, by the great Oz Eliot. He made his speech, and it was a very grand speech indeed, to the fresh-faced young journalists who were just about to leave and go off to work in the *New York Times* or CBS and he said, 'Now remember, all you kids, you are going out into the world with a very heavy responsibility on your shoulders. You are there as a component of the American constitution. You are going out as the informal legislators of mankind. You must be responsible. You must think seriously about your duty to the constitution of America every day of your life. Without you, the constitution won't work. You are the equivalent of any congressman'. Afterwards Eliot asked me what I thought of his speech, and I said, 'I will say one thing, you couldn't make that speech anywhere in Britain'. He was surprised, 'Why not? You've got wonderful journalists!' 'Oh no', I said, 'the British journalist is told that he is a ratfink reptile who is going out to kick a crutch from under a politician. You will never say he is the equal of any MP: he wants to kill every MP'. The most important thing, and the only sure way I believe you are going to do anything to curb the phenomenon that we are seeing at the moment, is by not relying on us journalists. Don't do that. But do make sure that whatever we can do to reveal the evolution of the surveillance society is actually heard.

My last point. Compare Lord Bingham's lecture this morning with Jack Straw's article in the *Guardian*, yesterday. Jack Straw would have been standing here twenty years ago, with Robin Cook, Patricia Hewitt, Harriet Harman. All these people would have been standing here castigating the Tory Government

> "We now apparently spend more money on surveillance equipment of all sorts than on arms."

for introducing the surveillance society. What happened to them? Are they all actually devious, venal liars? [*Audience cries: Yes!*] That was meant to be a rhetorical question. Um, no. Something happens to them when they get into power and we don't yet know what that is.

If I have one plea to all the lobbyists and think tanks who write endless articles and pamphlets on this subject, it would be this: 'For God's sake, stop writing about the importance of freedom! Try and find out what it is that works this poison inside Government on otherwise liberal people'. There is a sort of informal conspiracy operating against which even government ministers are not immune. Because unless you tell Jack Straw what he is, I am afraid that particular poison will go on operating and go on infringing upon our liberties.

Thank you very much.

Session 10
Child's Play? Equality and Young People
SUPPORTED BY LIBERTY

Children and young people deserve to be protected from harm, but this, in itself, is not enough. We must recognise that children and young people are the holders of a wide range of rights, including the right to express their views and to participate in the making of decisions which affect them. In recent years, there seems to have been a steady decline in respect for and equal treatment of young people: curfews for under-16s; 'mosquito' devices (using technology originally designed to scare away vermin) being used to deter young people from particular areas; the roll out of ContactPoint, the children's database; anti-social behaviour orders (ASBOs); and the naming and shaming of children, are just a few examples. The demonisation of children and young people can reinforce divisions between generations and damage young people's respect for law and order. So why are we seeing such a decline in respect for the rights of the young?

Children in the media spotlight
SAM DIMMOCK

In October last year, the United Nations Committee on the Rights of the Child (CRC) examined the UK government, and although the Committee noted areas where the Government has made progress in protecting children's rights, its concluding observations contained over 150 recommendations about what else needs to be done. These included concerns about child poverty, health inequality, the discriminatory treatment of traveller children and young asylum seekers, the participation of children with disabilities in society, and the education and treatment of children in custody. But emerging throughout all of this was a significant focus on children's civil rights - specifically in relation to their status in society and the human rights implications of current measures to address so-called 'anti-social behaviour'.

Unusually, and for the first time, the UN Committee has commented on the inappropriate characterisation of children in the UK. It has asked the Government to take urgent measures to address this. The UN Committee explicitly referred to the role the media plays in creating and perpetuating inappropriate images of children and young people. Intelligent news stories about human rights and children do exist, and many journalists pride themselves on accurate sensitive reporting. Some journalists even give children the opportunity to contribute their own perspectives to a story. They have shown it can be done, it can be cost-effective, and it can still be newsworthy copy. An awards ceremony is held each year by *Children & Young People Now* magazine to celebrate those that promote positive images of children. Organisations such as Headliners support children and young people to create their own news. But unfortunately, this isn't the norm. Negative stories about children dominate and negative images abound. There's a worrying intolerance of children in British media. Space is rarely given to the presentation of their world in the way in which they perceive it. There are few quotes from children in articles about them, despite the fact that they are ever-present in stories on a wide range of issues – and well able to comment intelligently about them.

We see evidence of these negative perceptions every day: complaints about children hanging around on the streets, in the assumption that they're all yobs in waiting and in public blogs on newspaper websites which roundly condemn any article that refers to the rights of the young. The media's overwhelming focus on the child, either as lawbreaker or victim, good or bad, achiever or non-achiever, results in a distorted and simplistic view of the role and experience of children in our society.

> "Unusually, and for the first time, the UN Committee has commented on the inappropriate characterisation of children in the UK. It has asked the Government to take urgent measures..."

The Children's Rights Alliance for England (CRAE) is not alone in believing that the media has a significant impact on the rights and status of children. The media can play the role of champion, exposing abuses of children's rights. Yet its coverage can also provoke policy makers into taking action resulting in ill-judged policy and legislation that does little to help. Ministers are rightly becoming critical of media coverage of children, yet they adamantly refuse to recognise the impact of their own actions. Widely reported was Jack Straw's assertion last year that 16 and 17-year-olds in custody are not children, but instead large, unpleasant thugs frightening the public. The removal of automatic reporting restrictions has allowed children as young as 10 to appear on the front page of national newspapers. The media's description of children frequently presents them as less than human. A 2007 article in the *Daily Mail* likened a 12 year-old boy to the demonic toy Chucky from the Child's Play movies. For these children, at best the public is encouraged to show little understanding of their difficulties, and at worst such reporting invites community hostility and vengeance. The UN Committee recently asked the Government to do more to respect children's privacy rights in the media, specifically avoiding naming and shaming. But to date, the Government has failed to take any action.

The unbalanced representation of children is not a new complaint by any means. Codes of conduct have been written to safeguard children's best interests. Commentators expound on the demonisation of children. There is now a growing body of research on children in the media. Some of the statistics bear repeating. One study by *Young People Now* in 2006 reported that 71% of stories about young people in one week of national newspapers were negative. Research by the British Youth Council found that this overwhelmingly negative portrayal of children, unsurprisingly, had an effect on their lives, with 98% of children considering that the media represent them as anti-social and a group to be feared. CRAE's own research in 2007, carried out by children and young people with over 1700 of their peers, found that 76% of them felt the media did not portray a balanced picture of children and young people. Research undertaken by CRAE for the Equality and Human Rights Commission in 2008 to determine the tone and content of reporting on children's rights and equality, looking at over two and a half thousand articles in the print media, found that 90% of articles about children did not contain a quote from a child. The difference in tone between articles focusing on children at large and so-called unpopular groups can be striking. The impact of broad assumptions about our most vulnerable children are far-reaching and immensely damaging. The language and imagery used has a pervasive and powerful impact that can embed or challenge prejudice. Children recognise this and they have themselves linked sensationalist reporting of children to many of the negative attitudes they are facing on a daily basis.

> "The impact of broad assumptions about our most vulnerable children are far-reaching and immensely damaging."

In March 2009, CRAE publishes its own guidelines for journalists, endorsed by the National Union of Journalists. These reflect the universality of human rights and equality issues in media reporting and highlight many of the concerns I have outlined. We detail for journalists the contribution they can make to the protection and promotion of children's human rights and the way in which they can effectively connect with children to better cover the real stories of their lives. CRAE's young activists are now embarking on a campaign to empower children to take action to address this issue of unbalanced reporting. Their Report Right campaign will produce a media charter for journalists, take action on naming and shaming based on children's own experiences of their coverage, and aim to secure the support of the media, the Government, parliamentarians, non-governmental organisations (NGOs) and other children for their campaign. It's admittedly ambitious, but will be a very exciting piece of work.

So, coming back to today's theme, is there a decline in respect for the young in the media? Respect for rights is certainly a work in progress and an international human rights treaty giving substantial rights to children is, quite frankly, terrifying to some. A widespread misunderstanding about human rights has had an undeniable impact on the reaction of the public to children's rights. But in response to such misunderstanding, lack of awareness and, at times, even open hostility, the UN has asked Government to ensure that the Convention on the Rights of the Child is widely known and understood, including by the public, and that training on it is systematic. It is not by chance that media professionals appear in the list of those requiring such knowledge.

We must recognise children as the consumers and producers of media that they are. It is in the world of blogs and social networking where most children and young people come into their own and seize the opportunity to express their views and assert their rights. It is time for the media to take a long hard look at its portrayal of children and childhood and take significant action to engage with children as they do with adults, reflecting their realities and their experiences. All we are asking for is balance.

Keeping tabs on every child
TERRI DOWTY

I want to nail this myth that ContactPoint and all its associated systems are something to do with child protection. The whole child database system has actually developed out of people's apathy towards children. I guess a lot of you are here today because you are worried about the increasing surveillance of the state. Forgive me if I say I want to go onto the main stage and shout, 'I told you so', because this all began back in 1998. The 'transformational government system' had already been piloted on children, in the name of 'child protection or curbing delinquent children', using young people as the crash test dummies.

Action on Rights for Children (ARCH) started life as a network of rather woolly-minded teachers, academics, lawyers and families concerned about issues of civil rights and education. And then one day, one of our number, who was head teacher of a large comprehensive said that he was rather alarmed, since he had been asked to hand over a huge amount of personal information on each pupil to the Government in what was the first of the pupil level school censuses. The power to do this had been forced through in the very end of the School Standards and Framework Bill, a very unremarkable and boring Bill. But somewhere tucked away, was a power to share individual information about every child who was in a state school in the country. Parliament never got to look at that provision. It was nodded through and suddenly we had a situation where head teachers were being told, 'You must give us personal information on every pupil next January'.

> "...suddenly we had a situation where head teachers were being told, 'You must give us personal information on every pupil next January'."

That was the start of the National Pupil Database in 2000. It was the first of the big databases and an experiment in having a large silo of

afternoon sessions

> "What ContactPoint is really doing is keeping tabs on children, as part of a 'risk management approach' to childhood and youth. It tries to spot problems early."

information that served no purpose other than statistical. The school censuses gradually accelerated, till it's now done every term with 41 data items stored on each child in every state school, as well in any state-funded childcare, so that babies from six months old are included, anyone with a childminder or in a nursery. This information is sent up to the National Pupil Database. At the time it was built, the National Pupil Database was designed as a statistical tool and access to it was quite tightly regulated. The Government was clearly nervous about collecting this amount of information and the possible backlash. So it was done very quietly, one step at a time, and now the National Pupil Database forms one of the foundation stones for the database everybody has heard about: ContactPoint, the national identity register of all children in the country.

At the same time as they were developing the National Pupil Database, they started an experiment on tracking young people called 'Connexions', which focused on 13 to 19-year-olds. The idea was for each local authority to have a central register of every 13 to 19-year-old, called the 'Connexions Customer Information System' and to actually track each young person to try and spot when they were developing problems, the idea being that any personal problem a child had was a potential barrier to their learning. Their words, not mine. The idea was that the child would be duly dealt with and returned to the learning environment in better shape, because the main aim under Connexions was to reduce the number of people over 16 'not in education, employment and training' - what they call NEETs, in the trade. At that time, the NEET rate was running at 8.7% of 16 to 18-year-olds, who were not in education, employment and training. So Connexions, this new system, was going to sort it all out and reduce that figure dramatically, so that more young people were being educated or gainfully employed. A personal adviser at the centre of the system collected information which could then be shared across youth justice, health, education, and social care agencies, ostensibly with a young person's consent. And it was this that formed the basis for the current Every Child Matters system.

Around 2002, a Cabinet office report called *Privacy And Information Sharing*

▶

– *The Way Forward For Public Services*, identified children's services as a place to make quick gains in transformational government. But note that at that stage child protection was not mentioned. Nor was it mentioned when the Minister, John Denham, the Minister for Youth at that time, announced something called Identification Referral and Tracking (IRT) which was the same sort of thing, keeping tabs on every child across the country to see who needed services.

Suddenly, a child protection green paper appeared in November 2003, as a response to the Laming enquiry into the death of Victoria Climbié. It was presented to the world as a Child Protection Programme and as a straight response to Lord Laming (although the strategy had actually been taking place over several years prior to that).

What ContactPoint is really doing is keeping tabs on children, as part of a 'risk management approach' to childhood and youth. It tries to spot problems early. There is a belief that future criminals have certain tell-tale signs about them, and that if you can wade in early with services, you can somehow head off criminal behaviour, unwanted teenage pregnancy, drug or alcohol abuse. Underlying it is a drastic shortage of child protection social workers, a drastic shortage of services. We are pumping money into IT, but actually the thresholds for getting services are climbing higher and higher as council budgets get squeezed more and more, quite often by the requirements to fork out for very expensive technology. We're in a very, very silly system at the moment.

This whole system, that's been going on for ten years, has allowed the 'transformational government' agenda as a whole to develop this idea of having a 'central information identity point' for each citizen, with services joined up around them.

We have just been conducting research into the legal capacity of children aged 12 to give consent to having their personal data shared. Separating out children and parents in this manner, has led to Government guidance that claims that a child can normally be presumed competent to share their personal data between agencies without the involvement of their parents from around the age of 12. So we were funded by the Nuffield Foundation last year to carry out a survey of all the leading lawyers and legal academics in the country who have specialist knowledge of consent issues. If anyone would like a copy, do come and help yourself to one before you go.

A sick society: that's enough
JENNI RUSSELL

We socialise children in order that they grow up within our society. They don't have equal rights to adults because they aren't yet fully capable of making decisions. But, as has been the case in all societies at all times, the point is that it's our responsibility as a society to teach and socialise them. We worry about how children get mistreated, whether they get demonised and whether they are treated with too heavy a hand by law enforcement authorities. But basically, in the guise of 'child protection', we have become absolutely terrified either that we will damage them, or that they will accuse us of assaulting or sexually abusing them.

We have created a situation in this country where normal adult interaction between adults and children, is now dangerous for adults to enter into. As a result, children are not being socialised or brought up by us in all the informal ways in which societies normally function. For instance, a couple of years ago, there were some teenagers kicking footballs on the rather wide pavement outside Sainsbury's, and a group of scared people including, as it happened, an old lady with a walking stick and a mother with a buggy were all standing around, unable to cross the pavement because there are about four teenagers kicking a football, clearly enjoying the fact that they were dominating the area so that nobody could move. So I stepped forward and said, 'Could you stop kicking the ball?', in that sort of, you know, working class mother way. They paid no attention at all. So when the ball bounced I picked it up. At which point one of the teenagers runs towards me, tears the

> "...in the guise of 'child protection', we have become absolutely terrified either that we will damage them, or that they will accuse us of assaulting or sexually abusing them."

ball out of my arms, tears my clothes and then kicks the football very hard at my back. When I worked out which school these children were from and ascertained the name of one of them, I rang their school's resident police officer. The only question the police officer wanted answered was if I had laid a hand on that child. I said, 'No, but he assaulted me'. And she said, 'Good, otherwise you'd be up on a court charge'. They were not interested at all in the event or the behaviour of these children. But this shows that it is now pretty much illegitimate for adults to interact with children.

> **I don't think it's a simple matter of telling journalists to act differently. I think we've got to say, this is enough. We have got to stop being frightened of one another.**

This leads to a situation where children are growing up without learning to react to, be helped by, respond to, or get on with adults around them. We then start to view them as threats because we don't know how to respond to them. I was sent a document last week from one of our country's leading music schools. It's a document that's just been issued to its staff and it begins by explaining that, from now on, they must be very careful in all their interactions with children, because any adolescent may, at any moment, be regarded as temporarily insane and could be a threat to their teachers. It said, 'Adolescents go through hormonal changes which means they may not recognise reality. They may not recognise the consequences of their actions and therefore you must, at all times, take care to protect yourself from ever being alone with a child'. 'When your lesson ends', it said, 'hustle the child out of the door in a no-nonsense manner. Do not, on any account, engage in conversation. Should you ever need to give a pupil a lift, you may not do so alone unless it is a medical emergency in which case you must place the child in the back seat of the car. You must immediately by mobile contact the parents and teachers to let them know what you're doing and you must make a record of the time, date and reason for your being alone in a car with a child'.

Now, this is a kind of absolute insanity and it is creeping into our society without anyone discussing it, without anyone legislating for it. What began as a proper concern that children must not be left at the mercy of paedophiles, has now become the view that, any adult who wants to speak to children is probably a threat to them. And if they aren't a threat to them, then the children are a threat to the adults. I was just talking last week to a man who became a father in his forties. He said the greatest joy for him is children. As an adult male, he said he has all his life thought he's got to avert his eyes from children and can never interact with them. Suddenly, as long as he's got his child next to him, he can smile at them and engage with them.

Last week, as it happened, I was skiing in Spain and I was so struck by the different approach there. I had just been there for a handful of days and was standing by the ski lift, when a small child aged about five was slightly separated from its mother, and fell on its face, screaming. A man immediately stepped forward, picked the child up, put it on its feet, handed it the skis and dusted the child down. The mother turned around to see what was happening and the child was beaming. The small children are plonked on the end of the adult lift when they're with ski school groups and the assumption is that the adult sitting next to them will take care of them. There's just an absolutely healthy response. So I don't think it's a simple matter of telling journalists to act differently. I think we've got to say, this is enough. We have got to stop being frightened of one another. Because if children grow up in these circumstances, the one thing we can guarantee is that they are not going to turn into adults who trust others around them. It's a very sick society that we're building. That is a children's right which we are damaging and we ought to do something about it.

Giving respect back
ALEX GASK

I'm going to talk about unequal treatment in the context of what is being called 'Antisocial Behaviour'. In December 2008, Barnardo's published the results of a survey they had conducted among more than 2000 adults on their perceptions of children. 54% of the adults surveyed agreed or strongly agreed that British children were beginning to act like animals and less than half of those surveyed considered that descriptions of children as 'feral' in the media were inaccurate. I think those are profoundly disturbing views. I have worked as a public lawyer, and think the Government has used this kind of fear as a way to justify increasingly oppressive laws directed at young people.

The first of those I will touch upon is probably the most well-known; the Anti-Social Behaviour Order (ASBO), which was introduced in 1998 with the Crime and Disorder Act. It seems 'antisocial behaviour' was part of a political discourse coined by Tony Blair when he was the shadow Home Secretary. Once Labour got into government they decided to deploy it. The ASBO is a civil order given in courts. If you breach that order - whatever that may be - it's a criminal offence. The ASBO can be given to adults and young people alike. Now the problems with ASBOs are many, but firstly, the term covers any behaviour considered likely to cause harassment, alarm and distress. That is a remarkably wide definition. There is also a lot of second-hand, untested, hearsay evidence that goes into these orders. Allegations can even be made anonymously, so that the person who the ASBO is sought against doesn't even know who is making the complaint. This means there could be hidden agendas at work.

> "I have worked as a public lawyer, and think the Government has used this kind of fear as a way to justify increasingly oppressive laws directed at young people."

Of the 5,557 applications for ASBOs made since 2006, 58 were refused, so appealing successfully is unlikely. Most of the lawyers I have dealt with who practice in this field don't even try to protest against an ASBO brought against a client. They simply try and limit the particular restrictions on that young person. So, ASBOs are very easy to get. And once you have an ASBO, it can contain prohibitions in anything the court considers necessary. I've worked with clients who had ASBOs that ban them from shouting in public anywhere in England and Wales. Being in a group of four or more in public has become a criminal offence. I saw a decision in November of last year when the divisional court upheld an ASBO to ban the wearing of hooded tops. The hurdle can be so low that breaching an ASBO becomes almost an inevitability, for example,

> "Government brought out a written policy on naming and shaming, declaring that publicity after an ASBO should be the norm, not an exception."

if you're not allowed to cross a certain road on a map and it happens to be on your route to school. These crazy things happen all the time. You have to go back to court to get it addressed. But if you do breach it, the penalties are potentially very severe.

For an adult, breaching an ASBO can mean up to five years in prison; a similar prison sentence to the maximum for dealing in arms. It sounds like a ridiculous comparison, but it's true. And under-18s can face up to two years in prison. Happily, imprisonment is not usually seen as the first option in a breach in criminal proceedings nowadays. But for breaching an ASBO, it is still a disturbingly high likelihood that a custodial sentence will follow.

Since the change in the Labour leadership, ASBOs have dropped from the peak of over 4000 orders in 2005 to approximately 2700 in 2006. But one thing that doesn't appear to have improved is the approach to naming and shaming young people and children with ASBOs. This has been actively encouraged in the past and I think this is a really sad indictment of our society.

I was involved in a legal challenge to the naming and shaming of young people while working at Liberty. A group of boys who had been given ASBOs - one of them as young as 14 - had their names, faces and street addresses (not their actual homes) put on leaflets and distributed to 5000 homes. The leaflet said this was keeping crime off the streets, and various terms were used for these 'young yobs', 'thugs' and 'Billie boys'. We challenged this naming and shaming and, on that occasion, the courts upheld the ASBO, effectively saying that it was reasonable and fair for the local authority to have done that. In the aftermath, the Government brought out a written policy on naming and shaming, declaring that publicity after an ASBO should be the norm, not an exception. It acknowledged that under-18s are different and in the same sentence said that the fact that they are young should not make you underestimate the impact of their antisocial behaviour on people around them. That was that.

The presumption of anonymity which is usually given to under-18s in far worse criminal proceedings, was explicitly withdrawn for circumstances of breaching ASBOs. I did a brief search on the internet and there are various places where Antisocial Behaviour publicity can be found. Every local authority has a website with pictures of those who have ASBOs, many of them quite young. The worst case I came across was a 12-year-old boy whose face appeared on posters put up around the town. I really don't think that, if these young people are antisocial and causing problems, this kind of publicity is going to help them to change their ways.

Under the Antisocial Behaviour Act which was brought in a few years later, the most obvious powers include the ability to take under-16s off the street, often referred to as 'the curfew power', and the dispersal power that comes with it. Police officers can designate an area 'at risk of Antisocial Behaviour', and then within that area, police officers are allowed to disperse any group of two or more. This is to do with the fact that people do not like seeing young people congregate in public spaces or on the street. If a police officer, in his discretion, decides that they are likely to cause some 'harassment and distress', he can disperse them. There's no definition of what this means. If they walk in different directions until they are 20 feet apart, that's dispersal. But if they don't disperse, it's a criminal offence. Anyone who is under 16 and out after 9pm, police officers are allowed to take them home. It doesn't matter if the person involved is behaving absolutely angelically, the police officer is entitled to remove them.

> "Young people need more support. They need more crucial services. And they need more respect given to them, so that they can learn about giving respect back."

That again was subject to a legal challenge brought by Liberty, and happily the courts did say that this curfew should not be allowed unless the police officer considered that the child is causing or is at risk from Antisocial Behaviour. That is in the legislation now. But I've seen police reports that still refer to a ban on under-16s who are out on the streets. So, the police still haven't quite got the message. This power is still very widely used: there are six dispersal zones in Ealing alone. I was talking to a 30-year-old youth worker who happens to be rather diminutive, last summer. She said she was out in a park chatting to some young people who live in her area and that a police officer approached them and told her they had to disperse. Apparently someone in a house on the other side of the park was in their kitchen, looking out of the window. They had seen four figures, called a policeman and said they were causing distress and the police officer came over and dispersed them. He did nothing wrong: he is entitled to do that.

It is inappropriate to give public authorities these very broad, ill-defined powers. Young people need more support. They need more crucial services. And they need more respect given to them, so that they can learn about giving respect back.

Session 11
Can Liberty Survive the Slump?

Economic opinion sees the current economic crisis as the most severe since 1929 with the possibility of a global depression. In the 1930s, this fed the rise of Fascism and Communism. But talk like this itself feeds an atmosphere of anxiety and fear that encourages people to look for strong government. Wildcat strikes over contractors restricting who they employ to foreign workers has already raised fundamental issues. Protectionism might prolong the economic downturn, but a free market in labour increases a sense of democratic disenfranchisement as the law favours international corporations. Does the failure of the economic system stem in part from a flawed political system? If so, what should be a democratic response to the downturn? How can people exercise their rights as free citizens in pursuit of good government as the financial system totters?

"One of the reasons I can remain slightly optimistic is because, all around us now, people are making the obvious connection between what has been regulated and what hasn't been regulated. What hasn't been regulated are the huge financial institutions. What has been over-regulated is our private lives, and people are really feeling this. This is no longer theory, this is no longer stuff that obscure columnists write about. We feel it…

How did we get to that position? We didn't get to that position just because of the recession. We have been in that position for about ten years. What's happened is that there has been this whole layer of experts brought in, experts in every field. Culture always precedes political change and if you watch TV or read newspapers or anything like that, you will know that you have an expert telling you how to live almost every single part of your life. They will tell you what not to wear, what not to eat, what not to smoke, what not to drink. We are all infantilised. We are all on the naughty step. That is what culture has been telling us for the last ten years and we have all bought into that in some way. But the message is also that we need protecting, not really from terrorism, but ourselves. That is where we have lost a lot of real, personal liberties. The idea is that if we are left to our own devices, not only will we be fat and smoke or get ill, we won't look ten years younger, we won't be able to clean our houses, we won't be able to pluck our eyebrows or we won't even know how to have sex unless somebody actually explains it to us…

What I am hoping, what I would really like to see start happening and do see happening with young people, is that we will have to go back to the 1960s and a counter-cultural movement, as we had against Margaret Thatcher. It will be against the new Tory government and it will be about liberty."

SUZANNE MOORE, PANEL SPEAKER AND COLUMNIST, MAIL ON SUNDAY

The neglected constitution of capitalism
WILL HUTTON

This convention does take place against an astonishing economic background. Just last week, we learned that in January, Japan's industrial production fell by 10%. It fell by 12% in December, it fell by 12% in November - in other words, it's fallen a third in three months. Japanese exports in January 2009 fell by an astonishing 46%.

Spool across the Pacific to the United States of America, and over three months - the last quarter of 2008 - their exports fell by 24% and their gross domestic product (GDP) declined at an annualised rate of 6.2%. There are astonishing decreases in industrial production in the European Union. In Britain, the Bank of England says that the decline in GDP between the summer of 2008 and the summer of 2009 will be 4%, and it will carry on falling after that, so that it will fall by about 6% in total over a period of 18 months. In Britain, over a four-year period between 1929 and 1933, GDP declined by 5.5%. So GDP in our country is declining faster than it did in the early 1930s, in a shorter period of time. And as Charlie Bean, the Deputy Governor of the Bank of England alerted us to, there is a 75% chance that that's too optimistic.

I am beginning to think that what is taking place internationally is graver than what took place in the early 1930s. The fall in house prices, the rise in unemployment, the collapse in wealth - you can see it yourselves with your own eyes in Britain, and it is an international phenomenon. It is the result of an extraordinary ten-year period which, in many respects, was also more extraordinary than the 1920s in Wall Street. When John Kenneth Galbraith wrote his book on *The Great Crash: 1929* about leverage in American investment banks and margin trading, that was child's play compared to what we have seen in the last decade. In June 2007, just a month before Bear Stearns had to declare three of their hedge funds bust on 31 July, followed the next day by Banque Paribas, one quarter of the balance sheet of American investment banks was being turned over every day, re-financed in these wholesale money markets that everyone thought were like the sea: here to stay. They have rolled back, those investment banks. All of them are no more.

In Britain, the building societies that used to borrow in those markets cannot do that anymore. We are watching the most spectacular implosion of credit and asset prices. The UK commercial property market has closed. There hasn't been a significant deal in UK commercial property for four or five months. What's the impact of all this going to be on liberty?

Already, internationally, you can see that the auguries are not terribly auspicious. In the European Union, are we going to put our hands in our pockets - the British, the Germans and French - to bail out the East Europeans and the Austrians in particular, where a first order crisis is going to emerge in the next three months? Is there enough European solidarity to do that?

Angela Merkel says we must coordinate the bonds we issue and was given a kind of quiet diplomatic raspberry by the rest of the European Union. There's a real sense of *sauve qui peut* at the moment. The Americans shrank from protection in the physical stimulus measures, but Sarkozy says he will not put any money behind the French car industry if that industry starts relocating production to the Czech Republic. This is completely against the spirit of the free movement of goods and the whole purpose of the European Union.

Everyone knows the story of the 1930s. When unemployment climbs as precipitately as it does, and when the safety net is as weak as it is, people blame 'the other'. The 'other' is the person that is outside the national community, outside the tribe. They blame other races, other ideologies - anyone but themselves. And in Britain - let's be brutal - unemployment will rise by a million by July or August of this year, and maybe another million after that. We have, over a 25-year period, made the social security net incredibly threadbare. When you were made unemployed in the early 1980s, broadly speaking, you were asked to live on two fifths of the average wage. We got through that in relatively good order, albeit with people quite frightened about social unrest, as there were riots in places like Toxteth.

Spool forward 25 years, and we are asking unemployed people to live on a fifth of average earnings when they go on Jobseekers Allowance, which is £60.50. Remember, the average wage in this country is £25,000 a year. It's an absolute calamity. And I think that as escalating numbers of people find that the social safety net is as threadbare as it is, hard questions are going to be asked of the way in which our affairs have been run these last ten years and the way they are going to be run in the future.

There will be demands for vengeance. We have heard about the undeserving poor; we now have the undeserving rich. The way we all feel about Sir Fred Goodwin's pension is going to become a generalised anger about the way things were run.

> "Everyone knows the story of the 1930s. When unemployment climbs as precipitately as it does, and when the safety net is as weak as it is, people blame 'the other'."

And this could go either way. This could be a moment for the left or it could be a moment for the right. But whether right or left, the conversation will be about closure, about more state, more surveillance and intrusion, and less openness. It is going to qualify not just economic liberties - many of which got us into this trouble in the first place - but political liberties too. I think that there will be a rise of parties all over Europe which will be extremely unpleasant, and I think there will be extremely unpleasant evolutions in places like Japan, where it will be the right that takes over. In Russia, nationalist forces to the right of Putin are in the ascendant. These are the terms of trade in our times.

I think that it behoves us at this Convention - people who think along these lines - to argue our heads off that the way through this recession - the way to prosperity on the other side - is to recommit to the great Enlightenment traditions. The reason why we got into this mess was that we didn't have sufficient checks and balances inside the banking system. The constitution, if you like, of capitalism was neglected, and left to free-market fundamentalists to argue the toss. There must not be, resiling from that world, a migration to a world of authoritarian statism on either the left or the right. A world of checks, balances, pluralism, entrenched liberties, and deliberation, justification, many voices. It is that kind of discourse that is actually the genius of Western societies. If we resile from it faced by a slump, we won't get to the other side without, I fear, more slump and even war.

The danger is that this recession is going to take out lots of pluralism. All these things weaken pluralism, weaken diverse voices and undermine a capacity to speak back to power. It's a very dangerous moment.

Paranoia?
VINCE CABLE

The word I reach for when I try to capture the spirit of a lot of the debate on crime and civil liberties, is 'paranoia'. Whatever the reason for it, there is an enormous disjuncture between what is actually happening on the ground - which is often improvement - and people's perceptions - which are of fear and alarm about crime. This also applies with respect to terrorism. There have never been any terrorist offences that I am aware of, in my part of London. At the last protest against airport expansion I attended, there were about 100 people, middle-aged mostly, half of them I guess were *Guardian* readers and the other half, *Daily Telegraph* readers. They had hit on the idea of throwing paper darts outside the Department of Transport as a way of expressing their strong feelings. After a few minutes of this, a senior policeman who was observing proceedings read out a document that he had come along pre-prepared with, saying, unless we dispersed within five minutes, he would invoke the terrorism legislation.

Anybody who now goes to a demonstration on aircraft noise or a power station will know these are the powers that are being invoked. Another anecdote: I was approached by one of my party activists who is well into his 60s. Like a lot of Lib Dem activists, he always wears a tie, is very polite and middle-class, and he had been driving around Twickenham Rugby Union stadium. He got a bit lost, and had been around the stadium two or three times. He was pulled over by an auxiliary police officer, and stopped and searched under terrorist powers, held for several hours, and asked to explain why he was behaving in such a strange way in front of an important national institution.

Now I take these cases very seriously and I worry about them. But I am also reassured, for two reasons. First of all our police culture is not – at least yet - particularly oppressive. A whole generation of police officers have been trained to police by consent rather than fear. I think many police officers are deeply uncomfortable with the role they are often placed in, and I take some comfort in that. The second factor is

> **"** ...in this economic crisis, the general environment is going to deteriorate and the kind of powers that people worry about, could be invoked."

the sheer incompetence of the British state. If you have to deal, as MPs do, with the Immigration and Nationality Department or Her Majesty's Revenue and Customs (HMRC) over tax credits, you see incompetence on a daily basis such as papers getting lost or files getting mixed up. I am reassured by the fact that the system simply cannot manage the data it has got on us.

Nonetheless, in this economic crisis, there is a risk that the overall environment will deteriorate and the kind of powers that people worry about, could be invoked. Let us look at who is going to be affected by this crisis. How will they react to it? Initially, what we are seeing is large numbers of individuals who - almost at random - are being affected by unemployment or having to work part-time. I meet many of them. Even in a fairly prosperous area like my constituency, there are growing numbers of people who are losing their jobs and are desperately worried about keeping up with their mortgage payments. So far, they see this very much in individual terms, not as a community being hit. These are scattered individuals in pain and confused and angry about their personal circumstances, trying to hold their marriages together and trying to keep their homes. They are more likely to be on antidepressants than part of a militant movement. Initially, this is how the crisis is manifesting itself.

But one of two things will happen that could change that and make opposition more concrete. One of them is that the next wave of victims will be students. If you reflect on what is currently happening in universities, I meet quite a few lecturers and professors who estimate that, of the current cohort who will graduate this summer, half of them will not have jobs. Some will find work on a part-time basis, some will go home to Mum and Dad, some will become permanent students. But there will be growing numbers - we are talking hundreds of thousands of people here - who don't have worries about their families and their homes, but who will have been bitterly disillusioned. They will have paid for their education in part, and suddenly find that society doesn't want them.

If this goes on for a couple of years, we shall have a large army of angry, educated, highly disillusioned young people, many of whom inhabit the inner cities of Manchester, Leeds, Sheffield, Bristol and London and who have serious political potential. How they will express that anger, I do not know, but we can see that it is coming.

The next wave of anger will come from the public sector. At present, the public sector is a safe haven. You probably read this morning that enormous numbers of people are now applying for jobs as teachers. It is a safe job in a slump, and the public sector is currently keeping the economy going. But public sector finance figures are awful, and all that money going into saving the banks is not sustainable. In two or three years' time, there is going to be the most ferocious crackdown on public spending and investment, and, if there's a change of government, I think probably even more ferocious than otherwise. I don't want to make a party political point, but certainly in a few years' time, the public sector will really be under the cosh. And we know from experience in this country, and also in continental Europe, that these are people who are better organised, more conscious of their rights and more able to protest than others. These are the groups that will start to feel the pain and will express it.

> "But the paradox at the end of all this is that countries will become more nationalistic in an environment where they have to cooperate even more than before..."

I will just mention one other group. It's probably not a group in any sociological sense, but I'm very conscious of it. Large numbers of people have serious debt problems. Much of the current crisis originates from large amounts of personal debt. I don't know how many of you have experienced this, but I am encountering growing numbers of people who are at the receiving end of bailiffs. Just ordinary people who have, for example, been given a parking fine, and have then moved house and so did not get the court notice. And then before they know where they are, there is a team of people at the front door with a sledgehammer. Under legislation this Government passed in 2004, bailiffs are allowed to use forced entry. Under legislation that went through last year - and not many people spotted it - they are allowed to use force on individuals. This is called 'reasonable force'. We are going to get growing numbers of people whose homes are going to be invaded by their creditors. And when large numbers of people realise this - and it may be in respect of a small amount of credit card debt or unpaid fines or other things of that category, which I don't want to trivialise - we are going to get some real, middle-class anger going on and this will add fuel to the fire.

There are potentially large numbers of people whose expectations of society are going to be severely dashed, and they will find an outlet for their frustration. Maybe we are going into a period where people will be able to think about more radical solutions than they were able to before. In this new environment, people will be willing to look at solutions that hitherto would have been regarded as impractical, such as the Dutch idea that, in every organisation, there should be a maximum salary differential of ten to one between those at the top and those at the bottom. Up till now, people say that you couldn't make that system operate. But I think, in this environment, where people are becoming highly conscious of unfairness, the time has come for radical solutions. Tax policy is the other, obvious, way to address concerns over unfairness.

When one looks at what is happening in this crisis to the ownership structure across the economy, there is more and more evidence of concentration. We will have fewer banks. We will have fewer big developers and fewer of everything, and the ones that are left will be much more powerful. If I were looking to the end of this crisis, what we could finish up with is a kind of Italian-style state capitalism, where there is a handful of very big powerful groups with enormous political and commercial power. And that is as relevant to the media as to everyone else.

In the kind of area I represent, the British National Party (BNP) is not a force. Politics is more subtle. But the paradox at the end of all this is that with rising frustration and insecurity, countries could become more nationalistic in an environment where they have to cooperate even more than before, especially if issues such as tax havens are going to be dealt with. One of the difficult contradictions that we are going to have to grapple with is this tension between national politics and the demands of a globally integrated economy. ■

Keynote Addresses and Closing Plenary

How do we secure modern liberty?

Government policies that threaten our liberty are taking place in a wider context. The most ominous and fast-moving is the economic crisis. With a further million people likely to lose their jobs in the UK in the coming year alone, amid resentment at the seemingly shameless aid and succour afforded to bankers from the public purse, we face a toxic combination of fear, anxiety, anger and helplessness. A classic background for even greater authoritarian measures and police repression than happened in response to the 'new' threats of terrorism and organised crime.

We want to secure our fundamental rights and freedoms in modern times. But it seems clear that it isn't going to be sufficient simply to defend what we have and recuperate what we have lost. How, then, is liberty to be secured?

"The first thing I would say we need, is to frame this debate not only in terms of incursions by the state into freedom, but to marry it with huge incursions made by corporate interests. We have to marry the two issues together to make it resonate. I don't think a lot of people are aware of the incursion of the state into their personal freedoms, but I think in some respects, they are quite aware of how big business interferes with them. For instance, how many people have had these direct marketers calling and disturbing them while trying to relax at home? I think that needs to be thrown in together. We shouldn't only be calling for an end to the database state, but we should be calling for an end to Big Brother business too.

We also need to define the way we talk about liberty. Particularly in the tabloid media, civil liberties are portrayed as protecting the rights of people suspected of blowing up buses down the road from here. I think we need to frame it in a much more positive way, where we are talking about civil liberties making us all safer.

And people like me in the political parties need to make this an election issue. Civil liberties issues are, strangely, quite unique in the sense that there are bodies of people in each of the main political parties who care passionately about personal freedom. We should all be demanding of the people drawing up election manifestos for the election 15 months away, that some concrete pledges are made in this regard, and we also need to show there is a political election imperative to make some pledges on this."

CHUKA UMMUNA, PANEL SPEAKER AND LABOUR PARTY CANDIDATE, STREATHAM

The Freedom Bill
CHRIS HUHNE MP

I am reminded of a very old quote which dates back to the 19th century: 'a liberal is a conservative who has been arrested by the police.' There is no substitute for personal experience of the abuse of power to turn anybody into a great believer in entrenched rights, and in the built-in ability to complain and make sure those complaints are taken seriously. I very much agree that there are people motivated by these issues in all political parties and I sometimes think of this as a parliamentary liberal party with a small 'L'. I would say there are 50 very clear Labour MPs signed up: those are the 50 who voted against 90 days with great courage, and we should show them due respect. There are some here today. And I would say probably about half of the Conservative parliamentary party are also part of the 'parliamentary liberal party'.

One of the reasons why the Liberal Democrats have put forward the Freedom Bill, which is in your packs today, is precisely because it is important now, first of all, to make the point that we have suffered a major cumulative loss of liberties since 1997. But two of those changes date back to the Conservative Government before 1997. We need to be pretty specific about what we want to repeal; what we want to turn back. It is there as a draft consultation document: go on the website, argue about it, put other things in. It is not an exhaustive list but is designed to try and create a debate, so that when we are actually arguing what should be in each of the main parties' manifestos, we can see very clearly who is committed to what. Ideally, we can make commitments in all of the parties to repeal some - if not all – of the most intrusive changes we have seen introduced since 1997.

There are still debates. We have proposed reducing the period of detention without charge from initially 28 days down to 14. We would make it very clear that that is an absolute commitment that we would vote for. No ifs, no buts, no timing, no Augustinian attitudes like 'Lord, make me virtuous but not yet'. That is something that we think needs to be changed and it is important to hold the other parties to account on that as well. Remember what happened on the Belmarsh provisions allowing terrorist suspects to be locked up indefinitely. We were the only party to vote against those, and when they were finally overturned by the judges and the control orders were introduced to replace them, we were also the only party to vote against control orders. Control orders are an absolutely fundamental breach of civil liberties. They allow ministers to put people under house arrest. We need to hold all the parties to account on the detail and actually make sure that we have a clear understanding across the 'parliamentary liberal party', if not more widely, of exactly what it is that we have lost, and what we intend to change.

It is also essential in my view that we don't abolish the Human Rights Act. Both Labour and Conservative politicians are now talking about how we need a British Bill of Rights and Responsibilities. The Conservatives have actually said they want to repeal the Human Rights Act, as opposed to adding further rights as some countries have done. Now we must remember why the Human Rights Act is so important, as opposed to British rights alone. Eleanor Roosevelt was not foolish when she championed human rights in the 1948 Universal Declaration. The British lawyers involved in the drafting of that process were making a fundamental point about human rights, rather than citizens' rights. Any society, at some point in the future, can decide who its citizens are and who they are not. That is what happened in Nazi Germany. In Nazi Germany, they defined the Jews as non-citizens - outside the pale, no longer deserving of German citizens' rights. If we define rights as British, that is a risk that we run again, and we must not allow that to happen. Human rights are the irreducible minimum that a civilised society wishes to afford to people by virtue of their humanity, not their citizenship.

And let me make one final point, which is that if we want to achieve that consensus that I very much want to see, we must certainly build a popular campaign. That is absolutely crucial. But the end of that popular campaign, to my mind, should be an entrenchment of our civil liberties in a way that cannot be challenged in the future in the way that it has been challenged in the last ten years in particular. I am thinking here of a written constitution.

What has happened in this country could not have happened in the United States. It could not have happened in Germany. Why were we so keen to entrench civil liberties in the German constitution after the Second World

War? My liberal colleague, Gerhard Baum, is now getting the German federal government to strike out data sharing powers from one part of the federal government to the others. That is the sort of entrenchment of civil liberties which we will never have in this country - unless we too have a written constitution - to guarantee that judges can oversee laws and can make sure that they do not contravene fundamental civil liberties.

> "...if we want to ensure that our freedoms are secure, we must have a parliament which is independent of the executive. We must be able to hold the executive to account properly..."

I don't mind whether we decide that we are going to separate the powers exercised by the executive and the legislature in the American way, through a very clear division between Congress and the executive, or in the less formal way that every other European democracy has done effectively by way of electoral reform. This ensures that parliamentary scrutiny committees are typically composed of a majority not of the minister's party. Having been in the European Parliament and now in the Westminster Parliament, one thing that I am totally convinced of is that, if we want to ensure that our freedoms are secure, we must have a parliament which is independent of the executive. We must be able to hold the executive to account properly and surely in the way that other mature democracies do.

A sensible guarantee of freedom will not happen until we have a very clear division of responsibility between the Government on the one hand, and the elected legislators on the other. We confuse these roles significantly in this country. We need to disentangle them and make sure there is a tension there, because it is that tension which will guarantee us our civil liberties in the future.

On the imagination
BRIAN ENO

I will talk about something that interests me and I think frames this discussion, which is about imagination.

What distinguishes human beings from all other creatures in the universe, as far as we know, is that we can imagine things. We can imagine things that don't yet exist. We can invent a course of action and then play it out in our heads. We can entertain the future; several alternative futures. Equally, we can imagine alternative pasts. So we can think of actions we have committed and we can think of other things we could have done and how they would have played out. That is the basis of regret, which, of course, is a great feat of imagination and one of the things that make humans develop in the ways that they do; it makes them pull themselves up by their own bootstraps.

We are able to imagine because we practise it all the time. We practise it by engaging in art forms, like novels and films, where we imagine ourselves to be in another world. We have professionals who help us do that called artists or futurists or cosmic physicists or astronomers (not astrologers, who don't help very much actually…). Essentially, we conceive of our great creations with our imagination. We don't do it empirically: a lot of the time, we do it in our imagination.

We also have the great human talent of empathy. Mary Kaldor, in a session this morning, said it was interesting that, since the end of the last war, we have really stopped seeing other people as the enemy in the way we used to. It is very difficult for us now to regard another bunch of humans as the enemy, when what we see on our television screens are women and children who look like they are made of pretty much the same stuff as us, suffering in pretty much the same way we suffer. In a sense, our circle of empathy, which one imagines in the past extended to family, clan or tribe – or, at best, our nation - now almost extends over the whole globe.

It expresses itself in other ways as well. We are concerned about the fate of people that we have nothing whatsoever to do with. When the tsunami happened in 2004, a lot of us sent money to people that we would never meet in places we would never go, suffering in ways that we were not even particularly concerned to find out about. But we did extend our circle of empathy in some way; perhaps because it was Christmas when it happened. Nonetheless, if you track the contributions to charities over the last 50 years or so, they increase year on year. That is except if they are given by governments, of course, when they go down year on year.

But whilst we have extended our circle of empathy, we have, I think, shortened our vision of the future. Because the rate of change is so fast, we do very few things with a very long view. Businesses, for example, are revving themselves up into shorter and shorter cycles: they are terrified of the next shareholder meeting; they are terrified of what the *Financial Times* is going to say. The share-price oscillates wildly every day. Unfortunately, governments have rather copied that model. Governments are terrified of the next election - I don't blame them - but they are equally terrified of the next by-election and the next edition of the Sunday papers and the next opinion poll. This means it puts governments in the position of being extremely reactive and carrying out decisions that are dramatic and incendiary: they look good in the papers, and really plant the seeds of very bad legislation.

In the longer view - which isn't really encouraged by anybody, particularly the media - one would be thinking about what a systemic change causes in the long-term, in the way Chris Huhne was saying. We have to think about legislation, not in terms of how it plays out on the front page of the *Daily Mail*, but in terms of what it will mean in 20, 30 or 40 years' time. What we have succeeded in doing is an act of anti-imagination. It is carefully taking apart what was a very beautiful structure. The British law, for all its bolted-on, ramshackle quality, was nonetheless a very effective structure. In 10 or 15 years, we have managed to take a lot of that apart.

It has not affected most of us directly. I have not personally been arrested or

> "Since working with the Stop the War Coalition, I have noticed that when we are organising a big demonstration, the computers go down before the demonstration."

harassed by the police. I have recently been told that, at the demonstrations I have attended, I am no longer allowed to take photographs of policemen, which starts to get a bit disturbing. Since working with the Stop the War Coalition, I have noticed that when we are organising a big demonstration, the computers go down before the demonstration. It is not a piece of paranoia, it actually happens. It happened in the Gaza demonstration. I am starting to become aware that there are intrusions being made. You know about all of those; you have been listening to that all day.

What I want to argue for - one frame we should put this whole discussion in - is how we operate in a socially creative way? What keeps the conversation of democracy going? What keeps us renewing ourselves, rethinking things, looking at new situations, finding new ways of adapting to them, watching the changing flux of populations and technologies? And what allows us to operate without becoming totally paralysed?

The problem with the kind of legislation that we have been seeing is that it is so security-oriented that, in fact, it is a form of paralysis. Governments actually like paralysis because it is easy to deal with. They don't really like a vigorous democratic conversation because it is messy and very unpredictable. You get a lot of nutters in those conversations and unpredictable, wild things happen. As Dominic Grieve said this morning, quality of life and security are not necessarily the same thing. If we want total security, we can have it and we will be hidebound. We will be in a straitjacket. Total security was what was achieved in the Soviet Union in the 1930s. I am sure it was achieved in Maoist China. The Khmer Rouge probably did well. It is very clear that it causes a stifling of the imagination and it creates a place where people stop talking to each other, stop trading wild ideas, stop tolerating the nutcases and become insular.

We need to do the job. We are facing humanity's biggest challenge. We have a few years to respond to it. We need to create a climate of completely unrestrained public discussion; social experimentation of a kind never seen before, because we are going to need every hand on deck to deal with climate change. It is the biggest issue. We are going into it with exactly the wrong set of social tools. That includes saying things like, 'Governments are trying to do that', or 'our Government'.

What we ought to be doing is looking at what is happening now with younger people. Younger people are starting to have conversations with each other through social networking sites, which are unparalleled. They are starting to do things with exactly the same technology the police are using to paralyse the situation. We should be helping them. Governments, as I say, like tools of control. Technology boys trust technology and like dealing with it more than humans. What we have now is a vast technology which is so much more complex and detailed than you can imagine and has two possible futures.

One is the future of the kind of total control that some people would like. The other is the future of possible total chaos, because the software won't work. If we can't even get a National Health Service (NHS) piece of software working, even at double the original budget, we won't be able to get this kind of software working. Vince Cable said he was very reassured by the fact that nobody will ever get it all to work. I am sort of reassured by that as well, but what I am also very aware of, is that they will still carry on using it even if it does not work.

Education ought to be the place where children are taught to swim in liberty, to be able, for once in their lives, to try any experiment, as long as it does not directly hurt somebody else. Unfortunately education has also adopted the business model and gone in exactly the opposite direction. This is something we should be talking about in schools. We should be preparing a generation to be able to use liberty, to understand what it means, and to be able to use their creativity freely without the kind of constraints we are seeing now.

> "Education ought to be the place where children are taught to swim in liberty, to be able, for once in their lives, to try any experiment, as long as it does not directly hurt somebody else."

Keynote Address

We are a better people
PHILIP PULLMAN

I want to say something about this nation as it might be, and about the virtues that sustain a working nation. I'm not going to spend much time on the vices that undermine it, although, as every storyteller knows, it's easier and more fun to talk about vice than about virtue. There are plenty of things to say about the vices of this nation, but I shan't dwell on them now. Hard as it is, I will stick with virtue.

So, which virtues does a nation need in order to be a state fit for human beings to live in? First of all, it needs courage. Courage is a foundational virtue; it's what we need in order to act kindly, even when we're afraid; in order to exercise good judgment even in the midst of confusion and panic; in order to deal with long-term necessity even when short-term expediency would be easier. A courageous nation would not be afraid of its own newspapers; it would continue to do what was right even when loud voices were urging it to do what was wrong.

It would stand up to economic interests when others were more important, and yes, there are interests that are more important than short-term economic benefits. Such a nation, for example, would rule out new coal-fired power stations, full stop. It would have the guts to say to the financial interests that wanted to build them: 'No, you can't do it and that is the end of the matter. Find something less destructive to invest in'. When it came to the threat of external danger, a courageous nation would take a clear look at the danger and take realistic steps to avert it. It would not take up a machine gun to defend itself against a wasp.

Another virtue that a nation needs is intellectual curiosity; wakefulness of mind, one might say. A nation with that quality would be aware of itself, conscious of itself and its history, and every separate thread that makes up the tapestry of its culture. It would believe that the highest knowledge of itself had been expressed by its artists, its writers and poets, and it would teach its children how to know, how to understand and how to love. We have to be taught how to love these artists' work, believing that this activity would give them, the children, an important part to play in the self-knowledge and memory of the nation.

> "So, which virtues does a nation need in order to be a state fit for human beings to live in? First of all, it needs courage."

A nation where this virtue was strong, would be active and enquiring of mind, quick to perceive and compare and consider. Such a nation would know at once when a government tried to interfere with its freedoms. It would remember how all those freedoms had been gained, because each one would have a story attached to it, and an attack on any of them would feel like a personal affront. That is the value of wakefulness. I never imagined, when I agreed to speak today, that I would find myself talking about virtue, but thinking about what this nation might have been, and might still be, makes it impossible to avoid.

The next virtue I will praise is perhaps even more unlikely at the moment. It is modesty. Modesty, which is not at all the same as humility, prudishness or self-abasement. Modesty in a nation consists, among other things, of fitting the form to the meaning, and not mistaking style for substance. A modest kingdom, for instance, would have to think for a moment or two whether or not it was a republic, because its royal family would be small, and its members would be allowed to spend most of their time in useful and interesting careers as well as being royal, and because their love affairs would remain their own business, and people would always be glad to see them cycling past.

Why does this matter? 21 years ago, Charter 88 began to show us that every part of our complex and bewildering unwritten constitution was tangled up with every other part. In order to improve this, we had to alter that. In order to let information flow properly here, we had to remove an obstruction way off over there. These things are all connected. So acquiring modesty, a proper sense of our size and position in the world, would be a big step towards reducing the self-importance of politicians who imagine they are defying existential threats to

▶

Western civilisation when they are merely throwing their weight around behind the bicycle sheds like a playground bully.

There are many more virtues I could consider, but there's one I can't leave out, and that is honour. Whatever made members of our Parliament think it was honourable to pocket large fees in exchange for pushing legislation? Whatever persuaded a minister of the crown to think it was honourable to conceal the truth about how this nation's cabinet led us to war? Whatever led a government to think it was honourable to spy on its own people? These things are a continuum. The small offenders get caught; the big ones smirk as they talk about realism and efficiency and extraordinary times needing extraordinary measures.

> "The small offenders get caught; the big ones smirk as they talk about realism and efficiency and extraordinary times needing extraordinary measures."

Just imagine for a moment a nation with that courage, with that modesty, with a simple wakeful clarity of mind that are so near at hand, so easy to find, if only we knew how. Imagine a government that trusted the people who elected it. Imagine agencies of the state that regarded the people's privacy as something it was the state's duty to guard, rather like the value of their money and the historic individuality of their town centres and their freedom to speak and write as they like. Imagine a nation that cherished these things as a kind of natural blessing, as something obviously good that needed no justification, like sunshine or kindness or clean water. Or honour.

Before I finish, I want to say something briefly about how virtue manifests itself in daily life and local life. I saw three things - three little things - recently in this nation of ours which gave me hope that the spirit of virtue - common, public, civic virtue - is still alive where people are free to act without interference.

One of the examples I call 'folk traffic calming'. People living in a residential road in the city I live in - a road that is home to a lot of families and children, a road that normally functions as a rat-run for cars - recently decided to take matters into their own hands in order to demonstrate that the street is for everyone, not just for people in large, mobile, heavy steel objects. They set up a living room in the road, with a sofa, a carpet, a coffee table and held a tea party. They put plant planters along the road containing bushes and small trees. This did not block the traffic, it just calmed it down. They set up a very funny walk-in petrol addiction clinic. The result was that cars could get through but drivers couldn't see easily and didn't think it was just for driving along at 30 miles an hour. Everyone shared the whole space. It was a triumph: inventiveness and wit in the service of a decent human standard of life.

The second thing I saw was a foundry of an industrial estate in Gloucestershire. They make castings for sculptures from the minute to the monumental. The company was founded 20 years ago, and, after starting from nothing, they now have over 80 craftspeople working flat out, many trained by the company itself. When I visited them a couple of weeks ago, every corner was full of busy, vital, creative activity. That is another example of what I mean by virtue: the goodness of productive work. The nation is a better place because of it. John Ruskin would have recognised that, and he would have seen the economic threat that hangs over it, too.

The third thing I saw was a television programme. We have a poet laureate in this country and we also have a children's laureate. At the moment it is Michael Rosen, a great man, I think. The programme was about a project he undertook with a school in South Wales where books had been undervalued for one reason or another. He showed the children, their parents and the teachers the profound value of reading and all it can do to deepen and enrich our life, and he did so, not by following curriculum guidelines and aiming at targets and putting the children through tests, but by beginning and ending with delight. Enchantment. Joy. The librarians there were practically weeping with the relief and pleasure at seeing so many children coming in to search the shelves and sit and read and talk about the books they are enjoying. But the libraries are still under threat of course.

Now what have these things to do with freedom and the threats to freedom we have been hearing about today? What has the virtue of delight to do with the virtue of liberty? Everything. A nation whose laws express fear and suspicion cannot sustain delight for very long; joy does not flourish in the garden of anxiety. The society these laws seem to be designed to bring about is one of institutionalised paranoia, of furtive hatred and low-level panic. Every scrap of delight and gladness we can find is a blow against that fear; every instance of civility and kindness we come across is a clean wind dispersing a foul vapour. Every example we cherish of imaginative play, of the energy of creation, of the enchantment of art and the wonder of science is a weapon in the arsenal and I say weapon, advisedly: we have a fight on our hands. 'I will not cease from mental fight', said William Blake, and this is the fight he meant. The fight to defend, to restore, and to sustain the virtue which is not now, but could so easily be, the natural behaviour of the state.

We are a better people than our government believes we are; we are a better nation.

Closing Keynote Address

Is that a police state, Jack?
DAVID DAVIS

The paradox of individual liberty is that it never depends on one individual, as the number of people in this hall demonstrates. Behind me there are 60 million others.

When I was shadow Home Secretary, I used to address all sorts of interesting groups. Some of them were prisoners. They gave me a paradoxical problem to solve. How would I start the speech? In prison, starting with 'it is a privilege to be here', did not seem right. And with this band of villains, murderers, fraudsters, thieves, 'it is an honour to meet you', didn't seem right either. I lit upon a formula, which was; 'I am so glad to see so many of you here'.

Well, it's in a slightly different context that I say it again today: I am so glad to see so many of you here. It has been a fantastic day with absolutely fantastic speakers. So much so, that an hour ago, in some alarm, I said to somebody: 'We have got to the point where just about everything has been said', and the lady turned to me very calmly and said, 'Everything may have been said but it has not yet been said by everybody'…

afternoon sessions

It is astonishing that we have so many people here at a freedom conference at whatever outrageous price Anthony chose to charge for it: we still ended up turning people away. It says something about the age and it says something about the battle we are undertaking.

> "Tell me, Jack, when does it become a police state? When the Government knows everything?"

I think it is a fateful battle, for my own beliefs are that freedom isn't just an abstract virtue. It defines our society. It defines, frankly, the spirit and soul of our nation and it defines our civilisation. It is not just about the right of the freeborn Englishman; they are fundamental rights for everyone. That's why I stood up and argued about Binyam Mohamed a few weeks ago, because these rights are fundamental, not limited to citizens of the United Kingdom.

That being said, we have in this country the longest tradition of freedom in the world. Frankly, one of the most magnificent speeches I have heard was the one by Lord Bingham today. I particularly liked the fact that he finished with my favourite quotation. I will show off and try to remember the full quotation about a light that will never be put out. If I remember correctly, it was Bishop Latimer who said: 'Stand up, Master Ridley and play the man, for today, by God's grace, we shall light a flame which will never be put out in England'. I have to tell you, they were both burned at the stake five minutes later. So, our freedoms have not been won easily and should not be lost easily either.

But they are not abstract. Freedom of speech is the midwife to the freedom of thought which is the parent of creativity. That's why we had Newton, Shakespeare, Faraday and all the other great geniuses in our history; probably more than we deserve to have had, given our size. It is what creates character, energy, and vigour and integrity, which is why we had the industrial revolution before anybody else and it is why everybody else got it when they got their freedoms. Freedom from oppression: that gives you dignity, individualism and character. It is one of the reasons that many of our country's institutions of democracy and justice have been copied around the world, mostly with success. So freedom isn't abstract. It is very real. It makes us what we are. Most important, in the context of the government and the government's actions, we should recognise that freedom is not a weakness. Freedom is a strength. And

▶

that is why, as a British Member of Parliament, I say to myself, 'What is the point of Britain if it does not adhere to the freedoms that made it?' What is the point of Parliament if it does not uphold its most sacred trust as a guardian of our liberty? What is the point of government if its principles aim to maximise fear and minimise our freedoms?

Earlier this week, Jack Straw said that this is not a police state. And I agree with him: Britain is not a police state. If it were, we wouldn't be having this meeting. Many of us would be locked up and we wouldn't have the right to debate. But that does not actually let the Government off the casual, careless corrosion of our freedoms that has been going on for the last decade and more.

In fact, I would like to respond to Jack Straw, not with an answer but with a question. Tell me, Jack, when does it become a police state? When the Government knows everything? When the Government knows - this is a long list I am afraid - everything about every citizen anywhere in the country? When they know every text, our every email, our every web access, our every phone call? When they can track every citizen through their car, to wherever they are in the country? When the police are able to enter your computer and search it without you even knowing about it? When virtually any state organisation can put you under surveillance without supervision or control, even including Local Government? When the police can arrest you for heckling the foreign secretary? (Quite frankly, you deserve a medal!) Or for wearing a *Bollocks to Blair* T-shirt, or reading out the names at the cenotaph? The police can now arrest you for photographing a London Bobby, which will lead to a lot of very surprised Japanese tourists, at some point.

Is that a police state, Jack? Or does it become a police state when MPs are arrested simply for doing their job of holding the Government to account and, yes, occasionally embarrassing them? Or, very much more seriously, is it a police state when the Government colludes in or condones torture as an act of policy? Is that a police state, Jack? Are we there yet? And if the answer is no, let's turn it round and say to him: OK, how many photographers do we arrest before it becomes a police state? How many innocent people are put on a DNA database before it becomes a police state: a million, as now, or 2 million? How many days do you lock people up without charge before it becomes a police state? 42? 90? And before you answer, Jack, remember that 90 days detention without charge was the first number picked by South Africa under apartheid. And then

> **" I also know this: that by the time we know it is a police state, it will be too late."**

it becomes 180 and then indefinite. I am glad to say that state fell and was replaced by a better one.

I don't know the answer to those questions. But I do know this: every erosion of our freedom diminishes us as a people, as a nation, as a civilisation. I also know this: that by the time we know it is a police state, it will be too late.

Because, of course, then it will be too late to do anything about it: the death of liberty will lead to the death of dissent. Because justice demands two views, when we have the end of dissent, it will mean the end of justice. And our country will not be the same again. That is the reason why we fight now. That is the reason why we seek today to ask, 'why?' We seek, today, to stop, check and reverse and put back the erosions of our freedoms that we have seen in the last decade.

We have had some spectacular victories in the last year and it really would be remiss if I didn't congratulate Liberty, Human Rights Watch and NO2ID. All the people and organisations in this hall that have been part of the battles that we have won this year all have reason to be proud. The political defeat of 42 days and, with it, the collapse of the authoritarian agenda; the psychological defeat of ID cards; the legal defeat of the DNA database of innocent people; the massive retreat on the communications database that the Government has had to undertake; not putting the bill in the Queen's speech (it was going to this year); and the pending retreat on database sharing that Jack Straw has trailed this week. Even (and this is particularly delicious for me), David Blunkett is giving a lecture this week on the dangers of the database state. Not since Frankenstein met his monster! But Blunkett's very partial change of heart tells you something important. Because, although David - and I love him dearly - is an authoritarian in his DNA to his fingertips - back to Frankenstein again - he is also an acutely clever politician. He can sense a change of wind almost before anybody else. So when he makes that speech, something is happening.

The British people, as we all know, are terribly casual about liberty. They treat it carelessly, like a very old suit of clothes, very comfortable, that they have had for a very long time. Because, that is precisely what it is. Only when it is under visible threat do they come out and are willing to die in their hundreds of thousands to defend it. But mostly they just treat it casually. But that is changing.

Cast your mind back. When we first fought the battle over ID cards, it was very hard for the politicians who did it because 80% of the public supported it. 80% of the public supported it then and now, about 70% oppose it. And my thanks to the Government who made it all possible! When we were fighting 42 days a year ago, 71% thought they supported it. Today, 70% oppose it. Something is happening in the hearts and minds of our countrymen. And the next test of this will be if and when they choose to introduce the communications database. Because then, unless I judge my people very wrongly, there will be uproar. There will be uproar and I do hope that you are all leading it.

That is important because we must ask why governments do this? Why do they set about taking away our liberties and our privacy? Why do they appropriate our identities? It is not just Labour governments - I will grant you that - though it has been worse recently. Is it misplaced machismo? Are David Blunkett, John Reid and Jacqui Smith and the Right going on an exercise to look tough on terror and make the opposition parties look weak? Of course, it is partly that. But it is also based on something else. It is based on fear. It is based on fear of failure. Fear of the *Daily Mail* headline when they can't quite do what they said they were going to do about crime or immigration, or, in particular, preventing terrorist attacks. These so-called tough policies - never be put off by that - are actually driven by the fear of difficult headlines. They are not tough; they are not courageous. They are actually cowardly. Don't ever forget that.

And what ministers do is that, in desperation, they reach out for the nearest glittering toy, the nearest piece of magic that will solve their problem: databases, face recognition programmes, number-plate recognition programmes, biometrics, cameras, DNA databases, electronic surveillance of all sorts. And, as Robert Heinlein once said, 'to a primitive people: any sufficiently advanced technology appears magic'. There is no more primitive group of people than ministers in a funk. It will magically solve their problems. And so, piece by piece, they have eroded our liberty, our privacy, our control of our own identity. One tiny step at a time. Every action was apparently reasonable. So slowly, without realising it, almost by accident, we lose our liberty. We acquired it by accident: if we are not careful, we'll lose it the same way.

So, everybody in this hall faces a momentous battle: but it won't be a battle of Arthurian legends. It won't be a great battle between good and evil which is won and over once and for all. It will be skirmishes – tough, difficult, frightening skirmishes, year in and year out probably for a decade or more. Each individual incremental decision, attacks on our shrinking liberty and shrinking privacy, will have to be fought time and again.

We'll have to fight the principle of expedience every time. It sounds easy does it not? Actually, sometimes you will find you are on the unpopular side. I repeat ID cards, 42 days, control orders, DNA databases, all popular when they started. But we won the arguments. You won the arguments. And we have to win those arguments time and again, over and over.

I ask the non-Conservatives in the hall, of which I suspect there are a few, to forgive me for a second while I give a message to my own party. Please keep my promises. Please abolish the ID cards, the first day you get into government. Please reduce 28 days to a more civilised level as soon as you possibly can, and please look at every law you pass and study it so that it gives freedom, privacy, and dignity back to the people, even if it is at the price of taking power away from the Government from time to time.

That is my message to the Party. Now my message for you. Abraham Lincoln once said, 'to sin by silence when they should protest makes cowards of men'. This is not going to be easy or straightforward. We are all here with people who agree with us but out there, they don't all agree with us. If the argument is unpopular and your opponent is intimidating, you must fight it time and again. It was interesting listening to Vince Cable earlier about the effect of the economic downturn. I had a conversation just before Christmas with a journalist – one of our rather swaggering Westminster members – who came up to me and said: 'Well, now people are afraid of losing their jobs and savings, their mortgage, houses, pensions. Isn't this liberty thing just a luxury?' And I said to him: 'Well, you tell me. When was the last time that liberty collapsed in Europe?'

He looked at me and I could almost see the penny drop. 'Oh', he said, 'the 1930s. I see what you mean'. And people are beginning to see what we mean on this. It reinforces the fact that we have a lot to do.

Since I have been rather sombre, I will finish with a story which seeing you here reminds me of. When he was getting on in years, in his seventies, one of the great defenders of the last century, Winston Churchill, was attending a meeting in the Guildhall and he was addressing the Women's Temperance Association. He looked just the same really, and they approved of his statesmanship, of course, but didn't always approve of his other habits. The Lady Chairman got up and said, 'Sir Winston', added something thankful about the war and then: 'I have to tell you, my members don't approve of your bibulous loose habits. When you add up all the port, wine, gin, brandy, whisky and other alcohol beverages you have taken in in your lifetime, we have calculated it will fill the Guildhall up to your chin'. Churchill got to his feet, looked up at the vaulted ceiling of the Guildhall. 'Madam', he said, 'when I think of my advanced years, I look at this building and I think to myself, "So little time, so much to do"'.

> "You won the arguments. And we have to win those arguments time and again, over and over."

So I say to you all: get out there; fight the good fight. You have only the future to win. Thank you.

ELSEWHERE IN THE UK...

Photo courtesy of Ciara Regan

Parallel conventions took place on the same day in Belfast, Bristol, Cambridge, Cardiff, Glasgow and Manchester
WATCH AND LISTEN AT: HTTP://WWW.MODERNLIBERTY.NET/PROGRAMME/ REGIONAL-PROGRAMMES

"With the interesting claim 'Despite continuing party political division, there is evidence of growing support for a Bill of Rights at a community level in Northern Ireland', the Belfast session covered human rights on a wide waterfront and featured cross-community debate on policing and justice, which looks as if it sprung no surprises. Each of the panel members also noted the need for restraint, without appeals to populism that may exacerbate the ethno-religious divide in Northern Ireland. Yet a central paradox remains concerning public confidence in the criminal justice system; that adequate public confidence is required to facilitate the transfer of criminal justice, but only the transfer and effective governance of criminal justice shall create adequate public confidence."

SLUGGER O'TOOLE BLOGS THE CONVENTION, 1 MARCH 2009

Cambridge Union Society Debate

In Cambridge, presented by NO2ID, a series of panels culminated in the afternoon in a Cambridge Union Society debate:

"This House believes that its civil liberties are under grave threat."

**PROPOSING: DAVID HOWARTH MP
(LIBERAL DEMOCRAT SHADOW SECRETARY OF STATE FOR JUSTICE)**
SECONDED BY PROFESSOR ANDREW GAMBLE
(PROFESSOR OF POLITICS, UNIVERSITY OF CAMBRIDGE)
OPPOSING: BILL RAMMELL MP (MINISTER OF STATE FOR FOREIGN AND COMMONWEALTH AFFAIRS)
SECONDED BY TARIQ SADIQ
(LABOUR PARLIAMENTARY SPOKESPERSON FOR SOUTH CAMBRIDGESHIRE)

David Howarth proposes

This is a very important day because it is the start, I think, of a fightback of what we, as a people, believe to be important. Because it seems to me that the gravest threat of all to civil liberties comes not from the Government, but from ourselves. If we forget how important liberty is and if we forget how important democracy is, then political leaders with other agendas will follow those other agendas. The one thing you can say about Britain is that it is - at least to some degree - a democracy. And if people like Bill Rammell think that we as a people don't care about democracy, then he won't care either.

So what are the threats to our freedom? Well the whole day has been about that and I don't want to repeat everything that has been said both here and in London. The central threat is still the threat to privacy: the threat to the idea that as individual people, we have a sphere of personal exclusion around ourselves which is no affair of the state. So the discussions on the database state, on the surveillance state, on the ID cards, on the national identity register and on the massive expansion of the DNA database to include many innocent people, the ContactPoint database which will track every single child born in this country – all that is at the heart of a project which profoundly undermines personal liberty.

What comes next in this development is the idea of data sharing. We are discussing a proposal for information sharing orders to be made easy for the Government to make even now in Parliament. We spent most of Thursday on that as well as techniques of data mining, with which we shall be able to bring together all the little bits of information that Government has on people and draw conclusions about those people that can be used for the purposes of control.

I just want to spend a second on a very important paper that David Omand, the former Head of Intelligence and Security at Number 10 under Tony Blair, has just written for the Institute for Public Policy Research (ippr). What that paper illustrates is the incredible breadth of the state's ambition to know everything there is about us.

The vision is of an intelligence–gathering system unparalleled anywhere in the Western world. In fact, in terms of technology, it would be unparalleled by anything that happened in the

> "...these oversight arrangements that sound very good on paper, don't work, because they themselves are subject to the executive branch of government."

former Soviet bloc. David Omand says that this is all fine, as long as there is some authority for it, and as long as there is some oversight of what happens. I'm afraid that just isn't enough. We need individual rights.

Just to give you an illustration of this, many of you will have come across the case of Binyam Mohamed who was tortured, not directly by our own agents, but certainly by the agents of several other states. In his case, a number of documents - the '42 documents' - which revealed a great deal about his torture and who knows what else, were never revealed to the overseeing bodies that have been established in this country. For example, they were never revealed to the Intelligence and Security Committee which is drawn from the House of Commons, although it isn't technically a House of Commons Committee. The existence of those documents only came to light after an individual court case based on Binyam Mohamed's individual rights. And now, shockingly, these documents are known to exist and only now will they be sent to the Intelligence and Security Committee. What this illustrates is that these oversight arrangements, that look very good on paper, don't work, because they themselves are subject to the executive branch of government. You can't trust the Government to control itself. There has got to be external control, and that is what individual rights are about.

But there are other things, grave dangers to individual freedom such as restrictions on the right to protest. I could go on all day about individual cases like the fact that it is now illegal for two or more people to gather when the police don't want them to gather, under the 2003 Anti-Social Behaviour Act; the fact that under Section 44 of the Terrorism Act, police can carry out a stop-and-search without any reason at all. I have spent a lot of time working on an environmental protest at the Kingsnorth Climate Camp. What has happened there strikes me as frightening. The police routinely see their role as disrupting

▶

a protest – not disrupting criminality that might accompany protest, but disrupting protest itself. And you may have noticed, any of you who have been on demonstrations recently, that the police spend all their time photographing you. I have been on two demonstrations recently, both to do with Bill's present and former ministerial duties, so perhaps he might explain why this is.

I was on a very quiet demonstration against student fees walking down Silver Street, and noticed that the police were photographing me. Obviously it is a very subversive thing to do: to protest against the Government's fees policy! And then, a couple of weeks later, I was on a demonstration outside Guildhall about Gaza and the same police were there, photographing again. There are signs that the police now routinely treat anybody who disagrees with the Government as a potential political extremist. That strikes me as a grave threat to civil liberties as well. And of course, to accompany this, under the Counter-Terrorism Act, it is now illegal for us to photograph the police! I will come back to that point later.

> "There are signs that the police now routinely treat anybody who disagrees with the Government as a potential political extremist."

We have also had erosions of the criminal justice system itself, erosions that make miscarriages of justice and abuse of power more likely: 28 days without charge; changes to the hearsay evidence rules; changes to the bad character evidence rules; undermining the jury system. And the latest attempt to undermine the jury system is a move to allow the Government to remove juries from inquests simply by issuing a certificate. You may not think that is important but it is vitally important. Deaths at the hands of the state are the most important violation of human rights possible. And to remove a jury in those circumstances strikes me as, not just grave, but very dangerous indeed.

There have also been attacks on the accountability structures - not just on the jury, but the ministerial veto on freedom of information. And the fact that parliament is controlled by the executive is the biggest of these. All these Henry VIII clauses in legislation which allow ministers to change the law by themselves are attacks on accountability.

What we must do now is look at the cumulative effect of all these things. The

> "We should look at the whole range, every single one of these instances together, and ask ourselves if this is proportionate to the threat."

Government says that, for each individual measure, the threat - the terrorist threat, for example - is 'so big' that we have to give way on this particular point. But that is not the way we should look at it. We should look at the whole range, every single one of these instances together, and ask ourselves if this is proportionate to the threat. Although the threat is real - and Bill will tell you that it is real - it is not the individual measure that we need to look at, but the whole lot, and the direction that we are going in.

Why is it dangerous? Normally on these occasions, people say: 'It's dangerous because, although people like Bill Rammell are fine, upstanding, decent chaps, think about what would happen if the British National Party (BNP) were in power with these powers!' That is a very good argument. But I'm starting to get worried about these guys as well. And I'm starting to get worried because I think there is a dissolution of the sense of moral limits on government that has been going on since 1997, which I don't think the Government itself notices, because it is like the boiling frog problem. Because it is so slow, I don't think they realise that the temperature is well over boiling point and that they are being boiled. Mention torture, Binyam Mohamed and extraordinary rendition episodes; mention David Omand's paper, which says that 'everyday morality cannot be upheld in the sort of operations that are going to go on'. But there is also the habit of government of basically making up threats, and operating on the basis of people's fears of a made-up threat - the weapons of mass destruction is the most obvious example.

What about the fact that, in the Binyam Mohamed case, the alleged threat from the US as far as we can tell, was asked for by the British Government: they produced the very thing that they tell us to be afraid of. I suspect that exactly the same thing happened in the infamous BAE Systems case. I can't believe that our strong ally, Saudi Arabia, would just turn up one day in Whitehall and start threatening us with terrorist attacks. I just do not believe that happened. I believe that that was also asked for by the British Government.

But above all, and this comes back to the point about photography, they photograph us but we are not allowed to photograph them. It is the entire

▶

loss of the idea of reciprocity between Government and the governed. It is the idea that they are more important than we are, and that they can tell us to do things on the basis of standards that they do not apply to themselves. That is the most fundamental aspect of this moral collapse. The Government says, on the issue of the surveillance state, that if you have nothing to fear, then you have nothing to hide. The very same Government then vetoes the information request on cabinet minutes on Iraq. That is what we are talking about; the fact that they apply different standards to us than to themselves. And that is why, fundamentally, there is a grave threat to all our liberties today.

Bill Rammell opposes

It's a pleasure to be here and a real pleasure to take part in this debate. Let me start with an admission: do I worry about getting the balance right between individual freedom and collective security? Yes, I do. Do I, however, believe that our civil liberties are under threat and that we are on the road to a police state – that was the thrust of David's argument? No emphatically, I do not. But we do need, I believe, to think long and hard about how we can get that balance right.

Let me lay out some of my own credentials. I am not by nature an instinctive 'banner' or a 'prohibitor'. Before I was Minister of State for the Foreign Office, I was Minister of State for Higher Education for three and a half years. One of the things I was responsible for was guidance to universities on tackling violent extremism. That covered issues such as safety by highlighting how violent extremist groups seek to recruit and groom students. But the centrepiece – the most recent guidance – was the argument that I put forward very strongly that, in academic freedom, free and open and challenging debate, we have at our disposal one of the most effective rebuttals to violent extremism in existence. That is one of the reasons why I have consistently argued, for example, against 'no platform' policies. Because I think instinctively that you don't rebut the arguments of extremism by banning people, by pushing them into corners. You actually need to beat them by the

> " ...do I worry about getting the balance right between individual freedom and collective security? Yes, I do."

persuasion of argument.

I recount that to demonstrate that I hold that view strongly, and also to give a sense that those kinds of actions do not accord with the caricature of a government minister wanting ipso facto to suppress freedom. But I am also confronted by the reality informed particularly by my experience as a Foreign Office minister: that the threat of the world that we live in today is, in many senses, much more dangerous than the world that I grew up in. Yes, I grew up in a world where we lived on a weekly basis with the danger of Irish Republican Army (IRA) terrorism, but both qualitatively and quantitatively, that was not the same scale of threat as we face today, from Al-Qaida and associated groups who were prepared to fly planes into the twin towers and kill hundreds of people. It was not the same as Al-Qaida using mentally impaired teenage girls as suicide bombers in Iraq, and not the same as Al-Qaida activists accusing Muslim victims in the December bombings in Algeria, many of whom were children, of crimes of apostasy.

I didn't grow up with the very real risk of proliferation of chemical, biological and nuclear weapons putting deadly and devastating capabilities into the hands of terrorists. Now I know that some people - and probably some of them are in the room today - will dismiss all of this and say that if only we understood what motivates such extremism, better! It's all the fault of the United States and Britain invading Iraq and Afghanistan! Yet I think we need to remember that the planning for the twin towers actually took place while Bill Clinton was still in the White House, and we were closer to a resolution of the Middle East conflict than we had been in generations.

The rejectionists of the threat that we face, particularly from Al-Qaida, forget one very important point: that the values that they and Al-Qaida-related groups despise most and want to destroy through a global jihad – the values of liberty, democracy, sexual equality, art and culture as a means of personal self-fulfilment - are actually the values of a tolerant, liberal left. We are all targets for those groups in a way that I don't think we were in the past.

I also think when we debate civil liberties, that the biggest affront on civil liberties is someone taking your life in their supposed cause. So the scale of the threat that I think we face is different. We do, therefore, have to consider the balance between individual freedom and collective security. I also very strongly believe that we need to understand that the world in which we live today, and particularly the means by which we communicate, has gone bluntly through a revolution in the last ten to fifteen years, the like of which we have never seen before. When I grew up, if you had told me you could go on Google Earth and look at anyone's house anywhere in the world, or that with the flick of a switch you could download a manual that could teach you chemical bomb-making, or that you could transfer money thousands of miles across the world at the flick of a switch regardless of the purpose of those resources, I would have thought that you had gone stark, staring mad. But that is the reality of the world in which we live. And as that technological capability has developed and has enabled very bad people to do very bad things, I think it has been both inevitable but also desirable that the state has looked to use that technology to counteract such efforts. That use of technology and that refinement of the law has brought real benefits to our collective and individual security.

> "...you don't rebut the arguments of extremism by banning people, by pushing them into corners. You actually need to beat them by the persuasion of argument."

To take just one example, often debated within these discussions, closed circuit television (CCTV) cameras. When those were brought in in my constituency in the town centre of Harlow, there was a 50% reduction in crime levels. It was CCTV camera footage that was crucial in prosecution of the men who planned the suicide bombings on public transport in London on 21 July 2005. And it is CCTV that is regularly used in anti-social behaviour cases where people's lives have been made an abject misery by irresponsible and inconsiderate people who don't take account of their civil liberties. I don't apologise for those measures because I think they have fundamentally improved people's lives.

I also reject the view, and this is very much the thrust of David's argument, that this government is intent on suppressing civil liberties, without regard for

> " It was CCTV camera footage that was crucial in prosecution of the men who planned the suicide bombings on public transport in London on 21 July 2005."

the consequences. As a Government Minister who sat for over two years on the Crime and Terrorism Cabinet Sub-committee, where for example, we debated virtually on a weekly basis the merits of 28 and 42 days' detention – you can believe me or believe me not – but I genuinely know how much agonising consideration was given to the pros and cons of such measures. I also – and again I think this is part of David's argument – reject the dewy-eyed notion that there were in the past some kind of halcyon days for civil liberties that have since been eroded. Jack Straw's argument in the *Guardian* newspaper yesterday was very powerful, when he said, the 1960s, 1970s and 1980s were, 'decades, for example, of informal judges' rules and of the absence of statutory protection of suspects where "fitting up" of suspects seemed to take place on a regular basis. We had massive miscarriages of justice such as the Birmingham Six and the Guildford Four and we had phone-tapping without any basis in statute law'.

They are just a few of the miscarriages of justice that took place. And it was this government which ended the situation where there was no overriding and systematic protection for people's rights and liberties with the Human Rights Act in 1999. We followed on by opening up the system with a Freedom of Information Act. Whatever you think about this government, whatever you think about what we are doing, governments that are unconcerned about the balance between individual liberty and collective security do not deliver legislative measures such as these two Acts.

But we do, I believe, need to maintain our vigilance, to be genuinely sceptical about new legislation, to expect governments to have to demonstrate beyond reasonable doubt the need for new measures, and we need to maintain a free media and a healthy debate such as the one that is taking place here today - and across the country - to ensure that we get that balance right. All of that, I genuinely welcome. What I don't welcome is caricature, distortion and exaggeration of what is taking place and what the Government is doing, not because it irritates me - although I would be less than honest if I didn't say it does irritate me sometimes - but much more importantly, because it actually undermines the real cause of real and genuine concerns about proposals that may be put forward.

And when some, as has happened in recent weeks, compare this country to Burma, or East Germany under Communist control – I say, bluntly, 'Get real!' Go to those countries where the internet is jammed, where people are executed for converting to another religion, where people are locked up in forced labour camps without trial and then you will see the real difference between there and here. Scepticism, vigilance, free debate and challenge to ensure that we get the balance right – emphatically yes. But please don't exaggerate, distort or mislead. Those arguments are not listened to. This is an important debate and it is genuinely important that we get it right. There are differences of view which we have got to air and expose. We live in a very different and more dangerous world than the one we lived in before, and that means that we will have to compromise something that we previously took for granted. The best way to discuss those is to open up a rational debate. That is an important thing to do. The kind of exaggeration I hear in that debate sometimes does not serve that debate one iota. Thank you for being here today. Thank you for taking part. I urge you to reject the resolution before you.

> "...when some, as has happened in recent weeks, compare this country to Burma, or East Germany under Communist control – I say, bluntly, 'Get real!'"

Bill Rammell sums up

Let me try briefly to respond to some of the issues in debate. Firstly, David, the only reason why some of the information about Binyam Mohamed is in the public domain is because this Government, rightly, did everything within its power, to ensure that the information was given to his defence lawyers. Before this ever became a public issue, we went out of our way to ensure that he had that information and was able to properly instruct his defence. Secondly, you made a big issue about the freedom of information case with regard to Cabinet minutes. I believe in freedom of information, but I also believe that there has to be space for private political discussions. David, you used to be a Liberal councillor. Did you publish your Liberal Group discussion minutes of your private meetings? No you didn't. Political groupings do not do that and the idea that we would enhance our democracy by having the detailed discussions in Cabinet being published, is not the case. You would then force private discussions to take place elsewhere and I don't think that serves democracy. Thirdly, you actually said, David, that the intelligence gathering system that we have in Britain is 'unparalleled anywhere in the world'. Members of Parliament can travel, David: go to North Korea; go to Libya; go to Zimbabwe; go to Iran; go to Burma and please come back and tell me that you really still think that the intelligence system that we have in this country is unparalleled anywhere in the world. Yes, there are legitimate criticisms you can make, but that kind of distortion, that kind of exaggeration undermines the arguments that are being made.

I thought Andrew Gamble's arguments were much more balanced and much more persuasive. One of the most telling points that he made – and I think this is one of the political dilemmas that we are dealing with – is that there is a collective aversion to risk within society and therefore there is an expectation from both the public and the media that the Government has to and should protect people from all sorts of ills where sometimes that is not necessarily the case. That is the kind of grounds on which we should be having a rational debate.

The point has been made that, at the height of the Cold War, we didn't ban the Communist Party of Great Britain! No, and neither are we currently banning Hizb ut-Tahrir. But this government - rightly or wrongly - is criticised by all sorts of people and all sorts of newspapers for allowing so-called 'preachers of hatred' to put their arguments forward. As long as you stay within the law and you are not threatening people with violent terrorism, that is the right thing to do. I also agree with you on the issue of the BNP. I was the Minister of State for Higher Education when – either the Cambridge Union or the Oxford Student Union – invited the British National Party (BNP) to speak at their union. And as long as the BNP remains within the law, my view then and my view now, was that they shouldn't be banned from that platform. Because the most effective way to rebut their arguments is to expose them and to take them on.

> "...the idea that we would enhance our democracy by having the detailed discussions in Cabinet being published, is not the case. You would then force private discussions to take place elsewhere."

I now turn to the arguments about explaining and justifying ID cards. Maybe I have got it wrong - I don't think I have - but frankly I find some of the arguments about ID cards amazing. ID cards, in one form or another, have existed on the mainland of Europe for most of the last fifty years. In my experience, as an active constituency MP who does regular meetings, this issue will come up from time to time and I ask people what their views are. Maybe Harlow is unique, but overwhelmingly people back the principle of ID cards. With the greatest respect, this is something of a self-selecting audience here today. If you go out and debate these issues with people, you will find that at the very least, there is a much more balanced view about ID cards than the one that has been put forward here this evening. [*Speaker: Order, order!*] Yes – freedom of speech, civil liberties! People have rightly had an opportunity to comment. Let's respond to that.

Several people have picked up on what I said about the situation being more dangerous. I said carefully that, qualitatively, I do think it is different than before. People who lived under the threat of IRA terrorism did not live with the threat of some of our fellow citizens being prepared to act as suicide bombers

> "...at the height of the Cold War, we didn't ban the Communist Party of Great Britain! No, and neither are we currently banning Hizb ut-Tahrir."

and take their own lives in taking ours. That is a different scale of threat. And when you listen to the Director General of Security Services who said recently that it was his estimate - you can believe him or believe him not – that there were some two hundred groups with some two thousand individuals engaged in terrorist activity within this country, I think that is cause for concern.

To the gentleman who took up the issue of weapons of mass destruction, let me be very clear: yes, the intelligence was flawed. It wasn't just our intelligence agencies... Even those countries who took a different view about the need to go to war with Iraq – the French, the Germans, the Chinese and the Russians – all their intelligence agencies were telling them exactly the same thing, and they also believed, based on that evidence, that Saddam Hussein had those weapons. I was a Junior Foreign Office Minister at the time of the run-up to the war with Iraq, and my biggest fear as we went into that conflict was that chemical weapons would be used against our troops. I would not have held that view if I hadn't genuinely believed the evidence before me. So, disagree with the decision that we took, but let's not have this ongoing debate about us misleading people. If we misled people, then even countries who opposed the war misled people.

Two final points. On the argument about the Dutch MP, there was a lot of consensus politically. It wasn't just the Government who took that view - and I think there are arguments both ways on a difficult issue. The Liberal Democrats also took the view that Geert Wilders should be banned. David said that it was one Liberal Democrat who took that view, but it was the Shadow Home Affairs spokesman for the Liberal Democrats, so perhaps he no longer speaks for the party!

The final point that I would make is that I started by saying that there is a genuine balance to be found between upholding individual freedoms and collective security. But I honestly believe that some of the exaggerations and distortions serve no purpose and actually undermine the case for that serious debate. And it is on that basis that I would ask you to reject the resolution.

David Howarth wraps up

Thanks. I suppose it is fair to say that there are matters of judgment and balance here and that it isn't all absolute. There are different views on the Wilders case, which all depended on whether you thought that that man's intention was to commit crimes and incite violence when he came to this country. If that is what you thought then you took one view, and if you didn't, you took the other view. As someone who hasn't seen the film, *Fitna*, I couldn't really say what I thought on this, though I suspect I may have taken a different view from my colleague.

But on other issues, I think there is more clarity. It is obvious, I think, from the debate, that part of the problem is that the Government – and perhaps most governments – don't understand that when you pass general legislation to give someone a power for one purpose, it is inevitable that the state will use those powers for other purposes. And if you don't understand that, you don't understand politics, you don't understand government, you don't understand human nature.

Let me just now cover some of the other points that Bill Rammell has made. On the Binyam Mohamed case, the fact remains, not only that this Government was using the results of torture to some degree at high levels of Government (the case says that a decision [to refuse to release information so obtained] had been endorsed at ministerial level), but also that the oversight system they had put in place failed. And it failed precisely because the Government didn't let the documents on '42 days' go to the Intelligence Security Committee in the first place. And that's how these systems always fail, because if you don't have individual rights and independent courts, then the executive always gets its way.

The case of the Cabinet minutes was very exceptional. This was the legality of the Iraq war, and if Bill was right in his remarks about how that war came about, he would be the first person to say those minutes should be released. It's very interesting that he's not saying that. What really annoyed me about what happened then, is that the Government could have appealed to the High Court to make an objective decision on whether its case for keeping those minutes private was a good thing

▶

> "...when you pass general legislation to give someone a power for one purpose, it is inevitable that the state will use those powers for other purposes."

or not. But it didn't, of course. It chose to stop the whole thing dead by its own fiat, by the exercise of a unilateral power, because that is the way that people start to think when they have those powers. If you have got them, use them.

As to whether the intelligence-gathering capacity of this country is unparalleled, I don't want to give away national secrets, but if you look at the UK-US Treaty and combine our capability with that of the United States – which is what you have to do because of that relationship – then in terms of SIGINT, ELINT, IMINT and MASINT, to go through four of the sources, our capacity is immensely greater than that of North Korea! They just don't have the technology.

The question is: what are we going to do with that technology? What do you do with the powers you have? You use them. What do you do with the intelligence you have? You use it. And that's the basic problem. As for ID cards, in this audience, I don't have to say anything more than, 'It's the database! It's not the cards! It's the database!'

I don't have time to go through all the very good contributions. But I just want to mention a couple of things, especially Tariq Sadiq's central point – 'The imperative for all governments is to uphold security. Governments can't act with hands tied behind their back. Governments should use all means – (yes, all means) – to protect security'. That is what he said. That is where we have got and that is what we have to move away from. We have got to stop that way of thinking, and I should say that that phrase, 'One hand tied behind its back' comes from an extraordinary judgment of the Israeli Supreme Court in something called the 'ticking bomb case', where the Israeli Supreme Court said in a torture case that a democracy has to act as if it has got one hand tied behind its back, because otherwise it wouldn't be a democracy!

But to come back to this central question, how did we get to this state where politicians say, 'Let's use all the powers we have, all the technical means, regardless of the consequences' – so that we drift into the removal of individual freedom? And the answer lies precisely in what Andrew Gamble was saying. There has been - if you read the 2008 White Paper on National Security – a fundamental shift in the definition of national security that does explain why we are where we are. It used to be that national security was something about defending the state against external attack or internal subversion, like all the trouble in the years of the previous Conservative Government and the years of the previous Labour Government, because I'm old enough to remember the ABC trial, and the Ex parte Leveller case(the Colonel B case). When I first came into politics, the reason why I didn't join the Labour party was precisely because they were the people taking away civil liberties at that point. It goes back, but at that point it was all about the abuses of internal subversion. And we still have that going on now. I must admit to having lost my place about what counts as internal subversion today. I suppose I must be an internal subversive because I go on about climate change and go on demonstrations against Gaza.

> "...that's how these systems always fail, because if you don't have individual rights and independent courts, then the executive always gets its way."

But it has gone beyond that. The definition of national security now, in the 2008 White Paper, is one that has to do with protecting everybody – all families, all individuals, all businesses – from all risks. And Tony Blair was always saying: 'I don't want to be responsible for the loss of one life if there is something more that I could have done'. So you think, oh yes, 'if there was some other freedom that I could have taken away to prevent that loss'. Of course, that fails what I call the '1940 test', because if you had taken that view in 1940, we would have given in because we were risking lives then to keep our freedom.

What we have now is a definition of national security which is impossible to fulfil while maintaining individual liberty, because it means the sacrifice of all liberties to a level beyond anything that has ever been achieved in a free society. Worse than that, it won't even be security because handing over all these powers to the state in the end makes you less secure, not more secure. The citizens of the Soviet Union were not exactly the most secure in the world, even though their state was very powerful.

There is one personal comment that I want to make to Tariq Sadiq. He used

> **As for ID cards, in this audience, I don't have to say anything more than, 'It's the database! It's not the cards! It's the database!'"**

an argument which you never hear anymore in the House of Commons and it is a shameful argument. You never hear it anymore because of what happened when Jacqui Smith used it last time. This is the argument that the friends of liberty are really the friends of terrorism. That is what he is saying. That is shameful and not worthy of democratic debate. And when Jacqui Smith used that argument in the final round of the 42-day fiasco, she was howled at on all sides, including her own. And that's why that argument will never be used, I hope, ever again at the centre of our democracy.

But I suppose the final point is this. We need to ask ourselves: why now? Why do we have to think about these issues at this point in time? We are not yet a police state. But there is a danger that, if we do nothing, we might well become one. And as Churchill said – and Henry Porter is very fond of quoting this – 'If you don't fight at the point when victory is certain and the costs of victory are low, then you may find yourself fighting at a time when the costs are very high and the odds are against you. Or even worse than that, fighting at a time when defeat is certain, but dying in defeat is better than a life in slavery'. I beg you to support the motion.

IN THE DAYS THAT FOLLOWED...

Photo courtesy of Mike Goldwater

CHECK OUT THE IMMEDIATE COVERAGE:
HTTP://WWW.MODERNLIBERTY.NET/COVERAGE

"In British public life, loyalty and service to power can sometimes count for more to insiders than any tricky questions of wider reputation. It's the regard you are held in by your peers that really counts, so that steadfastness in the face of attack and threatened exposure brings its own rich hierarchy of honour and reward. Disloyalty, on the other hand, means a terrible casting out, a rocky and barren Roman exile that few have the courage to endure. So which way will our heroes jump?"

KEN MACDONALD, 'INTOXICATED BY POWER, BLAIR TRICKED US INTO WAR', THE TIMES, 14 DECEMBER 2009 in the days that followed...

Joni Mitchell was right, you don't know what you've got till it's gone
SUZANNE MOORE

It's the little things, always the little things, that get you in the end. For me, it was having to be police-checked to take my child on a school trip to our local High Street. Sure, I realise that, for quite some time, the usual suspects have been banging away about the erosion of our civil liberties, but it's easy to turn a blind eye when you are not actually being arrested. Laws were being passed one after another, changing our rights. But, to be honest, most people just don't understand or have enough time to read the small print of legislation. Not even the MPs who vote it through.

Never have the lyrics of Joni Mitchell rang so true, as our civil liberties are slowly eroded. A lot of the time, we feel it has nothing to do with us. We noticed the smoking ban as we huddled under patio heaters, but took little notice of the odd person being locked up for 28 days for having a beard and having looked at some odd websites.

We have become so inured to the continual health warnings that emanate from this Government of puritans, that sometimes I think our culture of public intoxication is, in itself, a simple form of resistance to it all.

We were led to believe that the world changed so much after September 11, that endless checks on freedoms were necessary. We were scared and therefore allowed security to trump liberty, as there is no liberty for the dead, is there? We accepted this notion passively, but are now agitated in airport queues. I always struggle with the difference between lipstick and lip gloss as a matter of national security. The armed police stalking around frighten rather than reassure me. Now, they have the right to stop and search anybody and any car in designated areas, but I do not feel safer.

Should I want to protest about this, I could, of course, go on some kind of demonstration, as long as I pre-arrange it with the police and if I make sure that I do not go within 1km of the Houses of Parliament.

▶

357

convention on modern liberty

> " We have sleepwalked into a society in which, because technology watches us, we no longer watch out for each other."

This is part of another ridiculous new Act. And there is a law that means that if I took a picture of a policeman standing still I could be liable for a ten-year prison sentence. Why? We are now all suspects and subject to a massive amount of surveillance. Thousands of CCTV cameras record endless footage. They don't prevent crime but blurrily remind us that no space is unobserved. We have sleepwalked into a society in which, because technology watches us, we no longer watch out for each other.

All of us will have felt the chipping away of small freedoms. I was astonished to know that because I had more than 20 people to my last party it was legally classified as a rave. At my age! Read the Anti-Social Behaviour Act of 2003. But even to spin a few records in a pub, one now has to declare what kind of music will be played. It's a kind of insanity. Mozart or Basement? You can see how racially sensitive this legislation is.

Perhaps, though, freedom of expression and association are rather vague terms until some New Labour apparatchik starts reining them in, all the while talking to us as if we were five.

This weekend, all over the country, the Convention on Modern Liberty organised a series of events to discuss these issues. Have we left it too late? I think not. Now is the right time to put our feet down. Why, for instance, must I be made to think of myself as a potential paedophile, rather than a parent?

Something has gone badly wrong. Culturally we could read the runes. Although we have less faith in politics and institutions than ever before, they have been shoring up their power. Simultaneously, we have been bombarded by advice from lifestyle experts. Smoking, eating and drinking are no longer regarded as private choices but are subject to public scrutiny. Much of what we do is bad for us. Television reinforces this with experts who make people examine their own faeces or get 'made over'. We have not been nannied, but bullied onto the naughty step, forever infantilised.

More seriously, we have been lied to. While freedoms have been curtailed at home, we have flown people round the world to be tortured. In the dying days of this administration, Jack Straw and David Blunkett have been wheeled out to

▶

in the days that followed...

> "We have not been nannied, but bullied onto the naughty step, forever infantilised."

tell us that comparisons with a police state are crazy.

No one is saying that; we are simply staging a fight-back. Liberty does not belong to any particular party. The Convention on Modern Liberty brings together Left and Right in a powerful coalition. Something that has been fairly abstract in people's minds, is being made real. And part of that is surely connected to the economic downturn. Every day, it becomes more clear that where this Government, and indeed the one before it, should have regulated our monstrous financial institutions, they didn't.

They gave them freedom. The free market, remember, would save our souls and supposedly our public services. Now it all looks crazy because, instead, they over-regulated everywhere else. We cannot know what data is kept on our own children. Surveillance is hard-wired into every aspect of our lives. Big brother-like CCTV cameras capture our every move on film. All this is done because we need protecting, not only from terrorists and criminals, but from ourselves.

> "In the name of keeping us safe, they have imprisoned us. Time to break out."

The truth is, though, no one feels more secure, they just feel their liberties being shut down bit by bit. As Joni Mitchell sang all those years ago: 'Don't it always seem to go / That you don't know what you've got till it's gone.'

But we are starting to know, because, though we feel bewildered by all the jargon and legalese, we feel it in our bones that we are losing what made this country great. Times have changed, yes, but ancient and hard-won freedoms, which may make things difficult and messy sometimes, are part of our quality of life. The challenge for the next government is how far it is prepared to restore what has been lost.

Freedom is not a theory, it's a practice. It is precious. We don't need protecting from ourselves. We need protecting from those who would take away our freedom. The enemies of freedom have shown themselves to be not simply murderous bombers, but smiling legislators who know what is best for us.

In the name of keeping us safe, they have imprisoned us. Time to break out. ■

DAILY MAIL, 2 MARCH 2009

England: nothing to be scared of
PAUL KINGSNORTH

Ros Taylor's report on Saturday's panel discussion about English liberty, at the Convention on Modern Liberty, summed up well the problems that much of the political left still have with the idea of England. I believe, however, that virtually all of these perceived problems are based on either prejudice or misinformation.

Let's start at the beginning. In response to our discussion about the need, or otherwise, for an English parliament (though not for English independence, which wasn't discussed), Taylor writes that, 'sections of the left are deeply unhappy with the notion that an English consciousness and an English Parliament to express it are the remedy for public inertia. Firstly, an English legislature would probably be dominated by the Conservatives'.

Well, to argue that a people should be denied democracy because you might not like the result, is a pretty outrageous position. In any case, as Gerry Hassan, another panelist, pointed out, the last time a clear majority of the people of England voted Conservative, was back in 1955. So the left, it seems, can relax on that score.

Then there's the question about the place of ethnic minorities within England. 'Many first- and second-generation immigrants to Britain … find "Britishness" a more comfortable concept than "Englishness",' asserts Taylor. This has long been a claim of the left. As well as being confused ('Englishness' is not racial, it's cultural; there are plenty of non-white English people around), it, too, is misleading.

Last year, Ipsos MORI carried out a poll for the Ministry of Justice on this issue. The ministry was hoping the results would bolster the government's campaign for 'Britishness', but it got something of a shock. It found that England's black and minority ethnic populations identified more strongly with England than with Britain.

Taylor then mentions the appearance of an apparent white supremacist in the audience of our event, and suggests this is 'a warning'. I would ask: 'a warning' of what? For decades, elements of the left have suggested that the English are a dangerously racist people.

in the days that followed...

As well as finding this assertion offensive, I find no evidence for it. For my money, England is one of the most tolerant developed countries in the world. A non-white person living in France, Italy, Switzerland, Spain or Australia might be able to confirm this. Our most prominent far-right grouping, the British National Party (BNP), are a British, not an English, party who wave union flags and whose leader has declared his support for Welsh nationalism.

Finally, Taylor suggests that 'appeals to nationhood ... are the very stuff that oppressive anti-terrorist legislation feeds upon'. I'm not sure how this follows. Many of the legislative destructions of our liberty by New Labour could not have happened in the US, for example, because it has a written constitution. The defence of that constitution against a marauding president – an 'appeal to nationhood' if ever there was one – has been a rallying cry for the US left for the last eight years.

> "A culture that is comfortable in itself is more welcoming and outward-looking than a sullen, angry culture whose desire for self-expression is denied by its political elites...."

Personally, I think that the expression of a positive English identity is essential. A culture that is comfortable in itself is more welcoming and outward-looking than a sullen, angry culture whose desire for self-expression is denied by its political elites.

Indeed, Taylor didn't report what I thought was one of the most interesting results of this discussion – that Yasmin Alibhai-Brown, who came to the event set against the idea of an English Parliament, appeared to be willing to change her mind by the end of the session, having heard our arguments. Maybe there was something in them after all.

THE GUARDIAN, 2 MARCH 2009

No broken society here
HENRY PORTER

I can tell you what was impressive about the Convention on Modern Liberty in a second. It was the complete lack of cynicism; it was people giving of their best, listening without interrupting, rising to the occasion, finding others as worried or as inspired as they were, making connections across the political spectrum, speaking with extraordinary eloquence and clarity, reaching out to the other point of view.

This is something you see very rarely in our institutions and media. Halfway through the morning sessions I realised that those attending the Convention had designated the Institute of Education in Bloomsbury a neutral space, where the only currencies accepted were common ground, reason and humanity. That applied to the politicians too – exchanges took place that I did not believe were possible. Billy Bragg complimented David Davis on what was, by common consent, a very good speech. I watched Labour, Liberal Democrat and Conservatives nod with agreement and passion as they listened to Lord Bingham's speech and the oration by Philip Pullman, which, together with his article in the *Times* will become important texts for understanding history and our freedoms. It was extraordinary.

> "I can tell you what was impressive about the Convention on Modern Liberty in a second. It was the complete lack of cynicism; it was people giving of their best..."

This was the British – the modern British – at their very best. No broken society here; indeed it seemed like the virtues of old and new Britain mingled in a way that I had not seen before. There was so little rancour; the air shone with good nature. This was not simply an event about the attack on liberty, but something far more moving – an assertion of a culture. After years of watching the slow extinction of

in the days that followed...

> **After years of watching the slow extinction of parliamentary debate and the triumph of irony and cynicism in the media, it was a sheer delight to hear people talk so earnestly.**

parliamentary debate and the triumph of irony and cynicism in the media, it was a sheer delight to hear people talk so earnestly. Talk, discourse, parleying is ever more important in an age that has found so many ways to insult remotely.

Writing in the *Times*, Michael Gove MP said he had been put off attending the Convention because of his 'prickly antipathy to barristerial cant'. He continues: 'There's a certain sort of silky smuggery about some of freedom's defenders that I can do without'. This seemed a bit daft to me. Surely he cares more about the attack on freedom than the supposed manner of its defenders. He should have been there, because the speeches by Lord Goldsmith and Lord Bingham, Baroness Helena Kennedy, Sir Ken Macdonald QC and Edward Fitzgerald were direct and compelling. No cant, little flourish, just talk.

It was a great day and wonderfully organised by my co-director Anthony Barnett. There was an important message in this: we want the main parties to understand that an opposition is forming which is light on its feet and self-organising. We had one or two disappointments. The BBC took little notice on the day, which, given the quality of the speakers, was bizarre. No matter. Someone suggested that, for a little extra money, we could broadcast live to 150,000 people on the web.

Things are moving fast. Being ignored by a big broadcaster suddenly seemed to matter less than it once did.

THE GUARDIAN, 3 MARCH 2009

The database state and the true cost of Labour's free lunches
JAMES GRAHAM

During the Unlock Democracy debate at the Convention on Modern Liberty last month, Justice Minister Michael Wills defended the growth of the database state by arguing: 'We've heard a lot about data sharing today. But that data sharing, that so many here today say is an unacceptable intrusion of privacy by the state, can actually help thousands and thousands of children who are eligible for free school meals but don't get them at the moment... Look, it's all very well for you to sit here. You've probably all had a hot meal in the last week. One in five of the children in my poorest wards have not had such a hot meal in the last week... You can't walk away from this.'

Now, leaving aside the tendency of Labour politicians to come over all prolier than thou when backed into a corner (and they have the cheek to call us self-righteous...), it is an interesting point. Because, however we might like to wrap ourselves up into the language of rights and freedoms, if the database state is working for the average man (or child) in the street, what hope do we have of curtailing it? And Wills' quote is important for another reason: it highlights the fact that there is a lot more at stake here than simply whether or not we should have to carry ID cards around with us.

This brings me neatly onto *The Database State*, a new report published by the Joseph Rowntree Reform Trust today. The researchers of this report – Ross Anderson, Ian Brown, Terri Dowty, Philip Inglesant, William Heath and Angela Sasse of the Foundation for Information Policy Research have looked into 46 separate databases currently being managed by government departments, and have assessed each one on its relative merits. Assigning each one a colour according to a traffic light code, this is more than simply a polemic about the 'transformational government' agenda but a far broader assessment.

Where the researchers have identified a good example of how data can be managed by Government, they have said so. Sadly, however,

in the days that followed...

they have only green-lighted six projects, including the National Fingerprint Database and the TV Licensing Database. Of the remainder, ten have been issued a red light (suggesting the project should be scrapped or fundamentally redesigned) while 29 have been given an amber light (suggesting significant, worrying failings which may fall foul of a legal challenge).

You will probably have heard of many of this report's main targets: the National DNA Database, the National Identity Register, ContactPoint (the national database of all children), the National Health Service (NHS) Detailed Care Record and the putative communications database which the government wants to use to store all our itemised phone bills, email headers and mobile phone location history. But that is only the tip of the iceberg. Did you even know we had a National Childhood Obesity Database for instance, tracking the Body Mass Index of every single child in state education?

> "What is most striking from this report, is the extent to which so many of these databases use hearsay and subjective value judgments by public sector staff."

What is most striking from this report, is the extent to which so many of these databases use hearsay and subjective value judgments by public sector staff. The NHS Detailed Care Record for instance, will allow anyone with access to the database to write anything on a patient's record and has no system for quality control. The Common Assessment Framework database, which is a record for sharing information about vulnerable children, is essentially a pool of subjective information about a child and his or her family which will be shared by professionals. A couple of weeks ago, Gordon Brown pledged to make our public services more like eBay in terms of allowing people to rate them, but the truth is, it has effectively been government policy for public officials to issue the public with eBay-style ratings for years now.

The fundamental question is, will any of this actually help? The researchers here recognise the potential value of a lot of these projects, and have shown significant restraint in only red-lighting 1-in-5 of the projects discussed. But they raise serious questions. For instance, despite the National DNA Database doubling in size in recent years, the number of crimes solved using DNA has

▶

> **"Throughout history, badges of shame have been used to stigmatise people, not help them; why would the modern, whizzy, virtual version be any different?"**

remained steady at 1-in-300 (and actually fell slightly in 2007). That is a pretty damning statistic. The introduction of the social services' Integrated Children's System did not stop Baby P's murder and despite the litany of errors that have now been highlighted, Ofsted rated Haringey as 'good'. Even before this case, social care professionals were expressing concern about how the system had shifted the balance away from professional analysis and towards compliance with a standardised system.

To return to Michael Wills and the children in his constituency who are not getting the free school meals they are entitled to, it is not clear how exactly all this data storage will help them, but let's assume for a moment that it will. At what cost, however? The downside to all this data storage and sharing is that every minor indiscretion, and even mistakes on the database, are set to be stored for the perusal of public service professionals for years to come. The report opens with a fictional account of how all this information could be actively harmful for the very children so much of it is intended to help. How will a school teacher, for instance, treat a child who is marked on the ContactPoint register as having had contact with social services (but not specifying the nature)? If a child is listed on the Home Office's ONSET system for predicting offenders because of their father's criminal record, will the police treat her or him differently if they get in a fight? Will they be treated as a victim or a suspect?

Even if the databases themselves were perfect, the people using them can never be. Throughout history, badges of shame have been used to stigmatise people, not help them; why would the modern, whizzy, virtual version be any different? They say there's no such thing as a free lunch, but this appears to be a particularly heavy price.

It seems that only now are we waking up to the extent of the modern database state, and this report is a major contribution to that awakening. That it has been allowed to progress for so long with so little parliamentary or public oversight is itself a serious indictment of our political system. £100 billion is slated to be spent over the next five years, during an economic downturn when we simply cannot afford it. Yet at the same time, Michael Wills' Government blocks legislation such as the Fuel Poverty Bill - something that will save the lives of some of the most vulnerable, create jobs and protect the environment. If we are to be lectured that these projects are ultimately about helping the most vulnerable in society rather than treating them as suspects, they will have to do better than this.

LIBERAL DEMOCRAT VOICE, 23 MARCH 2009

Publisher's foreword to *The pro-Israel lobby in Britain* by Peter Oborne and James Jones
TONY CURZON PRICE

What happens in Israel matters to many of us, and for all sorts of reasons. So it is absolutely right - as this pamphlet emphasises - that Britain's political system should have pressure groups whose concern focuses on Israel. Among the hugely important reasons are: the realpolitik of the Middle East and its central place in the world's energy supply; Israel's important role in the globalised world of products and culture; the profound humanitarian impulses that extend sympathy to all those who have suffered; and above this, many of us have personal stories that give us direct or tangential interest in the fate of this young State and the possibility of an even younger Palestinian State. Welcome to globalisation.

The fates of nations and peoples are intertwined. A central theme of openDemocracy's publishing throughout the last decade has been that globalisation does not flatten the world (as the narrow-minded Washington consensus of the 1990's would have had it); rather, it layers yet another level of complexity and particularity to every social existence. Andre Malraux boasted that 'every human being has two countries: his own and France'. We can now extend his thought in all humility. All of us have many, and perhaps all of the world's countries within our lives, and all of us in different ways.

> "...the MPs expenses scandal has left...every class and section of British society with a sense that our system cannot be trusted to give us good politicians."

I am not just father, husband, brother, colleague, friend and monarch's subject... My computer uses an Intel chip designed in Ra'anana, my utility bills vary with the geopolitics of oil, I am the grandson of a Galician Jew executed by the Nazis in 1939 and of a British diplomat who directed refugees - some of them Jews to Palestine - this way and that in the confusion of the end of the Second World War. From the mundane to the fundamental, I have my own relationship to Israel.

But how exactly should our British interests be aggregated so that together we may have an effect - be it large or small - on what happens in Israel? The answer will be determined by our political process. Or, as we would like to say, by our democracy.

And it has been a very bad year for democracy in the UK, as 'OurKingdom', the British politics section of openDemocracy, has been chronicling. Alongside the undermining of liberty and the still-born promises of constitutional and democratic reform, the MPs expenses scandal has left many us - perhaps for the first time most of us - in every class and section of British society, with a sense that our system cannot be trusted to give us good politicians. From the pressure group-dominated response to the financial crisis to the prospect of no meaningful deal on climate change at Copenhagen, we feel that our political and financial class are part of a system that fiddles as the rest of us burn.

This sense of a wider crisis is expressed in all kinds of ways, whose larger significance is becoming apparent. This is why James Jones, Peter Oborne and the *Dispatches* team at Channel 4 have not only produced a very important and brave piece of journalism in investigating how our political machinery aggregates interests about Israel, but in doing so they also make a significant contribution to unveiling the nature and weakness of party politics in the UK.

At openDemocracy and 'OurKingdom', we are very proud to be associated with their research and making it more widely available because it shows that our political system is not working as it should. To have democracy in Britain, we need a process that is transparent, accountable and open. Where we do not, the country's interests are all too likely to be misrepresented and the process of our democracy captured.

> "...we need a process that is transparent, accountable and open. Where we do not, the country's interests are all too likely to be misrepresented and the process of our democracy captured."

By showing in calm, careful and authoritative detail how this may happen Jones and Oborne's work is a contribution to making political life in the UK more principled and trustworthy.

OPENDEMOCRACY, 13 NOVEMBER 2009

Britain's new Internet law - as bad as everyone's been saying, and worse - much, much worse
CORY DOCTOROW

The British Government has brought down its long-awaited Digital Economy Bill, and it's perfectly useless and terrible. It consists almost entirely of penalties for people who do things that upset the entertainment industry (including the 'three-strikes' rule that allows your entire family to be cut off from the net if anyone who lives in your house is accused of copyright infringement, without proof, evidence or trial), as well as a plan to beat the hell out of the video-game industry with a new, even dumber rating system (why is it acceptable for the Government to declare that some forms of artwork have to be

> "It consists almost entirely of penalties for people who do things that upset the entertainment industry (including the 'three-strikes' rule that allows your entire family to be cut off from the net)."

mandatorily labelled as to their suitability for kids? And why is it only some media? Why not paintings? Why not novels? Why not modern dance or ballet or opera?).

So, it's bad: £50,000 fines if someone in your house is accused of file sharing; a duty on ISPs (Internet service providers) to spy on all their customers in case they find something that would help the record or film industry sue them (ISPs who refuse to cooperate can be fined £250,000).

And that's just for starters. The real meat is in the story we broke yesterday: Peter Mandelson, the unelected Business Secretary, would have the power to make up as many new penalties and enforcement systems as he likes. And he says he's planning to appoint private militias financed by rightsholder groups who will have the power to kick you off the Internet, spy on your use of the network, demand the removal of files or the blocking of websites, and Mandelson will have the power to invent any penalty, including jail time, for any transgression he deems you are guilty of. And of course, Mandelson's successor in the next government would also have this power.

What isn't in there? Anything about stimulating the actual digital economy. Nothing about ensuring that broadband is cheap, fast and neutral. Nothing about getting Britain's poorest connected to the net. Nothing about ensuring that copyright rules get out of the way of entrepreneurship and the freedom to create new things. Nothing to ensure that school kids get the best tools in the world to create with, and can freely use the publicly funded media - BBC, Channel 4, British Film Institute (BFI), Arts Council grantees - to make new media and so grow up to turn Britain into a powerhouse of tech-savvy creators. ■

(cc) *2009 CorDoc-Co, Ltd. Some rights reserved under a Creative Commons Attribution-ShareAlike license.*

BOING BOING, 20 NOVEMBER 2009

in the days that followed...

An Afterword from Anthony Barnett

What is the point of gathering together the contributions from the Convention on Modern Liberty in this book? We can admire their range, their richness, their potential (or be annoyed by their brevity and other shortcomings). We can speculate how others could have contributed in an original way (some wanted to come but were away – this collection is, after all, drawn from invitees to a one-day event[1]). We can enjoy looking back at an interesting moment for what it *was*. The main purpose, however, in reading or dipping into this collection, is to respond to the challenge of the day.

A wager I was willing to lose

The Convention was a 'wake up call'. It was a gathering of those who feel there is a growing range of threats to our fundamental rights and freedoms in Britain, who wanted to test out whether this was the case in public and debate, if the argument held, why this is so and what could be done.

The arguments of the Convention set out here, and in the associated documents and videos to be found on the Convention's archived website, their energy, clarity and care, demonstrate that there is indeed a case to answer. They also show it can be communicated in a way that touches regular people and builds on their experience. Just take a look at the column published the day after the Convention in the *Mail on Sunday* by Suzanne Moore and some of the responses it provoked (pp 357).

As a Downing Street advisor to the Prime Minister said to me, the Convention took the issue of liberty 'out of Henry Porter's ghetto'. It was said with some admiration. It left in the air the thought that, even if those in the Government agreed that Porter's warnings were not without cause (and he had had an email exchange with Tony Blair in the *Observer* in April 2006[2]), in New Labour terms they could be ignored so long as they could be projected as a 'maverick's' concern. For the Government, what matters is the crude 'politics' of the issue, not its truth or validity. What matters is whether it is a story 'with legs'.

Well, the Convention showed that the issues could walk and that significant numbers among the public walk with them. With some modesty, David Davis

371

> **"Ours wouldn't be a country worth living in if its people wilfully didn't care about the creation of a potentially despotic database state."**

alludes to this in his contribution in discussing public opinion on 42 days which, despite almost the entirety of the political class sneering at his 'gesture' of resigning to take the matter to voters, shifted as the arguments were made[3].

This, then, was our first objective: to demonstrate that there are a set of hugely important issues that matter to people about the way the masters of the state are reshaping official power. Important, both because they threaten to hobble democracy and also because they may poison how we regard and think about ourselves. Ours wouldn't be a country worth living in if its people wilfully didn't care about the creation of a potentially despotic database state. At the first planning meeting I said that if we couldn't fill the hall with 900 people, especially with the *Guardian's* generous promise of sponsorship, I'd emigrate. It wasn't a boast: it was a wager I was willing to lose. Knowing the case, if there *wasn't* any public interest in a call to debate the state of our liberties in a modern form, there would be no point in living here.

The Convention demonstrated that there is great interest, especially among the young. This is a country worth living in for those who want to be free, those who are not the friends of friends of oligarchs and who confuse security and even community with the ubiquity of CCTV.

We wanted more

But as Co-Directors, Henry and I wanted more. We hoped that if we proved this point and touched a public nerve, then a movement would begin.

So far, no such movement has stirred. Why hasn't it? Why should such a magnificent event, far larger and with much more publicity and impact than many Compass, Fabian and ResPublica rallies and launches, not have led to a wider public response? Why, if it demonstrated what was possible, didn't the possible happen?

One simple answer is that it was stopped in its tracks when two of the main sponsoring organisations, Liberty and NO2ID, ruled out any further use of the Convention database apart from a final 'thank you' email. How this occurred

in the days that followed...

is partly recorded in the minutes of the meeting (which I chaired) that took place five days after the Convention at which, for example, Liberty's Shami Chakrabarti said:

> 'As long as no-one breathes more life into the Convention on Modern Liberty, we don't have a problem.'

When a funder who was present remonstrated,

> 'It would be madness to throw away the energy created',

Phil Booth of NO2ID replied,

> 'Let each debate form and push the argument forward. NO2ID has not changed stance throughout the whole process.'[4]

A parallel may be drawn with other occasions when NGOs insisted on the destruction of databases or of wider public alliances with high profiles. For example, Kumi Naidoo reflected on the fate of Make Poverty History in a recent *Guardian* interview with Annie Kelly, who reported:

> 'There is a thin line between focus and parochialism,' he says. 'While it is clearly justifiable that organisations seek to promote their own brands, this should not rule out greater co-operation, exploring how different social agendas intersect and global concerns articulate with each other. There is much room for improvement here.' Naidoo points to what he considers the 'betrayal' of the 2005 Make Poverty History campaign by UK development agencies.... Naidoo is bitter about the disbandment of the campaign, prompted by what he says was the reluctance of the big UK development groups to subordinate their own brands to the greater good.
>   'In 2005, Make Poverty History had 85% brand recognition,' he says. 'The disbandment of the campaigning was a fundamental mistake and one that has significantly strained the UK development community's relationship with their southern counterparts.'[5]

In the case of the Convention, there was no way to resist disbandment,

▶

because its potential solely relied upon a palpable feeling of a common interest not scarred or determined by tribalism. The spirit of the day was that its passions were open to anyone to join it, its arguments based on good faith, not instrumental calculation of organisational advantage or the old politics of territorial fights and branding.

But while important, I am not sure, even if everybody had wanted it and had there not been profound differences of perspective, that the Convention itself could have started a movement that remained free of heated rows and traditional conflicts.

> **...independent popular judgement is growing in self-confidence, having become altogether more threatening for our masters when it proved wiser than theirs over their 2003 decision to invade Iraq."**

For the internal tensions can also be seen as an expression of concern at high energy independence of any kind, linked to a desperation for funding and the need for dedicated support. Despite itself, this was perhaps another expression of the profound opposition across the whole political-media class to the spirit of liberty and independent popular judgement we advocated.

Because independent popular judgement is growing in self-confidence, having become altogether more threatening for our masters when it proved wiser than theirs over their 2003 decision to invade Iraq.

For me there is still something of a larger mystery, however. I'd echo Simon Jenkins' question (pp 287) when he asked a session of the Convention: what happens to people when they get to high office? What drives the creation and support of the hyper-centralised state by people who seem convinced that they are benevolent and acting in the public good?

To sketch an answer, first I want to summarise the case as restated recently by Porter in a single paragraph. Then I want to list some of the forces which strain their sinews to damp down and prevent independent debate of modern liberty. Then I want to touch on some of the ideological arguments that have the potential of dividing any movement for modern liberty as the fight-back builds, as it will. Finally, I want to address the paranoia question.

Here is the quote from Porter, from an end-of-year post in his *Guardian* blog where he set out the broad 'pattern in the powers endowed to the state by Labour'.

> ...the national DNA database, which despite the unanimous ruling of the European court of human rights retained the genetic profiles of the innocent; the plans to access the data of all communications; Police Forward Intelligence Teams building a database of legitimate protesters; the automatic number plate recognition system covering all major road and tracking "tagged" vehicles; the eBorders scheme that will collect and store information from all journeys across UK borders; the children's databases that prohibit access by parents; the Criminal Records Bureau checks of teenagers helping out at school; and the ID card scheme that will record all the major transaction of a person's life.
>
> There are many more but ... one point is crucial – we have moved into an era of official mistrust and suspicion that places the individual at a considerable disadvantage in relation to the state.

Porter goes on to say the trend is morbid and will be repaid with 'the people's mistrust of the state'[6].

This description is important: the process gets into the imaginative system of society and how we relate, not just to the state, but to public life and therefore to each other. It threatens to dissolve trust between us, members of the public, as it institutionalises distrust between the public and official power.

I now want to suggest that there is a network of interests that, by instinct and prejudice, do not want this to be debated, who are uncomfortable with the public being interested in positive solutions (that don't sell newspapers, etc).

Here is a list of the forces that 'don't want' an uncontrolled public debate about modern liberty:

1. The BBC
2. Political parties
3. The Government
4. Civil servants
5. NGOs
6. The left
7. Official Conservatives

8. To which, alas, we can also add the Lib Dems who, it seems, never fail to lose an opportunity if they can do so (though they will protest that they do *everything they can* to encourage such a debate).

1. *The BBC:* By coincidence, across the period of the Convention, the BBC was running a series of ads saying it knew where people lived so they had better pay their licence fee. The Corporation understands itself as part of the database state and sees nothing wrong with this, given that it is clearly acting in the larger public interest. Despite considerable press coverage, the BBC decided that the Convention was not a story, its extraordinary platforms of speakers not worth filming, recording or reporting. Ironically, the Russian arm of the BBC's World Service covered it with some success before the Putin lobby convinced British officialdom to cut back its Russian coverage.

2. *Political parties:* Representative democracy was developed as a way of political parties organising and shaping public opinion and remaining in control of it. The mass media have both subverted and replaced this relationship, which is why spin doctors and PR gurus now play the role the party chairman used to have. The potential independence of public opinion remains a felt threat to those who believe they are in charge, especially as the public becomes more articulate and demanding. All the more reason to keep them under surveillance for their own good.

3. *The Government:* From its point of view, the Government and its ministers are innocent fall-guys of malign conspiracy theorists and raving individualists who understand neither the public good nor the feelings of regular voters. Because the agenda is so vast, I'll just mention one example of the problem, the original creation of an 11 million plus child protection database. Legislated in 2006, when it finally went live in 2009, there was such an uproar that Ministers had to hastily establish a commission to cut back the numbers. But how could it have been created in the first place? Catherine Bennett has provided a biting and brilliant account of the parliamentary debates at the time,[7] that is well worth reading. The Minister told the Commons:

> "There are between 7.5 million and 9 million people involved in work with children or with vulnerable adults in one way or another, so it will not be possible to legislate to cover all those people in one fell swoop," he

said. "It will take time."

After the Soham murders, there was a call for a database of those who worked with children – even though the murderer, Huntley, was the boyfriend of the teacher the girls were looking for, so he'd not have been picked up by any vetting system. It was irresistible! To hugely increase the powers and knowledge of the central state and local government in pursuit of the protection of the vulnerable while being egged on by the tabloids – no magic potion could have brought together a more pleasing combination of substances: it was pure Viagra for social democracy. The odd warning voice even then that it would generate undue suspicion and turn childcare into a 'no-go' area could be ignored. Why should anyone want to question such progress?

4. *Civil servants:* What needs to be said? Weakness, arse-covering, fear of Freedom of Information. Actually, a great deal of the problem lies here - as in our informal constitution they are supposed to provide a vital 'check' if not balance against over-mighty politicians. But while politicians can supposedly be controlled by playing on their weakness in a game of *Yes, Minister* (now overtaken by the hollow yelling and swearing of *In The Thick of It*), the public is really dangerous and not to be trusted.

5. *NGOs:* There was a time when there were always one or two MPs who were the public spokesmen of important causes unpopular with the powers that be. They were the 'voice in the House' for the cause, and personified it with national as well as procedural influence. Of course, they were also the gatekeepers, cautioning about not going 'too far'. They moderated demands to ensure they remained achievable as well as being outspoken - even radical - in terms of the Westminster routines. Today, perhaps only Frank Field preserves this honourable, if exhausting, role. The rest are mostly lost. But NGOs have taken over. While MPs are reduced to constituency case workers, NGOs articulate the demands of campaigns and causes, holding the balance between being outsiders making demands and insiders participating in implementing reforms in committee and by advice. They have become the new gatekeepers.

6. *The left:* There is no such one thing, but then all these categories are generalisations with exceptions. But there is a strong feeling across the institutionalised London left, its think tanks and campaigns, that *of course*

they support freedom and liberty and open criticism - how could they not? - but that, without all the other things that need to be said about why electoral and constitutional reform and social policy are so important, just going on about liberty 'helps the Tories'. There is a profound reluctance to concede that anything fundamentally new is happening to the organisation of the state that demands a different response in this area. At the Convention, I found it striking that the traditional pro-Labour campaigns I am close to turned up as if fulfilling a routine obligation as one must in politics, unlike the radicals of the blogosphere led by Sunny Hundal of Liberal Conspiracy who generated some genuine excitement. Indeed, one of the speakers he hosted, Heather Brooke, shortly proved to have been single-handedly responsible for a more far-reaching and cleansing exposure of the British political system, thanks to her pursuit of and research into MPs expenses, than a dozen, profoundly thoughtful Fabian/ ippr/ Demos/ Compass/ Progress/ Prospect efforts to investigate what progressives should do about Britishness or consumerism.

7. *Official Conservatives:* There was an interesting Tory presence at the Convention, but not an official one. All one needs to say is that Cameron and Gove once saw themselves as the 'heirs to Blair' to understand the risks of continuity reinforcing traditional fear of the unwashed in new Conservatism. David Davis resigned from the Conservative leadership almost certainly because he did not feel liberty was safe in their hands.

Added to all these institutional forms of resistance to the politics of liberty, there is an argument over the role and place of human rights. Perhaps its clearest exponent is Shami Chakrabarti who, alone among those asked by the Editor, declined to have her contribution to the Convention republished in this book. As can be seen from the online Convention transcript, before introducing her opening keynote speech, I started by welcoming everyone as fellow citizens. Shami refused this description. Human rights are universal – to embrace the status of citizen suggests discrimination, ID cards, and immigration procedures.[8] In a way, David Goodhart, Editor of *Prospect*, takes the opposite, equally bizarre, view (pp 264) by insisting that we are indeed only members of our own communities and cannot incorporate universal values into our politics without undermining social democracy. Porter was scathing about this dispute after the Convention:

in the days that followed...

This being Britain, an entirely unnecessary dispute is laden with tribal symbolism. The rights side is characterised as representing the left while the constitutional side is deemed be full of Tory individualists. If we could only stop being so damned stupid and unite around a common cause, we would be able to confront those in the Conservative party who desire to seriously harm the redress available under the Human Rights Act (HRA), at the same time as those in the Labour party who have done so much to attack liberty.

Liberty and rights, or rights and liberty: it doesn't matter which comes first as long as we use them in the same sentence.[9]

As humans, we all share the universal condition of being born into the valley of tears and joy, but we are also all born into particular valleys – of gender, time and place – particularity and our efforts to negotiate it being intrinsic to our universal humanity. Really, there is no need for philosophy or theory about this. Philip Pullman's speech breathed humanity but was devastatingly accurate about, and demanding of, our government here in Britain.

If we want a democratic politics, we have to be able to build trust in ourselves and our fellow citizens. But distrust of an autonomous, free public is the name of the game. Human rights authoritarians say we must trust the judiciary; populists say we can only trust strong leadership; broadcasting fat-cats say we can only trust those like them who plumb the depth of public taste in their viewing stats; the police say we have to trust them because the rest of us are under suspicion; the NGOs say they are the ones to be trusted to know what the public needs; as for the political parties, evidently their leaders don't even trust their own membership!

Up against this lot we have a fight on our hands.

Are we paranoid?

It also poses the question, are we paranoid? Are *they* really out to get *us* as the argument seems to imply? It is very important to address this as it is the simplest way of dismissing all the concerns of the Conventioneers.

At the end of his marvellous account of the 1970s, *Strange Days Indeed*, about the madness and the insanity of those in power and out of their minds, Francis Wheen gently chides Porter for excessive alarmism and possible inheritance of the 'fusion paranoia' he traces back to the seventies, with his claim that the National Identity Register is designed to record 'every important transaction in a person's life'.

Wheen's study makes it evident that those in high office often really are out to get us, even when they are also consumed by the belief that others are out to get them. The classic British trope designed to deflate public concern about all this is to contrast the 'conspiracy theory' of history with the 'cock-up theory'; the latter being far more plausible, of course. In fact, the two are not opposites. History, or at least British politics, is mostly made up of non-stop incompetent conspiracies that prove to be cock-ups. Their fate should not blind us to the baleful intent.

In one case - in her account of the child protection database quoted above - Catherine Bennett, it seems to me, gets it exactly right. Having shown how the politicians embraced legislation that would 'generate paranoia' she concludes that they were:

> ...a body of people, acting without thought, in a mood of crowd-pleasing over-excitement, amid a succession of equally superfluous and ill-considered acts...

and asks whether they can be said,

> ...to have consciously intended anything at all?

I think in a general sense, they can. They intend to carry on.

Look at the line-up of general forces that I suggest resist the potential of modern liberty, with its celebration of autonomous, public politics that isn't dependent on those above us. And think about where they were after the expenses crisis broke. You might see more clearly what I mean. Whereas one can just about retain credibility while arguing that the public does not share the Convention's concerns about liberty (as Justice Minister Michael Wills does in his session), it is impossible to suggest that the public was not aghast and filled with contempt at the culture of entitlement the expenses crisis revealed.

Yet here again the BBC showed itself to be a regime and not a public broadcaster, itself riddled with the cancer of expenses and excessive pay. Where were the NGOs gathering together to shake a fist at the weakness of the political system, the party leaders able to drive through changes they claim it demonstrated were essential, the civil servants resigning at the suborned status of their precious culture of integrity? The whole political class reacted as if the voters' reaction was 'unpolitical'. Of course, they were protecting themselves.

One result is a resentful, cynical public whose political imagination is being devalued by a cycle of distrust. The best thing of all about the Convention was that it showed that a counter-imagination is possible - intelligent, open, and vigorous with disagreement and respect for the rights of others. Viva modern liberty!

ANTHONY BARNETT

(ENDNOTES)

1 For example, Juliet Stevenson who directed *Motherland,* on the imprisonment and the treatment of mothers and children asylum seekers in Yarl's Wood, was on stage on 28 February 2009; or Susie Orbach, who was speaking in Ireland; or David Marquand, who was unwell; or Nick Clegg, who was on paternity leave.

2 http://www.guardian.co.uk/commentisfree/2006/apr/23/humanrights.constitution

3 I discuss this episode in my contribution to Unlock Democracy's collection on 20 years of Charter 88, *Unlocking Democracy: 20 years of Charter 88,* Peter Facey, Bethan Rigby, Alexandra Runswick, eds, Politicos, 2008, pp 27-32.

4 Document 18, http://www.modernliberty.net/making-cml/history-of-cml/brief-history-making-the-convention-on-modern-liberty/the-documents/cml-doc-18-extracts-from-minutes-of-sponsor-meetings-showing-tension-between-event-movement

5 http://www.guardian.co.uk/society/2009/jul/22/kumi-naidoo-interview-social-justice-campaigner

6. http://www.guardian.co.uk/commentisfree/henryporter/2009/dec/09/big-state-hansard-society-civil-liberties

7 http://www.guardian.co.uk/commentisfree/2009/sep/20/catherine-bennett-safeguarding-children

8 http://www.modernliberty.net/read/transcripts/shami-chakrabartis-keynote

9 http://www.guardian.co.uk/commentisfree/henryporter/2009/mar/03/human-rights-act-modern-liberty

CONTRIBUTOR BIOGRAPHIES

Photo courtesy of Miki Yamanouchi

CML Biographies
(in alphabetical order)

GUY AITCHISON
Guy Aitchison is a contributing editor at openDemocracy.net and is currently working on the POWER2010 campaign for democratic reform. He was deputy director of the Convention on Modern Liberty.

ANTHONY BARNETT
Anthony Barnett is a writer and agitator. He was the Co-Director of the Convention on Modern Liberty, with Henry Porter. A founder of openDemocracy in 2001, he now edits its British blog, *Our Kingdom*. He was the first Director of *Charter 88*. Among his books are *Iron Britannia*, *Soviet Freedom*, *This Time* and, with Peter Carty, *The Athenian Option: Radical Reform of the House of Lords*. He writes regularly for openDemocracy.

PETER BAZALGETTE
Peter Bazalgette invests in digital media companies and acts as a consultant to such companies as Sony Music and Sony Pictures. Until 2007, he was Chief Creative Officer of Endemol and is a former Board member of Channel 4. He also serves as Deputy Chairman of English National Opera.

MOAZZAM BEGG
Moazzam Begg is one of nine British citizens held in US custody in Bagram and Guantanamo. He was released in 2005 without charge or apology. Since his release he has written an award-winning autobiography, *Enemy Combatant*, and appears regularly in the international media as a writer and commentator. As director of the human rights organisation, Cageprisoners, he lectures extensively around the country on issues surrounding imprisonment without trial, torture, anti-terror legislation and community relations.

FATIMA BHUTTO
Fatima Bhutto is a journalist and writer, born in Kabul in 1982. Her father was Murtaza Bhutto, who was killed by police in 1996 in Karachi during the premiership of his sister, Benazir Bhutto. Fatima's third book, *Songs of Blood and Sword*, a history of the Bhutto family and Pakistani politics, will be published

by Jonathan Cape in the spring of 2010.

GEOFFREY BINDMAN
Sir Geoffrey Bindman has practised as a solicitor in London for 50 years, specialising in civil liberties and human rights. He is a visiting professor of law at University College London and at London South Bank University and is chairman of the British Institute of Human Rights. He was knighted for services to human rights in January 2007.

TOM BINGHAM
Lord Bingham was called to the Bar in 1959 and was made QC in 1972. In 1980, he became Judge of the High Court and subsequently, Lord Justice of Appeal in 1986. From 1992 he was Master of the Rolls until he became Lord Chief Justice of England and Wales in 1996. He was then Senior Lord of Appeal in Ordinary from 2000-2008. Appointed a Knight of the Garter in 2005, he is the author of *The Business of Judging* (OUP, 2000). He will shortly publish: *The Rule of Law* (Allen Lane/Penguin) and *Widening Horizons* (Cambridge University Press). He is also the Chairman of the British Institute of International and Comparative Law and Reprieve.

ANDREW BLICK
Dr Andrew Blick is Senior Research Fellow at Democratic Audit. He is the author of *People Who Live in the Dark: the history of the special adviser in British politics* and *How to go to War: a handbook for democratic leaders*; and with Prof George Jones, the forthcoming *Premiership: the development, nature and power of the office of British Prime Minister*.

PHILLIP BLOND
Phillip Blond is director of ResPublica, a new public policy think tank. He is currently writing *Red Tory*, a book on radical conservatism. The New Statesman have called his thinking 'the only genuinely innovative political idea of the past few years.' He writes frequently for the mainstream press on economics, politics and social policy.

PHIL BOOTH
Phil Booth is the national coordinator of NO2ID, the UK-wide non-

partisan campaign opposing the National Identity Scheme and the database state. Founded in 2004, in response to the Government's stated intention to introduce the compulsory registration and lifelong tracking of UK citizens by means of a centralised biometric database, NO2ID seeks to put an informed case against state identity control to the media, to national institutions and to the public at large. NO2ID engages with all sections of the community, informs debate on database state issues and coordinates opposition to it.

CASPAR BOWDEN

Caspar is Chief Privacy Adviser in the Microsoft Worldwide Technology Office, providing expertise on the technology and public policy of privacy to 40 National Technology Officers around the world. He is a specialist in Data Protection and surveillance law, and privacy-enhancing technologies. In 1998, he co-founded the Foundation for Information Policy Research, with the late Professor Roger Needham and Professor Ross Anderson, an independent think-tank that studies the interaction between computers and society. He was appointed expert adviser to the UK House of Lords on three bills concerning privacy and surveillance. Previously he was a quantitative strategist with Goldman Sachs, and a software engineer consulting for clients including Microsoft, Acorn Computers, Research Machines, and IBM.

VICTORIA BRITTAIN

Victoria Brittain is a journalist and writer. Her most recent book is as co-author of Moazzam Begg's *Enemy Combatant*. She is on the board of the Institute of Race Relations.

GERALDINE VAN BUEREN

Geraldine Van Bueren, a barrister, is Professor of International Human Rights Law at Queen Mary, University of London and a Visiting Fellow at Kellogg College. Her forthcoming book *Law's Duty to the Poor* is commissioned by UNESCO. One of the original drafters of the United Nations Convention on the Rights of the Child, she is a recipient of the UNICEF Child Rights Lawyer Award. From December 2009 she was appointed as a Commissioner on the Equality and Human Rights Commission.

TONY BUNYAN

Tony Bunyan is an investigative journalist and writer specialising in justice and home affairs, civil liberties and freedom of information in the European Union. He has been the director of Statewatch since 1990 and edits *Statewatch bulletin* and *Statewatch News* online. He is the author of *The Political Police in Britain* (1977), *Secrecy and openness in the EU* (1999) and *The Shape of Things to Come* (2009) and edited *The War on Freedom and Democracy* (2005). He has taken ten successful complaints against the Council of the European Union and the European Commission to the European Ombudsman on access to EU documents.

JONATHAN BUTTERWORTH

Jonny previously held the position of President of the University College London Student Human Rights Programme (UCLSHRP) and now sits on the UCLSHRP Board of Advisors. He is currently employed by London School of Economics and Political Sciences as a Guest Teacher in the Law Department. Jonny is a human rights activist and campaigner, focusing on the protection of Economic and Social Rights, and is currently co-authoring a Democratic Audit publication, with Professor Stuart Weir, concerning the protection of Economic and Social Rights and Equality in the UK.

VINCE CABLE

Dr Vince Cable has been the Liberal Democrat Shadow Chancellor since November 2003 and is currently Deputy Leader of the Liberal Democrats. He founded and, until recently, chaired the All Party Parliamentary Groups on Police and Victims of Crime and has published several books and reports on international economics, trade and environmental issues. Most recently *The Storm* and *Free Radical* (both Atlantic Press).

DOUGLAS CARSWELL

Born in 1971, Douglas grew up in Uganda and Kenya where his parents worked as doctors amongst some of the world's poorest people. He read history at the University of East Anglia and King's College, London. Douglas had a proper job in business before politics, working in commercial television and then in fund management. Douglas has been the MP for Harwich and Clacton since May 2005. He is co-author of the best-selling book *The Plan: 12 months*

biographies

to renew Britain and has written for the *Financial Times, Sunday Times, Mail on Sunday, Telegraph* and *Spectator*, as well as appearing on the Politics Show and Radio 4's Week in Westminster and Westminster Hour.

TUFYAL CHOUDHURY
Tufyal Choudhury teaches international human rights law at Durham law school, is a Research Associate at the University of Oxford Centre on Migration, Policy and Society, a senior policy advisor to the Open Society Institute's 'Muslims in EU Cities' Project and a member of the EU Network of Experts on Violent Radicalisation. He is a graduate of the Universities of London (School of Oriental and African Studies, 1996) and Cambridge (Hughes Hall, 1998) and was called to the Bar as a member of Inner Temple in 1997.

CLARE COATMAN
Clare Coatman left school in Sheffield last year having completed A levels in Politics, Economics and Maths. She became active in politics due to the Iraq war and has since volunteered for a broad range of political parties (rapidly moving rightwards from Respect to the Liberal Democrats and most recently David Davis). She was the Participation Manager for the Convention on Modern Liberty and now runs Operations for POWER2010.

TONY CURZON PRICE
Tony Curzon Price is Editor-in-Chief of openDemocracy. He received a PhD in economics from University College London (UCL), and worked as a jobbing economist for more than ten years. He founded a high-tech electronics company, Arithmatica, in 1998 and lived in Silicon Valley from 2001 to 2004. He has lectured on economics and energy policy to postgraduates at Imperial College, London, and at the *École Polytechnique Fédérale de Lausanne* (EPFL).

DAVID DAVIS
David Davis was Parliamentary Secretary at the Office of Public Service and Science from May 1993 until July 1994 when he was appointed Minister of State at the Foreign and Commonwealth Office until April of 1997. From 1997 to 2001, he served as Chairman of the House of Commons Public Accounts Committee. In September 2001, he was appointed Chairman of the

Conservative Party, and in July 2002, he was appointed Shadow Secretary of State for the Office of the Deputy Prime Minister. From November 2003 to June 2008, David was the Shadow Home Secretary. As a backbench MP, he campaigns for civil liberties.

SAM DIMMOCK

Sam Dimmock is the Children's Rights Alliance for England's (CRAE) Head of Policy and Public Affairs. She is responsible for ensuring CRAE's human rights advocacy is focused on achieving the fullest possible implementation of the UN Convention on the Rights of the Child in England. She also oversees the strategic involvement of children and young people in CRAE's work. Sam began her career working in communications at the Imperial War Museum, after which she became the Education Co-ordinator at The Who Cares? Trust, a charity working with children in care. Prior to taking up her post at CRAE, Sam was the Regional Development Manager at Partnership for Young London, providing strategic development advice to youth services and organisations across London.

ANDREW DISMORE

Andrew Dismore is the Labour Member of Parliament for Hendon and is Chair of Parliament's Joint Select Committee on Human Rights. Prior to being elected to the Commons, Andrew was a solicitor specialising in personal injury and trades union law.

CORY DOCTOROW

Cory Doctorow (craphound.com) is a science fiction author, activist, journalist and blogger; the co-editor of *Boing Boing* (boingboing.net) and the author of the bestselling Tor Teens/HarperCollins UK novel *Little Brother*. He is the former European director of the Electronic Frontier Foundation and co-founded the UK Open Rights Group. Born in Toronto, Canada, he now lives in London.

TERRI DOWTY

Terri Dowty is Director of Action on Rights for Children (ARCH), a children's civil rights organisation with a particular focus on privacy and data protection. Terri is on the advisory councils of the Foundation for Information Policy

Research and of Privacy International, and is a co-author of the 2006 FIPR report to the Information Commissioner: *Children's Databases: Safety and Privacy*, and the recent Rowntree Reform Trust report *Database State*.

MICHAEL EDWARDS
Michael Edwards is a Distinguished Senior Fellow at Demos in New York, and a Senior Visiting Fellow at New York and Manchester Universities. From 1999 to 2008, he was the Director of the Ford Foundation's Governance and Civil Society Program, and also co-founded the Seasons Fund for Social Transformation. His latest book is *Small Change: Why Business Won't Save the World* (Berrett-Koehler).

BRIAN ENO
Brian Eno (born 1948) is an English musician and artist who lives in London. He has worked extensively in Ambient Music and Generative Music, and has collaborated with a wide range of other artists, including Roxy Music, David Bowie, Laurie Anderson, Talking Heads, U2, and Coldplay. He is a patron of British American Security Information Council (BASIC) and Client Earth.

EDWARD FITZGERALD
Edward Fitzgerald, the winner of the Silk of the Year award in 2005 and *Times* Justice Human Rights Award in 1998, specialises in criminal law, public law and international human rights law. In June 2008, he was awarded the CBE for services to human rights.

LIZ FORGAN
Dame Liz Forgan is Chair of the Scott Trust Ltd and also of Arts Council England. She was a newspaper journalist and later Director of Programmes at Channel 4 TV and Managing Director of BBC Network Radio.

TIMOTHY GARTON ASH
Professor Timothy Garton Ash is the author of nine books of 'history of the present', including most recently *Facts are Subversive: Political Writing from a Decade without a Name*. He is Professor of European Studies in the University of Oxford, Isaiah Berlin Professorial Fellow at St Antony's College, Oxford, and a Senior Fellow at the Hoover Institution, Stanford University. His essays

appear regularly in the *New York Review of Books* and he writes a weekly column in the *Guardian* which is widely syndicated in Europe, Asia and the Americas.

ALEX GASK
Alex was legal officer at Liberty between 2003 and 2008, in which time he developed an expertise on ASBOs - working as both a campaigner and a lawyer. He is now a barrister at Doughty Street Chambers where he has a broad civil and criminal practice, with a particular focus on human rights. Since coming to the Bar, Alex has been instructed in the fields of immigration, prison law, civil action, media law and criminal defence and extradition.

ANDREW GILLIGAN
Andrew Gilligan is London editor of the *Daily* and *Sunday Telegraph*. He was made Journalist of the Year in the British Press Awards for 2008. He clashed with the British Government over the weapons of mass destruction dossier used to justify war in Iraq. He has had a longstanding interest in civil liberties issues.

JO GLANVILLE
Jo Glanville is editor of Index on Censorship and a former BBC current affairs producer. Her anthology *Qissat: short stories by Palestinian Women* was published in 2006 by Telegram.

DAVID GOODHART
David Goodhart is the founder and editor of the London-based *Prospect* magazine. Before that he worked for the *Financial Times* for 12 years, including a stint as a correspondent in Germany during the unification period. He has written various books and pamphlets, the latest being *Progressive Nationalism: citizenship and the left* (Demos). He is married to the *FT* columnist Lucy Kellaway. They have four children and live in Highbury, North London.

JAMES GRAHAM
James Graham is the Campaigns and Communications Manager of Unlock Democracy and coordinated the online 'Carnival on Modern Liberty' on behalf of the Convention. A former Liberal Democrat staffer and election agent, he writes *Quaequam Blog!* which won the 2007 Best Liberal Democrat Blog Award. He is also the Secretary of the Social Liberal Forum and a regular

biographies

contributor to the *Guardian's* Comment is Free website. James is an avid comics reader, cinephile and player of German board games.

AC GRAYLING
AC Grayling is professor of philosophy at Birkbeck College, University of London. He has written and edited many books on philosophy and other subjects. Among his most recent are *Towards the Light: The Struggles for Liberty and Rights that Made the Modern West*, and *Liberty in the Age of Terror*.

DOMINIC GRIEVE
A barrister and QC, Dominic was elected as a Member of Parliament for Beaconsfield in 1997. Having previously held posts as Shadow Attorney General and Shadow Home Secretary, Dominic is now the Shadow Secretary of State for Justice.

GERRY HASSAN
Gerry Hassan is a writer, researcher and political commentator on Scottish and UK politics. He is the author and editor of over a dozen books including *After Blair: Politics after the New Labour Decade* (Lawrence and Wishart) and *The Modern SNP: From Protest to Power* (Edinburgh University Press). Future publications include an analysis of the nature and future of the United Kingdom with Anthony Barnett. Gerry's writings and research can be found at: www.gerryhassan.com.

IAIN HENDERSON
Iain Henderson works on Mydex, a social enterprise initiative planning to help individuals realise the value of their personal information. He also blogs about buyer-centricity/ VRM issues at *Right Side Up* and at *The Kantara Initiative* and carries out customer information strategy work for clients through Information Answers or H2X.

JERRY HICKS
Jerry Hicks joined AEU when he started work at Rolls Royce Bristol in 1975 as an apprentice. He was elected as Shop Steward in 1984, as Deputy Convener in 1987 and as Convener for the Test Areas in 1990. In 2003, he was elected to the Amicus National Executive Committee (polling the highest vote in the

393

Aerospace and Shipbuilding sector). In June of 2005 a 48-hour occupation of the 'Test Areas' saved the jobs of two fitters who were facing dismissal. Six weeks later, Jerry was sacked by Rolls Royce using trumped up charges based on unfounded allegations and anti-union legislation. A tribunal pre-hearing found in his favour and that in all probability he was sacked for trade union activities i.e. victimised. In 2008, though given 'no chance of success', his legal challenge forced an election for General Secretary of the Unite Amicus section when he came runner up to the incumbent GS and ahead of the other candidates, all of whom were national officials. Jerry has announced his intention to run again next year.

DAVID HOWARTH

David became Cambridge's MP in 2005 and is Shadow Secretary of State for Justice. He won his seat in Parliament after a 17-year political career with Cambridge City Council where he served in Castle Ward from 1987. He became leader of the Liberal Democrat group in 1990 and leader of the City Council in 2000. David was a member of the party's Federal Policy Committee from 1989 to 2000 and is a respected expert on economics and law, having played a leading role in formulating Liberal Democrat economic policy. Born in Walsall, near Wolverhampton, he went to a local state school before moving to Cambridge from where he graduated with a first class honours degree in law from Clare College. He took up postgraduate studies, gaining masters degrees in Law and Sociology from Yale University. David taught law and economics at Cambridge University and is a fellow of Clare College. He has lived in the city since 1977.

CHRIS HUHNE

Chris Huhne is the Liberal Democrats' shadow Home Secretary. He was an economic and financial journalist for nineteen years, writing for the *Independent* and the *Guardian*. He was also a City economist for five years, before being elected as a member of the European Parliament in 1999. Chris resigned from the European Parliament when he was elected as Eastleigh's MP in 2005.

SUNNY HUNDAL

Sunny Hundal is editor of the group blog/magazine *Liberal Conspiracy*, which aims to reinvigorate British left liberalism through online campaigning and discussion. He also blogs at *Pickled Politics*. As a journalist and commentator, he has written for the *Guardian*, the *Independent*, *Metro*, the *Times* and the *Financial Times* on media, the environment and race relations. He founded the think tank New Generation Network, which aims to challenge the thinking around race and faith politics, and is editor of the online magazine *Asians in Media*. In 2006, he was voted *Guardian* 'blogger of the year'. An ardent environmentalist and an unashamed lefty-liberal, he is vegetarian and cares strongly about the oppression of people and degradation of nature.

MURRAY HUNT

Murray Hunt has been the Legal Adviser to Parliament's Joint Committee on Human Rights since 2004. Before that he was a practising barrister at Matrix specialising in human rights and public law. He is the author of a number of publications concerning human rights and public law, including *Using Human Rights Law in English Courts*.

WILL HUTTON

Will Hutton joined The Work Foundation in 2000 and was Chief Executive until mid-2008 when he became Executive Vice Chair. He began his career as a stockbroker and investment analyst, before working in BBC TV and radio as a producer and reporter. Prior to joining The Work Foundation, Will spent four years as editor-in-chief of the *Observer* and he continues to write a weekly column for the paper.

NEIL JAMESON

Neil Jameson has been Executive Director of Citizens UK for the last 20 years and Lead Organiser with London Citizens for the last 15 years. As such, he and his colleague organisers are now driving the UK's largest and most diverse community-organising Training Institute, professional Guild of Organisers and a growing network of Citizens' Alliances like London Citizens. He is first and foremost a Community Organiser – seeking talented leaders and young Organisers who have the courage and commitment to work with others democratically to strengthen civil society and pursue the common good. He has travelled extensively and worked in the US and Sudan on civil society projects. Prior to Citizens, he worked for 20 years in the public and voluntary sector – with Somerset and Coventry Local Authority – and Save the Children and The Children's Society in the UK. He seeks a legacy of a much stronger, more powerful and better organised civil society sector in the UK, and knows that this will not just happen but needs sophisticated and creative citizens' organisers and leaders who see their primary role as institution builders and the development and political growth of the people they serve.

SIMON JENKINS
Simon Jenkins is a journalist and author. He writes columns twice weekly for the *Guardian* and weekly for the *Evening Standard*.

VAUGHAN JONES
Vaughan Jones is the Chief Executive of Praxis, a voluntary organisation working with vulnerable migrants in East London. He founded Praxis 26 years ago and today, the organisation provides extensive advice, guidance, interpreting, leadership development and community work to some of the most vulnerable in our society. He is also a non-stipendiary Minister in the United Reformed Church.

MARY KALDOR
Mary Kaldor is Professor and Director of the Centre for the Study of Global Governance at the London School of Economics and Political Science. She previously worked at the Stockholm International Peace Research Institute (SIPRI), and the Science Policy Research Unit and the Sussex European Institute at the University of Sussex. Her books include *The Baroque Arsenal* (1982), *The Imaginary War* (1990), *New and Old Wars: Organised Violence in a Global Era* (1999), and *Global Civil Society: An Answer to War* (2003). She was a founder member of European Nuclear Disarmament (END), founder and Co-Chair of the Helsinki Citizen's Assembly, and a member of the International Independent Commission to investigate the Kosovo Crisis, established by the Swedish Prime Minister and chaired by Richard Goldstone, which published the *Kosovo Report* (Oxford: OUP) in autumn 2000. Mary Kaldor was also convenor of the study group on European Security Capabilities established at the request of Javier Solana, which produced the Barcelona report, *A Human Security Doctrine for Europe* and in 2007 the follow-up report, *A European Way of Security: The Madrid Report of the Human Security Study Group*.

biographies

HELENA KENNEDY
Baroness Helena Kennedy is a leading barrister and an expert in human rights law, civil liberties and constitutional issues. She is a member of the House of Lords and chair of Justice – the British arm of the International Commission of Jurists. She is a bencher of Gray's Inn and President of the School of Oriental and African Studies, University of London. She was the chair of Charter 88 from 1992 to 1997, the Human Genetics Commission from 1998 to 2007 and the British Council from 1998 to 2004.

PAUL KINGSNORTH
Paul Kingsnorth is the author of *Real England: the battle against the bland*, and the co-founder of the Dark Mountain Project (www.dark-mountain.net).

FRANCESCA KLUG
Francesca Klug is a Professorial Research Fellow at the London School of Economics and Director of the Human Rights Futures Project. Francesca was previously a Senior Research Fellow at the Human Rights Incorporation Project at King's College Law School where she assisted the government in devising the model for incorporating the European Convention on Human Rights into UK law reflected in the Human Rights Act. From 2006-2009, Francesca was a Commissioner on the statutory Equality and Human Rights Commission. She is a frequent broadcaster and has written widely on human rights, including *Values for a Godless Age: the story of the UK Bill of Rights* (Penguin, 2000). She is currently writing a sequel to this book, to be published by Routledge.

MELISSA LANE
Melissa Lane is Professor of Politics at Princeton University, following fifteen years of teaching political thought in the Faculty of History of the University of Cambridge. Her primary expertise is in ancient Greek political thought and its modern significance. Her books include *Plato's Progeny: how Plato and Socrates still captivate the modern mind* (Duckworth, 2001) and a new Introduction to the Penguin Classics edition of *Plato's Republic* (2007); forthcoming is *Eco-Republic: Ancient Ethics for the Green Age*. She is a faculty member of HRH The Prince of Wales' Business and the Environment Programme and Fellow of the Royal Historical Society and the Royal Society for the encouragement of the Arts, Manufactures and Commerce.

KEN MACDONALD

Sir Ken Macdonald, QC, practises at Matrix Chambers and is a visiting Professor of Law at the London School of Economics. He was Director of Public Prosecutions, 2003-2008 where he was the first leading defence lawyer to have been appointed to that post. Since stepping down, he has been an outspoken critic of the communications database proposed by the government to track phone calls, emails, texts and internet use.

SUZANNE MOORE

Suzanne Moore is an award-winning columnist on the *Mail on Sunday*. She formerly wrote for the *Guardian* and the *Independent*.

IVO MOSLEY

Ivo Mosley is a freelance writer who is occasionally asked to write or talk on politics. A descendant of the notorious fascist Sir Oswald Mosley, he has thought long and hard about the perpetual inroads upon freedom made by those who seek power as an end in itself. He is at present working on a study of how electoral representation has empowered new, irresponsible and unaccountable elites.

PETER OBORNE

Peter Oborne is Political Columnist for the *Daily Mail*, Contributing Editor to the *Spectator*, and presents documentary films for Channel Four. Peter Oborne's films for Channel 4 *Dispatches* include: *Iraq: The Reckoning; Afghanistan: Here's One we Invaded Earlier; Mugabe's Secret Famine, Darfur: Into the Death Zone* and *Spinning Terror*. He is a regular presenter on BBC Radio Four's *The Week in Westminster*. His latest book, *The Triumph of the Political Class* (Simon and Schuster) is published in paperback.

HENRY PORTER

Henry Porter is a novelist and political columnist for the *Observer* newspaper in London. Since 2005, he has been chronicling the attack on liberty and rights in Britain. He has now written some ninety columns on the subject. In 2006, Tony Blair suggested an email debate with Porter and, after three robust exchanges, the correspondence was published in the *Observer*. Porter has written six novels. His latest title is *The Dying Light*, a political thriller set a few years in the future. He is also the UK Editor of the American magazine *Vanity Fair*. He lives in London.

STEVE POWELL

Steve works part-time for the Football Supporters' Federation (FSF) as Director of Policy. He is a former full-time official with the public service trade union Unison and has worked in the private, public and voluntary sectors. He has been an Arsenal supporter since 1968 and a season ticket holder since 1980/81. He is a life member of the Arsenal Football Supporters' Club and a founding life member and former chair of the Arsenal Independent Supporters' Association, both of which are affiliated to the FSF. He is also a founding life member and former board member of the Arsenal Supporters' Trust. He has been an individual member of the FSF and the Football Supporters' Association (FSA) (one of the FSF's two founding partners) since 1996.

PHILIP PULLMAN

Philip Pullman is a celebrated writer whose *Dark Materials* trilogy has drawn adult and children readers into a lively dialogue about faith. His interest in Milton illuminates his attitudes to liberty as rooted in an English tradition that he seeks to revive.

DOMINIC RAAB

Dominic Raab was an international lawyer at the Foreign Office, before working as Chief of Staff to respective Shadow Home and Justice Secretaries, David Davis and Dominic Grieve. In January he published *The Assault on Liberty - What Went Wrong With Rights*, and was selected in November by open primary to be the Conservative candidate for Esher & Walton at the next election.

BILL RAMMELL

Bill Rammell is the Labour MP for Harlow, and has served as a junior Minister at the Foreign Office, was Minister of State for Lifelong Learning, Further and Higher Education, Minister of State for the Middle East, and is currently Minister of State for the Armed Forces.

GEOFFREY ROBERTSON

Geoffrey Robertson QC is founder and head of Doughty Street Chambers, a

Recorder, a bencher of the Middle Temple and served as the First President of the United Nations Special Court for Sierra Leone. He is currently a member of the UN Justice Council. His books include *The Justice Game* – a memoir of some of his notable trials – and *The Tyrannicide Brief* – an account of how Cromwell's lawyers brought the King to justice.

PAUL ROGERS
Paul Rogers is Professor of Peace Studies at Bradford University where he teaches courses on international security, arms control and political violence. He has written or edited 26 books and his work has been translated into many languages including Chinese, Japanese, Turkish and Farsi. The third edition of his book *Losing Control: Global Security in the 21st Century*, will be published early in 2010. Paul Rogers is international security consultant for the Oxford Research Group, writes a weekly assessment of international security trends for openDemocracy and was Chair of the British International Studies Association, 2002-2004.

ALAN RUSBRIDGER
Alan Rusbridger has been editor of the *Guardian* since 1995. He has campaigned for changes in the libel laws and defended several large libel actions (mostly successfully!).

JENNI RUSSELL
Jenni Russell is a writer, commentator and broadcaster. She worked for many years at the BBC and ITN, most recently as editor of *The World Tonight* on Radio 4.

MICHAEL RUSTIN
Michael Rustin is Professor of Sociology at the University of East London, and a Visiting Professor at the Tavistock Clinic. He is author of *The Good Society and the Inner World* and many other writings. He was once on the Council of Charter 88, and is a founding editor of *Soundings*. He is a member and supporter of *Compass*.

HARRIET SERGEANT
Harriet Sergeant has written three books, one on apartheid in South Africa, and five reports for the Centre for Policy Studies on social issues, as well as a report

on the police for Civitas. She writes for the *Daily Mail* and the *Sunday Times* as well as appearing on TV and radio. Her most recent report published for the Centre For Policy Studies is *WASTED - the betrayal of white working class and black Caribbean boys.*

QUENTIN SKINNER
Quentin Skinner is Barber Beaumont Professor of the Humanities at Queen Mary. Professor Skinner was previously the Regius Professor of Modern History at the University of Cambridge. His work has won him fellowships of several academic Academies, including the British Academy, The American Academy and the Academia Europaea, and he has been the recipient of numerous honorary degrees, including degrees from Chicago, Harvard and Oxford.

ROGER SMITH
Roger Smith OBE is the director of Justice, the all-party human rights and law reform organisation. Justice is dedicated to improving access to justice, human rights and the rule of law. It has around 1500 members, largely lawyers. Justice supported the passage of the Human Rights Act and argues that considerable care must be taken to preserve its impact if it is to be, in any way, amended.

SAM TALBOT RICE
Sam Talbot Rice is Research Director at the Centre for Policy Studies (CPS). Before joining the CPS in 2007, he was a Policy Adviser in the Conservative Research Department, and a Researcher to two front-bench MPs. He graduated with a degree in history from Cambridge University in 2003. His areas of policy interest include media policy, public service reform and issues around privacy and the 'database state'.

UCLSHRP
The UCL Student Human Rights Programme (UCLSHRP) is a dynamic pro-active human rights organisation, led by students and advised by human rights academics and professionals, with members from all walks of life. Because our rights are worth protecting, the UCLSHRP seeks to foster a vibrant culture of human rights within UCL and wider communities by initiating awareness, instigating debate and inspiring action. The UCLSHRP was only founded in mid-September 2007 but within a year, had blossomed into lectures, panel discussions, research, a bulletin, a law journal, a moot competition and a

website. Above all, the Programme is proof that not all students are apathetic in the face of Bentham's charge that rights are 'nonsense on stilts'! For the UCLSHRP, the debate about our rights as human beings need not be confined to university lecture theatres and libraries, and certainly not the law section of the library. They want to see human rights introduced into the conspicuous elements of our culture: such as music, fashion, art, literature, food and academia. For more information and to get involved please visit: www.uclshrp.com.

DAVID VARNEY

Sir David Varney joined Shell in 1968 after gaining a BSc (Chemistry) from Surrey University. He gained an MBA at Manchester Business School in 1971. Returning to Shell, he worked in Australia, Holland and Sweden before becoming Head of Oil Products Europe. In 1996, he became Chief Executive of BG plc (previously British Gas). In 2002, he became Executive Chairman of Mmo2 plc. In 2004, he was appointed Chairman of HM Revenue & Customs.

MARINA WARNER

Marina Warner is a writer of fiction, criticism and history; her works include novels and short stories as well as studies of myths, symbols, and fairytales. She is Professor in the Department of Literature, Film and Theatre Studies, University of Essex.

STUART WEIR

Stuart Weir is Associate Director of Democratic Audit, the independent research organisation that audits democracy and human rights in the UK. He formerly founded Charter 88 and was the first director of Democratic Audit in which capacity he wrote and edited numerous books and reports (as he still does). He has written and edited joint guides to democracy assessment for the inter-governmental International Institute for Democracy and Electoral Assistance, and has acted as a consultant on parliamentary democracy throughout sub-Saharan Africa.

STUART WILKS-HEEG

Dr Stuart Wilks-Heeg is the Executive Director of Democratic Audit, an independent research organisation which monitors the quality of democracy in the UK, and Lecturer in Social Policy at the University of Liverpool.

MICHAEL WILLS

Michael Wills has been the MP for North Swindon since 1997 and the Minister of State in the Ministry of Justice since 2007.

INDEX

A
Aamer, Shaker, 240
Abbott, Diane, 6
ABC trial, 352
Abu Ghraib, military detention site, 246-7
academia, competitive, 271
accountability, 41, 196, 258, 265, 340, 369
  lack of, 103, 131
  MPs, 233
ACPO (Association of Chief Police Officers), 103, 111
Action on Rights for Children (ARCH), 294
Acton, Lord John, 201
Adams, John, 128-9
adult-child interaction, endangered, 297-300
advertising
  targeted, 78
  Web, 72
Afghanistan, 63, 343
  civilian deaths, 68
Al-Marri, Ali, 244
Al-Jazeera, bombing of idea, 96
Al-Qaida, 343
Algeria, 249
Alibhai-Brown, Yasmin, 4, 361
American Bill of Rights, 208
American Revolution, 280
American War of Independence, 128
Amicus trade union, 139
Amin, Idi, 204
'anchor institutions', 132
Anderson, Ross, 364
anger
  middle class, 313
  public sector, 312
  unemployed graduates, 311
anti-Muslim immigration politics, Netherlands, 59
Anti-Social Behaviour Act 2003, 18-21, 26, 302, 339, 358
Anti-Social Behaviour Orders (ASBOs), 14 197, 212, 289
  naming and shaming, 301-2
  varying scope, 299-300
Anti-Terrorism Crime and Security Act 2001, 14, 17, 26, 194
Appignanesi, Lisa, 270
Applebee, Humphrey, 203
Aristotle, 127
arms production, UK-US, 69-70
artists, role of, 268, 325
Arts Council, 370
Asylum and Immigration Act 2004, 15
asylum seekers, 17, 21
  Christian accommodation, 83
authoritarianism, 41
automated number-plate recognition (ANPR), 22, 96, 103, 332, 375
Azmeh, Umar, 23

B
Baby P case, 37, 366
BAE systems, 69-70
  Saudi Arabia case, 341
Bagram air base detention site, 245-7
bailiffs, new house entry powers, 4, 21, 312
balance, media concept of, 275
Ban Ki-Moon, 60
banks
  bail-out of, 220-1
  Banque Paribas, 307
  BearSterns, 307
  system regulation lack, 309
Barenboim, Daniel, Reith Lectures, 271
Barking and Dagenham
  employment decline, 125
Barnardo's, 299
Barnett, Anthony, 4-5, 9, 222, 329, 363, 371
Barrow, Simon, 80
Baum, Gerhard, 319
Bauman, Zygmunt, 218
Bazalgette, Peter, 76
BBC (British Broadcasting Corporation), 102, 275, 363, 370, 375

Licence Fee, 203
  pay excesses, 380
  World Service Russian Service, 376
Beacon, 77
Bean, Charlie, 307
Begg, Moazzam, 240, 247
Belarus, 209
Belmarsh prison, London, 194, 242, 248, 259, 265, 318
Bennett, Catherine, 376, 380
Berlin Wall, fall of, 144
Berlin, Isaiah, 87
Bhutto, Fatima, 94
Bill of Rights 1688, 50
bill of rights, contemporary, 207
  need for, 89
  Northern Ireland discussion, 336
  proposals, 209, 256, 263
  Tory suggestion, 250
  See also, British Bill of Rights
Bindman, Sir Geoffrey, 51
Bingham, Lord Thomas, 13, 47, 190, 240, 280, 286, 329, 362-3
biometrics, 17-18
Birmingham Six, miscarriage of justice, 345
Blackwater Company, 62
Blair, Tony, 6, 34, 96, 116, 118, 182, 247, 250, 338, 352, 371
Blake, William, 24, 328
Blick, Andrew, 185, 193
blogs, 170-1, 278-9
Blond, Phillip, 89
Blunkett, David, 331-2, 358
BNP (British National Party), 124-5, 313, 341, 348, 361
  free speech rights, 62
  leaked membership list, 126
Boing Boing, 370
Bolivar, Simón, 108
Booth, Phil, 10, 171, 373
Bosnia, 56, 67, 70
Bowden, Caspar, 72, 75
Bradford, 122
Bragg, Billy, 362
Brazil, 68, 219
British Library, 50
British Army, Iraqi death, 12
British Bill of Rights, 113, 259-60
  (and Responsibilities), 318
  need for, 57-8
  proposals, 208, 226, 253
  See also, Bill of Rights
British Film Institute, 370
British Institute for Human Rights, 253
British liberty, establishment myth, 225
British Museum, 280
British Muslims, loyalty to Britain, 123
British National Party, see above, BNP
British Youth Council, 292
'Britishness', 47, 115, 117, 360
Brittain, Victoria, 240, 249
Broadcasting Policy Group, 276
Broderick, James, 21
Brooke, Heather, 170, 378
Brown, Gordon, 51, 76, 113, 118, 281, 365
  'Britishness' project, 115, 117
Brown, Ian, 364
BT, 74
Bunyan, Tony, 178
Burckhardt, Jacob, 130
Burke, Edmund, 87, 90
Burma, rhetorical use of, 346-7
Burnley, 125
  Gaza support raids, 124
  job losses, 126
Bush, George W, 6, 63, 96, 200, 283
Butterworth, Jonathan, 23, 194

C

Cabinet Office, Security and Intelligence Coordination, 40
Cable, Vince, 323, 333
Cageprisoners, 239
Cambridge Union Society, 337
Cameron, David, 208, 247, 378
Campaign for an English Parliament, 113-14
Campbell, Alistair, 98
Canadian Charter of Rights, 207
Candler, Jean, 256
capitalism, corporate concentration, 313
Cardiff University, 121
Carroll, Malcolm, 104
Carswell Douglas, 202, 207, 211-12
cartel politics, 281-3
Carter, Lord Stephen of Coles, 52, 76,

CCTV cameras, 138, 198, 358-9, 372
  justification for, 344-5
censorship, 60-1
  journalistic self-97-8
  Pakistan, 94-5
  of English republican history, 227-8, 231
Centre for Policy Studies, 175
Chahal vs United Kingdom case, 248-9
Chakrabarti, Shami, 35, 55, 173, 264, 373, 378
Channel 4, 370
  Dispatches, 97, 368
Charles I, trial of, 227
Charter 88, 116, 325
  agenda, 222
  Bill of Rights campaign, 184
Charter of the Forests, England, 254
Chatham, Earl of, 47
children
  databases, 180, 375
  management approach, 295-6
  media negativity, 290-3, 298-9
  poverty, 254
  protection database, 297, 376, 380
  rights, 289
Children & Young People Now, 290
Children Act 2004, 188
Children's Rights Alliance for England (CRAE), 291-2
China, 69, 219
  climate change issue, 58
  Maoist, 322
  riot control outfits, 65
  sovereignty notion, 56
Choudhury, Tufyal, 121
Christianity, 235
  Church of England, 79-80
  Churches personnel international exchanges, 84
  English civil war tradition, 81
  practical, 236
Churchill, Winston, 209, 334, 353
CIA (Central Intelligence Agency)
  agents, 244
citizenship, 79, 266, 378
  non-citizens, 264
  people of faith, 80

Civil Contingencies Act 2004, 21-2, 26, 189
civil disobediance, 144
civil liberties, 34-5
  as 'maverick' portrayal, 371
civil partnerships, 269
civil rights, erosion monitoring, 12
civil servants, 377
Civil Wars
  English, 228
  US, 129
civilians, majority war victims, 67, 70
climate change, 58, 64-5, 68-9, 84, 322, 352
  Copenhagen conference, 368
  global warming, 88, 142
Climbié, Victoria case, 37, 215, 296
Clinton, Bill, 343
Coalition Provisional Authority Iraq,
  neoliberalism of, 63
Coe, Seb, 135
Cohen, Nick, 93
Coke, Sir Edward, 51, 226
Colnbrook Detention Centre, 82
Columbia School of Journalism, 286
Comment is Free, 170-1
Common Assessment Framework, 365
common law, 32, 35
Communist Party of Great Britain, Cold War era, 348
community organizing, 132
Comparative Media Law Centre, Oxford, 101
Compass, 218, 372, 378
'Connexions' experiment, 295
Connor, Leo, 96
Conservative Party, UK, 33, 42-3, 85, 113, 117, 220-1, 247, 254, 257, 317, 378
conspiracy/cock-up theory smugness, 379
Constable, Pamela, 62
consumer tracking, Web, 72
ContactPoint, children's database, 10, 17, 215, 289, 294-6, 338, 365-6
control orders, 13, 185, 242, 318, 333
Convention against Torture, 249
Convention on the Rights of the Child, 293

Cook, Robin, 286
Cool Britannia, 116
copyright rules, 370
Coroner's inquests, 12
  Coroners and Justice Bill 2009, 12, 16, 19, 22, 176
counter-insurgency, as terror, 67
counter-terrorism agenda, 119, 121-3
  Counter-Terrorism Act 2008, 15, 17, 19, 194, 340
  legislation, 187
  rationalisation use, 53
courage, political, 332, 334
courts, 190
  equal access to, 51
  House of Lords, see below
  role(s) of, 259, 263
  Star Chamber, 47
Cowley agency workers, sacking of, 138
credit monitoring, 38
Crick, Bernard, 228
crime
  alcohol-related, 105-6
  criminal justice politicization, 32
  - liberty trade-off, 33
  statistics obsession, 109-10
Crime and Disorder Act 1998, 26, 300
Crime and Terrorism Cabinet Sub-committee, 345
Criminal Justice Act 2003, 26
Criminal Justice and Immigration Act 2008, 21
Criminal Justice and Police Act 2001, 18, 26
Criminal Records Bureau (CRB) check systems, 18
Cromwell, Oliver, 228
Crouch, Colin, *Coping with Post-Democracy*, 282
cryptography, 73
curfew power, 302
Customer Relationship Management, 74
cyber crimes idea, Pakistan, 95
Czech Republic, 308

D

Daily Mail, 32, 42, 55, 57, 99, 210, 278, 291, 321, 332, 359
Daily Telegraph, 42, 310
Daly, Tony, 23
Dangerous Dogs Act, 206
Data
  Data Protection Act 1998, 16, 215
  mining, 40, 181
  private communication, 41
  protection regulation, 73
  retention, 77, 179, see also, DNA
  sharing, 6, 37, 213, 338
  state database, see below, state
  UK collection, 8
Davies, Gavyn, 275
Davies, Nick, *Flat Earth News*, 275
Davies, Simon, 174
Davis, David, 228, 362, 371
De Menezes, Jean-Charles, 97, 103
  death cover-up, 143
debt, personal, 312
Declaration of Arbroath, 50
delight, virtue of, 327
democracy, 128
  Direct notion 212
  property-owning, 91
Democratic Audit, 183
Democratic Republican Party USA, 130
demonstrations
  limitations on, 20
  police photographers, 340-1
Demos, 378
Denham, John, 296
Denning, Lord Alfred, 258
deportation(s)
  bail conditions, 241
  irresponsible, 84
Detainee Treatment Act, US, 208
detention without charge/trial, 248, 317, 345
  28 days, 340
  42 days proposed/defeated, 79, 87, 113, 331-2, 353, 372
  90 days, 317, 330
devolution UK, 116-17
Digital Britain, aspiration, 76
Digital Economy Bill, 369
Dimmock, Sam, 290
Diplock courts, 33-4
disestablishment, UK, 81
Dismore, Andrew, 260
dispersal zones UK, 302

displaced people, war aim, 67-8
DNA database, 10, 18, 36, 43-4, 259, 330-3, 338, 374
  crime-solving ratio, 365
  samples retention, 18, 111, 280
Doctorow, Cory, 369
Domestic Violence Crime and Victims Act 2004, 22, 26
domination, urge to, 273
Dowty, Terri, 294, 364
Draft (Partial) Immigration and Citizenship Bill, 17
Dutch Muslim Broadcasting Association, 59
Dutch Press centre, 59
Dyke, Greg, 275

E

E-Borders Scheme, 17
East Germany, rhetorical use, 346
economic recession, 280, 333
education, business model, 323
Education Act 1997
  National Pupil Database, 189
Edwards, Michael, 271
Egypt, torture assurances, 250
Eisenhower, Dwight, 285
Ekklesia, 79-80
elections
  mechanism importance, 234
  proportionate representation, 196, 284
  reform need, 202, 205
  system of representation, 128, 130, 199-200
'elective dictatorship', UK Constitution, 258
electronic monitoring, 13, 15, 242
ELINT, 351
Eliot, John, 226-7
Eliot, Oz, 286
elite(s), 65
  American Founding fathers, 128-30
Elstein, David, 276
empathy, global, 320-1
'Employment law'/anti-Union legislation, 138, 144
England
  minority ethnic populations, 360
  racial tolerance, 361

English Bill of Rights 1689, 209
English Revolution, 229-30, 232
Enlightenment, the
  European models of, 91
  Traditions, 309
Eno, Brian, 320
Europe
  aggressive policing, 181
  ethnic scapegoating, 56
  soldier numbers, 68
European Convention on Human Rights (ECHR), 12-13, 19, 22, 44, 55, 57, 88, 209, 253, 256-7, 259-60
European Court of Human Rights, 18, 55-8, 184, 247, 250, 257, 259
  Chahal vs UK, 248
European Parliament, racists, 180
European Social Charter, 254, 256
European Union, 6, 116
  bail-out role doubt, 308
  data retention, 178
  human rights norms, 265
  Posted Workers Directive, 139
  'security-industrial complex', 179
  shift to the right, 180
Evening Standard, 99
Every Child Matters system, 295
evidence
  character rules change, 340
  raw intelligence as, 241
  secret, 240, 246
Ewing, Keith, 190, 195
Ex-parte Levellers case, 352
Experts, media dominance, 305
Extradition Act 2003, 26
extraordinary rendition, 246, 341

F

Fabian Society, 217, 372, 378
face recognition programmes, 332
Facebook, 39, 74, 170
  financial model lack, 76
  private data profligacy, 77
Facey, Peter, 198
Factory Acts, 220
Fairclough, Anna, 105
fairy tales, 269
faith communities, 81, 83
Fallujah, November 2004 assault on,

62-3, 118
family, the, 268-9
Faraday, Michael, 329
Federalist Papers, 198
feminists, 268, 270
Field, Frank, 377
file sharing, criminalised, 370
financial crisis, global contemporary, 7, 65, 69
Financial Service Authority, 203-4
Financial Times, 65, 321
fingerprint passports, 178-9
FIT database, 103
Fitzgerald, Edward, 363
Focus on the Global South website, 66
Football Supporters' Federation, 105, 108
Forgan, Liz, 277
Form 27, 103
Fortress Europe, 181
Foundation for Information Policy Research (FIPR), 72-3, 364
Fox, Liam, 282-3
France, car industry, 308
Franklin, Benjamin, 49, 129
Freedom of Information (FOI), 170, 215, 377
freedom, as absence of impediments, 229-30
Friedman, Edie, 120
'function creep', National Pupil Database, 189

G

G8, 178
Gaddafi, Muamar, 249
Galbraith, John Kenneth, The Great Crash 1929, 307
Gamble, Andrew, 218, 337, 347, 351
Gandhi, Mahatma, 272
Garnier, Edward QC, 86
Garton Ash, Timothy, 55, 69
Gaza
  Blackburn 2008 convoy to, 124
  demonstrations for, 322, 340, 352
  Israeli invasion, 66-7, 143
gender stereotyping, 270
Geneva Conventions, 53, 209, 247
Germany, post-war constitution, 318

Giddy, Pam, 127
Gilligan, Andrew, 96, 275
Gladstone, William, 185
Glanville, Jo, 59
global warming, 88, 142
globalisation, 66
Goldacre, Ben, 170
Golder case, 88
Goldsmith, Lord Peter, 363
Goodhart, David, 260, 264, 378
Goodwin, Sir Fred, 309
Google, 77, 95, 216
  Google Earth, 344
Gove, Michael, 363, 378
government
  coalition, 284
  'first duty' argument, 213-14
  health warnings, 357
  IT project costs, 176
  marketisation of, 51
  patronage, 187
  'transformational', 175, 294, 296, 364
graduates, unemployment, 311
Graham, James, 364
Grayling, A C, 202, 213
Green Party, UK, 222
Green, Damian, 103
Grieve, Dominic, 42, 196, 221, 240-1, 322
Guantanamo Bay prison camp, 209, 240, 243, 245, 247
  Combatant Status Review Tribunals, 246
  torture, 244
Guardian, the 40, 42, 88, 99, 101, 104, 122, 125, 216, 241, 264, 277, 281, 286, 310, 345, 363, 372-4
  Public magazine, 37
  Scott Trust, 279
  tax avoidance series, 278
Guildford Four, miscarriage of justice, 345
Gulf War, first, 187

H

habeas corpus, 90, 186, 244, 246
Hain, Peter, 283
Hamburg, bombing of, 67
Hamilton, Eddie, 185-6

Hamilton, Alexander, 128
Hampden, John, 226
Harman, Harriet, 286
Harvard University, 280
Hassan, Gerry, 115, 360
Hayes, Ben, 179
Hazell, Robert, 117
hearsay evidence rules changes, 340
Heath, William, 364
Heathrow airport
  Harmondsworth Detention Centre, 82
  3rd runway decision, 222
Heinlein, Robert, 332
Helsinki accords, 93
Henderson, Iain, 74
Henry, Patrick, 48
Her Majesty's Revenue and Customs, 203, 311
Herbert, Guy, 10, 173
Hewitt, Patricia, 286
Hicks, Jerry, 138
history, British schools teaching, 228
History Today, 225
Hitler, Adolf, apologists, 61
Hizb-ut-Tahrir, 348-9
Hogg, Quentin (Lord Hailsham), 200, 258
Hollis, Thomas, 280
Holocaust-deniers, expression rights, 61
Home Office, UK, 32, 39, 249
  citizenship surveys, 122
  ONSET system, 366
  technocrats, 203
Homeland Security Act, USA, 208
Horsham Property case 2008, 261, 263
house arrest, 13
House of Commons, 282
  failures, 196
  42 day detention support, 184
  potential power of, 200
  Select Committees, 195, 206
  weaknesses, 50, 194, 205
  See also, Parliament
House of Lords, 33, 188, 193-6, 232, 243, 259
  Constitutional Committee, 8, 15, 189
  See also, Parliament
housing
  repossessions, 261

  right to, 255
Howard, Michael, 32, 198
Howarth, David MP, 337, 338, 344-5, 347, 350
Huhne, Chris, 317, 321
'human rights', 35, 70
  censorship use, 61
  erosion of, 81
  fundamentalism, 266
  impact assessment need, 193
  imperialism, 88
  'liberal conservative' case, 87
  non-negotiable, 211
  tabloid scorn, 9
  violations, 68
Human Rights Act 1998 (HRA), 8, 11-12, 22, 35, 50, 57, 88-9, 113, 184-5, 190-1, 193, 197, 205, 207-9, 215-16, 247, 249-50, 255, 257-8, 264, 318, 345, 378
  positive effects, 210-11
Human Rights Watch, 53-4, 58, 61, 331
Hundal, Sunny, 378
Hunt, Murray, 190
Hussein, Saddam, 349
Hutton, Lord, Inquiry, 98, 275
Hutton, John, 282

I

Identification Referral and Tracking, children, 296
ID cards, 6, 10, 36, 43, 137, 142, 173, 184, 203, 206, 286, 331-3, 338, 348, 364, 375, 378
  biometric, 176
Identity Card Bill, 85, 199
Identity Cards Act 2006, 16, 188
identity documents, 18
imagination, 320
IMINT, 351
Immigration and Asylum Act 1999, 17
Immigration, Asylum and Nationality Act 2006, 13, 22
Immigration and Nationality Department, 311
  Officers' increased power, 13
immigration legislation, bail hearings, 14
Imprint Academic, 127
Independent Police Complaints

Commission (IPCC), 97
Index on Censorship, 53, 61
India, 65, 69
  Sovereignty notion, 56
  the 'market', 219
indigenous peoples
  Latin America, 82
inequality
  Britain, 124
  global, 64-5
'inevitability', as justification, 177
infantilisation, 306, 358
information
  individual disclosure control, 74-5
  Information Commissioner's Office, 71, 215
  pro-active management of, 173
  profile use, 72
  verifiable, 276
Inglesant, Philip, 364
Inquiries Act 2005, 12, 23, 26
Institute for Public Policy Research (IPPR), 40, 113, 338, 378
Institute of Race Relations
  website, 243
Integrated Children's System, 366
Intel chip, Ra'abnana designed, 368
intellectual curiosity virtue of, 324
intellectual property, 78
Intelligence and Security Committee, 339, 350
International Commission of Jurists (ICJ), 240-1
International Covenant on Economic Social and Culture, 254
International Criminal Court, 53
International Law, 8, enforcement need, 68
International Olympic Committee (IOC), 134
Internet, 39, 280, 344
Iran, rhetorical use, 347
Iraq invasion and occupation, 343
  British soldiers, 211
  civilian deaths, 12, 63, 68
  legality question, 350
  London demonstration against, 145
  sectarian conflict, 67
  Tory-Labour conspiracy, 282

WMD hype, 98, 349
Ireland, 115-16
Irvine, David, 61
Islamic banking, 120
Islamov vs Russia case, 250
ISPs (internet service providers), 19, 72, 370
Israel, 367
  as exceptionalist, 209
  Gaza invasion and punishment, 66-7, 143
  Supreme Court, 351
IT (information technology)
  public sector budgets, 296

J
Jackson vs Attorney General, 196
Jackson, John, 46
Jacqui Smith vs Mitting case, 240-1
Jameson, Neil, 132
Japan, 65, 307, 309
Jefferson, Thomas, 128-9
Jenkins, Simon, 284, 374
Jewish Council for Racial Equality, 120
Jews, mass killings of, 368
Jobseekers Allowance, 308
Johnson, Boris, 133-4
Joint Committee on Human Rights (JCHR), 187-8, 190, 194-5, 204, 260
Jones, James, 367-9
Jones, Vaughan, 81
Jordan, 248-9
Joseph Rowntree Reform Trust, 364
journalism
  confidential sources need, 96
  economics of, 278
  'embedded' journalists, 62-3
  encryption learning need, 99
  investigative, 278
  persecuted journalists, 97
judiciary, UK, 93, 204, 258
  life experience, 255
  political attacks on, 283
  potential role, 260
July bombings, UK, 249
jury trials system, government undermined, 22, 33, 340
Justice, 253, 259

K

Kaldor, Mary, 63, 66, 320
Kandahar, military detention site, 245-6
Katwala, Sunder, 217
Katz/Mair thesis, 281
Keep Sunday Special, 84
Kelly, Annie, 373
Kelly, David, 98
Kennedy, Helena, 32, 207, 233, 363
Key, David, 96
Khmer Rouge, 322
King, Martin Luther, 267, 272
Kingsnorth Climate Camp, 339
Kingsnorth, Paul, 360
Kipling, Rudyard, 130
Kirby, Jill, 175
Klug, Francesca, 88, 195, 202, 211, 214-16
Knowles, Robin QC, 120
Kosova, 56
Kumar, Satish, 272

L

labour, free market in, 305
Lamb, Charles, 270
Lamb, Mary, 270
Laming enquiry, 296
language, of slavery, 231
Latimer, Bishop Hugh, 329
Latin America, conquistadores, 82
Lavalette, Michael, 124-5
law
  corporate firms, 52
  Legal Aid, 51-2
  retrospective changes, 201
Lawson, Neal, 218-19
Lawyers, libel fees, 100
Lay, Paul, 235
Leaks, importance of, 97
Learned Hand, Billings, 208
Levellers, 225, 229-30, 232-4, 237
  Bill of Rights, 227
  defence of liberty principle, 235-6
  language of, 231
leverage, US investment banks, 307
libel laws, UK, 99, 102
  costs, 101
  London tourism, 100

Liberal Conspiracy, 170, 378
Liberal Democrat Voice, 367
Liberal Democrat party, 222, 349
  Freedom Bill, 317
Liberty, 105-6, 199, 289, 301-2, 331, 373
  Decade of Decline, 210
liberty
  as shared social value, 236
  - liberalism dichotomy, 90
  martyrs for, 237
  tradition of, 50
Libya, 248-9,
  rhetorical use, 347
Lilburne, John, 230, 236-7
Lincoln, Abraham, 333
Lindsey Oil Refinery dispute, 139-40
living wage, 134
Livingstone, Ken, 133-5
lobby system, 275
Locke, John, 49, 87, 201
London Citizens organisation, 132-4
London left, institutionalised, 377
Long Lartin prison, 242
'love', 268-9
  unconditional, 272-3
Lucas, Lord Ralph, 22
Luddite labelling, 177

M

Maastricht Treaty, 206
Macdonald, Sir Ken QC, 39, 356, 363
Machiavelli, Niccolo, 127
MacPherson Report, backlash against, 121
Madison, James, 128-9, 198
Magna Carta, 11-13, 47, 50, 209, 226, 230, 244, 254
Mail on Sunday, 306, 371
majority rule, 214
Make Poverty History, 84, 373
Malik, Kenan, 61
Malraux, Andre, 367
Mandleson, Peter, 281, 370
Manning, Bernard, 130
marginalisation, self-awareness of, 64
market, the, 220, 271, 359
MASINT, 351
mass migration, 54, 81

Mavor Carol, 270
maximum salary differential, idea of, 313
Maynard, Sir John, 237
Mbeke, Thabo, 263
media
  children negativity, 290-3, 298-9
  digital impact, 76-7
  politicians' relation to, 275-7
  publicly-funded, 370
  under-resourced, 279-80
medical records, 10
Merits of Statutory Instruments Committee, 188
Merkel, Angela, 308
Methodist Central Hall, Westminster, 132
Mexico, 'drug wars', 68
Microsoft, 72-3
Middle East realpolitik, 367
migrant workers, human rights confiscation, 82
Miliband, David, 283
military-industrial complex, 285
Mill, JS, 87, 201
Milne, AA, 48
Milton Keynes Citizen, 96
Milton, John, 280
  Aeropagatica, 93, 227
  The Ready and the Easy Way, 231
Ministry of Justice, 2008 survey, 88
miscarriages of justice, 34
  pre-New Labour, 345
Mishcon de Reya, 46
Missionary societies, disbanded, 84
Mitchell, Joni, 357, 359
Mitting, Judge John, 241
mixed belief society, 79
mobile phone companies, 77
'modernisation', 174
modesty, virtue of, 325
Mohallem, Michael, 23
Mohamed, Binyam, 43, 239-40, 243-5, 329, 339, 341, 347, 350
monarchy, 232
Moore, Suzanne, 306, 357, 371
Morocco, torture, 244
Mosley, Ivo, 128
MPs, expenses scandal, 368
Murdoch, Rupert, 102, 117

Murrer, Sally, 96
Muslim Safety Forum, 119
Muslim Youth Helpline, 122
Mussolini, Benito, 283
My Society, 170
Mydex, 74-5

N

Naidoo, Kumi, 373
Nairn, Tom, 115
Naseby, 228
National Childhood Obesity Database, 365
National Curriculum SATS, 204
National Fingerprint Database, 365
National Health Service, 204, 212
  Computer, 286, 323
  constitution, 262
  Detailed Care Record 365
  development aid ratio, 265
National Identity Register (NIR), 18, 199, 365, 379
National Institute for Health and Clinical Excellence (NICE), 204
National Pupil Database 2000, 294-5
  'function creep', 189
national security, new definition, 352
National Socialism, 283
National Union of Journalists, 292
National Union of Mineworkers, 141
Nationality Immigration and Asylum Act 2002, 13, 17, 21-2
Nazi Germany, 318
NEETs, 295
Neier, Aryeh, 53, 61
Neo-Nazis, right to march, 61
'neoliberalism', 219-21
Netherlands, the, anti-Muslim immigration politics, 59
New Labour (Labour Party), 32, 35, 51-2, 57, 116-17, 215, 218, 220, 247, 284, 358, 361, 371, 379
  hollowing out of, 222
  1997 administration, 257
  regional employment failures, 125
New Model Army, 234
Newton, Isaac, 329
NGOs (non governmental organizations), 380

new gatekeepers, 377
NO2ID campaign, 10, 171, 331, 373
non-citizens, 318
Northern Ireland, 221
  Bill of Rights discussion, 261, 336
  miscarriages of justice, 34
Northern Rock, nationalisation of, 88
Norway, 284-5
nuclear energy, propaganda for, 143
Nuffield Foundation, 296

O

O'Toole, Slugger, 336
Obama, Barak, 39, 69, 132, 220-1, 234-5
Oborne, Peter, 281, 367-9
Observer, The, 93, 277, 371
  Scott Trust, 279
OFCOM, 97
Ofsted, 366
oil, dependence consequences, 69
oligarchy, 285
Olympic Games, London, 2012, 134-5
Omand, David, 40-1, 181, 338-9, 341
openDemocracy, 267, 367
opposition political parties, 'self-binding' commitments, 235
Orwell, George, 1984, 49
'other', the, 308
'Our Kingdom', 225, 368
oversight system, weakness, 339, 350
Overton, Richard, 230
Oyster card, 138

P

Pakistan
  Federal Investigative Authority, 95
  intelligence agents, 244
  Taliban compromise, 96
  torture, 8
  Urdu Press, 94
Palestine, 277
  Jews to, 368
  Possible Palestinian state, 367
Parenting Orders, 14, 18
Parliament, 190, 283
  debate lack, 175, 263
  Foreign Affairs Committee, 98
  'hung', 222
  idea of English, 360-1
  independent-minded MPs need, 199
  Leveller election ideas, 233
  open primary selection, 205
  role of, 191, 194
  scrutiny committees and obstacles, 192, 319
  weakness of, 6, 186-7
  See also, Houses of Commons and Lords
Patriot Act US, 208
pattern recognition software, 181
Pax Britannica, 64
Pearson, Lord Malcolm, 60
Peel, Sir Robert, 111
  Nine Principles of Policing, 109
Peirce, Gareth, 243
persecution, faith communities' experience of, 83
personal data, as media content payment, 78
Petition of Right, 50, 226
PFI (Private Finance Initiative), 221
PHORM, 78
photographing of police illegality, 19, 104, 138, 195, 322, 330, 340, 358
Plane Stupid, 104
Plato, 268
Plymouth Argyle, football supporters, 107
police
  Discretion, 111, 302
  Federation, 108
  Fortress police stations, 138
  Forward Intelligence teams, 375
  Greater Manchester, 106
  Nottinghamshire CID, 140
  pre-emptive actions, 7
  West Midlands, 97
political asylum, UK, 245
political theory, liberal contractualist, 90
political-media class, new, 281
Poll tax, 144
Porteous, Tom, 54, 58
Porter, Henry, 4-5, 7, 23, 50, 353, 362, 371-2, 374-5, 378-9
post-sentence restrictions, 14
postal service, 16

Powell, Steven, 105
Power 2010, 127
power
  arbitary, 230-2
  electoral, 233
Preston, police raids, 124
presumption of innocence, 35
  weakened, 15
Prevention of Electronic Crimes Act, 94
Prevention of Terrorism Act 2005, 13, 26
Price, Tony Curzon, 367
Primary Care Trusts, 203
printed press, financial difficulty, 102, 278
privacy, 77
  children's rights, 291
  enhancing technology, 73
Privacy International, 174, 179
'private credentials', 73
Private Eye, 275, 278
private health care industry, 52
private security companies, 104
Project for the New American Century, 63
proportional representation, 196, 284
Prospect, 378
Protection from Harassment Act 1997, 26
protectionism, 305
protesters, database of, 375
public good, notion of, 236
public inquiries, 23
'public opinion', 50, 129
  potential independence of, 376
public services
  delivery, 36-8
  'personalising, 178
  'predict and provide' mindset, 176
  Public Services Agreement, 26, 187
  spending crackdown, 312
public trust, 41
Pullman, Philip, 24, 324, 362, 379
Putin, Vladimir, 56, 309, 376
Putney Debates, 225, 228
Pym, John, 226

Q

Qualifications and Curriculum Authority (QCA), 204

Qudsi Rasheed, 23
Question Time, 204

R

Raab, Dominic, 228
racism, 121
radio frequency electronic microchip (RFID), 18
Rainsborough, Colonel Thomas, 225, 227
Raleigh, Sir Walter, 226
Rammell MP, Bill, 337-8, 341-2, 347
Random House, publishers, 60
'Raves', definition of, 20
Rayner, Emily, 23
Reagan, Ronald, 219
Real ID Act US 2005, 208
Red Pepper, 103
referendums, manipulation risk, 212
refugees, 68
Regulation of Investigatory Powers Act 2000 (RIPA law), 2, 16, 19, 26, 72
Reid, John, 283-4, 332
religion
  Christianity, see above
  freedom of, 236
  identity as 'ethnic social capital', 122
  mainstream traditions, 82
  tolerance, 227, 237
Renan, Ernest, 48
reporting restrictions removal, children, 291, 301
Republican Party, US, 220
Republicanism, English, 226-7
Research Assessment Exercise points, 271
Respect party, 124
ResPublica, rallies, 372
Resurgence, 267
Right to Know, 170
rights
  children, 289-93
  implementation, 256
  language of, 89-90
  of suspects, 41
  social and economic, 254-5, 260-2
  to medical care, 259
  to protest, restrictions, 339
  to silence, eroded, 15

welfare, 257-8
risk, 69, 43, 347
Roberston, Geoffrey, 226
Robinson, Mary, 88
Rogers, Paul, 69
Roosevelt, Eleanor, 226, 260, 318
Roosevelt, FD, 48, 209, 260
Rosen, Michael, children's laureate, 327
Rousseau, J-J, 204
Rowbotham, Sheila, 268
rule of law, 51, 283
Rump Parliament Statute, 227
Rusbridger, Alan, 99, 276
Ruskin, John, 327
Russell, Jenni, 297
Russia, 58, 69
  nationalists, 309
  sovereignty notion, 56
Rustin, Mike, 219
Rwanda, 70

S

Saadi vs Italy case, 248
Saatchi, Maurice, 218
Sachs, Albie, 260
Sadiq, Tariq, 337, 351-2
'sanction detections' target pressure, 109-11
Sankey, Lord John, 48, 240
Sarkozy, Nicolas, 308
Sasse, Angela, 364
Scarlett, John, 98
Scarman, Leslie, 46
Schiller, Friedrich, William Tell, 55
School Standards and Framework Bill, 294
Scott, CP, 277-8, 281
Scott, Jonathan, 234
Scottish National Party, social democratic values, 117
Second World War period, 48
Secret Immigration Court (SIAC), 241
sectarian wars, 67
Section 106 agreements, 135
secure authentication online, 72
security
  international 'control paradigm', 64-5
  meaning of, 69
  national rhetoric, 56

prioritisation, 39, 41, 49
'total', authoritarian fantasy of, 39, 44, 202, 322
security services UK, 41
  Director General, 349
  MI5, 8, 55-6, 245
  MI6, 245
self-sufficiency, notion of, 91
September 11th attacks, 179, 180, 198, 275, 357
Sergeant, Harriet, 108
Serious Crime Prevention Order (SCPO), 15
Serious Organised Crime and Police Act 2005, 26
sexuality, 269-70
Shakespeare, William, 329
Shameen, Naureen, 23
Sharia Law, poor understanding of, 122-3
Sharp, Andrew, 236
short-termism, 321, 324
SIGNIT, 351
Sinn Fein, airwaves ban, 210
Skinner, Quentin, 228, 233
smears, tabloid, 98
Smith, David, 71
Smith, Elias, 130
Smith, Jacqui, 243, 282, 332, 353
  See also, Jacqui Smith vs Mitting
Smith, Roger, 257
Smith, Sam, 170
SNP (Scottish National Party), 118
social enterprise, 74
social justice, 81
social networking, online, 77, 323
Socrates, 268
Soham murders, 37, 376
Sontag, Susan, 270
Sophie Electress of Hanover, 229
Soros, George, Open Society Institute, 61
South Africa
  apartheid end, 144
  Constitution Report, 263
sovereignty, 69-70
  absolutist view, 56, 116-17
Stasi, 55
State, the

as 'market' regulator, 220-2
authoritarian, 309
British, 81
centralised, 91
data losses, 176
'database', 6, 10, 15, 17, 79, 119, 170, 173, 177-8, 184-5, 194, 216, 331, 338, 364, 366, 372, 376
hybrid, 221
increased powers, 49
liberal legacy of, 89
mutating, 259
nation, 264
neoliberal weak, 116, 221
quango, 203
surveillance, 100, 254-5
'union'/'unitary', 115
Statewatch, 179
statutory instruments, unscrutinised, 193
Steiner Academies, 203
Stockholm Programme, EU, 178
Stoke City
 football supporters, 106, 107
Stoke
 employment decline, 125
 football supporters, 106-7
Stop the War Coalition, 322
Stop-and-Search ('Sus') laws, 34, 339
'Strangers into Citizens' campaign, 133
Straw, Jack, 12, 19, 40, 176, 254, 286-7, 291, 330-1, 345, 358
subsidies, privatised railways, 221
suicide bombers, 343, 348
Sun, The, 39, 44, 57, 98, 284
superiority assumption, North Atlantic countries, 66
surveillance, 16
 CCTVs, see above
 equipment spending, 286
 international, 53
 of migrants, 181
 police political, 140
 society, 4, 6, 8, 285, 287
 state, see above
 workplace, 137, 141-2
Swat valley, Pakistan, 96
Sweden, Riksdag Constitutional Committee, 195

Swindon, Pinehurst Estate, 197
swipe cards, workplaces, 141
Syria, 248

T

'Taking Liberties' exhibition, British Library, 225
Talbot Rice, Sam, 175
target culture, crime figures, 110
tax avoidance schemes, 101
Taxi to the Dark Side, 246
Taylor, Ros, 360-1
technological determinism, 182
Teheran, Holocaust conference, 61
'Tell Us Once' argument, 176
terrorism
 blanket legislation, 310
 State fear use, 57, 87, 341
 IRA, 343, 348
Terrorism Act 2000, 14, 20, 26
Terrorism Act 2006, 19
 Section 44, 339
Tesco, 216, 270
 'Clubcard' argument, 177
 Guardian libel action, 101
Thatcher, Margaret, 93, 117, 144, 210, 218-19, 306
The Independent, 133
The Jewel of Medina, Censorship of, 60
think-tanks, 378
Tibet, 56
Tokyo, bombing of, 67
Tolpuddle Martyrs, 144
torture, 8, 227, 244-5, 251, 282, 341, 350-1, 358
 common law position, 259
 regimes, 247-50
 UK collusion, 43, 58, 69, 239, 330
totalitarianism, 20th century, 214
Toxteth, riots in, 308
trade union movement, 144
 attacks on, 143
 membership advantages, 141
 sequestration fear, 139
traffic calming, self-organised, 327
Treatment of Claimants Act 2004, 20
Tribunals Courts and Enforcement Act 2007, 21
Trident missile, 69-70

Tsunami 2004, response to, 321
TV Licensing Database, 365
Twitter, 39

U

UCL Student Human Rights Programme (UCLSHRP), 11-12, 194, 196
UK (United Kingdom)
  as unitary state, 116
  Borders Act 2007 and Agency, 13, 18, 84
  children negativity, 290, 299
  credit implosion, 308
  democratic culture, 98
  development community, 373
  GDP decline, 307
  miners strike, 66, 139
  Muslim communities, 119, 121
  'national question', 114
  torture collusion, 58
  -US arms production, 70
  -US treaty, 351
Ul Haq, Zia, 94
Ummuna, Chuka, 316
UN (United Nations)
  Charter, 260
  Committee on the Economic, Social and Cultural Rights, 255
  Committee/Convention on the Rights of the Child, 253, 290-1
  Convention of Torture, Article 3, 250
  Declaration to the Equality and Human Rights Commission, 262
  Human Rights Council, 59-60
  special rapporteur on freedom of expression, 59
unemployment, 54, 308, 311
Unite trade union, 139
Universal Declaration of Human Rights, 60-1, 209, 226, 254, 264, 318
universalism, 264
  French revolutionary, 91
  human rights, 257, 378
University College London, 176
Unlock Democracy, 197, 222, 364
'unprecedented threats', repression rationalisation, 87
US (United States of America), 43, 58
  Afghanistan war, 67
  Bill of Rights, 209
  civil liberties, 200-1
  Congress, 100
  'enemy combatant' prisoners, 243
  'Founding fathers', 128-9
  GDP decline, 307
  Marine Corps, 62
  neocons, 63
  partisanship, 234
  Presidential election 1800, 129
  sovereignty notion, 56
  surveillance specialist corporations, 6
  torture role, 239
  UK client relation, 69, 283
  written constitution, 361
USSR (Union of Soviet Socialist Republics) 1930s, 322
Uzbekistan, torture assurances, 250

V

Van Bueren, Geraldine, 254, 260, 264
Varney, Sir David 2006 report, 36, 175-6
Violent Crime Reduction Act 2006, 20
  Section 27, 105, 106, 107
Voltaire, 199, 237

W

wakefulness, need for, 325
Walker, Clive, 21
Walker, Richard, 23
Walwyn, William, 236
Wandsworth, William, 270
'War on Terror', 6, 64, 68, 116, 142, 239, 243, 245, 247, 275
  rhetoric, 42
Warner, Marina, 268
Washington Consensus, 367
Washington Post, 62
Washington, George, 128
Weber, Max, 204
Weir, Stuart, 184
Wellcome Institute, 269
Wells, HG, 48
Wheen, Francis, Strange Days Indeed, 379
whistleblowers, 100
  crackdown on, 96
White Paper on National Security 2008,

351-2
Widdecombe, Anne, 32
Wilders, Geert, 60, 349
  Fitna, 59, 350
Wilks-Heeg, Stuart, 123
Wills, Michael, 186, 196-7, 364, 366-7, 380
Women's Temperance Association, 334
Wootton, David, 234
Wordsworth, Dorothy, 270
Wordsworth, William, 270
workers
  'freedom of movement', 139
  rights undermined, 137
  solidarity action, outlawed, 138
World Health Organisation, 63
World Wide Web, advertising business model, 72
written constitution(s), 200
  UK need for, 232, 319

X
xenophobia, 121, 124

Y
Young, Gareth, 114
Young, Hugo, 277, 281
young people
  oppressive laws, 300
  UK hostility to, 301-2
Young People Now, 292
YouTube, 60, 202

Z
Zhang, Kai, 23
Zimbabwe, 56
  as exceptionalist, 209
  rhetorical use of, 347